# POLITICS AND WOMEN EMPOWERMENT IN THE HIMALAYAN STATES

*Himalaya Past and Present Series*

# POLITICS AND WOMEN EMPOWERMENT IN THE HIMALAYAN STATES

*Editor*

***K. S. Gulia***

**ISHA BOOKS**

**DELHI-110 009**

**Politics and Women Empowerment in the Himalayan States**

ISBN : 81-8205-424-9



Published in 2007 in India by
Isha Books, B-63, Ist Floor, New Gupta Colony,
Near DDA Market, Delhi-110009
Phone: 9212142040
E-mail: ishabooks@hotmail.com

*Laser Typesetting by*: Tact Computer Graphics, Delhi
*Printed at*: Salasar Imaging System, Delhi

## Contents

# Introduction

The ecological degradation taking place all over the world is due to a complex array of factors like global warming, pressure of population growth, deforestation, soil erosion, loss of biodiversity, urbanization and over-exploitation of natural resources. All this is adding to the woes of people living from Kashmir to Sikkim and other States of the Northeast. Encompassed are also Nepal and Bhutan. Apart from these factors, in the aftermath of the war with China in 1962 and with Pakistan over Kargil in 2001, all the along the border in Kashmir, Ladakh, Uttranchal, Sikkim and Arunachal, militarisation has left its mark on the ecosystem of the Himalayas.

In our book *Politics, Security, People's Movement and Women Empowerment,* we are discussing at length how the Himalayas affect the lives of the Indians in general and those who are living in their lap in particular. One cannot think what life would be in the subcontinent without Himalayas – its demography, its weather, the way people live. When the great poet Kalidas wrote Meghdhoot fifteen hundred years ago, trying to find his plot in the dark clouds floating high in the sky, he had opined: "Himalayas is a measuring rod of Earth". It was not a flippant expression as we can today vouch for.

In Chapter One we have taken up Ecological Security of the Himalayas. The mountain chain of Himalayas is nature's gift to India and other countries in the Far East in its lap. They are natural storehouse of water for the perennial rivers. Sindh in Pakistan, the five rivers of Punjab, Ganga and Yamuna and many of their tributaries, Brahmputra in the East India and many other rivers in Thailand and Cambodia have their source in the Himalayas. They prevent the icy winds of the north from reaching the plains of South Asia. This fragile ecosystem supports the entire population of the plains in these countries. The ecological services they provide are difficult to quantify in real terms.

In light of this, the issues of environmental security provided by the Himalayas in South Asia have a unique importance.

Chapter Two discusses ancient communities of the Himalayas. Since the dawn of civilization, communities have been the same the world over. To say that the primitives did not have political organizations because they had no territorial ambitions is wrong. Riches, women and land have been the most important factors ever since man first constituted a community. Such opinions may not hold good when examined against the functioning of some of the age-old political institutions, time-honoured practices, popular traditions and beliefs. This chapter to a reasonable extent helps us to understand this aspect, which was prevalent among our predecessors in the early period of history of mankind.

Indian civilization is distinctive in the sense that it evolved in the forests, not in the cities. Forests in India have remained central to India's civilisational evolution. Forest based *ashramas* (settlements) produced the best scientific research and cultural writing and India thus came to be known as an *Aranya Samskriti* (forest culture). The protection and propagation of forests as a deeply ingrained civilisational characteristic in the South Asian region is evident from the existence of sacred groves in river catchments, foreshores of tanks and village woodlots. The planting of trees, either for their fruit or for the purpose of obtaining shade was an act, which was held in high esteem in India since ancient times. Centrality of forests in Indian thought is discussed in Chapter Three.

Chapter Four discusses People's Ecological Movement in Kumaon and Garhwal over Forest Rights. While the absence of popular protest in the first century of British rule had given rise to the stereotype of the simple and law abiding hillman, the reservation of the Kumaon forests between 1911 and 1917 met with violent and sustained opposition, culminating in 1921 when within the space of a few months, the administration was paralysed by a strike against statutory labour. This transformation in peasant consciousness and peasant revolt that was closely related to the more subtle but equally enduring changes in the structure of colonial administration has been detailed in this chapter.

Year after year, for almost a century, the floods in the North India seem to be getting worse. Some time they are absolutely devastating. This means that there is something radically wrong in the Himalayas, and that 'something' without doubt, is connected with forests. This 'something' was elaborated by Mira Behn, an associate of Gandhiji. She had settled in Uttranchal after Gandhiji's death. It was she who had sowed the seeds of Chipko movement. Sunderlal Bahuguna who from the seventies headed the Chipko movement got inspiration from her as a fifteen years old. Chapter Five gives in detail the genesis of Chipko movement in Uttranchal. This idea has spread like a mushroom all over the world where because of excessive exploitation ecosystems are under threat.

Chapter Six takes a look at the progression of Chipko movement. Environment and ecological crises had been looming large on the Himalayas; this Andolan forced the attention of the people of India to danger to ecosystem. The social changes that have created a money-order economy and a lopsided demographic profile in Uttaranchal have also helped fuel this movement. Chipko has turned to be a response to the fragmentation of the village community in recent decades. Women have always played an important role in economic life of a village and this structural constant may explain the widespread participation of women in contemporary social movements. The association of women with this movement has influenced recent economic changes in intensifying their traditional dependence on the natural environment.

Chapter Seven is about Sikkim. The development projects, as the term implies, are meant for the upliftment of society, for material benefit of common man. These are the mechanisms, which any government ought to put in place. In a closed society that Sikkim has been for centuries, one such project has created undue confusion among the masses, created in the name of religious sentiments by the Lamas and other religious leaders. This Chapter delves deep into the controversy raised by these vested interests in the development and construction of Tathong Chu dam in Sikkim.

Chapter Eight is a backgrounder to Politics in Nepal. The foundation of the modern State of Nepal was laid in AD 1769. Nepal's peculiar geographical position of being hemmed in the two giant powers of Asia dictated the policy of isolation, which her rulers followed until very recently. The Ranas ruled the land with an iron hand for two hundred years.

While political upheaval in India was going on, they did not read the writing on the wall, which led to a popular upsurge against them. This Chapter traces the history of Rana rule in Nepal for over two centuries.

The country's location bordering the Ganga belt, where an enormous share of its human and natural resource base is concentrated, makes it critically important from the perspective of India's security and stability. Nepal's social-cultural ties with and economic inter-dependence on India are extensive and deep and is dependent on latter's seaports for trade. For China the possibility of Nepal acting as a springboard for anti-Chinese activities in Tibet is the most paramount and sensitive issue. Nepal Security and Political Environment have been discussed in Chapter Nine.

Amidst the continuously expanding sphere of Maoist influence, political uncertainties and growing international interest, Nepal continues to remain one of the most volatile countries of South Asia. The Maoist insurgency has emerged as one of the most serious political and security challenges in Nepal, with its disturbing implications for the adjoining regions in India. Political vacuum and government incompetence are further giving a push to the insurgency, which is bleeding Nepal continuously. Chapter Ten and Eleven and Twelve discuss Peace, Emergency and Maoist movement in Nepal.

For Tibetans, their country is the center of the earth and the earthly reflection of all-embracing cosmos. With a present population of five million, about a third of whose men live as Lamas in the monasteries of the country, Tibet in the past centuries has lived on the edge of events.

Tibet moved into the bright light of the present when insistent forces in the Indian continent and later in China brought about a reorganisation of their State. Tibet too was caught up by the tide of political reorientation. This Chapter also discusses the influence that Mongolia had over Tibet for centuries. History of Tibet and present day Tibet has been discussed in Chapters Thirteen and Fourteen.

Bhutan is a frontier society away from the riverine centers of civilization. Though lamaist ethnic groups existed, it was the Drukpa theocracy that provided the social base of the contemporary Bhutanese social structure. Chapter Fifteen discusses Bhutan at length.

Chapter Sixteen discusses ethnic stalemate, the crisis brought about by migration of Nepali Hindus to Bhutan. In a predominantly Buddhist society, this has definitely given rise to racial tension. The recent ethnic conflicts have necessarily exposed the hollowness and limitation of the politics of consensus as a state policy in Bhutan.

The last Chapter, Seventeen, discusses gender disparity in literacy in Uttranchal. Uttranchal is one of the better literate States of India. It has shown continuous rise in literacy over the years. But the State still has a wide range of sex disparity when quesition of giving education to girl child comes up. All the facets of literacy have been gone into in this Chapter.

# 1
# Ecological Security of the Himalayas

"Himalayas is a measuring rod of Earth"

— Kalidas *in Kumar Sambhav*

## Background

They Himalayan extend west to east, from the Pamir Knot in the north-west to the valley in the Brahmaputra river in the east. The ranges pass through Afghanistan, Pakistan, India (J&K, Himachal Pradesh, Uttaranchal, Sikkim, Assam, Arunachal Pradesh, Manipur, Meghalaya, Mizoram, Nagaland, Tripura and Darjeeling district of West Bengal), China, Nepal, Bhutan, Bangladesh and Myanmar.

The Himalayas which date back to 40 to 45 million years are among the youngest folded mountains in the world, and the youngest in India. They traverse an arc of about 2,500 to 3,000 km between the Indus and Brahmaputra and the average width varies from 100 to 400 km. Total area covered is 4.6 million sq km above 1500 m, 3.2 million sq km above 3,000 m and 0.56 million sq km above 5400 m. The Himalayas are still geologically active and structurally unstable. For this reason, earthquakes are frequent. Being the world's highest mountain chain, the Himalayas are characterised by a complex geological structure, snow capped peaks, large valley glaciers, deep river gorges and rich vegetation. A complex interplay of climatic and geological processes, patterns of resource use and economic conditions has led to resource degradation, and environmental threats to the ecosystems.[1]

## Nature's Gift

The mountain chain of Himalayas is nature's gift to India and this part of Asia. They are a natural storehouse of water for the perennial rivers. The ecological services they provides are difficult to quantify in real terms. In the 20th century, due to geopolitical reasons between nations, the Himalayas were witness to long drawn military actions ranging from a general war to insurgency and terrorism. Security managers were justified in defending the borders with military might. However, it was not realised that while the players played their great games of geopolitics due to national interests, the ecological interests were either ignored or were too vague to be considered in security thinking.

Now, at the start of 21st century, new thinking on security is influencing the mainstream security agenda. The truth is that the ecologically vital Himalayas are now under threat, and military means are unable to protect them. Rather, militarisation of the Himalayas is one of the reasons for the ecological degradation combined with other causes like global warming, population growth, urbanisation and waste disposal and unsustainable practices. A greater threat is that that proponents of modern development want to convert nature into cash. Many seminars and workshops have been held, and would continue to be held, on the socio-economic aspects of the Himalayas and eco-tourism. Some vital ecological factors due to the militarisation of the mountains have come to the fore. This chapter attempts to throw some light on the socio-economicproblems currently being faced.

**Mountains—International Year**

The United Nations declared 2002 as the International Year of the Mountains. In the global .......... it places ......... Agenda 21 is about "Managing fragile ecosystem: sustainable mountain development". In the global debate on environment and development,[2] 'it places mountains on an equal footing with climate change, tropical deforestation and desertification as a key issues.

**The its fragility Himalayan Ecology**

The Himalayas have a unique importance. In issues of environmental security in the South Asian context. They comprise about 16 per cent of the geographical area. As Table 1.1 shows it, there are just over 6 per cent of the national population (6.26 crore) or people in the hills proper. The population supporting capacity of the mountains is obviously less than that of the fertile plains in the south. This fragile ecosystem supports the entire population in the plains below. The fragility of the system is more sensitive and it can be degraded easily.

**Refugees from Shangrila:** The book on Refugees from Shangrila is the source of the influential theory of Himalayan Environmental Degradation. The narrative goes as under:

> Migration up hillsides is seen to increase population and livestock density and thus the demand for food, fuel, fodder and timber. Firewood shortages result in the burning of cow dung previously used as fertiliser and thus fertility already declining due to soil erosion, falls sharply. Lower output leads to the clearing of even larger, even steeper tracts of forests, intensifying the erosion and landslides hazard. Deforestation increases run off of water and sediment, which exacerbates flooding in India and Bangladesh. The additional sediment blocks irrigation channels and silts up the dams, generating further migration.

Thus, mountain people have little choice but to follow their souls down the slopes.[3]

Thus, the ecology of the Himalayas is under a multiple attack. State governments are in any case attempting to resolve the socio-economic problems. Many social tensions are due to these reasons.

**TABLE 1.1**

**Population of the States in the Himalayas (Less Hill Districts of West Bengal)**

| *State* | *Population* | *Percentage* | *Round Figures* |
|---|---|---|---|
| India | 102.7 crore | - | 102.7 crore |
| J & K | 10,009,917 | 0.98 | 1 crore |
| Himachal Pradesh | 6,077,248 | 0.59 | 60 lakh |
| Uttranchal | 84,779,562 | 0.83 | 84 lakh |
| Sikkim | 540,493 | 0.05 | 5 lakh |
| Arunachal Pradesh | 1,091,117 | 0.11 | 10 lakh |
| Nagaland | 1,988,636 | 0.19 | 20 lakh |
| Mizoram | 891,058 | 0.09 | 9 lakh |
| Manipur | 2,388,634 | 0.23 | 24 lakh |
| Tripura | 3,191,168 | 0.31 | 31 lakh |
| Meghalaya | 2,306,069 | 0.22 | 23 lakh |
| Assam | 26,638,407 | 2.59 | 2.6 crore |

*Source: Census of India,* Provisional Population Totals, 2001.

The Himalayas stand between the icy winds of the north and the plains of South Asia. At the same time they force the monsoon clouds to shed their moisture over the fertile plains. Water, land and forests in the Himalayas are mutually inclusive and are delicately balanced. The areas, more so the northeast Himalayas, are rich in biodiversity, with rain forests. The most vital aspect of the Himalayas is that the rivers are a perennial source of water and nutrients in the river basins of southern Asia. The Indus, Ganga, Brahmaputra, Meghna basins are vital crankshafts of the agrarian economy of countries like Pakistan, India, Nepal, Tibet, Bhutan, Bangladesh and Myanmar. Even the east or south-east flowing rivers like the Salween, Mekong, Yangtze and Hwang Ho originate in the Tibetan/Himalayan region affecting the agrarian economies of China and Indo-China. Besides being part of the spiritual culture, the Himalayan rivers are also a great source of hydroelectrical potential. Due to population growth, industrial and commercial activity, the fragile ecology has come under great stress. The common threats are deforestation, soil erosion and pressure on restricted land.

The Himalayas have nearly one-third of our national forest cover. The cutting down of trees leads to soil erosion and landslides. This loss in tree cover also reduces local rain. Massive blasting and road construction, if not properly done, leads to further destabilisation of the soil. The Ganga-Brahmaputra basin deposits three billion tons of silt a year. This is the highest figure in the world. This leads to overflowing of rivers from top of the banks and increased flooding in the lower basin. One of the most serious indicators of this environmental degradation in the water regime are the wide annual variations in the maximum and minimum flow of the Himalayan rivers. This is 70:1 at Haridwar for the Ganga. Rivers in Nepal originating from the hills below 2,000 metres have a ratio of 1,000-30,000:1. Those in Nepal originating at higher altitudes have a ratio of 40:1.[4]

**Ecological Threats to the Himalayas**

The ecological degradation is due to a complex array of factors like global warming, population growth, urbanisation, over exploitation by humans, and militarisation of the Himalayas. What is of great relevance is that the ecological loss is now being reported by veteran mountaineers and mountain lovers as well as locals. S.P. Chamoli, while traversing across the Himalayas, reported encroachment and deforestation which had denuded the green mountains. Forest species like pine in the lower altitudes and oak in the higher reaches were threatened due to clearing land for potato cultivation. Construction of roads and the resultant communications have introducted the vices of modern civilisation. The first victims have been the hand-spun woollens due to the introduction of synthetic materials. Roads also lead to the deodar and pine being cut, and the timber smuggled to the plains.[5]

Though a common geomorphologic phenomenon, abnormal retreat due of the glaciers has been observed. Also there have been drastic changes and reduction in snowfall patterns. Deforestation, soil erosion and loss of biodiversity are also widespread. Mosquitoes and the use of fans which were unheard of till some time back in the hill stations, are now common.

**Effect of Global Warming**

The LUNEP in June 2002, reported startling evidence of the effect of global warming on the Himalayas. A UN backed mission to the area found that the glacier from where Sri Edmund Hillary and Tenzing Norgay set out to conquer Mount Everest nearly 50 years ago has retreated by around five kilometres up the mountain. Locals have also reported rapid and significant changes over the past 20 years in the ice fields. UNEP scientists have used satellites and on ground studies to pin-point 44 glacial lakes in Nepal and Bhutan that are now so swollen that they could burst their banks in as little as five years.[6] Centre of Science and Environment has carried out a series of studies and field work. In their journal Down to Earth. They have reported serious ecological changes.

(a) Shift in local weather in Kumaon/Almora (Uttaranchal). Delay/ shift in the monsoons. Prolonged rains, no clear weather post-monsoon as was the case earlier. The summers are longer and hotter, and winters shorter and less cold.
(b) Increased rainfall in Leh (J&K). No snowfall in the year 2000.
(c) In Shimla (Himachal Pradesh), the seasons are late, with less snowfall. The cold wave is prolonged.
(d) In Gangtok (Sikkim), the summers are hotter, and winters shorter. There is also less rainfall.[7]

**Meltdown of Glaciers**

It is feared that the end of the 21st century may coincide with the meltdown of glaciers. The west flowing rivers to Pakistan are fed by the Himalayan glaciers: any ecological loss is also a loss to the water regime of the Indus plains. Similarly, Tibet is the roof of the world and the source of not only the south flowing rivers but also the Hwang Ho and Yangste which flow eastwards into mainland China. The hydrology and ecology in that part is dependent on permafrost, which may melt and thus turn Tibet into quagmire, soon to die. Melting permafrost also emits carbon dioxide gas into the atmosphere, thus adding to the alarming levels of excess human-induced greenhouse gases. A small change in climatology may have a massive impact on the Himalayan ecology where about 15 crore people living in the mountains and adjoining foothills. About 30 crore people live in the adjacent plains. The total of 45 crore people is no small a figure. Thus global warming may have a very cataclysmic effect.

**Over Exploitation:** Gangotri is the most polluted areas in the Himalayas today due to the influx of 1.5 lakh pilgrims, 10,000-15,000 trekkers and 3,000-4,000 mountaineers.[8] According to another account, 75 mountaineering expeditions, 25,000 trekkers and 2,50,000 pilgrims visit the areas of the Gangotri Conservation Project annually. It is the most polluted areas in the Himalayas today. Even the rare *Bhojpatra* tree has been vandalised by visitors and is nearly extinct.[9] The alarming retreat of the glacier due to excessive human interference is the most serious ecological concern. Till about 1971, the glacier had retreated 2 km in 200 years. But in 25 years since then, it had retreated 850 metres.

Ecological crises would lead to resource scarcity, economic loss, breakup of the social fabric, and to violent conflict. We all need to take parallel and simultaneous measures in our own fields, regions and countries to preserve the common and global Himalayan ecology. The effect caused by human disturbance is there for every one to see.

**Militarisation of the Himalayas**

In the early sixties we had problems with China. A short duration was also took place, leading to establishment of permanent military camps on both sides of the border. The massive militarisation in the eco-sensitive Himalayas has not been of our choosing. It has been thrust upon us by our adversarial neighbours due to geopolitical reasons. From a long-term perspective, we may find that in our myopic vision of realism we may be fighting amongst ourselves as the Titanic prepares to sink. In that case, we all are destined to perish. This calls for a new approach to peace and security in the Himalayas through ecological security. Like maritime security and the health of the Indian Ocean, the Himalayan ecology is a multi-disciplinary and international affair. Better solutions are to be found through cooperation and peace rather than conflict and competition. Military posturing and weapons can in no way solve the impending ecological crisis that may occur in the Himalayan region. Ecological problems are best tackled by consultation, cooperation and knowledge. We all seem to agree on this. Thus, peace may well dawn through preserving the Himalayan ecology in the future. This is will help in keeping the ecological balance in tact.

Peace research is still not the dominant and senior partner of security studies. Either we may all be jolted one day to give it priority like the way the world gives priority to fighting terrorism. Alternatively, diplomacy and political will applied with imagination and courage may provide answers to the looming crisis.

## Preparation for War and Counter-insurgency the Himalayan Impact

No major military campaigns ever occured in the Himalayas. It was hoped by sincere idealists that the Himalayas would provide us military and national security. But since 1947 all the major threats that the country has faced has been through the Himalayas.

### The Wars in the Himalayas

The first Indo-Pakistan war was over J&K from October 1947 to 31 December 1948, and was fought in the Himalayas. Nearly half of J&K still remains as Pakistani Occupied Kashmir (POK), as viewed from the Indian perspective, and Azad Kashmir as viewed by the Pakistanis. The war led to the eyeball to eyeball deployment of armies along the ceasefire line. From the 1950s onwards, as India languished in ignorance, the Chinese constructed a road through the Indian territory of Aksai Chin in J&K to build up forces in Tibet. The road they built crossed a flat plateau and was serviceable in winter, whereas a direct route from the centre of China into Tibet would have encountered hazardous terrain and climatic conditions.

Later, in 1955, the route was used for suppression of the Khampa rebellion and consolidated Chinese hold over Tibet.[10] We reacted late and militarily lost the bitter 1962 war which was fought in Ladakh and the North East Frontier Agency (NEFA) now reorganised as the state of

Arunachal Pradesh. This was yet another setback to the Himalayan ecology. It made us reassess national security from a realist perspective and soon many newly raised mountain divisions moved into deployment in permanent defences. There was also a great deal of road building for better military communications. As it was a war time requirement, the roads had to be built keeping the military needs in view. Roads were built for troops build-up, switching of forces and dominating ground with tactical and strategic considerations. It is obvious that cutting and blasting roads provided a logistic capability but it also led to felling of trees, and to soil erosion and landslides.[11] Many pristine areas with a sensitive ecology had to be converted into military bases.

The Himalayas borders, from J&K, Himachal Pradesh, Uttaranchal (hills of the erstwhile Uttar Pradesh), Sikkim, Arunachal Pradesh (NEFA) and other north-east states became permanent field and operational areas or permanent military stations. Trees were felled as rush jobs for road building and defence works as also for better fields of fire for military weapons. Massive digging and blasting was undertaken. Many areas for troops deployment were high altitude alpine and Tundra zones where the ecological system is very fragile. In such areas, defences had to prepared with a military angle.

**Ecology, a lower priority**

In the preparations for war, as we all know, ecology is at a lower priority. This probably is one important factor in the ecological health of the Himalayas. We realise now that the regenerative capacity or recovery at high altitudes is slower than in tropical rain forests.[12] At those heights, the birch tree attains a diameter of two centimeters in six years, and the juniper bush takes 20 years for the same growth.[13]

But as realist based national security was paramount, not much could be organised to save the ecology during those terrible times of war. We had to save the Himalayas from the enemy. Later, in 1965 another war broke out with Pakistan, and J&K was witness to military operations from August to September.

The Indian and Pakistani forces firmed in better on the ceasefire line. More mines were laid to protect the posts and the old mines could never be removed. More roads were built from the military point of view. More natural resources were consumed for national security. In 1971 again, a war was fought in December. Massive field defences were constructed/improved along the Line of Control in the entire state of J&K. Troop strengths kept on increasing as devastating firepower improved with time.

**Karakoram Highway**

In the 1970s and 1980s, the Pakistanis built the Karakoram Highway. This was a network of strategic highways through the Khunjerab and

Mintaka Passes across the fragile Karakorams linking Pakistan with Kashi (Kashgar) in Xingiang province of China. Line of communications were also ruthlessly built, using brute force, in other POK areas by Pakistan and by the Chinese in Tibet.

**Siachen Glacier**

In 1984, to preempt Pakistani intrusion in the Siachen glacier, Indian troops occupied the Saltoro ridge. This gave rise to a unique type of low intensity fire-fights, small scale infantry operations and artillery duels at extremely high altitudes. Unlike adventure loving mountaineers who get themselves photographed on the summit of a conquered peak, Indian troops occupied summits and mountain passes permanently for three to six months tenure in rotation at heights nearing 20,000 feet without oxygen. Changeover of personnel was done by helicopters as it was not possible on foot. No one could have imagined that the glaciers would be converted into a battle ground from being pristine places for the passionate eccentricity of mountaineers. It is reported that probably due to warming at the local or global level, the snout of the glacier is breaking causing a sudden surge of water. Militarisation of the glacier is also considered as one of the reasons for this.

In spite of the best efforts to preserve the ecology, annual waste generated per year by Indian troops is about 1,000 tons. Pakistani forces may also have similar figures. This is the massive waste accumulated, and is much more than the 100 tons of total garbage which remains on Mount Everest.[14] The degradation of the Siachen glacier is now being written and talked about a lot by the military establishment and ex-soldiers. It is of interest to study the change in perception on the glacier. Initially, in the 1980s and 1990s, there was a gung ho attitude, asking for better equipment and means of survival. It was the "show piece of national interest". Slowly, due to ecological reasons, the Siachen glacier and the Karakoram region is coming under ecological scrutiny by the military. A serving Indian corps commander in December 2000 gave a presentation to the PHD Chambers of Commerce on the ecological problems being faced by the glacier due to military operations.[15] The major ecological problems identified were human waste and garbage disposal, and environmental changes and degradation due to smoke pollution caused by kerosene oil and diesel that are needed for survival. Eco cleaning by the Indian Army is another innovation which has been given media coverage.

**Ecological Management**

The local army formation has set up an Ecological Management Cell to clean up the area with whatever resources they can muster. Recovery of packing material besides,[16] clean up also saves about Rs two crore per year as the material is recycled. In 2002, a book by an ex-general officer commanding, and articles by senior retired officers referred to an attempt on conflict resolution through "peace park" proposals, as suggested by the Sandia National Laboratory of USA.[17] They referred to the idea of a joint Indo-Pakistan Siachen Peace cum Scientific Park to facilitate research and end this bizarre conflict. In June 2001, before the failed Indo-Pak Agra summit, Pakistan had sent a proposal for converting the region into a park on lines similar to the Khunjerab National Park and Central Karakoram National Park. The concept is not new: there are 136 trans-frontier peace parks on the border of 98 countries.[18] If replicated here it save hundreds of crocres rupees to both the government, will save many lives which lost in incessant firing and save the ecology of the region.

**Future of the Siachen Conflict**

When viewed from the overall perspective of glacier retreat, it appears that some changes would have taken place even if there had not been any militarisation. The Baltoro glacier holds 124 billion cubic metres of water, that is about one and a half times the flow of the Niagra falls. Any abnormal glacier melt would have a greater impact on Pakistan as the western rivers are mostly snowfed. It may be premature to predict disaster due to the meltdown, but realist and hawks in Pakistan and India may like to factor this as well, as both countries and regions are affected. It is not a zero sum game in any case. Any man-made change brought about in Siachen can play have with the system in Pakistan as well as India.

What lesson does this bring out? The most important one is that neither the Indian nor the Pakistani militaries would ever wear out. All units would seek combat and perform well, in keeping with the traditional regimental spirit. Both are professional and competent enough to battle it out as long as deemed proper by the political leadership. The threshold for acceptance of casualties due to weather and firepower is also there. Human security or troop morale remains unchanged due to changeover of units and professionalism of both armies. But what the battle brings out clearly is that for the first time in the history of wars, the degradation of the terrain and a larger ecological threat due to war are going to be the reasons for end of hostilities. The changed perceptive and intense comparison of national, ecological and human security concerns is shown as a bar chart, in Fig. 1.1.

**Impact of 1999 Kargil Conflict of 1999**

One important factor which probably has not been highlighted by the various authors on the Indo-Pakistan conflict of 1999 at Kargil is the reduced snowfall on the Himalayan range at Zojila. If one sees the history of past wars and snowfall, many a times, heavy snow has blocked the opening up of the snowbound Zojila through which the main road runs from the Srinagar valley to Ladakh. In spite of remarkable efforts by the Border Roads Organisation in cutting through snow to clear the road, the timing, intensity and quantum of snow are the deciding factors in opening up a snow covered motor road in high altitudes. Somehow,

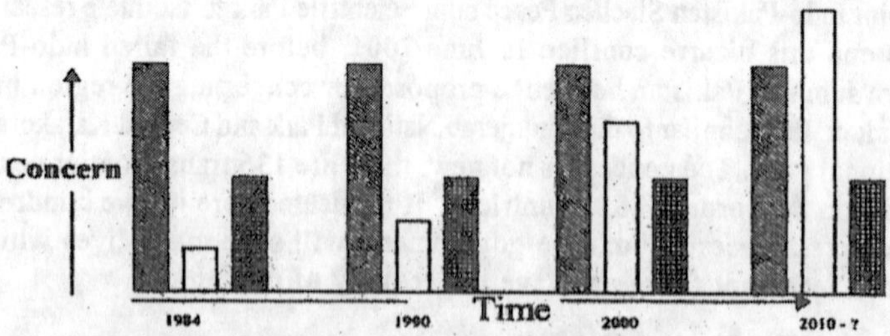


*Notes:* National security concerns do not change.
Ecological security concerns keep increasing.
Human security of troop morale remains unchanged dueo to changeover of units and professionalism of both armies.

Fig. 1.1. Siachen Glacier—Inter-se Comparison of National, Ecological and Human Security.

Himalayan degradation in 1999 gave the last blessing in disguise to the Indian Army to save the Himalayas. Due to the reduced snowfall, Zojila opened up well in advance and the induction of 8 Mountain Division, army artillery and logistic loads could be carried out using surface transport in the month of May. One shudders to think of what could have happened if there was snow "business as usual" and 3 Infantry Division had to evict the intruders using its own resources and limited air transport. That would have prolonged and expanded the war over two to three seasons and would have caused far greater degradation of Himalayas. Probably in a year of normal snow, the Pakistan army could have cut off and captured the road from Zojila to Kargil and cut off the approaches to Leh. Nature same time play its own part in human schemes.

**Himalayan Ecology and Insurgency**

In 1989, insurgency, proxy war and terrorism erupted in the Kashmir valley and even the virgin and pristine areas of Doda were affected. In 2001, it was feared that drought, not bullets, may spark an exodus from Doda, since for the last three years, there had been a widespread drought[19]. The proxy war being spread to Doda together with natural resource scarcity comprises a potent mixture for further ecological degradation.

On the other end of Himalayas, in the mid-1950s insurgency erupted in Nagaland. This was followed by other insurgencies in the Northeast. Till today, many parts of the north-east are under the strain of military operations by the security forces to counter insurgency. In insurgency prone areas, economic development gets a low priority. Ecological and environmental issues, though the first casualty, are way down in the order and exist only in research papers or dissertations. On the ground militancy converts to felling of trees by the militants or the security forces for better observation in conditions of jungle warfare.[20] The politics of greed and widespread insurgency are causing serious damage to the incredibly rich forest wealth in the Manas National Park and the foothills of Bhutan. ULFA (United Liberation Front of Assam) militants have shelters in these fragile areas.[21] In 1996, a log of pine cut by the militants was noticed rolling down every 15 minutes in Kashmir.[22]

**Felling of Trees**

Felling of trees by militants and even by pro-security forces oufits[23] has led to deforestation in the catchment areas of the Dal, Wullar, Anchar and Nagina lakes.[24] Recently, *The Hindustan Times* reported:

> Forests were the first victims. Militancy spurred building construction across the valley. People believed that whatever Kashmir's status, the property would remain an asset. Trees were ruthlessly cut and militants smuggled timber at a time when vigilance system in forests had collapsed. Trees were felled and sold at dirt cheap rates............[25]

On a rough calculation the loss in the valley alone has been 150 sq km of forest cover in the past 12 years due to militancy. However, some help has been forthcoming. The media reported that Norway is offering Rs. 150 crore for a/reforestation in J&K.[26] The irony is that even without any militant action, the number of Chinar trees in Srinagar had dropped to 1,500 from a figure of 10,000 in 1985.[27] Indirect influence of militancy in the delicate ecological areas, has been great and direct.

**Nuclear Weapons**

With the threat of nuclear weapons, a new dimension has been added. Although from the comfort of our strategic vision, we may say that nuclear weapons are political weapons for deterrence, never to be used, there may, however, be some remote possibility of a nuclear weapon being used for a tactical or strategic purpose in the Himalayas. There may be a nuclear accident or inadvertent use. Terrorists may also get hold of a crude radiological nuclear weapon.

Studies conducted by think Tanks in Europe and some Indian strategists believe that the Chinese have tactical nuclear weapons in Tibet. Some Indian nuclear theologians suggest that we may consider nuclear area denial munition (ADM) being placed in the passes against the Chinese to be set off once they attack over the passes, to block them. This option is fraught with ecological danger as we are a downstream country and all the rivers from the Himalayas and Tibet flow into India. With ADM, we may get the worst of nuclear contaminated silt.

In any case, even the Chinese plan, as reported in some sections of the media, to use a peaceful nuclear explosion to dam the Brahmaputra in Tibet before it enters India has generated fears of nuclear contamination and silt harming the ecology of downstream countries. In the case of Pakistan, though politically it is a separate country climatically and weather-wise we are one entity in Southern Asia. Western disturbances during winter are broadly from west to east. Fallout of a nuclear weapon in these areas during the winter would be over the Himalayas due to the Western disturbances. In the other seasons, barring the monsoon winds which flow from India towards Pakistan, most winds flow into India and to the Nepal Himalayas.[28] What it means in simple terms is that all the countries sharing the Himalayan ecological system would be affected directly or indirectly by the fallout of a nuclear explosion, irrespective of who uses the weapon first. For the sake of their countries, which every politician and military man swears by, they will have to think over and over before they unkash any nuclear device over the Himalayas or in the region.

## Conclusion

Let us understand and admit that ecological degradation of the Himalayas has been caused due to ignorance, mismanagement, intention, and a mix of natural and human actions. Of the various factors that are a threat to the Himalayas, the military dimension may be the most relevant. Our national strategy should take the long-term ecological degradation into account. Short-term tactical successes should not make us complacent. We need to identify the factors that are leading or may lead to a catastrophe in the Himalayas. A general war which may turn into a nuclear war should never be allowed to occur. Confidence building measures on ecological aspects need to be initiated to tackle common concerns. De-militarisation of eco-sensitive spots, like Siachen should be addressed.

## References

1. 'Background Paper on Himalayan Ecology: Main Issues and Concerns', Tata Energy Research Institute (TERI). Joint Indo-US seminar on Himalayan Ecology of November 2001.
2. *UN Newsletter*. January 19-25, 2002.
3. J.D. Ives and B. Messerli, *The Himalayan Dilemma: Reconciling Development and Conservation*, (London and New York: Routledge, 1989) quoted by Patricia L. Saunders, "Environmental Refugees: The Origins of a Construct" in Philip Stott and Sain Sullivan (edited), *Political Ecology*, (London: Arland Publishers, 2000), Chapter 10.

4. Sailender Nath Ghosh, "Highly Vulnerable", Seminar 378, *The Himalayas,* (February 1991).

5. S.P. Chamoli, *The Great Himalavan Traverse: Kanchengdonga to Karakoram,* (New Delhi: Vikas Publishing House, 1993), pp.150 and 165.

6. *UN Newsletter,* June 8-14, 2002. India did not participate in this UNEP programme probably due to security reasons. Two experts, Jagdish Bahadur, former advisor of the Department of Science and Technology and Syed Iqbal Hasnain from the Glacier Research Group of the JNU, in an interview indicated that awareness in government circles about GLOF is minimal. Too many agencies overlap, with concomitant confusion and grey areas. The Union Ministry of Science and Technology deals with glaciology, whereas ecology comes under the Ministry of External Affairs. While water is looked after by the Ministry of Water Resources. A single agency to mange problems of Himalayas is suggested by them. See, "Ministries play the blame game", *Down to Earth,* (June 30, 2002), pp. 52-53. It is evident that like the complex interdepartmental maze in the issues of the Indian Ocean, the Himalayas also need one single agency as suggested by scholars of maritime security in the draft Indian Ocean Policy.

7. "Nature's Whims and Fancies", *Down to Earth.* (February 28, 2001), pp. 49-50. For an alarming and disturbing report of the result of global warming on abnormal melting of glaciers by group of scientists from Indian Space Research Organisation and Snow and Avalanche Study Establishment, see Anil V. Kulkarni. P. Mathur, B.P. Rathore, Suja Alex, N.Thakur and Manoj Kumar, 'Effect of global warming on snow ablation pattern in Himalaya', *Current Science,* Vol. 83, No. 2, (25 July 2002), pp. 120-123. The glacier degradation due to urbanisation of the Himalayas is 67 per cent as reported by the findings of Delhi University Project in Himachal Pradesh, see, Shruti Maheshwari, "Kuu Valley Paying a Heavy Price for Development: Study", *Hindustan Times (*New Delhi), 21 October 2002.

8. K. Bhupinder Singh, Brigadier "Gangotri is the Most Polluted Area" in Captain M.S. Kohli and Yogendra Bali (edited), *Himalaya: Ecology and Environment,* (New Delhi: Har Anand Publications, 2000). Chapter 5.

9. Sushil Kumar, Lieutenant General (retired), "Gangotri Conservation Project" in Kohli (edited). Ibid, Chapter 34.

10. Mahnaz Z. Ispahani, *Roads and Rivals: The Politics of Access in Borderlands of Asia,* (London: I.B. Tauris and Co. Ltd. 1989), p. 170. Also see Satyanarayan Sinha, *The Chinese Aggression,* (Ram Krishan and Sons/Times of India Press, 1961).

11. A Public Works Department type of road causes 40,000 to 80,000 cubic metres of rock/soil to slide down per kilometre of road. Over 45,000 km of roads are reported to have been built on the Indian Himalayas (as in 1991). Maintenance each year creates yet more debris. See Sanjeev Parakash, "The Problem", *Seminar,* 378, The0Himalayas, (February 1991).

12. Maneka Gandhi, "We Preserve Our Himalayas or We Perish", in M.S. Kohli and Yogendra Bali (edited) *Himalaya,* n 8.

13. H.C. Sarin, "Preservation of Ecosystem in the Himalayas", in S. Kohli and Yogendra Bali (edited), *Himalaya'* n 8.
14. Noguchi Kan, "Cleaning Up Mount Everest", *Japan Quarterly,* (October-December 2000).
15. Gautam Navlakha, "Whither People's Security", *Economic and Political Weekly,* June 9-15, 2001, p. 2038.
16. Srinjoy Chowdhury, "Army Does an Eco Clean Up in Siachen", *The Statesman* (New Delhi), January 2, 2002.
17. V.R. Raghavan, Lieutenant General, *Siachen: Conflict Without End,* (New Delhi: Vikings/Penguin, 2002), p 204, and N.K. Pant, Wing Commander (retired), "Saving Siachen from Ecological Decay", *USI Journal,* (January-March 2002) and A.M. Cariappa, Air Marshal (retired), "Battle Fatigue", *Down to Earth,* (November 15, 2002) and Nanda Cariappa, 'The Siachen standoff', *The Hindu* (New Delhi), November 26, 2002.
18. Atul Aneja, "Siachen as peace park will help", *The Hindu* (New Delhi), June 22, 2001.
19. Arun Joshi, "Not Bullets, but drought may spark exodus in Doda", *Hindustan Times,* New Delhi, March 27, 2001.
20. Romesh Bhattachari, "Fading Forest: North East Faces Disaster", *Frontline,* March 13, 1992.
21. B.P. Singh, "The Eastern Himalayas: Wet Lands, Forests, and Beliefs", *Economic and Political Weekly,* August 4-10, 2001.
22. Max Martin, "Kashmir: Barren Hills and Barren Smoke", *Hindustan Times* (New Delhi), January 8, 1996, reproduced in *Bulletin of Himalayan Research and Cultural Foundation,* Vol. 1, No. 3, (Fall 1996).
23. Harinder Baweja, "Special Report, Interview of Renegade Militant Kuka Parray", *India Today,* December 15, 1995. Kukka Parray explained that to support a cadre of 6,000 men getting salary of Rs 4,000-5,000 per month, he had no other option than to sell trees rather than accept money from the adversary/Pakistan.
24. Sharad K. Soni, 'Himalaya Faces Ecological Threat', *Bulletin of Himalayan Research and Cultural Foundation*, Vol. 1, No. 3. (Fall 1996). The author quotes Max Martin, note 9.
25. Arun Joshi, "Kashmir on the Brink of Eco Disaster", *Hindustan Times,* March 29, 2001.
26. *Ibid.*
27. Rashid Ahmad, "Chinar Trees Victim of Neglect, Greed', New Delhi, *Hindustan Times,* May 2, 2001.
28. Amitav Ghosh, *Countdown*, (Delhi: Ravi Dayal Publishers), pp. 90-95.

# 2

# Ancient Communities of the Himalayas

## Political Aspects

Money, land and woman have been the most important factors in the society over since man first constituted a community. Many scholars have tried to establish that the primitive people did not have political organizations because they had no territorial ambitions. But such opinion may not hold good when examined against the functioning of some of the age-old political institutions, time-honoured practices, popular traditions and beliefs and through some reliable source, which help us to a reasonable extent in having a clear understanding of the 'system' which was prevalent among them during the early period.

## Political Scenario

The central Himalayas had two communities, Kirats and Kols. Neither the political set up of kols nor their societal set up is known. Perhaps they followed the organisational structure of the Kirats. They also had to accept the authority of kirats who were better organised. The political system of the Kiratas was preceded by the social organization in a normal and natural manner. Their kingdom or *rashtra* contained clans *(jana),* communities, *(vish),* families a *(griha* or *kul),* and villages *(grama).* History records that the first stage in political evolution of the tribal people was their clan organization which was followed by the families, bound together by kinship and the formation of villages. Those village-units constituted the nucleus for the whole system.

That proved to be a stepping stone for the organized civil administration. Each of the villages belonging to a group of families or households was governed by a headman. Several clans constituted a larger group, known as the community. The head of community was known as the chief. The phratry was the cementing force between the families, the clans and the state. Their political-evolution resembles, to some extent, to that of the Aryans of the early Vedic age and of the Greeks before the city-states in the Hellenic age. Their political evolution more or less follows the 'Social

Contract Theory', postulated by Rousseau. They had independent or semi-independent tribal forms of government. The magnificent superstructure of their indigenous democratic system was built on the foundation laid in the primitive age.

It is worthy of note that before the formation of tribal states in the early medieval period and the germination of sophisticated political ideas and institutions, the villages were the pivot around which their whole administration revolved. In the primitive days open assembly was held, wherein everything was decided on the basis of collective wisdom. The villagers used to assemble in groups; they used to sit on different stones, placed in different rows in an open ground and, both male and female members used to take part in the deliberations. In the beginning, they had no conception of chieftaincy or kingship.

**Emergence of Chieftainship**

Chieftainship constituted the most important element in the political system of the ancient communities. The emergence of the institution of chieftainship among them goes as far back as the age of *Mahabharata*, which suggests that the Kiratas, Khasas and other tribes of the Himalaya had their own chiefs or kings. From the *Sabha Parva*[1], it is quite evident that Pulinda and Sumana, the two illustrious and virtuous Kshatriya chiefs of the Kiratas and numerous other tribal chiefs attended the imperial assemblage of Yudhishthira.

The classical account bears witness to the fact that the chieftainship had existed among the Kiratas of the Northwestern region much before the 5th century B.C. The epigraphic evidences also prove the existence of the popular political institution among the Kiratas in the ancient times. The Kirata chiefs were nominal heads. They were not acknowledged as the 'rulers' in strict sense rather, they were the 'elders' and spokesmen of the villages. They were assisted by advisers, councillors and other local functionaries in running the day-to-day administration. Any decision pronounced in the village council was considered a mandate for the whole population. They used to manage their affairs in accordance with the republican principles of governance. On the whole, they had a democratic and oligarchic or republican system of government.

**Village Panchayat System**

When village Panchayat system emerged, it constituted the most significant aspect of the local self-government. The self-governing villages were the cornerstones of the political system of both the Aryan and non-Aryan administration. The role played by the entire population in the conduct of administrative business in the village council, an open assembly and a supreme parliament of people, remarkably testifies to the existence of a long standing democratic tradition. A.S. Altekar has rightly stated that, "in historic times republics were flourishing in ancient India in north-western and north-eastern zones."[2] K.P. Jayaswal also affirms that the *parvatiya ganas* were the republican communities.[3] The Puranic and the Epic accounts of the *parvatiya janapadas* of the Kiratas confirm this statement. The Kiratas of the Himalayan region ruled over the entire Central Himalayan region even before the rise of the Buddha as the organized groups, constituting what may now be called as the republics.

V.A. Smith[4] is of the opinion that the customs of hill men give the best clue to the working of the *ganas.* His appreciation of the tribal republics of the so-called Mongoloid origin is very striking. The essence of republican form of government of the Kirata was that the decision was taken on the basis of free and frank discussion in public meetings or in open councils and assemblies. The administration of justice furnishes an illuminating example of their developed democratic system. There was a complete absence of the central authority. Kinship groups were the judicial body. They had a rude but mature sense of jurisprudence. They had disproportionately a small body of civil law under the archaic conditions.

**Penal Laws of Ancient Communities**

The civil jurisprudence, penal law, the unwritten customary law, etc. were generally obeyed. Henry Maine's observation that, "the penal law of ancient communities is not the law of crimes, it is the law of wrongs or to use the English technical word Torts"[5] is absolutely correct. Their customs, conventions, usages, ancient practices, ethical codes, percepts, fables, antecedents, etc. formed the part of their customary laws, which can be fairly compared to the *Dharma Sutras* (600-300 B.C.), a record of social customs and usage, on which civil and criminal laws were based. The tribal justice was guided by the customary laws exactly in the same way as in the pre-Kautilyan age. Hindu system of justice was guided by the *Dharma Sutras.* Their village councils used to function as an open court, where disputes were heard and decided according to the established customs and practices. The village councils constituted a 'supreme court of justice'. They used to decide the civil and criminal cases according to the ancient practices. In ancient times they used to hold open courts for dispensing the justice through arbitration, mutual reconciliation, persuasion and other means.

Their judicial procedure, crimes and punishment, oaths and ordeals were based on the traditional practices. It is worthwhile to note that the political institutions of the Kiratas stand in a marked contrast to the Vedic bicameral bodies—*sabhas* and *samitis,* the *parishads* of the Brahminic or Upanishadic period, the *sanghas* and *ganas* of the age of Panini and Patanjali, the *gana-rajya* of Buddhist India, the Hellenic institutions known as *yepovia* or *senatus*, the folk-assemblies *ayopa* of Homeric age, democratic and oligarchical institutions of Pericles age, Public Councils of Burma known as *hiuttaws* and *byedaiks*. These were also different from the minor republics of Chumbi valley in Tibet and other folk-assemblies, senates and tribunals of western countries.[6]

Just like the Kiratas, the Khasa-polity and their political organizations were also based on the democratic pattern. They formed some sort of oligarchic republics in the hills. The Aryan kingdoms in the plains had contact with those Khasa republics, which find mention in the *Mahabharata* and later in Panini's *Ashtadhyayi*. Besides trade and commerce, these republics had political relationship with the Kauravas and Pandavas. The Khasas, Eksanas, Paradas and Kulindas visited Yudhishthira during his *rajsuya yajna*.

**Republican States**

The families, clan, tribes and village communities were often formed into republican states which evolved a strong and settled organization no less significant than the organization of an empire.[7] The existence of Indian republics is attested by the Greek writers too. The *Santiparva* of the *Mahabharata* throws light on the working of republics. It may be assumed that the other tribal groups followed almost the same pattern of political system as of the Kiratas on account of their contemporaneity and also geographical contiguity. The Khasas are considered republican by the scholars. Dr. Rhys Davids, K.P. Jayaswal and Dr. R.K. Mukherjee agree to the fact.

The Kunindas had a republican form of government. They had a constitution which provided for the election of a king's consul, and was the type what Kautilya calls a *rajsubdin sangha*, a republic which recognized a title of the *rajan*. The Kuninda coins were struck in the name of king and the political community. The Kuninda king was always mentioned there as *amoghabhuti*, i.e., of the unfailing prosperity; and that appellation appears for centuries (150 B.C. to 100 A.D.). This was an official title, and not a personal name. Varahmihira mention the leaders of the *gana* of the Kunindas. In the Constitution of the Kuninda republic "the Council of Elders" ruled. There were hereditary royal families in republican bodies, those have also been mentioned in the *Mahabharata*. The 'kings' were responsible to the Council, which was probably elected by the whole community. Being a democracy, the Central Assembly consisted mostly of the members of the landed military aristocracy of the Kshatriya class.

**Popular Councils**

The towns and villages, however, had their own popular councils consisting of elders, hailing from all the classes and professions. The executive authority in some of those republics was in some constitutions delegated to a second chamber or the house of elders, while in others it remained with the general *gana* or parliament. The officers, called the chiefs or leaders of the *gana* formed the executive body or the cabinet. The elders formed another body. They were like a second house. They had varying powers according to individual constitutions.[9] The central executive of the republic was originally elected by the central assembly. That seems to have been a sort of corporate body. But, from the coins of Kunindas, issued in the 2nd-1st century B.C., the *rajanya* or *rana* seems to have gathered power and that office had become confined to a few hereditary royal families.

The membership of the central executive became hereditary in the course of time, and with the disintegration of democracies during the supremacy of Indo-Greeks, Sakas and Kushanas in the northwest of India, those *ranayana* or *rana* families became supreme and independent in their territories That way *ranayana* age was ushered in at least in the Himachal hills. Similarly, the petty principalities, with feudals assuming title of king, may be observed in Garhwal and Kumaon region. Thus, the Kuninda republic was broken into small fragments under many petty chiefs or *ranas.*

As is revealed from the vastness of the area in which their coins have been found. The Yaudheyas were perhaps the largest republic.

The chiefs of the Yaudheyas adopted the viceregal title. The adopted a system which Lichchhavis in earlier times had been following. The Yaudheyas used a term *gana* for themselves. According to Jayaswal,[10] that *gana* may be considered the same as the modern democracy. He quotes references in support of the fact that the Yaudheyas existed much earlier than their coins. This has been doubted by P.L. Gupta,[11] who considers that the word *gana* must not have meant the same thing in the later period. He thinks that the terms *janapada* and *gana* referred to a democracy. But these terms must have meant to two different forms. In his opinion the word *gana* should mean some sort of federation. We know of their federal communion with the Arjunayanas and the Kunindas at the time, when they had decided to overthrow the Kushana power. Yaudheya coins of 3rd and 4th century A.D. bore the legend *Yaudheya Ganasya Jayah'*[12] which may reveal that they reverted to a *gana-based* constitution and the presiding or tutelary deity or the leader had no relevance any more.

**Sangha and Gana**

Yaudheyas have called themselves as the *gana* on their coins though panini refers to them as *sangha*. In the *Mahabharata,* both those terms, *samgha* and *gana,* have been used to mean republican states in general.[13]

K.P. Jayaswal asserts that the democracy of Yaudheyas was not a conservative and narrow setup, but a tribal one in a strict sense of the term. He refers to the *Mahabharata* to define tribal set-up based on legal and communal understanding. Panini also mentions that the martial states had men of all castes and not of one *gotra* or one tribal origin.

One set of the Yaudheya coins was struck in the name of the *Mantradharas* and the *gana,* while the other set was struck simply in the name of *gana.* It, therefore, appears that the chief or leaders of the *gana* formed the executive body or the cabinet. And, as the *Mahabharata* says, the main difficulty with the *gana* type of constitution was about the maintenance of secrecy among the numerical strength of its members. It is probable that they might have formed a 'second house' of the 'elders' who had varying powers, differing according to their individual status.

In times of war and difficulties, aristocratic families used to manage administration and lead the armies, though they did not usually had the title of *raja* and *maharaja.* The Central assemblies of the Yaudheyas used to elect central executive of the republics[14] The head of the Yaudheya state was given the regal title of *maharaja* but the post was elective[15] and he was not permitted to put his name on the state coinage. The so-called *maharaja* used to be the commander-in-chief of the tribe, besides being the head of the state.

Dr. P.L. Gupta has critically examined various other factors and has confirmed that the successors of the Yaudheya republic were nominated by the ruling heads, approved by the *gana (puraskrita).* The *maharaja* (the head of the tribe) was also a *mahakshatrapa, mahasenapati* or a *senapati.*[16] It is not established as to how those *maharajas* were elected. It is presumed that the presidents of the city councils and village *panchayats* and also the members of the families might had been putting their candidates for that election.

**Political Confederation**

In 200 A.D., the Kunindas, Yaudheyas and Arjunayanas formed a union of tribes. This has been confirmed by many scholars. The foreign and military affairs remained centrally controlled, probably by a council of presidents of those republics, elected by the federating units. These presidents enjoyed the title of *maharaja mahasenapati*[17] That is further confirmed by the prevalence of the word *dvi* and *tri* on some of the coins of that community, which indicates that they belonged to the second or third section of the confederation.

In the 5th century A.D., the federal set-ups disappeared totally and their coinage also came to an end by c. 400 A.D. The communities in the Central Himalaya during ancient period were largely democratic and based on the republican political system. The maturity of that system may be noticed in the republics of the Kunindas and the Yaudheyas. However in the later times, we find the rise of feudal system and the emergence of monarchical form of government. We see that the Katyuris in Garhwal and Kumaon region ruled from 6-7th century to 10th century. They established monarchical form of government. The king was all in all in the polity of the state. This form of government became a rule over India in the subsequent period of its history.

## References


1. *Mahabharat, Sabha Parva,* Section IV, p. 7.
2. Altekar, A.S., *State and Government in Ancient India,* p. 118.
3. *Journal of the Bihar and Orissa Research Society,* Vol. L, Part. II, pp. 173-78.
4. *Indian Antiquary,* 1905, pp. 233-35.
5. Lowie, Robert H., *Primitive Society,* pp. 4-5.
6. Singh, G.P., 'A Study of the Tribal Republic of North-East India', *North-east Affairs, Quarterly Study of Trends and Events,* 1986, pp. 79-103.
7. Mukherjee, R.K., *Democracies in the East,* p. 76.
8. Varahamihira, *Brihatsamhita:* Ed. by S. Dvivedi, Eng. trans. H. Kern, pp. 81-86.
9. Jayaswal, K.P., *op. cit.,* pp. 74-75.
10. *Ibid.,* p. 148.
11. *Indian Historical Quarterly,* Vol. XXVII, No. 1, p. 200.
12. Allan, J., *British Museum Catalogue of Ancient India,* CLI.
13. *Mahabharata, Shanti Parva,* 82 and 108.
14. Altekar, A.S. and Mazumdar, R.C., *op. cit.,* p. 266.
15. Jayaswal, K.P., *op. cit.,* p. 43.
16. *JNSI,* Vol. XXXII (1970), part. II, p. 154.
17. A fragmentary inscription depictings these designation has been found at Bharatpur.

# 3
# The Survival Economy and Forest Conflicts in Himalayas

## Indigenous Management for Satisfaction of Basic Needs

According to Tagore, 'Forests have nurtured India's mind and India's civilization. Intellectual growth in India did not take place in enclosures made of brick, wood and mortar, but was inspired by the life of the forests in which nature's living forces express themselves in daily variation, creating a diversity of life and sounds, providing the context for the understanding of nature and man. Human understanding in such a context, could not be restricted to perceiving nature as inert, as an accumulation of dead resources waiting for exploitation. Nature provides light, air, food and water through living processes of creative renewal. This awareness of life in nature as a precondition for man's survival led to the worship of light, air, food and water and they were considered sacred. Indian culture has been cradled by the culture of the forest, first in the Vedic period and later during the times of Buddha and Mahavir."

Indian civilisation is distinctive in that sense it evolved in the forests, not in the city. Thus, forests in India had remained central to its civilisational evolution. The forest based 'ashramas' (settlements) produced the best scientific research and cultural writings and India thus came to be known as an 'Aranya Samskriti' or a forest culture. Human understanding of the fundamental ecological utility of forest ecosystems and their economic importance led to veneration of trees. This basic dependence on the existence of forests for human survival was the material basis underlying the worship of trees in almost all human societies.

## Aranyani

In the *Rig Veda,* forests are described as Aranyani or mother goddess who takes care of wildlife and ensures the availability of food to man. These ashramas and forests, not urban settlements, were recognised as the highest form of cultural evolution providing society with both intellectual guidance and material sustenance. This civilisational principle became the foundation of torest conservation as a social ethic through millenia.

Its erosion began with the spread of colonial methods of management of forests in India. Teak from the forests of the Western Ghats, sal from Central and Northern India and conifers from the Himalayas were felled to meet the timber needs of the British empire.

The result was not merely the destruction of forests but the destruction of a culture that conserved forests. India's forest wealth is characterised by richness of diversity which is related to the diversity of soil types and climate. Moist tropical evergreen and semi-evergreen forests are characteristic of the Western Ghats and the northeastern region. Tropical dry deciduous forests are seen in the north and the south with sal and teak being the dominant species, respectively. The Himalayan region has a diversity of moist and dry temperate forests changing into alpine vegetation at the highest altitudes. Each region of India had paid special attention to the growth of village forests with multipurpose tree species providing, fuel, fodder, fruits, fibre, green manure, etc.

**Ecological Role of Forests**

The ecological role of forests in soil and water conservation was widely recognised and social control over the felling of trees in ecologically sensitive areas like river banks was strictly exercised.The protection and propagation of forests as a deeply ingrained civilisational characteristic in the South Asian region is evident from the existence of sacred groves in river catchments and foreshores of tanks, and from village woodlots. These practices were, of critical value both ecologically and economically. Ecologically, indigenous and naturalised vegetation has provided essential life support by stabilising the soil and water systems.

Economically, trees have been a source of small timber, fodder, fuel, fibre, medicines, oils, dyes, etc. Indigenous medicines use more than 2,000 species of plants, both wild and cultivated. The centrality of trees to survival and economic well-being created the need for their conservation which was achieved through the concept of sacredness. In the archaeological remains of the Harappan culture, it is clear that even in the third or fourth millenia BC trees were held in high esteem and were worshipped.

The planting of trees, either for their fruit or for the purpose of obtaining shade, was an act which was held in high esteem in oriental countries, and especially in India, since ancient times.

The oriental appreciation of the luxury of shade led to the plantation of trees along canals and highways. In the Sunnud (Royal Order) of Emperor Akbar, it is directed that on both sides of the canal down to Hissar, trees of every description, both for shade and blossom, be planted, so as to make it like the canal under the tree in paradise; and that the sweet flavour of the rare fruits may reach the mouth of everyone. During the reign of Emperor Sher Shah a 2,000 km long Grand Trunk Road, connecting Punjab and Bengal, was planted with shade-giving trees on both sides. Travel along this route was increasing day by day and extreme chimates in India demanded this.

**Plantation of Trees**

Roadside plantations of trees constitute another vital source of tree wealth, not only providing ample shade to the traveller but also ensuring a steady flow of supplies of timber, fuel, fruits, green manure and animal feed. This was so in Mysore state in mid-nineteenth century. The access roads to the villages from the main highways were known for their leafy cover, generally of honge, neem and tamarind, and maintained by the village organisations themselves; and the avenues along the highways were covered by species such as ala, bage, neem, tamarind and jamun, and were managed by the services of the State administration.

A report on forest area of the princely State of Mysore: in 1880-81 reflects the importance attached to village forests and roadside plantations by the state administration village forests numbered 16,293 standing on a total area of 14,376 acres and containing 8,11,308 trees while 3,750 miles of public roads had been planted with trees on both sides, at distances varying from twelve to sixty feet.

Plants (oshadhis) and trees (vanaspatis) are personified as goddesses and deities and collectively invoked as the jungle goddess, 'Aranyani', in the *Vedas*. All religions and cultures of the South Asian region are rooted in forests, not out of fear and ignorance but due to ecological insights. This is true of all forest cultures in the tropics. As Myers observes,

> In contrast to the folklore of temperate zones, which often regard forests as dark places of danger, traditional perceptions of forests in the humid tropics convey a sense of intimate harmony, with people and forests equal occupants of a communal habitat. A primary source of congruity between man and nature.

**Conflicts Over Forests Resources**

Conflicts over forest resources in India can be demarcated into four phases. The first phase began when the British 'reserved' large tracts of forests for commercial exploitation to meet the military and other needs of the British empire. These conflicts led to forest struggles and forest satyagrahas during the late nineteenth and early twentieth centuries. The second phase was the post-colonial phase when the 1952 forest policy led to the rapid expansion of forest based industry, large-scale clear felling of natural forests, and their conversion to monocultures of commercial species. Conflicts generated by this intensification of forest use led to movements like Chipko.

In the third phase, spurred partly as a response to growing public criticism of the commercial exploitation of forests, and partly as a response to the crisis in the supply of raw materials for wood based industry, industrial plantations expanded on farm lands and village commons under 'Social Forestry' and 'Wasteland Development Programmes'. These afforestation programmes have become a new source of conflicts during the eighties. The fourth phase is expected to emerge in the future as international finance, changes in biotechnologies and biomass conversion into chemical and energy substitutes for petroleum based products, supported by major investments in forestry. A new level of transnationalisation of forest use and forest conflicts, are likely to emerge because of these new requirements and thursts.

**Colonial Forestry: Commercialisation Against Survival**

Colonial rule introduced dramatic breaks in the way in which forests in India were perceived and used. The perception of forest ecosystems as having multiple functions for satisfying diverse and vital human needs for air, water and food was superseded by the growth of one-dimensional scientific forestry during the colonial period which had as its only objective the maximisation of the production of commercially valuable timber and wood while ignoring the other ecological and economic objectives for the utilisation of forest resources.

In India, forests play three major economic roles. In order of their significance for economic development in a democratic society like ours they may be classified as contributions to:

1. Nature's economy through regulating the supply of water to the nation's water resources and conserving soil to support the viability of this vital economic function.
2. Survival economy by providing the supply of basic domestic biomass needs of fodder, fuel, fertiliser, etc., to three-fourths of the population.
3. Market economy by providing the supply of wood for satisfying industrial and commercial demands.

**Defence against Floods**

Obviously, the first contribution of forests to the national economy through maintenance of nature's economy is the defense against the threat to our survival from floods, droughts and soil erosion. Commonly this is characterised as conservation. Lack of recognition of this vital contribution led to the downfall of the Roman, Mayan, Harappan and Mesopotamian civilisations. The second contribution is the sustenance of nearly three-fourths of the people who depend on the free productivity of nature for the satisfaction of basic biomass needs. The process of growth of wood based industries which obviously comes after survival and sustenance is ensured, and not before it. This is also a very important contribution which the forests make to the natural economy.

Conflicts over forests emerged when colonial rule ignored nature's economy and the survival economy through indifference to the conservation and basic needs role of forestry, and developed forestry only along the one-dimensional criterion of commercial industrial requirements. Forest resources, like other resources needed for survival, have traditionally been common resources, collectively managed and utilised by village communities. They could not consistently with the principles of Hindu law and the customs of the country belong to any individual. To transform these common forest resources into commodities from which revenues and profits could be derived, it was therefore necessary to change property relationships. Through the Indian Forest Acts of 1865 and 1878, the British acquired a monopoly right over all valuable tracts of forests by converting them into 'reserved forests'.

The traditional free access to forests of the forest communities was therefore curtailed. British forest legislation aroused resistance from village communities, which were thus deprived. Local revolts broke out in all forest regions of the country. Forest struggles have been a sustained response to commercial forestry introduced by the British. The earliest records of commercial exploitation are of a syndicate formed in 1796 by Mr. Mackonchie of the Medical Service for the extraction of teak in Malabar to meet the demand for shipbuilding and military purposes. In 1806, a police officer, Captain Watson, was appointed the first Conservator of Forests in India incharge of Malabar and Travancore, to extract teak for the King's navy, indicating that policing not science, was needed in the colonial forestry of that period. Indigenous trade was sealed and peasants were denied rights.

> By 1823 the growing discontent of the forest proprietors and timber merchants, chafing under the restrictions of the timber monopoly, and the outcry of the peasants, indignant at the fuel cutting restrictions, came to a head. On the recommendation of the Governor of Madras, Sir Thomas Munro, and with the consent of the Supreme Government, the conservatorship, on which Captain Watson had been followed by several successors during the seventeen years of its existence, was abolished.

**Forest Act of 1927**

The traditional rights of local people had been denial by the government by the Forest Act of 1927. This aroused new response against the denial of these rights. During 1930-31 forest *satyagrahas* were organised throughout India as a protest against the reservation of forests for exclusive exploitation by British commercial interests and the transformation of a common resource into a commodity. Villagers ceremonially collected forest produce from the reserved forests to assert their right to satisfy their basic needs of forest products. The forest *satyagrahas* were particularly successful in regions where survival of the local population was intimately linked with the access to forests as in the Himalayas, the Western Ghats and Central India. These non-violent protests were suppressed by the armed intervention of the British rulers. In Central India, Gond tribals were shot down for participating in the *satyagraha*. On 30 May 1930 several unarmed villagers were killed and hundreds injured in Tilari village of Tehri Garhwal when they gathered to protest against the reservation of forests. Following the loss of many lives, the *satyagrahas* were finally successful in reviving some of the traditional rights of the village communities to forest produce as recognised privileges. The British government had to concede many of the demands.

The imperative for increasing revenue and profits in a growth economy, however, drives resource utilisation patterns in directions which maximise production of the commercially valuable components of the ecosystem at the cost of destruction of those components which are commercially valueless but essential to survival. The forest *satyagrahas*, like the Salt Satyagraha, were generally protests against legislation introduced by the British administration which transformed vital common resources into resources reserved for revenue and profit generation through the establishment of monopoly rights and control. These *satyagrahas* were a response to conflicts which were based on the exclusion of the competing demand on the resources for survival needs.

**Exclusion of Local Communities**

Thus, in the case of forest resources it was not enough to manipulate policy and legislation to exclude the local communities from free access to forests. It also became imperative to manipulate nature to increase the production of biomass for commerce at the cost of decreasing and destroying biomass for survival. Systems of science and technology thus combined with systems of policy and legislation in becoming essential tools for the appropriation of vital common resources for commerce, revenue and profits. Scientific and technical aspects of forestry determine prescriptions for the functioning of forests which maximise immediate production of wood of commercial value through the destruction of other biomass forms that have lower commercial value but may have very high use value. Silvicultural systems of modern forestry are prescriptions for destruction of non-commercial biomass for the increased production of commercial biomass.

Ultimately, this increase in commercial production is achieved by mining the ecological capital of the forest ecosystem and disrupting the essential hydrological and nutrient cycles of nature which make plant, animal and human life possible. The growth of commercial economic activity through the manipulation of nature generates second order conflicts over natural resources which arise not merely from issues of how a particular resource is distributed, but also how it is utilised and how it affects related resources. Thus, in the case of forest resources, contemporary conflicts are being generated by silvicultural systems aimed at maximising the production of commercially and industrially valuable species like eucalyptus, pine and teak, through the destruction of natural indigenous mixed forests which have a high use value for basic needs and for ecological stability.

In Bihar, the conversion of sal forests into teak plantations has been resisted by the tribals. In 1980, a violent confrontation between tribals and the forest officials and police in Gua resulted in the death of thirteen tribals and three policemen. This clash was the outcome of the conflict between two types of silviculture, one based on trees for the people and the other based on trees for commerce. Movements arising from conflicts over natural resources at this level are ecologically rooted since they do not merely emerge from an unfair distribution of a single resource, but from the unjust and unsustainable use of an ecosystem as a complex of interrelated resources. In ecologically sensitive regions, the destruction of forest ecosystems has in turn threatened the survival of the forest dwelling communities.

**Ecological and Economic Crisis**

The people's response to this deepening ecological and economic crisis induced by the commercial exploitation of resources has been the emergence of movements for the conservation of forest resources throughout the country. The most well-known and successful among these is non-violent Gandhian movement called the Chipko (hug the tree) movement. Chipko as a national campaign for forest conservation is a response to the multidimensional conflicts over forest resources at the scientific, technical, ecological and economic levels. Beginning in the early seventies in the Garhwal region of Uttar Pradesh, the methodology and philosophy of Chipko has now spread to Himachal in the north, Karnataka in the south, Rajasthan in the west and Bihar in the east.

The British were hardpressed for hardwood since their own oak forests were destroyed and rendered unproductive in the second-half of the eighteenth century through unscientific management. Stebbing has recorded the situation in India after the arrival of the British The arrival of the British and their exploitation of India's forest resources marked a new phase in the use of forest produce in India:

> The new Administration possessed no knowledge of tropical forestry, nor, indeed, of European forestry, since British forestry had almost ceased to be understood as a commercial enterprise in Great Britain. With the realisation of the value of teak the British Admiralty were soon engaged in enquiries with the object

> of replacing (local) oak timber by teak from India for use in the construction of the Fleet. For the supplies of first-class oak timber were falling short in England owing to the cessation of the planting, which had fallen off to a great extent early in the later part of the eighteenth century.

**Requirement of Oak by British Navy**

In 1805 there was no oak available in England any more. The Directors of East India Company received a missive from the King, enquiring to what extent the King's navy might, in view of the growing shortage of oak in England, depend on a permanent supply of teak timber from Malabar. This despatch led to the immediate formation of a forest committee charged with a comprehensive programme of enquiry both into the capacity of the forests themselves, and the status of proprietory rights on them. Thus, the first real interest expressed in the forests of India and the subsequent study of those accessible at the time originated from England, and the reason was the same which had kept forestry in the forefront in England for a period of three centuries—the safety of the empire, which depended upon its 'wooden walls'.

The planting of oak owing to the supineness of successive governments had fallen into abeyance for nearly a century, and the country was faced with a shortage in timber supplies which, in view of the bid of the French for sea supremacy, might well spell the doom of England. When the British started exploiting Indian timber for military purposes, they did it rapaciously, because the great continent appeared to hold inexhaustible tracts covered with dense jungles, but there was no apparent necessity for their detailed exploration even had this been a possibility. In the early years of our occupation the botany of the forests, the species of trees they contained and their respective values was an unopened book. No body knew what our jungles contained. The Indian rulers of the time never factored the jungles in their scheme of the things. The new British master did not bothes. The gabbed the jungles.

**Denuding the Jungles**

As far as the government and its officials were concerned, the important role played by forests in nature and the tremendous influence they had on the physical well-being of a country went unnoticed, neither were they able to, appreciate their importance to the people nor their revenue producing potential. In view of the tremendous forest wealth that existed, for some years the government obtained its full requirements without any difficulty and the people also managed to get all they wanted. The early administrators appear to have been convinced that this state of affairs could continue for an unlimited period of time; and that in many localities forests were an obstruction to agriculture and, therefore, a limiting factor to the prosperity of the country. The overall policy was to expand agriculture and the watchword of the time was to destroy forests with this end in view. On the one hand, they wanted land for agriculture. At the same time they wanted wood. they started ravaging the jungles.

The requirement of the military for Indian teak led to an immediate proclamation declaring that the royalty right in teak trees claimed by the former government in the south of the continent was vested in the East India Company. Under increased pressure from the Home government to ensure the maintenance of the future strength of the King's navy, the decision was taken to appoint a special officer to superintend the forest work; someone who was conversant with the language and habits of the people in addition to having a knowledge of forests. His duties were to preserve and improve the production of teak and other timber suitable for shipbuilding. A police officer, Captain Watson was appointed the first Conservator of Forests in India in November 1806. Under the proclamation of April 1807, he wielded great powers, which unfortunately were somewhat vague in both in scope and in the extent of interference he was permitted in the established order. He did not conserve the jungles. He started cutting them.

**Forest Conflicts in the Himalaya**

In the Garhwal Himalayas, an Englishman, Mr. Wilson, obtained a lease in 1850 to exploit all the forests of the Bhagirathi Valley for a low annual rental of Rs. 400. Under his axe several valuable Deodar and Chir forests were cleared, felled and completely destroyed. In 1864, inspired by Mr. Wilson's flourishing timber business, the British rulers of the Northwestern provinces obtained a lease for twenty years and engaged Wilson to exploit these forests for them. European settlements, such as Mussoorie, created new pressures for the cultivation of food crops, leading to large-scale felling of oak forests. The conservation of forests was not considered. In his report on the forests of the state, E.A. Courthope, IFS, remarked: 'It seems possible that it was not mainly with the idea of preserving the forests that government entered into this contract'. Inspired by the economic success of Mr. Wilson and the government, in 1895 the Tehri state took over the management of forests. Between 1897 and 1899 forest areas were reserved and restrictions were imposed on village use. These restrictions were resented and completely disregarded by the villagers, and led to incidents of organised resistance against the authorities. On 31 March 1905 a Durbar Circular (No. 11) from the Tehri King announced modifications to these restrictions in response to the resistance. These modifications, however, failed to diffuse the tension. Struggles took place throughout the kingdom, but the most significant one occurred in 1907 when a forest officer, Sadanand Gairola, was manhandled in Khandogi. When King Kirti Shah heard about the revolt he rushed to the spot to pacify the citizens. The Doon Valley in the Garhwal Himalayas is an example of how colonial forest policy eroded the traditional management systems for forest use for basic needs. Forests for commercial exploitation became the norm. Traditional system of forest use was completely ignorned systematic denuding of forests started.

**Himalayan Settlements**

Earlier settlements of Dehradun were located in the slopes of the Himalayan belt and the triangular plateau in the valley defined by the rivers Tons and Rispana. These settlements were of the agro-pastoral type and their requirements of forest resources were non-commercial in nature—fodder, fuel, structural timber for housing and agricultural implements. The exploitation of forests for the satisfaction of these needs was controlled by the social organisation of these villages. Clusters of several villages were called taluks. Each village was the property of a community of cultivating owners, managed by a headman or sayana who, as representative of the community, held his village in subordination to the sayana of the whole taluk.

The bond that held together the villages in a taluk was the community ownership and management of grazing and forest lands. The forests used by villages were traditionally under the ownership and management of an entire community and not of a private individual. It had also been reported in a letter to the Secretary of the Board of Revenue, which states that forests and wastelands:

> could not consistently with the principles of the Hindu law and the customs of the country belong to any individual and must ascertain to the state as public property.... By Hindu law a piece of land, sufficient for the pasturage of cattle was directed to be left uncultivated around each town or village, between it and the fields under cultivation.

Besides the social control built into the management of forests as commons, people also had their indigenous conservation strategies. As Pant reports, in the hill regions,

> A natural system of conservancy was in vogue, almost every hill top is dedicated to some local deity and the trees on or about the spot are regarded with great respect so that nobody dare touch them. There is also a general impression among the people that every one cutting a tree should plant another in its place.

**Management of Resources**

That this system of management of resources ensured the sustainable utilisation of forests is reflected by the fact that while this tenure system continued, village forests around taluks like Dwara and Malkot were in a very good condition as reported in accounts of the last century. The sustainable utilisation of forests near the villages ensured their health and limited the exploitation of forests in the rest of the valley, which remained virgin till the British entry in 1914.

The British were interested only making money. They did not require that much wood for ship-building, there was commerce to think about. The British rule introduced drastic changes in the pattern of forest produce utilisation. First, a new pressure was put on the virgin sal forests by linking them with far-reaching commercial demands outside the valley. Second, the British administration changed the ancient tenure pattern, overtly and covertly, by introducing the zamindari system, which destroyed the community organisation. Third, the large-scale colonisation of the valley through liberal land grants to Europeans converted large forest tracts into agricultural or plantation areas. The use of virgin forests as mines for sal (Shorea Robusta), sissoo (Dalbergia Sissoo) and tun (Tuna Siliata) timber under the free felling system led to rapid and severe degradation. The free felling system allowed uncontrolled extraction of timber in exchange for revenues on the produce. As William writes in his memoirs:

> Reckless waste was inevitable and the fine sal forests began to disappear rapidly. The absence of conservancy was absolute. The district still abounded in fine trees 100 to 200 years old and upwards. All these fell before the axe. And probably the rest would have gone with them had the roads been a little better. The consequences of this bad system are most perceptible in Western Dun.

Initially, the forests were leased against fixed revenues to individuals who farmed the dues from the actual extractors. For the period 1819-21 the average revenue for Dehradun was Rs. 4,000. In 1839 the forests were leased for Rs. 6,500 a year. However, when Mr. Vansitartt, the Superintendent of Dehradun, discovered that the actual amount collected was Rs. 80,000 a year, he discontinued the lease and took charge of the collection. Subsequently, the Forest Department was established in 1855. As the 1911 *Gazetteer* reports:

> The forest department instituted in 1855, concentrated its energies on the collection of revenue without making any attempt at systematic conservancy. It was in fact nothing but a forest revenue collecting agency. The effect of this neglect became apparent in 1867 when the revenue reached the low figure of Rs. 23, 333.

**Community Control**

Community control had been maintained on a sustainable basis. The new inequalities imposed on the region by the British administration through the introduction of the zamindari system became a source of degradation of village forests, In this process village forests were declared to be the property of zamindars of the villages to which they appertained. These zamindars, as new centres of economic and political power, completely destroyed the community organisation and its control over village forests. Thus, 'in Malkot *iliqua* (region) containing 31 villages the cultivating proprietors had lost their power .... a disability due to the aggression of the superior sayana, Surjan Negi, a man of capital and influence'. Surjan Negi's capital and influence was, in turn, derived from the fact that in 1822 forests in the valley were farmed to him. This economic power of a contractor coupled with the power of a zamindar completely destroyed the role and responsibility of the sayanas in the management of common resources for common use. As the control of the community was substituted by the control of the zamindars, the zamindars were only 'too anxious to make money as fast as possible out of their new acquisitions. In pursuance of this policy they prohibited the tenants from grazing and cutting wood in the village forests and sold the latter to charcoal burners who completely denuded the hillsides'.

The British wanted to colonise the valley. The climate in the valley was suitable to Europeans. In 1838, some did come. They were given ample grants. The *Gazetteer* of 1911 records that:

> the grantees were bound to clear the whole of their grants within 20 years with the exception of the irremediably barren land. The land was to be subject to a progressive rental until the tenth year when it reached its maximum of 12 annas with which may be compared the universal rate of 14 annas proposed by Maj Young in his settlement.[20]

These grants covered large areas with the original nine grants amounting to nearly 200 sq km. The best sites among these had been appropriated by the officers of the district or persons associated with them. The extent of clear felling of forests through a single administrative decision was the most significant factor contributing to the depletion of forest cover in the Doon Valley. This deforestation altered the face of the valley and reduced the stability of the river banks. Indicating this impact the *Gazetteer* of 1911 reported that 'near Dehra Dun the scenery has been somewhat spoilt by the rapid spread of cultivation and the cutting down of the sal trees that used to lie in the high banks of the numerous ravines in the neighbourhood'.

## Agricultural Surplus

British were thinking on two fronts. One, the trees would give them revenues. Once the land was cleared, it could be put to use for agriculture. Large-scale clear felling of forests for agricultural land use was a typical colonial phenomenon, which was the outcome of the colonial view of agricultural surplus as an important source of revenue. As the eighth settlement report admitted:

> Perhaps no mistake was more common in the early days of British rule than to suppose that the extension of the cultivation wherever culturable land could be found and the clearing of forest and jungle to extend cultivation, must necessarily benefit the country and the government, and should be encouraged and pushed as much as possible. It is now fully recognised that every country requires to have a certain proportion of its area under forests, and that in a tropical country like India, where the heat is so intense, and the very existence and well being of the people depend on a regular and sufficient rainfall, this proportion should be even larger than in European countries.

These ecological considerations were not, however, the central objectives of the reservation of forests through the notification of the Forest Act of 1878. The reservation of forests was guided largely by the fact that: 'Forests in themselves constituted a property of great value and might be made to yield an annual revenue equally with cultivation'.[23]

**Forest Reservation**

Forest reservation denied the local people access to the free use of forests. Village forests which were not reserved were declared to be the property of zamindars to which they pertained. While villagers thus lost their traditional resource bases, their requirements were not systematically included in the management of reserved forests. The reserved forests managed by the forest department continued to be guided by the objective of revenue maximisation through commercial exploitation of forests. The only difference between the earlier free felling system and the present system of scientific management through the working plans was that the same objective was achieved in a more systematic and regular manner. This conservancy was thus made an equivalent to maintaining revenues. Neither ecological considerations nor considerations of the basic needs of villagers were an intrinsic part of this scientific management. According to the 1911 *Gazetteer*:

> During the earlier years of conservancy the forest department denied that the villagers possessed any rights of any description. The government, however, called for a report from the Superintendent Mr. H.G. Ross who took a very different view of the matter. He described the most extensive prescriptive 'right' in grazing as having existed from time immemorial and he produced much evidence in support of his contention. The forest department, however, preferred to call the grazing facilities enjoyed by the people 'privileges'.

A systematic management for satisfying the basic needs of the local population never became an intrinsic part of the management of reserved forests. The direction in which the systematic approach did evolve was largely in the area of quantifying growing stock to guide felling to ensure steady revenue returns. When Mr. Ross's report became the basis of notification No. 702 of 1880, specifying the list of villages entitled to special grazing facilities, the forest department was successful in the battle of words, so that 'rights' were not admitted, but villages included in Mr. Ross's list were permitted to exercise certain privileges.

**Conflicts Over Forests**

Conflicts over forests emerged because colonial rule ignored the demands of nature's economy and the survival economy through indifference to the conservation and basic needs role of forestry, and developed forestry only along the one dimensional criterion of commercial/industrial requirements.

Subsequent to notification No. 702 of 1880 based on Ross's report of the villagers' rights to forest produce, notification No. 889F of 1893 very clearly spelt out the management framework for meeting local needs of grazing, fodder, fuelwood, poles and thatching grass for housing. According to this notification, the Divisional Forest Officer (DFO) was to prepare an annual list of forest areas which would be open to grazing. The list would specify which areas, in which block of the forest, would be open for grazing in that year. The grazing of cattle in the said reserve blocks was to be regulated in either of the following ways:

1. By arrangement to a fixed settlement every three years based on an enumeration of cattle they desired to graze.
2. By a yearly pass obtainable from the DFO.

On the basis of a list prepared in this manner the DFO was to issue herdsmen badges specifying the number of permitted cattle, the names of villagers owning the cattle and the names of the herdsmen. Only those cattle under the charge of a herdsman and certified by the number on his badge were permitted to graze.

**Removal of Fodder Grass**

Village communities enjoying these grazing facilities were also to be permitted to collect and remove headloads of fodder grass as well as fallen and dry fuel free of charge. Although operationalising this management scheme was the most important precondition for satisfying basic needs as well as protecting the reserved forests from degradation, they do not appear to have been enforced in the working plans.

In the Kumaon region there is evidence that the needs of the empire and not of the local people led to rapid forest denudation. According to Atkinson's *Gazetteer*,

> the forests were denuded of good trees in all places. The destruction of trees of all species appears to have continued steadily and reached its climax between 1855 and 1861 when the demands of the Railway authorities induced numerous speculators to enter into contracts for sleepers, and these men were allowed, unchecked, to cut down old trees far in excess of what they could possibly export, so that for some years after the regular forest operations commenced, the department was chiefly busy cutting up and bringing to the depot the timber left behind by the contractors.

While the local people were denied their traditional rights to forest resources, and while the colonial forest policy became a 'policy for deforestation', the local people were often blamed for the devastation of forests. As Pant observes:

> The tale about the denudation of forests by the hillman was repeated ad nauseum in season and out of season by those in power so much so that it came to be regarded as an article of faith .... By way of vindication of the forest policy it is claimed by its advocates that in the pre-British days the people had neither any rights in the soil nor in the forests.

**Opposition to Forest Policy**

Opposition to forest policy first came forth in 1906. Their ancient rights were taken into consideration by colonial masters. Their resentment was first manifested in 1906 in the state of Tehri Garhwal. On 27 December 1906, the forest surrounding the Chandrabadin temple about 14 miles from Tehri town was earmarked for reservation . The next day 200 villagers gathered to protest against state interference in their forests over which they claimed full and extensive rights.

Mass meetings started occurring in Almora to protest against the forest policy, which authorised the government to declare all forests and 'wastelands' ('benap' or unmeasured land) as reserved forests. Peoples resentment increased because they were unable to get a response. They set fire to government forests and resin depots in 1916. The Kumaon Association was also established in that year to look into the forest problems of Kumaon, with G.B. Pant as its general secretary. Increasing people's protests forced the government to set up a 'Forest Grievances Committee' to enquire into forest protests in Kumaon and Garhwal. Though the committee reclassified forests to pacify the villagers, yet people's rights were not protected.

As Pant concluded in *The Forest Problem in Kumaon,*

> The policy of the Forest Department can be summed up in two words, namely, encroachment and exploitation. The Government

> has gone on pushing forward, extending its own sphere and scope and simultaneously narrowing down the orbit of the rights of the people .... The memory of the 'San assi' boundaries (1880 predemarcation) is green and fresh in the mind of every villager and he cherishes it with a feeling bordering on reverence; he is simply unable to see his way to accepting the claim of the Government to the benap lands comprised within his village boundaries and regards every advance in that line as nothing short of encroachment and intrusion. Let the san assi boundaries be vested with their real character instead of being looked upon as merely nominal, and, to remove misgivings, let the areas enclosed within these boundaries be declared as the property of the villagers and all the benap lands included within these areas be restored to the village community, subject to such conditions as to impartiality, etc., as may be desirable in the public interest. It is a matter of common knowledge that a large number of memorials were sent by the villagers at their own instance, about the year 1906, asking the Government to restore the areas within the san assi boundaries to them: the unsophisticated villager spontaneously reiterates the same demand today. This is the minimum demand of the people and there seems to be no other rational and final solution. The simple fact should not be forgotten that man is more precious in this earth than everything else, the forests not excepted, and, also, that coercion is no substitute for reason, and, however stringent and rigid the laws may be, the forests cannot be preserved in the midst of seething discontent against the unanimous wishes and sentiments of the people . . . . The collective intelligence of a people cannot be treated with contempt, and even if it be erratic, it can come round only by being allowed an opportunity of realising its mistake. If the village areas are restored to the villagers, the causes of conflict and antagonism between the forest policy and the villagers will take the place of the present distrust, and the villager will begin to protect the forests even if such protection involves some sacrifice or physical discomfort.

**Start of Non-Cooperation Movement**

No agreement was in sight. The contradictions between people's basic needs and the state's revenue requirements, however, remained unresolved, and in due course these contradictions intensified. In 1930, the people of Garhwal launched the non-cooperation movement to draw attention to the issue of forest resources. Forest satyagrahas to resist the new oppressive forest laws were most intense in the Rawain region. The King of Tehri was in Europe at that time. In his absence, Dewan Chakradhar Jayal resorted to armed intervention to crush a peaceful satyagraha at Tilari. A large number of unarmed satyagrahis were killed and wounded, while others lost their lives in a desperate attempt to cross the rapids of the Yamuna river. Years later, the martyrs of the Tilari massacre provided inspiration for the Chipko movement when people pledged themselves to protect their forests. This incident could never be removed from the Oninds of people.

**The Tilari Declaration of the People of Tehri-Garhwal 30 May 1968**

From ancient times forests have been the foundation of our cultural and material life. We reaffirm our birthright to draw sustenance and livelihoods from forests while protecting them.

From time to time, our forest rights have been violated through brute force leading to a disintegration of our cultural and economic life. Sometimes the mirage of petty reforms and privileges have been put before us. But only a few vested interests have gained from changes in forest management. Governments will come and will go. But it is our firm belief that our happiness and prosperity are based on a harmonious relation between our forests and ourselves. This relationship must be allowed to continue forever.

Today, we remember the martyrs of Tilari and offer homage to them. Their peaceful and non-violent movement and sacrifices give us a timeless inspiration to protect our forests and forest rights. We, therefore, declare today as Forest Day and renew this pledge.

# 4

# Rebellion as Confrontation: People's Ecological Movement in Kumaon and Garhwal over Forest Rights

God sent Gandhi in the form of a Bania [merchant]
to conquer Bania government.

—Kumaun peasant leader, 1921

While the absence of popular protest in the first century of British rule had given rise to the stereotype of the 'simple and law abiding hillman',[1] the reservation of the Kumaun forests between 1911 and 1917 'met with violent and sustained opposition',[2] culminating in 1921 when, within the space of a few months, the administration was paralysed first by a strike against utar (statutory labour) and then through a systematic campaign in which the Himalayan pine forests 'were swept by incendiary fires almost from end to end'.[3] This chapter examines the trajectory of social protest in Kumaun division during the early decades of this century.

In view of the strategic location of Kumaun the demands of the state on the peasantry were extraordinarily light; moreover, the style of rule was a typically paternalist one, exemplified in the person of Henry Ramsay, commissioner from 1856 to 1884. This transformation in peasant consciousness and peasant revolt was closely related to the more subtle but equally enduring changes in the structure of colonial administration. It was the advent of forest management—with the hill conifers being arguably the most valuable forest 'property' in India—that indicated a growing intervention of the state in the day-to-day life of the peasantry. The workings of scientific forestry, in particular, by curtailing customary rights, drastically affected the mode of peasant social and economic organization. At the same time, the imperatives of exercising effective control led to a more general bureaucratization of state authority. This transition was succinctly expressed by a district officer in Almora in the late 1930s who recalled Ramsay's rule 'as a benevolent despot who could do as he liked and [which] would always remain an envious [sic] example to the present generation of civilians who are so much bound by red tape and the bulky Manual of Government Order'.[4] The trajectory of social protest in British Kumaun was intimately connected with the changes in administrative structures and styles.

The early phase of resistance to forest management and the *begar* system lay, in various ways, in a direct path of continuity with traditional methods of peasant resistance. As this resistance crystallized into a more widespread movement, it began to use new mechanisms of protest—chiefly in response to forest management—in addition to those traditionally used. These changes in the method of protest were matched by concomitant changes in peasant consciousness, both reflecting the rapidly fading legitimacy of the colonial state. The history of social protests in colonial kumaon vividly illustrated the transformations in peasant ideology and forms of resistance, and their interrelationship with changing structures of power and authority.

**Beginning of Resistance to Forced Labour**

Incidence of utar was resisted in various ways in the first century of British rule, though it was very hight to begin with. The village *pradhan* (himself exempt) occasionally concealed some of the *hissedars* in his village;[5] alternatively, travellers who indented for coolies found the headman being 'openly defied' by his villagers, who refused to supply labour or provisions.[6] When census returns from Garhwal reported a large excess of males over females in the ten to fourteen age group, this discrepancy was traced to the age (sixteen years) at which men were called upon to carry loads or furnish bardaish. Thus, all those whose age could possibly be understated were reported to be under sixteen.[7] Officials commented too that the hillman's aversion to being made to work under compulsion had led to his earning an undeserved reputation for indolence. While he worked hard enough in his fields, coolie labour—especially during the agricultural season—was performed in a manner that made his resentment apparent.[8]

Travellers and soldiers often found themselves stranded when villagers failed to oblige in carrying their luggage. White mountaineers on expedition found that villagers on begar duty, when pushed too hard, either refused requests to prolong the duration of the expedition or expressed their resentment by taking an 'unconscionable time' over meals.[9] It is reported that Henry Ramsay, the long-time commissioner of Kumaun, had once to levy a fine of Rs. 500 on a village near Someshwar in Almora district which struck against utar. Another strike in 1903 led to the imprisonment of fourteen villagers of Khatyadi.[10] Concurrently, opposition to the begar system was expressed in newspapers, edited by nationalists of the Gokhale school, from Almora, Nainital and Dehradun. The Kumaun Parishad, based in Almora, took up both the begar and forest issues, asking the forest department to hire its own coolies and build more roads.[11] Resentment against the British governments forest policy was summering below the surface.

With the advent of the forest department the burden of these services on the Kumaun villager dramatically increased. The reservation of the forests and their future supervision involved extensive touring by forest officials who took utar and bardaish as a matter of course. Coming close on the heels of the demarcation of the forest, the additional burdens which the new department had created evoked a predictable response. Forest officers touring in the interior of Garhwal were unable to obtain grain as villagers, even where they had surplus stock, refused to supply to a department they regarded 'as disagreeable interlopers to be thwarted if possible'.[12]

**Uttar**

Utar, in the words of the Kumaun Forest Grievances Committee, was 'one of the greatest grievances which the residents of Kumaun had against the forest settlement'.[13] When coupled with the abbreviation of customary access to the forest, it represented an intervention unprecedented in its scope and swiftness. Villagers looked back, not altogether without justification, to a 'golden age' when they had full freedom to roam over their forest habitat, and state interference was at its minimum. These emotions were poignantly expressed by a government clerk who applied for exemption from begar and bardaish:

In earlier times villagers could get their necessities of life form the forests without much effort. There were no such government laws and regulations prohibiting the free use of unsurveyed land and forest by them as they have now. The time itself has now become very hard and it has been made still harder by the imposition of different laws, regulations, and taxes on them and by increasing the land revenue. Now the village life has been shadowed by all the miseries and inconveniences of the present day laws and regulations. They are not allowed to fell down a tree to get fuels from it for their daily use and they cannot cut leaves of trees beyond certain portion of them for fodder to their animals. But the touring officials still view the present situation with an eye of the past and press them to supply good grass for themselves and their [retinue] without even thinking of making any payment for these things to them who after spending their time, money and labour, can hardly procure them for their own use. In short all the privileges of village life, as they were twenty years ago, are nowhere to be found now, still the officials hanker after the system of yore when there were everything in abundance and within the reach of villagers.[14]

**State Encroachment**

Unusual extractions and other forms of state encroachment upon the privileges of individuals or communities were regarded as transgressing the traditional relationship between ruler and ruled. New laws and regulations were already beginning to threaten the considerable autonomy enjoyed by the Khasa community. By clashing with his notions of economic and social justice increased state-intervention, breached the 'moral economy' of the peasant.[15] Anticipating that the hillman would react by 'throwing his forest loads down the khud and some day an unfortunate Forest Officer may go after them', Wyndham, commissioner of Kumaun, believed that the only way to prolong the life of the utar system would be for forest officials to use pack ponies. Government could hardly defend the use of utar by a money-making department which, if it continued to avail of begar, would hasten the end of the system.[16] Echoing the commissioner's sentiments, the Garhwal lawyer and legislative council member Taradutt Gairola pleaded for a 'vigorous policy of reform' failing which 'trouble [would] arise' at the revision of the revenue settlement.[17] These warnings were to prove prophetic, but in the meantime the state hoped to rely on a series of ameliorative measures. The Lieutenant-Governor had in 1916 rejected the possibility of the utar system itself being scrapped; while it had caused 'hardship' in certain areas, the government, he emphasized, was concerned merely 'with checking any abuse of the systetem'.[18]

In a move initiated by Gairola, coolie agencies were started in parts of Garhwal: by paying money into a common fund from which transport and supplies were arranged, villagers were not required to perform these tasks themselves.[19] In other parts registers were introduced to ensure that the utar burden did not fall disproportionately on any individual or village. Officers were advised to camp only at fixed places and procure grain from merchants subsidized by the government. Rules were framed prescribing what kinds of supplies could be indented for, and loads restricted to twelve pounds per coolie.[2o] In a bid to 'raise the status of the soldier', retired and serving members of the Garhwal regiments were granted personal exemption from utar in 1900, although they were required to provide a substitute.[21] This was extended during World War I into an unconditional exemption for all combatant members of the 39th Garhwalis, and for the direct heirs of soldiers killed in battle.[22] The introduction of these palliatives which afford a considerable measure of relief, it was hoped, would ensure the continuance of the system itself.[23]

### Resistance to Forest Management

Consequent on the imposition of forest management all these measures important the dislocations in agrarian practices. The working of a forest for commercial purposes necessitates its division into blocks or coupes, which are completely closed after the trees are felled to allow regeneration to take place. Closure to men and cattle is regarded as integral to successful reproduction and grazing and lopping, if allowed, are regulated in the interests of the reproduction of favoured species of trees. Further, protection from fire is necessary to ensure the regeneration and growth to maturity of young saplings. Thus, the practice of firing the forests had to be regulated or stopped in the interests of sustained production of chir pine. While the exercise of rights, where allowed, was specified in elaborate detail, rightholders had the onerous responsibility, under Section 78 of the act, of furnishing knowledge of forest offences to the nearest authority and of extinguishing fires, however caused, in the state forests. Control of forests was uppermost in the minds of the policy makers.

### Forest Management

Forest management had become a bone of contention between the villagers and forest officials. Evidence of protest at the contravention of traditionally held and exercised rights well before the introduction of forest management is available in plenty. Charcoal required for smelting iron in the mines of Kumaun was brought from neighbouring forests. Where these forests lay within village boundaries, villagers prevented wood being cut without the payment of *malikhana*.[24] In the years following the constitution of the DPF in 1893, the deputy commissioner (DC) of Garhwal reported that 'forest administration consists for most part in a running fight with the villagers.'[25] Even where discontent did not manifest itself in overt protest, the loss of control over forests was acutely felt. The forest settlement officer of British Garhwal commented thus at the time of the constitution of the reserved forests:

> The notion obstinately persists in the minds of all, from highest to the lowest, that Government is taking away their forests from them and is robbing them of their own property. The notion seems to have grown up from the complete lack of restriction or control over the use by the people of waste land and forest during the first 80 years after the British occupation. The oldest inhabitant therefore and he naturally is regarded as the greatest authority, is the most assured of the antiquity of the people's right to uncontrolled use of the forest; and to a rural community there appears no difference between uncontrolled use and proprietary right. Subsequent regulations—and these regulations are all very recent—only appear to them as a gradual encroachment on their rights, culminating now in a final act of confiscation . . . [My] best efforts however have, I fear, failed to get the people generally to grasp the change in conditions or to believe in the historical fact of government ownership.[26]

### Notion of Private Property

There did not exist a developed notion of private property among these peasant communities, a notion particularly inapplicable to communally owned and managed woods and pasture land. In contrast, the state's assertion of monopoly over forests was undertaken at the expense of what British officials insisted were *individually* claimed rights of user. With the 'waste and forest lands never having attracted the attention of former governments',[27] there existed strong historical justification justs for the popular belief that all forests within village boundaries were 'the property of *the villagers*'.[28] This brings out quite clearly that the root of the conflict between the state and hill villagers over forest rights lay in differing conceptions of property and ownership.

The option of flight was considered by a group of villagers belonging to Tindarpur patti in Garhwal, who approached an English planter for land 'as the new forest regulations and restrictions were pressing on them so severely that they wished to migrate into another district and climate rather than put up with them any longer.'[29] This was the way the villagers showed their discontent with the new forest regulations. Another time-honoured form of protest—non-compliance with imposed regulations—was evident when villagers gave misleading information at the time of fixation of rights.[30] As villagers were 'not in a frame of mind to give much voluntary assistance', one divisional forest officer (DFO) accurately predicted 'active resentment' at the fire protection of large areas and their closure to grazing and other rights.[31]

The year 1916 witnessed a number of 'malicious' fires in the newly constituted reserved forests. In May the forests in the Gaula range of Nainital division were set ablaze. The damage reported was exclusively in chir forests; 28,000 trees which were burnt had to be prematurely felled. For the circle as a whole it was estimated that at least 64 per cent of the 441 fires which burnt 388 square miles (as against 188 fires that had burnt 35 square miles in the preceding year) were 'intentional'.[32]

**The Protests**

Numerous fires broke out simultaneously over large areas, and often the occurrence of one fire was the signal for general firing in the whole neighbourhood: 44 fires occurred in North Garhwal division, almost all in order to obtain a fresh crop of grass. The 'deliberate and organized incendiarism' of the summer of 1916 brought home to the state the unpopularity of the forest settlement and the virtual impossibility of tracing those who were responsible for the fires. In Nainital and in the old reserves of Airadeo and Binsar of Almora district—areas which had been fire-protected for many years—an established crop of seedlings was wiped out. The area chosen for attack had been under both felling and resin-tapping operations.[33] In Airadeo the fire continued for three days and two nights, with 'new fires being started time after time directly a counterfiring line was successfully completed'.[34]

As a result of such 'incendiarism' several thousand acres of forest were closed to all rights for a period of ten years.[35]

The protests against the forest settlement were viewed with apprehension in Lucknow, where the Lieutenant-Governor anticipating the conclusion of World War I, observed that 'it would be a pity for the 39th Garhwalis to come home and find their villages seething with discontent.' Reporting on the situation the DC of Garhwal concluded, somewhat self-evidently, that government could not but affect village life in every patti by taking over the forests. The people's 'dislike of the forest department and the horde of new underlings let loose on the district' was shared by the soldiers, one of whom stated that if the war had ended before they left Europe they could have petitioned the king to rescind the settlement. The soldiers' discontent was evidently disturbing, for, as the district officer put it, 'if we can get them on our side it will be a great thing... They are already a power in the land and will be still more a power after the war.'[36] The forest department continued to be complacent about the possibilities of such discontent blowing over when the villagers had 'greater familiarity with the true aim of the department'.[37]

**A Considerate Officer**

Alternatively, they pointed to the strategic and financial results obtained in a few years of commercial working.[38] Percy Wyndham, as the Commissioner of Kumaun the senior official entrusted with law and order, was considerably less sanguine. He preferred that the hills continue to provide 'excellent men for sepoys, police and all such jobs'—a situation jeopardized by the forest department which had demarcated the 39th Garhwali villages as if 'the world were made for growing trees and men were vermin to be shut in'. In a situation where 'the Revenue Department holds the whole country by bluff', without the help of regular police, Wyndham was clearly not prepared to enforce new rules on a 'dissatisfied people.' According to him scrapping the forest rules and relocating the staff was the best action.[39]

**Table 4.1**
**Breaches of Forest Law in UP, 1911-22**

| *Circle* | *Western circle* | | *Eastern circle* | | *Kumaun circle** | |
|---|---|---|---|---|---|---|
| Year | A** | B** | A | B | A | B |
| 1911-12 | 786 | 1798 | 1167 | 2306 | 958 | 2159 |
| 1912-13 | 881 | 2182 | 1230 | 2424 | 1203 | 3374 |
| 1913-14 | 1006 | 2091 | 1365 | 2905 | 1309 | 3864 |
| 1914-15 | 1248 | 2681 | 1646 | 3293 | 1671 | 5857 |
| 1915-16 | 1401 | 2662 | 1514 | 3029 | 1610 | 5796 |

*... Continue*

*Continue*

| | | | | | | |
|---|---|---|---|---|---|---|
| 1916-17 | 1368 | 2517 | 1636 | 2944 | 2023 | 10264 |
| 1917-18 | 1242 | 2364 | 1530 | 2777 | 2197 | 11046 |
| 1918-19 | 1153 | 2058 | 1723 | 3167 | 2167 | 11024 |
| 1919-20 | 1162 | 2120 | 1378 | 2773 | 2136 | 13457 |
| 1920-21 | 926 | 1618 | 901 | 2154 | 1723 | 10328 |
| 1921-22 | 1248 | 2437 | 1622 | 839 | 2070 | 3799*** |

* The total area of reserved forest in UP equalled 4-32 million acres, of which 1.91 million acres lay in the Kumaun circle.

** A = cases; B = convictions (persons).

*** Cases dropped due to the recommendation of the Kumaun Grievances Committee.

*Source:* APFD, relevant years.

Friction was brewing. Regulations concerning forest operations like lopping grazng and duties of right holders was the evidence. Table 5.1 is inductive of that. Figures from other forest circles are given by way of comparison. While the number of yearly convictions in the Kumaun circle far exceeded those obtained elsewhere, a comparison with 'criminal justice' in Kumaun itself is no less revealing. Over a ten-year period (1898-1908) an average of only 416 persons was convicted annually in Almora district on account of cognizable crime of all kinds, ranging from non-payment of excise to murder.[40] Indeed, with the absence of an adequate patrolling staff, many breaches of the forest law went undetected.[41] Underlying the stiff resistance to the regulations of the forest department was a tradition of hundreds of years of unrestricted use.[42] The continuing opposition to forest administration bore a strong similarity to traditional methods of social protest in Kumaun and Garhwal.

The forms of protest—flight, strikes, occasional attacks on officials, marches—as well as its moral idiom, which reflected the state's failure to meet traditional obligations, were integral to the indigenous form of collective resistance known as the *dhandak*. As the distinctive form of social protest specific to this area, the *dhandak* continued to be used, albeit with variations, in both the colonial territory of British Kumaun and the princely state of Tehri Garhwal. Meanwhile, village oppositon to the begar system was matched organizationally by the establishment of the Kumaun Parishad in 1916. This association of local journalists, lawyers and intellectuals, chaired in its initial years by Rai Bahadurs professing loyalty to the King Emperor, underwent a rapid transformation with the setting up of the forest department and the increased requirement of customary services.

### The Utar and Forest Movement of 1921

The impact of village-level protest and, indirectly, of upsurges elsewhere in India, contributed to a growing radicalization of the Parishad, best exemplified in the person of Badridutt Pande of Almora. As Shekhar Pathak has compellingly shown, Pande, far more than other Kumaun nationalists (such as Govind Ballabh Pant), was acutely aware of the growing discontent amongst the peasantry.[43] Convinced of the futility of memoranda presented to government by a few individuals based in Almora, Pande and his associates sought to establish branches of the Parishad in the villages of Kumaun. Simultaneously, his weekly, *Shakti,* published from Almora, became an important forum in which the begar system and forest rules were made the butt of strident criticism.[44] In 1920 *Shakti* reported a strike against utar by villages in patti Kairaro, with villagers refusing to pay the fine levied on them. At the annual session of the Kumaun Parishad, held at Kashipur in December 1920, a major conflict arose between those who still hoped to negotiate with the state and village representatives who pressed for direct action.

After the reformists had walked out the latter urged Badridutt Pande and other Parishad leaders to come to the Uttaraini fair.[45] Held in mid-January at Bageshwar, the temple town at the confluence of the Saryu and Gomati rivers, this fair annually attracted fifteen to twenty thousand pilgrims from all over the hills. Here, matters came to a head. In early January the conservator of forests was refused coolies at Dwarahat and Ganai, and, anticipating a strike, the DC of Almora, W.G. Dible, urgently asked government for a declaration of its future policy—a request summarily dismissed.[46] At Bageshwar a crowd of over ten thousand heard Badridutt pass on a message from Mahatma Gandhi that 'he would come and save them from oppression as he did in Champaran.' When almost everyone responded to a call to raise their hands to show that they would refuse utar, Pande continued: 'After abolishing coolie utar they would agitate for the forests. He would ask them not to extract resin, or saw sleepers, or take forest contracts. They should give up service as forest guards which involves insulting their sisters and snatching their sickles.'

### Enter the Mahatma

Slogans in praise of Mahatma Gandhi and 'Swatantra Bharat' and cries that the government was 'anniyayi' (unjust) filled the air.[47] In a dramatic gesture, village headmen flung their coolie registers into the Saryu.[48] In the weeks following the fair, several officials were stranded when the villages neighbouring Bageshwar declined to supply coolies. Elsewhere, only *khushkharid* (on payment) coolies were available, at extraordinarily high rates. With schoolmasters and other government functionaries extending their support to the movement, Dible hastily summoned the regular police.[49] Pathak has uncovered evidence of at least 146 anti-begar meetings in different villages of Garhwal and Kumaun, held between 1 January and 30 April 1921.[50] When the DFO of Almora complained of the continuing difficulties faced by touring officials, he was tersely told that the district administration was not in a position to 'give you or your department one utar coolie'.[51] Requests for utar were not made in tracts when they were likely to be refused.[52]

In a matter of weeks the state's determination not to dispense with the system itself had broken down, and its abolition followed. In the following year over 1.6 lakh rupees were spent by the exchequer on the transport and stores of touring officials in the hills.[53]

The resistance to utar mirrored similar opposition in parts of Java, Africa and New Guinea, where attempts by colonial regimes to extract corvee labour were often met with sullen resentment. As in Kumaun, peasants sometimes expressed the wish that whites should carry their own loads, and in extreme cases by striking, made this inescapable. The sentiments of Sindano, a Watchtower-movement preacher in Zambia during World War I, could serve equally well as an expression of the anti-utar campaign conducted around the same time in Kumaun and Garhwal: 'There they are, they who overburden us with loads, and beat us like slaves, but a day will come when they will be the slaves.'[54]

**Loss of Forests**

However, in the Himalayan case resistance to corvee labour was greatly intensified by its association with the major indignity peasants had to suffer at the hands of colonial rulers: the loss of control over forests. And, as the press communique issued by the UP government emphasized, the growth of the forest department, with all that this implied for the social and economic life of the hill peasant, was at the root of the anti-begar movement.[55] Peasant opposition to utar was conducted at a different level and for quite different reasons from that symbolized by the periodic memoranda—appealing to the instincts of a benign and civilized government—that liberal nationalists continued to submit to the state.[56] An English planter based in Kausani reported that while Hargovind Pant, an Almora lawyer, was asking that coolies be not supplied for utar, village leaders were prepared to go even further. Thus, local activists insisted that no coolies should be supplied at all, i.e., they were against khushkharid coolies as well.[57]

After Bageshwar, the DC of Almora was tersely informed by a group of padhans that they had refused to supply coolies in order to compel attention to their grievances, chief among which was the taking away of their forests. Dible reported that proposals for closure to grazing had much to do with this intense feeling. A fund had been created by the villagers—anticipating punitive action for defending anyone against whom the state had initiated proceedings, and for paying fines where they were inflicted.[58] While this unity and sense of purpose necessarily made their actions political, the politics of the peasantry was clearly not derivative of the politics of urban nationalism. A hazy perception of Gandhi as a saint were invoked against the inimical powers of government.[59] Apart form that mention of Gandhi. there was nothing much in the movement to match the erusption taking place in other parts of the country. It was a non-cooperation movement of another hand.

**The Forest Movement of 1921**

Uttaraini in the mind of a villager was a success. Thereafter, Pande and his colleagues toured the different pattis of Almora, establishing local *sabhas* of the Parishad. Inspired by the success of the anti-utar campaign, Pande urged in his speeches the need for direct action in order to recover lost rights over forests. For, the 'government that sells the forest produce is not liable to be called a real government'—indeed, it was precisely these mercenary motives which had made God send Gandhi 'as an incarnation in the form of Bania to conquer Bania government'.[60] As the reference to Gandhi's caste indicates, the term 'bania' evoked images of power as well as deception; by selling forest produce the state was hastening the erosion of the legitimacy it had earlier enjoyed in the eyes of the peasantry. At Bageshwar Badridutt had depicted this transition in tellingly effective symbols. When forest resources and grass were plentiful and easily available, villagers had an abundance of food and drink. But now, he said, 'in place of tins of ghee the forest department gives them tins of resin.'[61] Sensing the peasantry's mood after the utar strike, Dible had with uncanny prescience predicted the shape of the impending agitation: '[The] next move will be against the Forest Department. Agitators will make a dead set for resin coolies and contractors' coolies engaged in sleeper work, and try to drive them from this work. The people will be incited to commit Forest offences and we shall have serious trouble with fires.'

In the coming months breaches of the forest law increased daily. These included not merely the firing of forests for grass but also 'wholesale cutting of trees'.[62] In British Garhwal, too, the popular feeling against the forest policy continued to be 'Very bitter'.[63] The summer of 1921 was one of the driest on record. The failure of the winter rains had contributed to a poor *rabi* crop and money was sanctioned as subsistence *taccavi* in the hill districts.[64] In Totashilling, where the campaign was to be at its most intense, the local branch of the Kumaun Parishad passed a resolution that the people were themselves to decide whether or not to set fire to forest land falling within 'san assi' boundaries.[65] From the last week of April a systematic campaign, especially in Almora district, had been launched for firing the forest. When called upon (under Section 78 of the forest act) to assist in extinguishing these blazes, villagers instead directed their energies towards helping the fire to spread. As a consequence the attempted fire protection by the forest department of commercially worked areas was a major failure. Of 4 lakh acres of forest in which fire protection was attempted, 2.46 lakh acres were burnt over.[66] An estimated total of 819 offences occurred, of which 395 were definitely known to be 'incendiary'.[67] The machinery for control of forest offenses, which had been in place earlier, was in shambles. There was no way for forest department, with its hinted resources to control this conflaration.

**Burning of Chir Forests**

On the one hand incendiarism represented an assertion of traditionally exercised rights—the annual firing of the forest floor—circumscribed by the state in the interests of commercial forestry. On the other the areas burnt over were almost exclusively chir pine forests being worked for both timber and resin, this wholesale burning of the chir reserves representing, as Wyndham acknowledged a 'direct challenge to government to relax their control over forests'.[68] The intensification of the campaign in Almora and Nainital was confined to those areas well served by a network of roads that had been under commercial working for some time. When fires swept through nearly all the areas being logged, young regeneration was wiped out. Covering nearly 320 square miles of forest, these fires destroyed 11.5 lakh resin channels and 65,000 maunds of resin.[69] As Eric Hobsbawm has argued, such destruction is never indiscriminate, for 'what is useful for poor men'—in this instance broad-leaved species far more than chir—is spared.[70] There is no evidence that the vast extent of broad-leaved forests, also under the control of the state, was at all affected. As in other societies in different historical epochs, this destruction by arson was not simply a nihilistic release, but carefully selective in the targets attacked.

**Similarity with France**

In the nineteenth century, similar occurrance had happened in France. There peasants' rights in the forest were curtailed in favour of producing wood for iron forges. Believing that the 'wood supplying the forges was in the domain of their traditional rights of usage', villagers burnt the forges to the ground.[71] Iron forges in nineteenth-century France, and resin depots in Kumaun a century later, both represented commercial uses of the forest that were taking priority over earlier subsistence-oriented uses. In either case this change, fostered from above, was fiercely resisted by peasants denied traditional rights of access and use. Indeed, as the analysis of court cases by the Collector of Almora indicates, the act of burning the chir forests represented a direct confrontation with the colonial authorities. The decision to burn the commercially worked areas was predicated not merely on their containing the locally almost useless (in comparison with oak) chir pine. Badridutt Pande well understood, that the export of forest produce by the state clashed strongly with the subsistence orientation of the hill peasant. In the collector's classification—typical in its detail of the concern of the colonial state to understand, with a view to suppressing, any sign of protest—the fire cases were broken down into the headings shown in Table 4.2.[72] On the other had, confrontation with forest department was invertable.

**Table 4.2**
**Fire Cases in Almora, 1921**

| *Head* | | *No. of Cases* | *No. of Persons involved* |
|---|---|---|---|
| I. Intentional | | | |
| A. | To paralyse forest department (FD) by destroying valuable areas | 8 | 21 |
| B. | To cause loss to FD by way of revenge due to hatred | 26 | 45 |
| C. | To have good grass for cattle | 11 | 17 |
| D. | To cause loss to resin mates out of enmity | 2 | 3 |
| E. | To spite another out of enmity | 3 | 5 |
| F. | Whose agitation was direct cause of fire | NA | 13 |
| Total | | 50 | 104 |
| II. Accidental | | | |
| (This includes smoking or carrying fire within the reserves, the spread of fire from cultivated fields or waste and not under government, etc. | | 23 | 45 |

*source:* Forest Department (FD), file 157/1921, UPSA.

The court cases slapped by the government did not made much headway in curting the protests. Further details which may reveal more about the nature of protest can be gleaned from summary accounts of court cases. Gangua, aged sixteen, was one of the several youths 'put up by non-cooperators' to destroy 'valuable regeneration areas' by fire. Nor was participation restricted to men: thus, one Durga was sentenced to a month in jail when she 'deliberately set fire to Thaklori forest'. In at least four different instances, witnesses set up by the prosecution were 'won over' by non-cooperators and the cases had to be dropped. Chanar Singh and four others of the Tagnia clan of Doba Talla, Katyur, were 'affected by lectures' by 'Non-cooperators and a Jogi' and set fire to regeneration areas.

This reference to Yogi was an attempt at giving the protest a religious tinge. In the circumstances it was not untowards. Every thing was fair. The yogi was later prosecuted.

The peasantry sought, as in the Uttaraini mela, a moral/religious sanction for their acts. No such sanction was required by Padam Singh and Dharam Singh of Katyur, awarded the maximum sentence of seven years rigorous imprisonment, who expressed their opposition to state monopoly in no uncertain terms. In the words of the magistrate: 'The compartment fired was near the village and used by them. They resented the work of the Department in this compartment since it interfered with their use of the compartment. Therefore they set fire to it deliberately.'[73]

**Pine Needles**

Pine needles were set on fire in Garhwal as well. With commercial forestry and the protection of regeneration areas from grazing and fire as yet restricted in their operations, the damage to the state-controlled forests was not as widespread as in Almora. Yet the DC had convicted 549 persons, 45 for 'direct or indirect incendiarism' and 504 for refusing to extinguish fires, before the recommendations of the grievances committee led to all pending cases being dropped. Fires were reported to be most acute in the areas bordering Almora, and in the southern pattis of Lansdowne subdivision in the outer hills. With resin-tapping in its infancy, fires were most often started with a view to obtaining fresh grass.[74] Fresh pan, and not resin ws their sustenance.

That is when the soldier, discharged from the army after the World War or those on leave entired the agitation against colonial government's forest policies. While all social groups participated, the involvement of soldiers in the forest movement of 1921—in the same way as the participation of village headmen in the utar campaign—bore witness to the failure of the attempt by the colonial state to create an indigenous collaborating elite. Like leaders of cargo cults in Melanesia, these soldiers were not always leaders in the old authority structure. However, they had a special experience of white rule, one that enabled them to exercise a moral claim on the rulers. When this claim was ignored and the forest regulations not withdrawn, expectation quickly turned to outrage; in consequence, soldiers were in the forefront of the opposition to commercial forest management.

**Kumaoni Soldiers**

The demobilized soldiers of the Mexican army in South America had led their fellow peasants in the Mexican Revolution. These soldiers of Kumaon were 'proud veterans now and still full of fight, their revolutionary consciousness ironically enhanced by the official discharge papers they carried, [who] went back home as missionaries of the new unruliness'.[75] Thus, in Garhwal the fires were most often started by soldiers on leave, but as '99 per cent of the population sympathized with them', their apprehension by the authorities became an impossible task.[76] After the Uttaraini mela, ex-soldiers were active among those who helped the Kumaun Parishad form sabhas in the villages of the Kosi valley. One soldier said in his speeches that 'Government was not a Raja, but a Bania and Rakshasi Raj and the King Emperor was Ravan.' Recounting his experiences in Europe, where he was wounded, the pensioner described the visit of the King Emperor to his hospital bedside. Asked to state his grievances, 'he complained against *Patwaris* and forest guards but all that has been given is the Rowlatt Act and Martial Law.[77] No longer was the king perceived as being bestowed with the quasi-divine powers of intervening to restore justice and a harmonious relationship between the state and the peasant. Ravan, the very personification of evil, was equated with the King Emperor, whose failure (or inability) to stem the expansive growth of the forest department and its minions had led to his rapid fall from grace. As expressed through the symbolism of the epics, the government now embodied not merely the rapacious bania but the evil-intentioned demons of Hindu mythology.

## Social Protest: 1921-42

Soldiers who had voiced their resentment while fighting in Europe and figured prominently in the 1921 movement continued to be in the forefront of the opposition to forest policy. The constitution of the Kumaun Forest Grievances Committee in the wake of the 1921 movement evoked mixed reactions in the hill districts. Meetings held at different villages expressed dissatisfaction at the composition of the committee. While the committee had only one non-official member, Jodh Singh, he too was regarded as being more on the side of the government than the people.[78] The chairman, Commissioner Wyndham, also came in for criticism for his attempts to drive a wedge between the two dominant communities in the hills, Rajputs and Brahmins. A famed *shikari*, Wyndham was held to be ignorant of 'true justice' *(asli-nyaya)*. An example of his insensitivity to public opinion was provided by the 1918 report on quli-bardaish, which he framed without asking the opinion of the inhabitants of Kumaun. As a consequence, the people had to take the initiative in stopping utar.[79]

The committee did not contain any representative of the people. Several villages resolved to boycott its sittings. A form was circulated, to be filled in by different villages in Garhwal and submitted to the KFGC. The form provided for the designation of different plots of forest near every village, over each of which peasants would have exclusive rights of fuel, fodder, building timber and wood for agricultural implements, bamboos for basket-making and other crafts, and so on. It asked for villages to be given full rights over nearby forests, which would be managed by the panchayats. Further, it designated forests where afforestation could be carried out by the villagers themselves. Finally, the form asked the government to provide a forest patrol to each village to aid in protection.[80]

## Forest Grievances Committee

The Kumaon Forests Grievances Committee toured the three hill districts in May-August 1921, examining 5040 witnesses in all. A particular source of bitterness related to the treatment of women and children who committed the bulk of the forest 'offences', but who did not appear in court as per custom. Attempts by forest officials to prevent them from lopping and cutting grass were greatly resented. Complaints were also made against the reservation of temple trees and oak groves which villagers had conserved for their own use. In some instances, forest boundary pillars were placed too close to cultivation, while 'in other cases the outcry against the forest pillars had been caused by a desire to get a freedom from the rules and restrictions which these pillars represent rather than by an existing need for more land.' The oft repeated act of the removal of these pillars symbolized the perceived threat to peasant autonomy and sovereignty that forest reservation represented.[81] In the circumstances, the committee concluded that 'any attempt to strictly enforce these [forest] rules would lead to riot and bloodshed.'

The committee recommended the division of the existing reserved forests into two categories:

(1) Class I—containing forests of little or no commercial importance; (2) Class II—containing forests stocked with chir, sal, deodar, kail and other commercially exploitable species. In Class I reserves, management was to be almost nominal.[82] Of the existing forests, 1986 square miles were covered by Class II and 1090 square miles by Class I forests, respectively.

Table 4.3 gives details regarding breaches of forest rules during 1926-33, i.e., after the recommendations of the KFGC had taken effect. Several features merit comment. Forest offences in Kumaun circle still consistently exceeded those in the two other circles of UP. Although the area under which the old restrictions operated fell away sharply, better supervision was possible in the commercial Class II forests to which attention was now confined.

**Table 4.3**

**Breaches of Forest Law in UP, 1926-33**

| Year | *Kumaun circle* | | *Eastern circle* | | *Western circle* | |
|---|---|---|---|---|---|---|
| | *Cases* | *Conviction* | *Cases* | *Conviction* | *Cases* | *Conviction* |
| 1926-27 | 1919 | 3661 | 1470 | 3078 | 1440 | 2646 |
| 1927-28 | 1992 | 3786 | 1435 | 3167 | 1568 | 2809 |
| 1928-29 | 2545 | 5482 | 1418 | 2740 | 1334 | 2323 |
| 1929-30 | 2675 | 6019 | 1457 | 3148 | 1531 | 2600 |
| 1930-31 | 2511 | 4500 | 1705 | 3821 | 1299 | 2226 |
| 1931-32 | 2534 | 5514 | 1621 | 3170 | 1524 | 2629 |
| 1932-33 | 2629 | 5968 | 1928 | 3085 | 1681 | 2871 |

*source:* APFD, relevant years.

A comparison with Table 4.1 is instructive, as summarized below:

| Period | *Cases* | *Convictions* |
|---|---|---|
| | *Per year* | *Per year* |
| 1916-22 | 2053 | 9986 |
| 1926-33 | 2401 | 4990 |

While there is an increase to the order of 17 per cent in cases per year, there is a corresponding decrease in the latter period of 40 per cent in convictions obtained. A plausible inference one can make is that while better supervision enabled detection of individual cases of infringement, such as fuel and fodder collection, collective or group infringement was no longer so common. The latter would typically include collective grazing of village cattle, burning of the forest floor, and failure to inform the authorities when a forest fire occurred. With the large area of Class I under light supervision, these activities were no longer as liable to be deemed infringements of the law. Another contributory factor was the introduction of controlled departmental burning (cf. chapter 3). In 1928-29, for example, 81,000 acres were departmentally burnt in Kumaun circle, of which 35,000 acres were burnt with unpaid voluntary labour.[83] In a way, modification in their perception helped the forest Department.

**Incendiarism**

The villagers resentment had not did down. An outbreak of what the state still preferred to call 'incendiarism' or 'malicious firing' did, however, take place in both 1930 and 1931. In the summer of 1930 a large number of fires occurred in regeneration areas of Almora district, notably within a few miles radius of Bageshwar, venue of the historic Uttaraini mela. Interestingly, the burning of the forest was contrary to the wishes of the Congress leaders. Of 63 fires that burnt 15,591 acres, 58 occurred in the two forest divisions of East and West Almora. As in 1921, peasants concentrated on the most vulnerable state-held areas—thus 21 per cent of the area under chir regeneration was burnt.[84]

According to a later estimate the reserved forests were fired 157 times, with 37,000 acres of chir regeneration (or 50 per cent of the total) being destroyed.[85] The campaign in 1931 was more widespread, with the abnormally hot weather favouring the spread of fires. It was observed that 'burning the hill forests in a dry year is so easy and the results obtained with the minimum of exertion so large that it is one of the first ways in which any general feeling of unrest manifests itself.' Not so localized, the campaign spread to the Kosi, Gaula and Ladhia valleys of Nainital, apart from Almora and some parts of Garhwal. Of 89 fires that burnt 38,512 acres, 34 occurred in Nainital, 49 in the two Almora divisions, and 6 in Garhwal.[86]

**Civil Disobedience Movement**

The year 1931 was a turning point in the history of Garhwal. It witnessed a burst of nationalist activity, coinciding with the Civil Disobedience movement. A procession bearing the national tricolour made its way from one end of the Nainital lake to the other. In Almora, on 25 May, an attempt to hoist the flag on the municipal board building was foiled by the police. The next day there was a lathi- charge when a crowd tried again to mount the tricolour at the same venue.[87] In Garhwal shops were closed in several towns when Mahatma Gandhi was arrested upon the completion of the Dandi March.[88] The incarceration of the popular local leader Anusuva Prasad Bahuguna in August provoked a *hartal* or general strike in Badrinath town. A half mile long line of demonstrators hoisted the tricolour on the highest point of the Badrinath temple. Unnerved, the rawal or head priest sent telegrams to both the Tehri Raja and the Commissioner of Kumaun.[89]

Simultaneously, there was opposition by villagers to the new land settlement, which had enhanced revenue by as much as 30 per cent. In Salt patti of Almora district, labourers were asked not to work for forest contractors. Several hundred villagers went to the forest to enforce a collective decision to ex-communicate anyone who did work. This culminated in a scuffle with the police and many arrests. In Garhwal telegraph wires were cut in Dontiyal and protests organized in Dugadda.[90] the protests wore spreading.

During the Quit India movement of 1942, when Almora was perhaps one of the most active districts in the state. Several strikes were organized in the towns. In Deghat police fired and killed two members of a crowd protesting the arrest of their leader. When the patwari of Salem, one of the most active pattis, fled, villagers burnt his records. A force sent to quell them was repulsed by the villagers, who confiscated their weapons. Another force comprising white soldiers was dispatched, but this force too was engaged by the villagers using sticks and stones. Two villagers were killed in the battle. In Salem's neighbouring patti of Salt, police fired on satyagrahis, prompting Gandhi to call the patti India's second Bardoli.[91] Things were taking a nasty turn for the British administration.

**Favourite Target**

A favourite target of the 1942 rebellion continued to be the forest department. Totashiling in Katyur, one of the most active localities in 1921, witnessed the burning of a resin depot. In Nainital district youths cut telephone wires and burnt the Mangoli forest rest house and the dak bungalow at Ramnagar. The office of the conservator of forests also went up in flames. In Garhwal the forest bungalow in Siyasen and the post office at Chamoli were burnt. Telegraph wires were also cut. An elaborate plan was framed to burn all the timber godowns from Hardwar in the west to Ramnagar in the east.[92] Either something went wrong with the planning or some wise counsel prevailed, this plan stayed put. It was never carried out.

The relative freedom enjoyed by the peasantry following the recommendations of the KFGC undoubtedly contributed to the diminution of social protest in the years following 1921. At the same time, Kumaun was more fully incorporated in the orbit of colonial capitalism, as males migrated outwards to be employed in the British Indian Army and in the lower echelons of the colonial administration. Yet the specific episodes mentioned above do exhibit a marked continuity with the rather more concentrated activity of 1916-21. Arson, neither haphazard nor indiscriminate, continued to be aimed at symbols of authority, such as forest offices or rest houses, or at points where the state was most vulnerable, e.g., chir areas under regeneration or, latterly, channels of communication.

No less striking was the refusal of the peasantry to merge fully with the structured and highly restrictive stream of Congress nationalism. While the spread of Congress activities played a role in the 1930 and 1942 movements, the defiance of orders from 'above' during 'incendiary' campaigns and the violent episodes of 1942—which, testify to the imperfect control exercised by the Congress over peasant protest. it must be admitted, were in conformity with the countrywide character of Quit India.[93]

**From Custom to Confrontation**

There is a parallel to the situation in Kumaon. Two American Michael Apdas and James Scott have studied the confrontation between peasantry and instituted authority in Malaysia they have made a powerful case for the systematic study of forms of protest. What Scott calls 'everyday forms of peasant resistance' and Adas 'avoidance protest' embrace a wide variety of protest forms, all of which stop short of directly challenging the legitimacy of the rulers.[94] Clearly, as the extraordinarily rich material collected by Scott in rural Malaysia suggests, avoidance protest is more easily discerned through ethnographic research in contemporary societies. However, while the archival record may obscure, it can never completely eliminate evidence of everyday resistance. As elaborated in this chapter, many of the weapons of the weak described by Scott for Malaysia—including foot-dragging, false compliance, feigned ignorance, migration, breaches of the law, and social appeals to 'custom'—were effectively used by Himalayan villagers in thwarting the aims of colonial forestry. Yet my evidence also suggests that, over a period of time, peasants tended to discard these weapons in favour of more open and confrontational forms of protest: attacks on channels of communication, on state buildings, and most frequently on commercial forests and resin depots. This transformation in strategies of resistance was accompanied by a radical change in cultural perceptions of the overlord. Undoubtedly, the first century of British rule and the paternalist style of officials like Henry Ramsay may have seen a partial transference of an allegiance earlier owed to native kings. If early resistance drew on the dhandak tradition, by 1921 hill villagers were viewing the British authorities in distinctly unfavourable terms, equating the King Emperor with the very personification of evil, Ravan.

**Kumaun Parishad**

As a resault of this radicalisation of the movement started in 1921. Nowhere was this transformation in rebel consciousness and forms of resistance more explicitly manifested than in the form of an organization originally set up to mediate between the state and the peasantry. Established in the afterglow of the Coronation Durbar of 1911, the Kumaun Parishad initially swore undying loyalty to George Pancham (George V).[95] But the pressure from below, as it were, egged the Parishad leaders, and most noticeably among them Badridutt Pande, to adopt a more directly confrontationist position. By July 1921 their philosophy was being described as 'the anarchist doctrine of direct action, which has been attempted in England by Labour Revolutionaries'.[96] Clearly, such a situation had been brought about by the 'inherent' elements of folk or popular ideology impinging upon, and transforming in the process, the 'derived' elements originating in the sphere of organized politics.[97]

In this instance, at least, 'primitive' rebellion proved to be several steps ahead of modern nationalism', the rationale of its acts and the success which attended them being attested by the rapidity with which the state capitulated on both the begar and forest issues. What are the sociological factors that explain the transition from custom to confrontation in the social history of protest in Kumaun? While early resistance may have utilized the idiom of the dhandak, Kumaun peasants later displayed, like their counterparts in Tokugawa Japan, 'the capacity, language and organisational ability to create a new world view when the old was inconsistent with reality'.[98]

Evidence from other societies suggests that the fabric of customary rebellion normally contains within it the latitude for rebels to step outside the traditional relationship of dominance and subordination and challenge the very foundations of authority. Thus,

> to express rebellion against a lawful master, the Javanese used the words *mbalik* (lit. to turn around and stand face to face), *mbeka* (to be recalcitrant), *mbalka* (to-revolt), and the phrase *madeq kranan,* which can be translated as 'to set up one's own government', obviously with the purpose of establishing a new and independent territorial power or even a new government challenging an existing one.[99]

Closer to Kumaon in Kathiawad in western India, peasants would resort to one of two kinds of protest against the government: (i) *risaaman,* indicating 'the temporary severing of relations between intimate friends or family members in order to emphasize one's grievances which, when applied to politics, led to peaceful protest and petition'; and (ii) *baharvatiya,* literally going outside the law—this implied the use of violence or other confrontational forms of protest.[100] Its flexible 'repertoire of contention', to use Charles Tilly's phrase, throws further doubt on the interpretation of customary rebellion as a periodic release of discontent crucial to the integration and persistence of a society. What is more germane to our purposes, perhaps, is that the transition from 'avoidance' to 'confrontational' resistance in Kumaun followed a pattern quite similar to that observed in other colonial contexts.

In China, for example, resistance to French colonialism in the early decades of this century 'passed from deferential petitioning in the tradition of Confucianism to an insurrection along anarchist lines'.[101] In Kumaun, as in Vietnam, Burma, Indonesia, and other parts of India, the imposition of colonial rule represented, in the Weberian sense, a transfer from traditional to legal/rational structures of authority. Traditional patterns of authority had, on the one hand, been flexible in their claims on peasant subsistence, and, on the other, bound by a cultural and personalized idiom of reciprocity.

**Bureaucratic State**

Under colonialism, however, a centralized and bureaucratic state apparatus increasingly impinged on village life; the rationalized and uniform tax structure, and the takeover of forests and other natural resources, rendered villagers far more vulnerable to economic fluctuations. As in Dutch-ruled Java, therefore, peasant risings in Kumaun 'can be regarded as protest movements against intruding Western economic and political control which were undermining the fabric of traditional society.'[102] The peasant rebels challenged the legitimacy of the colonial rulers in Kumaun from a vantage point which as been explained by Barrington Moore as under:

> Only when the obsolete character of a dominant group becomes blatantly obvious through *failure in competition with another society and culture* is it liable to lose its legitimate right to appropriate the surplus extracted from the underlying population. This is what happened to the Tsarist bureaucracy, the scholar gentry of China, and the armed knights of medieval Europe.[103]

When the white rulers were deemed unfit to rule, their performance was compared not to the authority of a future millennium, nor to the ruling class in an adjoining state, but to the traditional rulers of the same society. Moreover, the persistence of customary forms of protest in the adjoining state of Tehri Garhwal must have acted as a reference point by which Kumaun peasants judged the responsiveness (or lack of it) of British officials to their demands. In the examples advanced by Moore, the claim of the ruling class to rule was challenged from the perspective of the future, of a society in the making—state socialism in the case of Russia and China, capitalist democracy in the case of Europe. Colonialism, however, was challenged from the vantage point of the past, of the society which it had superseded.

**Challenge to Authority**

The actions of the Kumaun peasants no doubt represented a direct challenge to authority of government, nor does it, in any way, conform to the picture of violence drawn by scholars reporting tribal and peasant revolts in peninsular India. The methods of resistance characteristically used by the hill peasant were strikes and the burning of the forest floor; physical violence was very rarely resorted to. In this connection one might refer again to the unusual political and economic structure of Kumaun, where the state dealt directly with the relatively egalitarian village communities without the help of an intermediary class enjoying a vested interest in land. The dreaded triad of 'Sarkar, Sahukar and Zamindar [which was] a political fact rooted in the very nature of British power in the subcontinent', was here conspicuous by its absence, as indeed was the 'total and integrated violence' of rebellion observed elsewhere.[104] Although 'impatient of control',[105] the hillman enjoyed an autonomy rarely found in other parts of India, as this description of the 'Garhwal village *paharee*' testifies:

> I suppose it would be difficult to find any peasantry in the world more free from the *res angustae domi* [i.e., straitened circumstances at home] he is the owner of a well built stone house, has as much land as he wants at an easy rental, keeps his flocks and herds, and is in every sense of the word, an independent man.[106]

The suhukar was conspicuous by his absence in this struggle, between the body of cultivating proprietors and the state. The autonomy these proprietors continued to enjoy are germane to the particular forms assumed by the conflicts between the peasantry and the state. This was the manner in which these conflicts were represented in popular consciousness. Thus, in Kumaun the absence of violent protest may be related to the structure of domination in hill society—this being one that did not quite correspond to the forms of domination in other parts of India—as well as to the distinctive tradition of peasant protest embodied in the dhandak. Moreover, while Adas is correct in suggesting that '*most forms* of the protest of retribution represent very limited responses that flaunt laws and threaten individuals . . . [but] have little lasting impact on existing systems of peasant elite exchange and social control',[107] this was certainly not the case in Kumaun in 1921.

Hill forests were strategic to the colonial rule. Their vulnerability to fire left the state with no effective response but to abandon control over large areas of woodland. Likewise, labour strikes in an inaccessible and poorly connected region crippled the administration, forcing it to end the begar system. Clearly, the extent of violence will vary with different forms of domination. The peculiar social structure, cultural history of resistance, and the relative efficacy of different methods of protest. The protesters did not include in violence at all. There was the aparian rebels played on these strengths in Kumaon and never throught of physical intimidation.[108]

**Nationalism and the Vanguard Party**

The literature on Indian nationalism, in common with that on the Vietnamese and Chinese Revolutions, has focused on the role of the vanguard party—in this case, the Indian National Congress—in agrarian movements.[109] The history of social protest in the Indian Himalaya also calls into question the received wisdom on the participation of the peasantry in anti-colonial movements in the Third World. While this bias is in part a function of the historical record—namely the accessibility of source materials on organized nationalist campaigns—it is also informed by a scepticism of the power of the peasantry to act independently in defence of its interests. According to a prominent Indian historian, nationalism as represented by the Congress party 'helped to arouse the peasant and awaken him to his own needs, demands and above all the possibility of any active role in social and political development.'[110]

A Korean scholar has this to say on the links between the peasantry and communists in his country:

> If traditional peasant uprisings can be characterized as unorganized, amorphous and spontaneous, then modern peasant uprisings can be said to be more organized, systematic and contrived. The traditional uprising was a more or less natural phenomenon arising in the face of possible starvation; economic factors played a decisive role. The modern peasant uprising, in contrast, possesses a relatively clear goal as well as calculated strategies; political factors such as leadership and ideology play a decisive role.[111]

This perspective on the possibilities of peasant protest lies much in the tradition of social analysis that I called the S-O paradigm for the study of lower-class resistance. It posits a linear transition from unorganized to organized forms of resistance, with the former doomed to hopeless defeat, and the latter, by virtue of its association with an organized party, having a fair chance of success.

Curiously enough, scholars of diametrically opposed political persuasions are apt to overestimate the influence of the vanguard party.. In this vision peasants stand closer to nature than to culture; it takes the intervention of urban intellectuals, whether nationalist or communist, to transform elemental peasant needs into a social movement worthy of the name. For their own very different reasons intellectuals of the Rand Corporation and party historians would tend to magnify the role (conspiratory in one version, emancipatory in the other) of the Communist Party in the Vietnamese nationalist movements. Similarly, apologists of the British imperium as well as official Indian histories have, by and large, uncritically accepted the Congress party's projection of itself as the initiator, director, and guarantor of Indian nationalism. As Richard Cobb not unfairly observes, these party-centred perspectives assume 'that a popular movement cannot be self-led and that the common people are too stupid to look after things for themselves. It is a thesis that, for obvious reasons, has always had an appeal to the right wing mind and to the intellectual, two studies in arrogance.'[112]

**Peasant Nationalism**

Recent historical research has begun to challenge theories of peasant nationalism centring on a 'hegemonic' party. First, a reinterpretation of historical source material is shedding more light on the everyday forms of peasant resistance, the 'prosaic but constant struggle between the peasantry and those who seek to extract labour, food, taxes, rent and interest from them'. For, 'to understand those commonplace forms of resistance is to understand what much of the peasantry does "between revolts", to defend its interests as best as it can.'[113] Second, scholars have been recovering the numerous peasant revolts in the nineteenth and early-twentieth centuries (well before 'modern' nationalism penetrated the countryside), reconstructing the world view of the rebels and their own radical rejection of colonial rule.[114] Third, and perhaps most significant, recent work has stressed the relative autonomy of peasant participation in later movements formally led and directed by a nationalist party. While the rural masses joined the national movement for reasons of their own—which often did not coincide with the charter of demands laid down by the Congress Working Committee—on many occasions peasants on their own initiative adopted forms of struggle that broke the narrow confines of Congress-directed non-cooperation.[115]

My own research strongly suggests that peasants joined nationalist movements only when such participation could redress local grievances. Finally, the linkages between the educated leaders and the rank and file were by no means as one-sided as some party histories suggest. In many parts of India, and clearly so in Kumaun, the leaders of the Congress, like the leaders of the Indo-chinese Communist Party in another context, were 'overwhelmed by their subordinates'.[116] One could even argue that far from being stirred from their 'apathy' by larger political developments, peasants have historically seen these forces as an opportunity to settle old scores with their local oppressors. Within the restricted sphere of the conflict over forest rights, ample confirmation is provided by evidence from three continents of the links between political upheavals at the national level and the assertion of peasant claims at the local level: witness the massive invasions of forest and grazing lands during the Russian Revolution of 1905-07, and the affirmation of peasant (as opposed to landlord or state) control over forests during the Mexican Revolution, the latter occurring almost simultaneously with the movements in Kumaun.[117]

**Parallels with France**

Indeed, as far back as 1688 the Glorious Revolution was a signal for English villagers to mount a 'general insurrection against the deer' protected in royal hunting preserves.[118] Perhaps the best documented of all such cases concerns the French Revolutions of 1830 and 1848, which the French peasantry welcomed as a golden opportunity to recover their lost rights in the forest.[119] This is precisely how the villagers of Kumaun seem to have viewed the nationwide campaigns of 1919-22; in fact, peasants and tribals of other forest regions of India also rode the impetus of the Non-Cooperation movement and the promise of 'Gandhi raj' in pursuance of strikingly similar ends.[120] Larger historical forces—democracy in nineteenth-century France, mass nationalism in twentieth-century India—served to legitimize protests oriented towards forest rights, enabling peasants to claim these rights more insistently and with greater militancy. As the comparative history of peasant resistance so abundantly illustrates, there is often a yawning gap between the concrete reasons for which peasants join larger revolts, and the more abstract goals of 'democracy' and 'nationalism' invoked by the articulate leadership.

Thus in rejecting the idea that the national assembly and the urban bourgeoise organized the rural jacquerie at the time of the French Revolution, Georges Lefebvre comments sharply: 'The peasants had their own reasons for joining the conflict, and these reasons were more than sufficient.' Likewise, when Madeiro initiated the Mexican Revolution in November 1910, rural leaders in the province of Morelos 'did not flock to his cause without weeks of hard reckoning and calculation. And when they did join him, it was for conscious, practical reasons—to recover village lands and establish security.' Half a century later, peasants gleefully recalled a conversation between Madeiro and their leader Zapata. When Madeiro says he is 'fighting for Effective Suffrage, No Re election [for the strongman Porfirio Diaz]', Zapata replies that he, on behalf of the poor, is fighting for 'Water, Land and Justice'.[121] These complex and often unexpected interconnections between organized nationalism and lower-class resistance are sufficiently illustrated in the trajectory of social protest in British Kumaun. For the Himalayan peasant the cohesion and collective spirit of the village community, and not the organized resources of urban nationalism, provided the mainspring of political action.]

Congress leaders in the towns of Almora and Nainital very likely believed themselves to be fighting for the nationwide goal of Purna Swaraj (complete independence), yet peasants used the vehicle of nationalism to more effectively reclaim their lost rights in the forest. For forest administration had introduced a notion of property, one integral to colonial rule but previously foreign to Kumaun, which ran contrary to the experience of the Khasa village communities in which different *jatis* shared a 'remarkable amity', symbolized by their sharing of the common *hookah*.[122] Thus, the wide-ranging campaign of 1921, though differing from a modern social movement in its aims and methods, was far from being the spontaneous outburst of an illiterate peasantry, representing a blind reaction to the expropriation of a resource crucial to their subsistence. It expressed, albeit in a far more heightened way, the motivations which underlay the sporadic and localized protests in the early years of forest administration. Expressed through the medium of popular protest were conflicting theories of social relationships that virtually amounted to two world views. One can meaningfully contrast state monopoly right with the free use of forest by members of the village community as sanctioned by custom, a pattern of use, moreover, regulated by the community as a whole.

**Exploitation of Pine Forests**

The exploitation of the pine forests on grounds of commercial profitability and strategic imperial needs was at variance, too, with the use of natural resources in an economy wholly oriented towards subsistence. The invocation of the symbols of Bania and Rakshas, with all that they stood for, was a natural consequence of this discrepancy. As the paternalist state transformed itself into an agency intruding more and more into the daily life of its subject population, so its claim to legitimacy floundered. Peasant opposition to this encroachment took the form of consciously determined actions that were incomprehensible to an observer unfamiliar with the social and cultural heritage of the Kumaun peasant. But set in their socio-historical context, these actions' become intelligible and are seen to represent a frontal challenge to state authority. The seemingly docile peasantry had been thought incapable of this. From the perspective of the sociology of domination, we can observe considerable differences between popular perceptions of an ancient dynasty and of a government alien in terms of both race and language.

In Tehri Garhwal the king, sanctified as Bolanda Badrinath, enjoyed a status denied to representatives of the colonial state. The latter's workings were far more impersonal and lacked the sanctity of tradition. In Tehri it was the motif of the 'wicked official' that symbolized the impediment between raja and praja. As a consequence, peasant protest was directed exclusively at officials and the laws they implemented, not at the king as such. Rather, the monarch was required to restore justice by dismissing tyrannical officials or repealing unjust laws. Even the kisan andolan, which covered large parts of the state and led to the eventual fall of the monarchy, was not really anti-monarchical in its popular ideology. In Kumaun division, on the other hand, the social idiom of protest clearly revealed a growing separation of the state from the peasantry. Thus, the state was depicted as a Bania government, the caste appellation evoking images of power as well as deception. On another occasion it was called a Rakshas (demoniacal) government. In Kumaun division there had occurred by 1921 a near total rupture between the colonial state and its subject population. On the other hand the quasi-divine Tehri monarch exemplified the continuity—sometimes threatened but never fully breached—between the state and the people

## References

1. P. Mason, *A Matter of Honour* (London, 1975), p. 451; cf. also T.W. Webber, *The Forests of Upper India and Their Inhabitants* (London, 1902), p. 39.
2. E.P. Stebbing, *The Forests of India*, 3 volumes (London, 1922-26), III, p. 258.
3. E.A. Smythies, *India's Forest Wealth* (London, 1925), p. 84.
4. M.S. Randhawa, *The Kumaun Himalayas* (Delhi, 1970), p. 12.
5. J.H. Batten, 'Final Report on the Settlement of Kumaun', in Batten (ed), *Official Reports on the Province of Kumaun* (1851; rpt. Calcutta, 1878), p. 270.
6. 'Mountaineer', *A Summer Ramble in the Himalaya* (London, 1860), p. 167.
7. Census of India, 1891, Vol. 16, part 1, NWP & O, General Report, pp. 29-30.
8. V.A. Stowell, *A Manual of the Land Tenures of the Kumaun Division* (1907; rpt. Allahabad, 1937), pp. 150-06; H.G. Walton, *British Garhwal: A Gazetteer* (Allahabad, 1911), pp. 68-69.
9. Thomas Skinner, *Excursions in India, Including a Walk over the Himalaya Mountain to the Sources of the Jumna and Ganges* (London, 1832), Vol. I, p. 307; A.M. Kellas, The Mountains of Northern Sikkim and Garhwal', *The Geographical Journal*, Vol. 40, No. 3, September 1912, p. 257.
10. See Shekhar Pathak, 'Uttarakhand mein Coolie Begar Pratha: 1815-1949, unpublished Ph.D. thesis, Kumaun University, 1980; *idem*, 'Kumaun mein Begar Annulan Andolan', paper presented at Jawaharlal Nehru University, October 1982, pp. 4-14. Hereafter Pathak (1) and (2).
11. See letter from comm., KD, to chief secretary, UP, 18 September 1916, in FD file 164/1916, UPSA.
12. DO no. 10 x, 6 February 1917, from DFO, North Garhwal, to conservator of forests (CF), Kumaun circle, GAD file 398/1913, UPSA.

13. *Report of the Kumaun Forest Grievances Committee* (thereafter KFGC), in Progs A, June 1922, nos. 19-24, file no. 522/1922, dept of rev. & agrl. (forests), p. 2, NAI.
14. Petition to Sir James Meston, L-G, UP, by Pandit Madan Narayan Bist (village Ulaingad, patti Wallawigad, Almora), clerk on duty at the office of the director-general of archaeology at Ootacumund, 17 May 1913, GAD file 398/1913. Grammar and punctuation as in original.
15. J.G. Scott, *The Moral Economy of the Peasant* (New Haven, 1976).
16. 'Note on transport of Forest officials by Utar and pack ponies' by comm., KD, 17 August 1919, in file no. 21 of 1918-19, dept xv, Regional Archives, Nainital (RAN).
17. 'Report of the Kumaun Sub-Committee of the Board of Communications of coolie utar and bardaish in Kumaun', sd P. Wyndham, chairman, 9 October 1919: note on above report by T.D. Gairola, 17 October 1919, GAD file 739/1920, UPSA.
18. Speech by Sir James Meston at durbar held in Nainital on 30 September 1916, GAD file 108/1918, UPSA.
19. See, for example, 'Annual Report of the Coolie Agencies in Garhwal District for 1911-12', in GAD file 398/1913.
20. No. 6544/XV/50, 10 October 1916, from comm., KD, to chief secretary, UP; 'Rules for touring officials in the hill pattis of the Kumaun Division', sd comm., 18 October 1916, both in ibid.
21. No. 6056/XVI-19, 19 June 1900, from comm., KD, to chief secretary, NWP & O; no. 2503/1-303B, 4 August 1900, from chief secretary, NWP& O, to deputy adjutant general, Bengal, both in file no. 19 of 1899-1900, dept. xvi, RAN.
22. No. 1156/III/398, 5 June 1916, from chief secretary, UP, to officers commanding 1st and 2nd 39th Garhwal Rifles, GAD file 398/1913.
23. See note by under secretary to chief secretary, UP, 17 August 1913, in ibid.
24. J.O.B. Beckett, 'Iron and Copper Mines in the Kumaun Division', report of 31 January 1850, in *Selections*, Vol. II, pp. 31-38. 'There is *not a single* malgoozar of any of the villages in the neighbourhood of the iron mines who has not at one time or other endeavoured to levy a tax on *all* the charcoal burners . . .' Ibid., 36, emphasis added.
25. 'Note on forest administration for my successor', by McNair, DC, Garhwal, Feb. 1907, in FD file II/1908, UPSA.
26. J.C. Nelson, *Forest Settlement Report of the Garhwal District* (Lucknow, 1916), pp. 10-11.
27. E.K. Pauw, *Report on the Tenth Settlement of the Garhwal District* (Allahabad, 1894), p. 52.
28. T.D. Gairola, *Selected Revenue Decisions of Kumaun* (Allahabad, 1936), p. 211.

29. District and sessions judge, Moradabad, to private secretary to L-G, UP, 2 March 1916, in FD file 163/1916 (Forest Settlement Grievances in the KD), UPSA.
30. According to the settlement officer, 'much was omitted and much exaggerated, much extenuated and much set down in malice', while quarrels over rights 'were unfortunately always very bitter.' Nelson, 'Forest Settlement Report', pp. 2-4, 13, 25.
31. A.E. Osmaston, *WP for the North Garhwal Forest Division, 1921-22 to 1930-31* (Allahabad, 1921) p. 67.
32. *Report on the Administration of the United Provinces of Agra and Oudh, 1915-16* (Allahabad: Government Press, 1916), p. viii.
33. *Annual Progress Report of the Forest Administration of the United Provinces* (hereafter APFD), 1915-16, p. 7.
34. H.G. Champion, 'Observations on Some Effects of Fires in the *Chir (Pinus longifolia)* Forests of the West Almora Division', *Indian Forester*, Vol. 45 (1919), pp. 353-63.
35. H.G. Champion, *WP for the Central Almora For. Div.* (Lucknow, 1922), pp. 13-14.
36. J.G. Meston (lieutenant-governor) to comm., KD, 5 March 1916; DC, Garhwal to L-G, 27 March 1916; 'Note on the Forest Settlement and the Garhwali Officers of the Regiment', by DC, Garhwal, 20 March 1916, all in FD file 163/1916.
37. GO no. 197/XIV/163, 14 February 1918, appended to APFD, 1916-17.
38. See GO no. 114/XIVA/172 of 1918, 4 February 1919, appended to APFD, 1917-18.
39. Wyndham to Meston, 26 June 1916; *idem*, 3 July 1916; 'Subjects for discussion at the conference of selected officers to be held at Government House, Nainital at 10.30 a.m. on the 28th August 1916', sd P. Wyndham, 14 August 1916, all in FD file 163/1916.
40. Figures calculated from H.G. Walton, *Almora: A Gazetteer* (Allahabad, 1911), appendix.
41. See, for example, GO no. 123-XIV-209, 2 November 1922, appended to APFD, 1921-22.
42. See APFD, 1919-20, p. 8; Osmaston, 'North Garhwal WP', p. 89.
43. However, most Parishad leaders were small landholders, like the majority of their kinsmen, and perhaps less alienated from the villages than urban nationalists in many other parts of India. See G.B. Pant's evidence to the *Royal Commission on Agriculture in India* (London, 1927), Vol. III, p. 360.
44. Shekhar Pathak, *Badridutt Pande aur Unka Yug* (Lucknow, 1982), pp. 12-24. Hereafter Pathak (3).
45. Pathak (2), pp. 22-24. Prominent among the village activists was Mohan Singh Mehta of Katyur.

46. HG no. C.3, Bageshwar, 17 January 1921, from DC, Almora, to comm., KD; extract from confidential fortnightly report of comm., KD, 10 January 1921, both in police department (PD) file 1151/1921, UPSA.
47. Summary of Badridutt Pande's speech at Bageshwar, by S. Ijaz Ali, deputy collector, Almora, in ibid.
48. Pathak (2), p. 28.
49. DC, Almora, to comm., KD, no. C.3, 17 January 1921; *idem*, no. C.4, 20 January 1921; no. 43, C421, 29 January 1921, from comm., KD, to chief secretary, UP, all in PD file 1151/1921.
50. Pathak (1), appendix III.
51. No. 42, C.I, 21, 28 January 1921, from comm., KD, to DFO, Almora, in PD file 1151 /1921.
52. Comm., KD, to secretary to government, UP, 4 March 1921, in GAD file 739/192O-zero
53. Resolution passed by UP legislative council on 5 March 1921; table on transport of officers in camp, 1921-22, enclosed with DO no. 215, 17 June 1922, from comm., KD to deputy secretary, GAD, UP, both in ibid.
54. Karen Fields, *Revival and Rebellion in Colonial Central Africa* (Princeton, 1985), p. 135; see also S. Moertono, *State and Statecraft in Old Java* (Ithaca, 1968), p. 75; Peter Worsley, *The Trumpet Shall Sound* (London, 1957), pp. 104-06.
55. 'In recent years, mainly owing to the rapid expansion of the Forest Department, the demands for utar have greatly increased and the obligations of furnishing utar has caused growing resentment.' Press communique, 1 February 1921, sd H.S. Crosthwaite, secretary to government, UP, in GAD file 739/1920.
56. See memorandum on coolie utar submitted by Kumaun Association (Ranikhet branch) to L-G, UP, 16 October 1920, in ibid.
57. Letter from R.G. Bellaire, colonization officer of Soldier Settlement Estates, Kausani, to DC, Almora, 1 February 1921, in PD file 1151/1921.
58. DC, Almora, to comm., KD, 17 January 1921; *idem*, no. C.15, 24 January 1921, both in ibid.; Wyndham was clear that 'the root of the whole evil and discontent is our d—d forest policy': no. 2, C.II.21, 1 February 1921, from comm., K.D, to chief secretary, UP, in ibid.
59. Cf. Govind Chatak, *Garhwali Lok Geet* (Dehradun, 1956), pp. 261-62.
60. 'Report of Pandit Badridutt Editor's Speeches to Villagers in Almora District', in PD file 1151/1921.
61. See criminal case no. 7 of 1921, *King/Emperorus. Motliram, Budhanand and Badridutt* of Totashiling, at police station Palla Boraraw, in the court of W.C Dible, district magistrate, Almora, 7 July 1921, in FD file 157/ 1921 ('Forest fires in Kumaun'), UPSA. The implication, if it needs to be spelled out, was that while the forests had earlier supplied products like ghee and thus contributed to the local economy, now they were used to produce resin which was of no use to villagers. The use of such a metaphor, it may be added, reiterates the strong emphasis placed on village autonomy.

62. DC, Almora, to comm., KD, no. C.15, 24 January 1921; *idem*, no. C.63, 2 March 1921, both in PD file 1151/1921.
63. Extract from fortnightly DO from comm., KD, for second-half of March 1921, FD file 157/1921.
64. See file no. 56 of 1921, A. Progs, Nos. 1-2, May 1921, dept of revenue and agriculture (famine), NAI.
65. See resolution printed in the *Shakti* of 12 April 1921 (extract found in FD file 157/1921). All archival sources in the rest of this chapter, unless mentioned otherwise, are from this source.
66. Fortnightly DO no. CY.21, 23 May 1921, from comm., KD, to chief secretary, UP; DO no. 348, 28 May 1921, from chief conservator of forests (CCF), UP, to governor, UP; No. 53-CC/*xiv-i*, 2 June 1921, from offg CF, Kumaun circle, to CCF, UP.
67. APFD, 1921-22, pp. 7-8.
68. DO no. 31.CVI.21, 9 June 1921, from comm., KD, to home member, UP.
69. S. B. Bhatia, *WP for the East Almora Forest Division 1924-25 to* (Allahabad, 1926), p. 41.
70. See his *Primitive Rebels* (3 edn, Manchester, 1974), pp. 25-26.
71. John Merriman, 'The Demoiselles of the Ariege, 1829-1831', in Merriman (ed). *1830 in France* (New York, 1975), pp. 102-03.
72. This extremely revealing classification and the following paragraph are taken from the two 'Statements on fire cases in Almora', W.C. Dible, 23 July and 3 November 1921, respectively. Unfortunately, similar details could not he traced for Nainital and Garhwal.
73. Cf. Eric Hobsbawm on the Luddites: 'In some cases, indeed, resistance to the machine was quite consciously resistance to the machine in the hands of the capitalist.' See his *Labouring Men* (London, 1964), p. 10.
74. 'Fire cases in Garhwal district', sd P. Mason, DC, Garhwal, 9 September 1921; DC, Garhwal, to secretary, government of UP, 29 December 1921; DO no. 31.CV.21, 9 June 1921, from comm., KD, to home member, UP.
75. Worsley, *Trumpet*, p. 69; John Womack, *Zapata and the Mexican Revolution* (New York, 1960), p. 101.
76. DC, Garhwal, to secretary to government, UP, 7 September 1921.
77. FD file 156/1921 ('Forest fires in Kumaun'), UPSA.
78. *Garhwali* (hereafter GRH), 7 May and 21 May 1921.
79. A.P. Bahuguna, 'Kumaun aur Janglat ki Committee', GRH, 21 May 1921.
80. 'Garhwal Janta ki Janglat Sambandi Mang', GRH, 18 June 1921.
81. See Bhatia, 'East Almora WP', for details.
82. KFGC, pp. 2-10.
83. See APFD, 1928-29, pp. 5-9.
84. APFD, 1929-30, pp. 8-9.
85. See F.C. Ford Robertson, *Our Forests* (Allahabad, 1936).
86. APFD, 1931-32, pp. 4-6. etc.

87. D.S. Manral, *Swatantra Sangram mein Kumaun-Garhwal ka Yogdan* (Bareilly, 1978), pp. 70-74.
88. GRH, 17 May 1930.
89. GRH, 9 August 1930.
90. Manral, *Swatantra Sangram,* pp. 75-77; S.C. Dabral, *Uttarakhand ka Itihas,* Vol. 8, part 2 (Dugadda, n.d.), pp. 251-53.
91. Manral, *Swatantra Sangram,* pp. 85-93.
92. *Ibid*; Dabral, *Uttarakhand,* pp. 288-90.
93. See C.S. Mitra, 'Political Mobilization and the Nationalist Movement in Eastern Uttar Pradesh and Bihar 1937-42', unpublished D.Phil, thesis, Oxford University, 1983.
94. Michael Adas, 'From Avoidance to Confrontation: Peasant Protest in Pre-colonial and Colonial South-east Asia', *Comparative Studies in Society and History (CSSH),* Vol. 23, No. 2, 1981; J.C. Scott, *Weapons of the Weak: Everyday Forms of Peasant Resistance* (New Haven, 1986).
95. The Coronation Durbar was a lavish spectacle held in Delhi to commemorate the accession of George V.
96. Dible to Wyndham, DO no. C355, 24 July 1921, in FD file 157/1921, UPSA.
97. These terms have been used by George Rude, following Gramsci, in his *Ideology and Popular Protest* (London, 1980). Rude, like some other historians, is rather more conscious of instances where 'derived' elements transform folk ideology.
98. Irwin Scheiner, 'Benevolent Lords and Honorable Peasants: Rebellion and Peasant Consciousness in Tokugawa Japan', in Tetsuo Najita and Irwin Scheiner (eds), *Japanese Thought in the Tokugawa Period, 1600-1868* (Chicago, 1978).
99. S. Moertono, *State and Statecraft in Old Java* (Ithaca, 1968), pp. 78-79, emphasis added.
100. Howard Spodek, 'On the Origins of Gandhi's Political Methodology: The Heritage of Kathiawad and Gujarat', *Journal of Asian Studies,* Vol. 30, No. 2, February 1971.
101. Scott, *Moral Economy,* p. 125.
102. See Sartono Kartodirdjo, *The Peasant Revolt of Banten in 1888* (The Hague, 1966), pp. 3, 21-22, 28, 67, 94, 106, 321-22, etc. The framework of this fine work anticipates both the neo-Weberianism of Scott and Adas and the 'history from below' of the Subaltern Studies school; despite its unfortunate neglect by later scholars, it is a germinal contribution to the sociology of peasant resistance under colonialism.
103. Barrington Moore, *Injustice: The Social Bases of Obedience and Revolt* (White Plains, NY, 1978), p. 43, emphasis added.
104. Ranajit Guha, *Elementary Aspects of Peasant Insurgency in Colonial India* (Delhi, 1983). pp. 27, 157, etc.

105. *Report of the Kumaun Forest Grievances Committee*, Progs A, June 1922, nos. 19-24 file No. 522/1922, dept of rev. agl. (forests), p. 2, NAI.
106. Dr F. Pearson, 'Report on Mahamurree and Smallpox in Garhwal, in *Selections from the Records of the Government of the Northwestern Provinces*, Vol. II (Allahabad, 1866), p. 300.
107. Michael Adas, 'From Footdragging to Flight: The Evasive History of Peasant Avoidance Protest in South and South-east Asia', pp. 81-82.
108. The violence/non-violence debate acquires a particular significance in the context of Indian nationalism, with Marxist writers often accusing Gandhi of adopting non-violence to wean the masses away from the revolutionary path. See, for the classic statement, R. Palme Dutt, *India Today* (Delhi, 1948). For a different reading of Gandhi's methods, which stresses their roots in Indian political tradition, see Dharampal, *Civil Disobedience and Indian Tradition* (Varanasi, 1971).
109. Cf. Sumit Sarkar, *Modern India, 1885-1947* (Delhi, 1983); *idem*, *Popular Movements and Middle Class Leadership in Late Colonial India* (Calcutta, 1983).
110. Bipan Chandra, *Nationalism and Colonialism in Modern India* (Delhi, 1979), p. 345. For another commentator, 'the patronage of politics from above helped agrarian discontent to get organized [and] it was in that sense a child [sic] of the politics of Indian nationalism.' Majid Siddiqi, *Agrarian Unrest in the United Provinces, 1918-22* (Delhi, 1978), pp. ix-x.
111. Se Hee Yoo, 'The Communist Movements and the Peasants: The Case of Korea', in J.W. Lewis (ed.), *Peasant Rebellion and Communist Revolution in Asia* (Stanford, 1974), pp. 75-76.
112. Cobb, *The Police and the People: French Popular Protest*, 1789-1920 (Oxford, 1970), p. 78.
113. Scott, *Weapons of the Weak*, p. 29.
114. The major work for India is Ranajit Guha, *Elementary Aspects*. See also A.R. Desai (ed.), *Peasant Struggles in India* (Delhi, 1979).
115. The pioneering regional studies are G. Pandey, *The Ascendancy of the Congress in Uttar Pradesh, 1926-34*. (Delhi, 1978); D. Hardiman, *Peasant Nationalists of Gujarat: Kheda District, 1917-34* (Delhi, 1981).
116. Morche Commission Report, quoted in Scott, *Moral Economy*, p. 149.
117. Teodor Shanin, *Russia as a 'Developing' Society* (New Haven, 1986), Vol. II, pp. 36, 84, 90-91, etc., Oscar Lewis, *Pedro Martinez: A Mexican Peasant and His Family* (New York, 1964).
118. E.P. Thompson, *Whigs and Hunters* (Harmondsworth, 1975), p. 41.
119. A mayor in Ariege during the 1830 Revolution wrote thus: 'The liberty which his majesty Philippe I *[sic]* has just given the French nation has been misinterpreted by our mountain peasants, who now believe themselves authorized to violate the laws, in delivering themselves, without

any limit, to all the disorders that they can commit against the forest administration.' Thus, liberty in, the Ariege did not mean the "essential political liberties", the *charte,* or an extended electoral franchise ... it primarily meant the return of traditional rights of usage in the forest.' Merriman, *Demoiselles,* pp. 104-05. In 1848, at the first sign of the republic, peasants in the Var marched on a forest newly enclosed by a landlord, destroying his wall and uprooting newly planted fruit trees—'the idea was to regain the forest for the community . . . since "now we are a Republic".' Maurice Agulhon, *The Republic in the Village* (Cambridge, 1982), p. 172.

120. See Ramachandra Guha and Madhav Gadgil, 'Forestry and Social Conflict in Colonial India', *Past and Present, No.* 123, May 1989.

121. Lefebvre, *Great Fear,* p. 99; Womack, *Zapata,* p. 220; Lewis, *Pedro Martinez,* p. 88.

122. G.R. Kala, *Memoirs of the Raj: Kumaun* (Delhi, 1974), p. 20.

# 5
# The Chipko Movement

The significance of Chipko movement lies in the fact that it took place in post-independent India. Historically, philosophically and organisationally an extension of the traditional Gandhian satyagraha. The continuity between the pre-independence and post-independence forms of this satyagraha has been provided by Gandhians, including Sri Dev Suman, Mira Behn and Sarala Behn. Sri Dev Suman was initiated into Gandhian satyagraha at the time of the Salt Satyagraha. He died as a martyr for the cause of the Garhwali people's right to survive with dignity and freedom. Both Mira Behn and Sarala Behn were close associates of Gandhiji. They settled in the interior of the Himalayas and established ashrams. Sarala Behn settled in Kumaon, and Mira Behn lived in Garhwal till the time she left for Vienna due to ill health. Equipped with the Gandhian world view of development based on justice and ecological stability, they contributed silently to the growth of women power and ecological consciousness in the hill areas of Uttar Pradesh. The influence of these two European disciples of Gandhiji on the heritage of struggle for social justice and ecological stability in the hills of Uttar Pradesh has been immense and they generated a new brand of Gandhian activists who provided the foundation for the Chipko movement.

**Sunderlal Bahuguna**

Sundarlal Bahuguna is prominent among the new generation of workers deeply inspired by these Gandhians. Influenced by Sri Dev Suman, he joined the independence movement at the age of 13. Later, he worked with Mira Behn in Bhiiangana Valley and was trained in her ecological vision. In an article written in 1952, Mira Behn had stated that there was 'Something Wrong in the Himalaya'.

> Year after year the floods in the North of India seem to be getting worse, and this year they have been absolutely devastating. This means that there is something radically wrong in the Himalayas, and that 'something' is, without doubt, connected with the forests. It is not, I believe, just a matter of deforestation as some people think, but largely a matter of change of species.

> Living in the Himalayas as I have been continuously now for several years, I have become painfully aware of a vital change in species of trees which is creeping up and up the southern slopes—those very slopes which let down the flood waters on to the plains below. This deadly changeover is from Banj (Himalayan Oak) to Chir pine. It is going on at an alarming speed, and because it is not a matter of deforestation, but of change from one kind of forest to another, it is not taken sufficiently seriously. In fact, the quasi-commercial Forest Department is inclined to shut its eyes to the phenomenon, because the Banj brings them in no cash for the coffers, whereas the Chir pine is very profitable, yielding as it does both timber and resin.
>
> The Banj leaves, falling as they do, year by year, create a rich black mould in which develops a thick tangled mass of undergrowth (bushes, creepers, and grasses), which in their turn add to the leaf-mould deposit and the final result is a forest in which almost all the rain water becomes absorbed. Some of it evaporates back into the air and the rest percolates slowly down, to the lower altitudes, giving out here and there beautiful sweet and cool springs. It would be difficult to imagine a more ideal shock-absorber for the monsoon rains than a Banj forest.
>
> The Chir pine produces just the opposite effect. It creates with its pine needles a smooth, dry carpet, which absorbs nothing and which at the same time prevents the development of any undergrowth worth the name. In fact, often the ground in a Chir pine forest is as bare as a desert. When the torrential rains of the monsoon beat down on these southern slopes of the Himalayas, much of the pine-needle carpet gets washed away with the water and erosion invariably takes place, because these needles, being non-absorbent, create no leaf-mould, but only a little very inferior soil, which is easily washed out from the rocks and stones.

Mira Behn had thus identified not merely deforestation but change in species suitable to commercial forestry as the reason for ecological degradation in the Himalayas. She recognised that the leaf litter of oak forests was the primary mechanism for water conservation in the Himalayan mountain watersheds.

Inheriting these early lessons in ecology, Bahuguna was later able to transfer this ecological perspective to Chipko. The rapid spread of resistance in the hills of Uttar Pradesh and its success in enforcing changes in forest management was also largely due to the awareness created by folk poets like Ghanshyam Raturi, and grassroots organisational efforts of a number of people including Man Singh Rawat, Chandi Prasad Bhatt and Dhoom Singh Negi. Bhatt, who later became well known for his work, became an activist at the behest of Bahuguna in 1959 when they met at a bus station in Gopeshwar where Bhatt was working as a booking clerk and Bahuguna, along with Rawat and Raturi, was waiting for a bus during an organisational trip through Gopeshwar. Having found Bhatt a promising activist, Bahuguna invited him to join them.

In the post-independence period, under the coordination of Sarala Behn, the Gandhians organised themselves into the Uttarakhand Sarvodaya Mandal in 1961. The Chipko movement is this the contemporary expression of a continuing heritage of peaceful resistance by the people of Uttarakhand. The Sarvodaya movement in the sixties was organised around four major issues:

1. The organisation of women.
2. Fight against alcohol consumption.
3. Fight for forest rights.
4. The establishment of local, forest based small industries.

While the fight against alcohol consumption provided the platform for the organisation of women, the increasing conflict over forest produce between the local and non-local industries provided the rallying point for popular protest during the sixties. In 1968, the people of Garhwal renewed their resolve to fight for their forests in a memorial meeting held at Tilari on 30 May. The platform for the organisation of women was thus ready by the seventies and this decade saw the beginning of more frequent and more vocal popular protests on the rights of the people to protect and utilise local forests.

**The Movement Takes Root**

In 1971, Swami Chidanandji of Rishikesh undertook a month-long march to bless the people in their struggle. The year 1972 witnessed the most widespread organised protests against commercial exploitation of Himalayan forests by outside contractors in Uttarkashi on 12 December, and in Gopeshwar on 15 December. It was during these two protest meetings that Raturi composed his famous poem describing the method of embracing the trees to save them from felling:

*Embrace the trees and*
*Save them from being felled;*
*The property of our hills,*
*Save them from being looted.*

While the concept of saving trees from felling by embracing them is old in Indian culture, as was the case of Bishnois, in the context of the current phase of the movement for forest rights in Uttarakhand, this popular poem written in 1972 is the earliest source of the now famous name 'Chipko'. In 1973 the tempo of the movement in the two centres—

Uttarkashi and Gopeshwar—reached new heights. Raturi and Bhatt were the main organisers in these two places. While a meeting of the Sarvodaya Mandal was in progress in Gopeshwar in April 1973, the first popular action to chase contractors away erupted spontaneously in the region, when the villagers demonstrated against the felling of ash trees in Mandal forest. Bahuguna immediately asked his colleagues to proceed on a foot march in Chamoli district following the axemen and encouraging people to oppose them wherever they went.

**Non-violent Demonstration**

Later in December 1973, there was a militant non-violent demonstration in Uttarkashi in which thousands of people participated. In March 1974, twenty-seven women under the leadership of Goura Devi saved a large number of trees from a contractor's axe in Reni. Following this, the government was forced to abolish the private contract system of felling and in 1975 the Uttar Pradesh Forest Corporation was set up to perform this function. This was the first major achievement of the movement and marks the end of a phase in itself. Bureaucratisation, however, cannot replace a civilisational response to the forest crisis. The ecological limits of forest extraction was hardly recognised and estimated. Ecological problems were accentuated leading to increased suffering of women who were responsible for bringing water, collecting fodder, etc. During the next five years Chipko resistance for forest protection spread to various parts of the Garhwal Himalayas. It is important to note that it was no longer the old demand for a supply of forest products for local small industries but the new demand for ecological control on forest resource extraction to ensure a supply of water and fodder that was being aired.

In May 1977 Chipko activists in Henwal Valley organised themselves for future action. In June of the same year, Sarala Behn organised a meeting of all the activists in the hill areas of Uttar Pradesh which further strengthened the movement and consolidated the resistance to commercial fellings as well as excessive tapping of resin from the Chir pine trees. In Gotars forests in the Tehri range the forest ranger was transferred because of his inability to curb illegal over-tapping of resin. Consciousness was so high that in the Jogidanda area of the Saklana range, the public sector corporation, Garhwal Mandal Vikas Nigam, was asked to reguilate its resin-tapping activity. Among the numerous instances of Chipko's successes throughout the Garhwal Himalayas in the years to follow, are those in Adwani, Amarsar and Badiyargarh.

**Auctions**

The auction of Adwani forests took place in October 1977 in Narendernagar, the district headquarters. Bahuguna undertook a fast against the auction and appealed to the forest contractors as well as the district authorities to refrain from auctioning the forests. The auction was undertaken despite the expression of popular discontent. In the first week of December 1977, the Adwani forests were scheduled to be felled. Large groups of women led by Bachhni Devi came forward to save the forests. Interestingly, Bachhni Devi was the wife of the local village head, who was himself a contractor. Chipko activist Dhoom Singh Negi supported the women's struggle by undertaking a fast in the forest itself. Women tied sacred threads to the trees as a symbol of a vow of protection. Between 13 and 20 December a large number of women from fifteen villages guarded the forests while discourses on the role of forests in Indian life from ancient texts continued non-stop. It was here in Adwani that the ecological slogan: 'What do the forests bear? Soil, water and pure air' was born. The axemen withdrew.

They return on 1 February 1978 with two truckloads of armed police. The plan was to encircle the forests with the help of the police in order to keep the people away during the felling operation. Even before the police could reach the area volunteers of the movement entered the forests and explained their case to the forest labourers who had been brought in from distant places. By the time the contractors arrived with the police each tree was being guarded by three volunteers who embraced the trees. The police, having been defeated in their own plan and seeing the level of awareness among the people, hastily withdrew before nightfall.

A new auction was to take place at Narendranagar in March 1978. Demonstrated resisted and disturbed the auction. A large popular demonstration was organised against it and the police arrested twenty-three Chipko volunteers, including women. In December 1978 a massive felling programme was planned by the public sector Uttar Pradesh Forest Development Corporation in the Badiyargarh region. The local people instantly informed Bahuguna who started a fast unto death at the felling site, on 9 January 1979. On the eleventh day of his fast Bahuguna was arrested in the middle of the night. This act only served to further strengthen the commitment of the people. Folk poet Ghanashyam Raturi and priest Khima Shastri led the movement as thousands of men and women from the neighbouring villages joined them in the Badiyargarh forests. The people remained in the forests and guarded the trees for eleven days. Bahuguna was released from jail on 31 January 1979. After prolonged negotiation the contractors withdrew from the forests.

The cumulative impact of the sustained grassroots struggles to protect forests was a rethinking of the forest management strategy in the hill areas. The Chipko demand for the declaration of the Himalayan forests as protection forests instead of production forests for commercial exploitation was recognised at the highest policy-making level. The late Prime Minister, Mrs. Indira Gandhi, after a meeting with Bahuguna, recommended a fifteen year ban on commercial green felling in the Himalayan forests of Uttar Pradesh.

## The Respite

That was a respite that the movement got. The moratorium on green felling gave the Chipko movement breathing time to expand the base of the movement and Bahuguna undertook a 4,780 km long arduous Chipko foot march from Kashmir to Kohima to contact villagers in the long Himalayan range and to spread the message of Chipko. At the same time, activists found it opportune to spread the movement to other mountain regions of the country.

## Ecological Foundation of the Chipko Movement

What differentiates Chipko from the earlier struggles is its ecological basis. The new concern to save and protected forests through Chipko satyagraha did not arise from a resentment against further encroachment on people's access to forest resources. Both the earlier forest satyagrahas and their contemporary form, the Chipko movement, are rooted in conflicts over forest resources and are similar cultural responses to forest destruction. It was a response to the alarming signals of rapid ecological destabilisation in the hills. Villages that were once self-sufficient in food were forced to import food as a result of declining food productivity. This, in turn, was related to the decrease in soil fertility in the forests. Water sources began to dry up as forests disappeared. The so-called 'natural disasters', such as floods and landslides, began to occur in river systems which had hitherto been stable.

The Alaknanda disaster of July 1970 inundated 1,000 km of land in the hills and washed away many bridges and roads. In 1977 the Tawaghat tragedy took an even heavier toll. In 1978 the Bhagirathi blockade resulting from a big landslide above Uttarkashi led to massive floods across the entire Gangetic plains. The over-exploitation of forest resources and the resulting threat to communities living in the forests have thus evolved from concerns for distribution of material benefits to concerns for distribution of ecologically generated material costs. During the first stage, the growth of commercial interests resulted in efforts to exclude competing demands. The beginning of large-scale commercial exploitation of India's forest resources led to the need for a forest legislation which denied village communities access to forest resources. The forest satyagrahas of the thirties were an outcome of the Forest Act of 1927 which denied people access to biomass for survival while increasing biomass production for industrial and commercial growth.

## Second State of Conflict

The growth imperative, however, drove production for commercial purposes into the second stage of conflict which is at the ecological level. Scientific and technical knowledge of forestry included in the existing model of forest management, is limited to viewing forests only as sources of commercial timber. This gives rise to prescriptions for forest management which are basically manipulations to maximise immediate growth of commercial wood. This is achieved initially by the destruction of other biomass forms that have lower commercial value but may be very important to the people, or have tremendous ecological significance. The silvicultural system of modern forestry includes prescriptions for the destruction of non-commercial biomass forms to ensure the increased production of commercial biomass forms. The encouragement to substitute ecologically valuable oak forests by commercially valuable conifers is an example of this shift. Ultimately, this increase in production may be described as mining of the ecological capital of forest ecosystems which have evolved over thousands of years. The contemporary Chipko movement, which has become a national campaign, is the result of these multidimensional conflicts over forest resources at the scientific, technical, economic and ecological levels.

It is not merely a conflict confined to local or non-local distribution of forest resources, such as timber and resin. The Chipko demand, at one stage was for a larger share for the local people in the immediate commercial benefits of an ecologically destructive pattern of forest resource exploitation. It has now evolved to the demand for ecological rehabilitation. Since the Chipko movement is based upon the perception of forests in their ecological context, it exposes the social and ecological costs of short-term growth-oriented forest management. This is clearly seen in the slogan of the Chipko movement which claims that the main products of the forests are not timber or resin, but soil, water and oxygen. With proper social control the basic biomass needs of food, fuel, fodder, small timber, and fertiliser can, in the Chipko vision and the Garhwal practice, be satisfied as positive externalities of biomass production primarily aimed at soil and water conservation to stabilise the local agro-pastoral economy.

**Ban on Felling**

The government imposed a fifteen year ban on commercial green felling in the hills of Uttar Pradesh, in stopping clear felling in the Western Ghats and the Vindhyas, and in generating pressure for a national forest policy which is more sensitive to people's needs and to the ecological development of the country. This was the direct result of Chipko movement. Unfortunately, the Chipko movement has often been presented by vested interests as a reflection of a conflict between 'development' and 'ecological concern', implying that 'development relates to material and objective bases of life whereas 'ecology' is concerned with non-material and subjective factors, such as scenic beauty. The deliberate introduction of this false and dangerous dichotomy between 'development' and 'ecology' disguises the real dichotomy between ecologically sound development and unsustainable and ecologically destructive economic growth. The latter is always achieved through the destruction of life-support systems and material deprivation of marginal communities. Genuine development can only be based on ecological stability which ensures sustainable supplies of vital resources.

**Paradigm Conflict**

Gandhi and later his disciples, Mira Behn and Sarala Behn, clearly described how and why development is not necessarily contradictory to ecological stability. The conflict between exploitative economic growth and ecological development implies that, by questioning the destructive process of growth, ecological movements like Chipko are not an obstacle to the process of providing material welfare. On the contrary, by constantly keeping ecological stability in focus, they provide the best guarantee for ensuring a stable material basis for life. In the final analysis, the dichotomy between 'development' and environment can be reduced to what is 'development' and how scientific knowledge is generated and used to achieve it. This dichotomy is clearly enunciated in the two slogans on the utility of the Himalayan forests—one emanating from the ecological concepts of Garhwali women, the other from the sectoral concepts of those associated with trade in forest products. When the Chipko movement evolved into an ecological movement in Adwani in 1977, the spirit of public interest ecological science was captured in the slogan: 'What do the forests bear ? Soil, water and pure air'. This was a response to the commonly accepted, partisan science based slogan: 'What do the forests bear ? Profit on resin and timber'. The insight in these slogans symbolised a cognitive shift in the evolution of Chipko. The movement underwent a qualitative transformation from being based merely on conflicts over resources to conflicts over scientific perceptions and philosophical approaches to nature.

**Ecological and Cultural Content**

This transformation also led to that element of scientific knowledge which has allowed Chipko to reproduce itself in different ecological and cultural contexts. The slogan has become the scientific and philosophical message of the movement, and has laid the foundations of an alternative forestry science which is ecological in nature and oriented towards public interest. The commercial interest has the primary objective of maximising exchange value through the extraction of commercially valuable species. Forest ecosystems are therefore reduced to timber mines of commercially valuable species. 'Scientific forestry' in its present form is a reductionist system of knowledge which ignores the complex relationships within the forest community and between plant life and other resources like soil and water. Its pattern of resource utilisation is based on increasing 'productivity' on these reductionist lines. By ignoring the systems linkages within the forest ecosystem, this pattern of resource use generates instabilities in the ecosystem and leads to a counter-productive use of natural resources at the ecosystem level.

The destruction of the forest ecosystem and the multiple functions of forest resources adversely affects the economic interests of those groups of society, which depend on the diverse resource functions of forests for their survival. These include soil and water stabilisation and the provision of food, fodder, fuel, fertiliser, etc. Forest movements like Chipko are simultaneously a critique of reductionist 'scientific' forestry and an articulation of a framework for an alternative forestry science which, is ecological and can safeguard public interest. In this alternative forestry science, forest resources are not viewed as isolated from other resources of the ecosystem. Nor is the economic value of forests reduced to the commercial value of timber. 'Productivity', 'yield' and 'economic value' are defined for the integrated ecosystem and for multipurpose utilisation. Their meaning and measure is therefore entirely different from the meaning and measure adopted in reductionist forestry. Just as in the shift from Newtonian to Einsteinian physics, the meaning of 'mass' changed from a velocity independent to a velocity dependent term, in the shift from reductionist forestry to ecological forestry, all scientific terms change from ecosystem independent to ecosystem dependent ones.

Thus, for tribals and other forest communities a complex ecosystem is productive in terms of herbs, tubers, fibre, the gene pool, etc., whereas for the forester these components of the forest ecosystem are useless, unproductive and dispensable. Two economic perspectives lead to two notions of 'productivity' and 'value'. As far as overall productivity is concerned, the natural tropical forest is a highly productive ecosystem. Examining the forests of the humid tropics from the ecological perspective, Golley has noted: 'A large biomass is generally characteristic of tropical forests. The quantities of wood especially are large in tropical forests and average about 300 tons per ha compared with about 150 tons per ha for temperate forests. However, in partisan forestry, overall productivity is not important. It looks only for the industrially useful species and measures productivity in terms of industrial biomass.

Bethel states, referring to the large biomass typical of forests of the humid tropics:

> It must be said that from a standpoint of industrial material supply, this is relatively unimportant. The important question is how much of this biomass represents trees and parts of trees of preferred species that can be manufactured into products that can be profitably marketed .... By today's utilisation standards, most of the trees, in these humid tropical forests are, from an industrial materials standpoint, clearly weeds.

**Partisan Science**

With these assumptions of partisan forestry science wedded to forest industry, large tracts of natural tropical forests are being destroyed across the Third World. Though the justification given is increased 'productivity' yet productivity increase is only in one dimension. There is an overall decrease in productivity. The substitution of natural forests in India by Eucalyptus plantations has been justified on the grounds of improving the productivity of the site. However, it has been a partisan view of productivity in the context of pulpwood alone that has been projected as a universally applicable measure of productivity. What has been termed the 'Eucalyptus controversy' is in reality a paradigmatic conflict between an ecological public interest forestry and a reductionist partisan forestry, which only responds to industrial requirements. While natural forests and many indigenous tree species are more productive than Eucalyptus in the public interest paradigm, the opposite is true in the partisan paradigm of forestry. The scientific conflict is actually an economic conflict over which needs and whose needs are more important. In such paradigmatic conflicts, dominant scientific assumptions change not by consensus but by replacement.

Which paradigm will win and become dominant is determined by the political strength backing the paradigms. The utilisation of natural resources, is part of planned development, has been classically guided in India by the concept of maximisation of growth in the short-run. This maximisation is based on increasing the productivity of labour alone. Gandhi critically articulated the fallacy of increasing labour productivity independent of the social and material context. Gandhi's followers in the Chipko movement continue to critically evaluate restricted notions of productivity. It is this concern with resources and human needs which is symbolised in Bahuguna's well-known slogan— 'ecology is permanent economy'. These conceptual issues assume tremendous importance in view of the fact that we are entering into an era in which large amounts of financial resources are being handed over to Non-Government Organisations (NGOs) who are rapidly becoming the new managers of old development projects.

**Debate on Development**

The self-reliance, decentralisation and sacrifice intrinsic to voluntary action is being threatened by treating NGOs as the new delivery system. It is in this context that the debate on these two philosophies of nature and political action becomes central to the debate on development. The urgency of establishing a new economy of permanence, based on ecological principles, is felt with each new environmental disaster in the Himalayan region which spells destruction for the Gangetic basin. Chipko's search for a strategy for survival has global implications. Chipko's demand is conservation of not merely local forest resources but the entire life-support system, and with it the option for human survival. Gandhi's mobilisation for a new society in which neither man nor nature is exploited and destroyed, marked the beginning of this civilisational response to the threat to human survival. Chipko's agenda includes carrying forward that vision against the heavier odds of contemporary crises. Its contemporary relevance as well as its significance for the future world, is clearly indicated in the rapid spread of the ecological world view throughout the vast stretch of the Himalayan region, following the historical 5,000 km trans-Himalaya Chipko foot march led by Bahuguna, and subsequently through other vulnerable mountain systems such as the Western Ghats, Central India and the Aravallis.

# 6

# Chipko: Social History of an 'Environmental' Movement

All of a sudden, the Chipko Andolan drew the attention of the world forest conservationists and environment movements. Environment and ecological crises had been looming large on the Himalayas and this Andolan forced the attention of the people of India to this crises. The Chipko andolan provided the point of entry for the present work. In this chapter I explore the major dimensions of Chipko as a social movement. Essentially, a sociological study of the Chipko Andolan must grapple with three sets of issues.

Let in first understand the movement in its historical dimension. On the one hand, we need to interpret the social idiom of Chipko in the context of earlier movements centring around the question of peasant access to forests. On the other hand, we need to examine the interconnections between Chipko and different aspects of state intervention, both scientific forestry in particular and, more generally, the administrative policies followed by different governments. In keeping with the overall emphasis of this work, both social participation in Chipko and its reflection in popular consciousness are sought to be depicted in terms of the changing relationship between the state and the peasantry.

**Chipko: Fragmentation of Village Community**

Chipko movement in Uttarkhand has taken a special significance and form with respect to the social structure of the area. Here, one must emphasize the social changes that have created a 'money-order' economy and a lopsided demographic profile in the villages of Uttarakhand. Thus, Chipko can be read as a response to the fragmentation of the village community in recent decades. Again, women have always played an important role in economic life, and this structural constant may explain the widespread participation of women—marking an important departure from the pre-Independence period—in contemporary social movements.[1] At the same time, the participation of women in Chipko and its associated movements has been influenced by the impact of recent economic changes in intensifying their traditional dependence on the natural environment.

The enduring nature of Chipko and its assumption of an organizational form has raised major questions: the nature of leadership, the ideological clashes between different sub-cultures of the movement, and the redefinition of the relations between the sexes. These were absent from many of the earlier, largely 'unorganized', movements of social protest in Uttarakhand. While Chipko lies in a direct path of continuity with an earlier history of social protest and as an organized and sustained social movement, at the same time, it represents an expansion in the scale of popular mobilization and the development of popular consciousness. This extension has two distinct aspects. Second, notwithstanding its internal schisms, as an extension of popular consciousness Chipko attempts to combat the growing social and ecological disintegration of hill society. This attempt consists, on the one hand, of an expansion of the movement to embrace other social issues, and, on the other, of the presentation to the state and the general public with alternative strategies of resource use and social development. The nature of leadership as in every movement is of paramount importance.

## Chipko: Its Origins and Development

### The Background

Not surprisingly, the continuation by the government of independent India of forestry practices inimical to local needs generated a certain amount of discontent. In 1958 a committee was formed to 'investigate ... the grievances of the people' of Uttarakhand concerning forest management. It deplored the situation in the hill tracts where, even after the attainment of independence, 'not only great discontent against the Forest Department prevails at several places, but it is also looked upon with extreme suspicion and distrust.' While recognizing the need to locally develop the resources of the hills the committee considered as inevitable the continuance of restrictions viewed by the people as a 'forfeiture of their hereditary natural rights'. Its typically non-specific recommendations gave priority to the 'preservation, development and extension of the forests' and to meeting the 'genuine needs of the local people'. It also asked for a declaration from the government that it would respect village rights over forests and that, along with forest preservation, 'it would provide every opportunity for the economic progress of the people'.[2] In the absence of concrete programmes, local legislators warned, there was every chance of a popular upsurge in the tradition of movements against the British and the Tehri durbar.[3]

In fact, Communist Party of India activists in the Yamuna valley had organized several satyagrahas against the high-handedness of different state agencies.[4] Great resentment continued to be expressed against the practice of large timber coupes being sold to 'outside' contractors. Villagers also refused to help the forest staff extinguish fires, as they were bound to do under the forest act.[5] The undercurrent of protest against forest management was combined with opposition to other facets of commercialization and the continuing underdevelopment of the hills. Led by Sarvodaya workers, thousands of villagers, mostly women, opposed the widespread distillation and sale of liquor. Processions and the picketing of liquor stalls were organized in different districts of Garhwal. In Tehri the prominent Sarvodaya leader Sunderlal Bahuguna and several women were arrested for defying prohibitory orders.[6]

A partial prohibition was imposed on the occasion of the centenary of Gandhi's birth; when this was successfully challenged by liquor contractors in the high court, sale was recommenced. This led to a fresh wave of *dharnas,* with Bahuguna embarking on an indefinite hunger strike. Thirty-one volunteers were arrested in Tehri for picketing liquor shops.[7] Meanwhile the demand for a separate hill state gathered momentum. Students went on strike demanding the establishment of universities in the hills. *Bandhs* were successfully organized in several towns. In a metaphor reminiscent of the forest movement of 1921, the government was termed 'Bania', a government which yielded only under coercion. Consciously seeking to establish a continuity with earlier protest movements, the Uttarakhand Rajya Sammelan had organized a meeting at Bageshwar on the sacred occasion of the Uttaraini mela. Here, speakers stressed the looting of natural resources from the hills, the growing unemployment, and the cultural similarities between Garhwal and Kumaun. The government responded by setting up universities and autonomous development corporations in both Garhwal and Kumaun divisions.[8] These measures were long being considered by the government. The protest gave these measure a big peish.

## The 1970 Flood

In 1970, Alaknanda valley was hit by floods. No living person in the region could recall any sad devastation and flood. In the Alaknanda valley, water inundated 100 square kilometres of land, washed away 6 metal bridges and 10 kilometres of motor roads, 24 buses and several dozen other vehicles; 366 houses collapsed and 500 acres of standing paddy crops were destroyed. The loss of human and bovine life was considerable. The Gauna lake, formed by the Alaknanda flood of 1894, was filled with debris. Apart from the tributaries of the Alaknanda, the Kali and Bhagirathi rivers also spilled their banks. Houses in Rishikesh, where the Ganga enters the plains, were also destroyed. Due to the blockage of the Ganga canal, 95 lakh acres of land in eastern UP went unirrigated.[9] The flood marks a turning-point in the ecological history of the region. Villagers, who bore the brunt of the damage, were beginning to perceive the hitherto tenuous links between deforestation, landslides and floods. It was observed that some of the villages most affected by landslides lay directly below forests where felling operations had taken place.[10]

Preceding official initiative, 'folk sense was the only body that surveyed the grim scene and drew conclusions. The causal relationship between increasing erosivity and floods on the one hand, and mass scale felling of trees on the other, was recognized by [it].'[11] The villagers' cause was taken up by the Dashauli Gram Swarajya Sangh (DGSS), a co-operative organization based in Chamoli district. Organized by several local youths in the mid-1960s, the DGSS had as its major objective the generation of local employment. Despite serious obstacles it operated a small resin and turpentine unit, manufactured agricultural implements, and organized the collection and sale of medicinal herbs.

On 22 October 1971 the DGSS organized a major demonstration in Gopeshwar, the district town of Chamoli. The demonstrators called for an end to liquor sale and to untouchability, and for giving priority to the local use of forests. Arguing that they had nurtured the forest growth themselves, villagers demanded that local units be given preference in the allotment of raw material. Led by Sarvodaya workers, such as Gandhi's English disciple Sarla Devi (who had set up an ashram in Almora district in the 1940s) and the leading local activist Ghandi Prasad Bhatt, the procession was of a size never before seen in Chamoli district.[12] In the following year major public meetings were held at Gopeshwar and Uttarkashi. A charter of demand was submitted. The demands were very simple. They wanted to set up small scale industries which was beings permitted by the government. At the same time they demanded contractor-system be replaced and labour co-operatives the given the felling contracts. Their main thrust was on employment.[13]

## Mandal[14]

In early 1973 the DGSS had asked for an allotment of ash trees in order to make agricultural implements. The forest department refused to accommodate this request. Instead, they asked the DGSS to use chir trees, totally unsuitable for the purpose. However, the Symonds Co. was allotted ash trees in the forest of Mandal, barely several miles from Gopeshwar. This blatant injustice inspired the DGSS to organize several meetings in Mandal and Gopeshwar to discuss possible action. Two alternatives presented themselves: (i) to lie down in front of the timber trucks; (ii) to burn resin and timber depots as was done in the Quit India movement. When Sarvodaya workers found both methods unsatisfactory, Chandi Prasad Bhatt suddenly thought of embracing the trees. Thus 'Chipko' (to hug) was born. Led by their headman, Alam Singh Bist, the villagers of Mandal resolved to hug the trees even if axes split open their stomachs. Young men cemented the oath with signatures of blood.

The birth of Chipko preceded the actual advent of Symonds Co. in Mandal. Hearing of the villagers' plan, the district magistrate wired the

UP government, who responded by calling Bhatt for negotiations to Lucknow. A compromise was suggested, whereby the government would allot the DGSS ash trees on condition that the sporting goods firm could take away its quota. Despite, raising its offer from one ash tree to five, the authorities could not break down the stiff resistance. The labour and agents of the company could not fell a single tree they left Mandal.

In June Symonds was allotted trees near the village of Phata in the Mandakini valley, en route to the shrine of Kedarnath.[15] When the news reached the DGSS, they were able to contact (the late) Kedar Singh Rawat, a prominent social worker of the area. Despite heavy rainfall a huge demonstration was organized on 24 June. Dismayed, the company's agents returned to Gopeshwar, where they complained at the forest office that even after depositing the guarantee money they were unable to fell the trees marked for them.

**Reni[16]**

The government did not heed the protests. It went ahead with the yearly auction of forests in November. One of the plots scheduled to be assigned was the Reni forest, situated near Joshimath, in the Alaknanda valley—a locality affected by landslides in the recent past. Reni itself was a village inhabited by members of the Bhotiya community who had abandoned nomadic pastoralism in favour of settled agriculture. Hearing of the auction, DGSS workers contacted the block *pramukh* of Joshimath, Govind Singh Rawat of the Communist Party of India. While trekking through the area they noticed that over 2000 trees had already been marked for felling. Ironically enough, the labour for marking had been provided by the villagers themselves.

Meetings were organized at which the tragic 1970 flood was remembered, and the possible consequences of felling the marked trees highlighted. Bhatt suggested to the villagers that they adopt the Chipko technique. The village women huddled some distance from the meeting were clearly amused at the thought of 'Chipko'. The fellings were scheduled for the last week of March 1974. On the 25th a massive demonstration was organized in Joshimath where college students from Gopeshwar threatened to embark on a Chipko Andolan unless the fellings were called off. Fearing opposition to the felling operations, the forest department resorted to subterfuge. The conservator of forests, who was based at Pauri, hoping that Chandi Prasad Bhatt could be persuaded to stay on in Gopeshwar, arranged to visit the DGSS premises on the 26th. Bhatt stayed on to receive him.

The same day the men of Reni and neighbouring villages were called to Chamoli to receive the compensation long overdue for lands appropriated by the Indian army after the Chinese invasion of 1962. With both DGSS workers and local men out of the way, the lumbermen proceeded to the forest on the 26th. The same evening Govind Singh Rawat phoned Bhatt with news of the department's deceit. Now it was believed to be too late. A plan to *gherao* the conservator was foiled when the official fled from Gopeshwar.

At Reni events had taken a dramatic turn. The contractors' men who were travelling to Reni from Joshimath stopped the bus shortly before Reni. Skirting the village, they made for the forest. A small girl who spied the workers with their implements rushed to Gaura Devi, the head of the village Mahila Mandal (Women's Club). Gaura Devi quickly mobilized the other housewives and went to the forest. Pleading with the labourers not to start felling operations, the women initially met with abuse and threats. When the women refused to budge, the men were eventually forced to retire.

**The Government Steps in Reni**

Reni's importance in the saga of the Chipko Andolan is twofold. It was the first occasion on which women participated in any major way, this participation, moreover, coming in the absence of their own menfolk and DGSS activists. As Gaura Devi recounted, it was not a question of planned organization of the women for the movement, rather it happened spontaneously. Our men were out of the village so we had to come forward and protect the trees. We have no quarrel with anybody but only we wanted to make the people understand that our existence is tied with the forests.[17]

Until then, Reni was an archetypal hill village isolated from the market and dependent on the forests only as an input for subsistence agriculture. From now on Chipko was to come into its own as a peasant movement in defence of traditional forest rights, continuing a century-long tradition of resistance to state encroachment. No longer could the government treat Chipko merely as the reaction of motivated local industry deprived of raw material. The Chief Minister of UP, H.N. Bahuguna, who himself hailed from Garhwal, had earlier told the Chipko leaders that he could not meet their demands as he was 'the chief minister of the entire state, not only of the hill districts'.[38] After the Reni incident he conferred with them and agreed to set up a committee to investigate the incident. Headed by a botanist, Virendra Kumar, the members of the committee included Bhatt and secretaries of several government departments. Later, its terms of reference were extended to include the entire upper catchment of the Alaknanda. The committee concluded that one important reason for the 1970 flood was the widespread deforestation in the Alaknanda catchment. Accordingly, commercial fellings were banned for a period of ten years in the upper catchment of the river and its tributaries.[19] Tree plantation was also taken up at a trisk pace.

**Resin Tapping**

Existing practices of resin tapping were also required to be looked into a second government committee headed by KM Tiwari was formed.[20] The Tewari Committee found that tapping rules were rarely followed. In the several forest divisions toured by it, irregularities concerning the width, depth and length of cuts were observed to be widespread. Such maltreatment had made the trees particularly vulnerable to lightning.[21] The UP government also promised to review the lease granted to Star Paper Mills. Proposals to set up units in the hills were examined by another committee, headed by a paper technologist from the FRI, and included Bhatt. The latter proposed that a number of small units, spread over the entire hill region, should be set up. Although eight sites were identified for the purpose, the scheme was found economically unviable. However, the committee found two sites suitable for the setting up of units of a capacity of 25 tonnes per day, and where infrastructural and raw material facilities were available. Although detailed project reports were prepared, these recommendations were never implemented by the government.[22]

One proposal that did materialize in response to Chipko was the constitution of a forest corporation or Van Nigam, to takeover all forms of forest exploitation. As originally envisaged, the auction system would be abolished and a large proportion of forest lots were to be allotted to FLC's by the corporation. Over time, however, the corporation reverted to the old system. Subcontractor and their agents made their way into the system with their own labour.[23]

**Chipko Spreads to Tehri**

Following Reni, forest auctions were opposed in different parts of Garhwal. In Dehradun the auction of the Chakrata division forests had to be called off following protests led by local students. At Uttarkashi's Hanuman Mandir, Sunderlal Bahuguna underwent a two-week fast in October 1974, calling for a change in the existing forest policy.[24] That summer youths from both Kumaun and Garhwal had embarked on a 700 kilometre trek from Askot village—the eastern extremity of Kumaun—to Arakot on the borders of Himachal Pradesh. The marchers traversed the breadth of Uttarakhand in forty-four days. Bahuguna accompanied them over some distance.[25]

The movement then turned its attention to the damage done to the Chir trees and the lack of co-operation between the newly constituted Van Nigam and labour co-operatives. This became central to the next major form the movement was to take. On the occasion of Van Diwas (30 May, the anniversary of the Tiladi firing), Chipko activists in Tehri district informed the forest department that the resin-scarred chir trees would be bandaged. When the department did not respond to the call to save the trees, a direct action programme was commenced on another historic day, the anniversary of Sridev Suman's death (25 July). Villagers of Khujni patti started pulling out the iron leaves inserted to extract resin. In Advani forest, close to the Hemval river, the Sarvodaya worker Dhum Singh Negi went on a fast which was called off when villagers assured him that they would save the marked trees. A reading of the Bhagavad Gita was also organized.[26] Signifying their close relationship with trees, women tied 'raakhees' around the wounded spots.

Bhagirathi valley saw another flood in 1978. The immediate cause was a blockage in the Kanodia Gad, a tributary of the Bhagirathi. The financial loss due to the flood was estimated at Rs. 25 crore.[27] Despite the flood, forest auctions were held at Nainital under heavy police protection. Opposition to forest felling also took place in the Chamyala forest, near Bahuguna's ashram at Silyara.[28] Elsewhere, people's committees were formed which successfully opposed felling at Loital and Amarsar. In Badyargarh, over 2300 trees had been marked for felling by the forest corporation Chipko moved to Badyagarh.[29]

**Chipko in Kumaun**

Its a result of introduction of Chipko movement at Nainadevi fair at in Nainital in 1974 forest auctions were opposed at several places.[30] However, it gathered momentum following the major landslides at Tawaghat, a village situated close to the India-Nepal border, in 1977. In the landslide 45 men and 75 heads of cattle perished. Young activists of the Uttarakhand Sangharsh Vahini (USV) opposed the auctions that were scheduled despite the Tawaghat disaster. In October 1977 large demonstrations were organized in Nainital. When several leaders of the USV were arrested, a crowd of a thousand people surrounded the Rink Hall, where the auctions were being held. The auctions were rescheduled for November. This time too Section 144 had to be enforced. In the presence of the police and the provincial armed constabulary, protesters sang the songs of the legendary folk poet, Gaurda. Again, the leaders were arrested.

In the following months different Chipko agitations were organized by the USV. On 15 December Chipko activities were commenced in the Hat forest of Almora, where 5,000 chir trees had been marked for felling. The USV demands included the revision of the forest settlement and a ban on the export of raw material from the hills.[32] In Chanchridhar forest, situated in the sensitive catchment area of the Gagas river, protesters marched into the block where the forest corporation planned to fell 6,000 trees. They camped in the forest for over a week till the foresters had to admit defeat. Later, fellings scheduled by the corporation were successfully stalled at Janoti Palri and at Dhyari on the Almora-Pithoragarh road.[33] The movement was becoming successful.

**Chipko Returns to Chamoli**

In Chamoli commercial fellings continued to threaten the ecological stability of different habitations. In the Bhyunder valley, adjoining the famous Valley of Flowers, oak trees were marked to meet the fuelwood needs of Badrinath town. In Badrinath, an important pilgrim centre, the temple alone consumed over 1,000 quintals of wood between May and November every year, during the pilgrim season. The total fuelwood consumption of the town was estimated at 2500 quintals. When trees were marked near Pulna village, the village panchayat wrote to the divisional forest officer and the district magistrate. Officials replied that 250 villagers could not get precedence over 1.5 lakh pilgrims. On the second day of felling operations (5 January 1978) the women of Pulna, despite 40 centimetres of snow, surrounded the labourers, took away their implements, and gave them a receipt for the tools. In this manner 621 trees were saved.[34] It was a resurgence of the movement.

**Potato Farm**

Another significant agitation occurred in the Pindar valley, near the village of Dungri-Paintoli. Here the men of the village wanted to sell their oak forest to the horticulture department, which intended to establish a potato farm on the land. If the forest, the only good one for miles around, had been cut the women would have had to walk a long distance every day to collect fuel and fodder. When the women voiced their opposition, it went unheeded. At this juncture Chipko activists intersvened and, helped by the district administration, ensured that the forest area remaining (some forest had already been cleared) was saved.[35] Angered at the women's success, the village headman threatened Bhatt and his colleague Ramesh Pahari with dire consequences if they came back to the area.[36]

Lured by promises of better communications and other 'modern' facilities, the men hoped to make some quick money. The women, for their part, 'raised some fundamental questions challenging the system. In their opinion, agriculture and animal rearing was entirely dependent upon them, both closely related to the forest, and yet they were not consulted with regard to any [decisions] taken relating to forestry.'[37] Therefore, this was an open conflict between the men and women of Dungri-Paintoli.

The next Chipko agitation took place at Parsari, near the army encampment of Joshimath. Here, kharsu and *moru* (high-level oak) trees were being felled to meet the fuel requirements of Joshimath town. The appointed forest provided fuel and fodder to four villages nearby which had appointed a watchman to guard it. In fact, the Kumar Committee had recommended that there be no felling in this area. A people's committee headed by Narendra Singh and Narayan Singh organized the village opposition. Not a single tree could be felled.[38]

**The Badyargarh Andolan**

Thus far, I have presented a broad overview of the major Chipko agitations that have occurred since the movement's inception. Let us now look more closely at one particular Chipko mobilization in order to properly appreciate its social and cultural idiom. The Chipko agitation that occurred in the Badyargarh patti of Tehri Garhwal district in the winter of 1978-79 forms the focus of the section, and my analysis of it is based largely on fieldwork conducted in early 1983. I present here an internal analysis of the movement, i.e., its patterns of mobilization and type of organization, the participation of different social groups, its ideology and methods, and the relationship between the leadership and the rank and file. I also highlight the changing perceptions of the state which has replaced the Tehri durbar as the unit of legitimate authority. The fundamental characteristics of Chipko, as the movement is conceived by its participants, may thereby become clearer.

The patti of Badyargarh is situated between the Bhagirathi and Alaknanda rivers, about 130 kilometres north-east of Rishikesh. The social structure, in conformity with the rest of Uttarakhand, is built around relatively homogeneous and cohesive village communities. For the past few decades, however, grain production has been inadequate to sustain the population. In this money-order economy, women labour hard to perform household and agricultural tasks.

**Erosion of Community Spirit**

Badyargarh is a relatively prosperous patti, containing a large number of retired and serving army personnel. The growing opportunities offered to individuals by commercialization, education, government employment, etc. have definitely contributed to the erosion of the community co-operative spirit. The possibility of individual social mobility that the outside world offers is reflected in the village by the return of successful individuals to build cement structures. Although the community spirit is still present, as shown by Chipko, there is, simultaneously, a slowly growing differentiation within the village due to the impact of commercialization. There is, too, a sense of disruption of the traditional social fabric that the opening out of Garhwal has brought, as well as anger at the comparative underdevelopment of the hills.

With the building of a motor road into the area 1965, commercial forestry started in the region. In the following years the extraction of resin and turpentine was commenced, alongside the felling of chir trees. In 1979, the Van Nigam gave out a big contract for the felling of chir pine in the area. The felling, which went on for several months, was, according to villagers, very destructive, with young regeneration being removed in addition to the logged trees. Several dozen trucks came and went daily, taking away all the wood, including the branches of trees. As people later reminisced, the contractor replied to early signs of protest by remarking that, he would not leave any part of the tree behind *('Hum ped ka koi hissa nahin choddenge')*.

**The Andolan**

Following upon this activity and just prior to the proposed logging in the Malgaddi forest, Sarvodaya workers, trusted associates of the Chipko leader Sunderlal Bahuguna, came to Badyargarh to enquire into the people's grievances. These leaders, Dhum Singh Negi, Kunwar Prasun, Pratap Shikhar and Vijay Jardari, among others, went from village to village informing people of the proposed felling and its harmful ecological consequences. At the same time Bahuguna's wife, Vimla, and other ladies mobilized the village women on the issue.

The andolan started on 25 December 1978 but acquired momentum only after Bahuguna went on a hunger fast from 9 January 1979. Conducted in a disused shepherd's hut in the forest, and in the middle of winter, the fast was a rallying point for people of the surrounding villages. Thus, over three thousand men, women and children participated, 'one for every chir tree in the forest'. An attempt at cutting by night was foiled by villagers taking night duty by turns. Classic non-cooperation tactics were adopted, there being no question of any violence used *('himsa ka koi saval nahin tha')*. Bahuguna was carried away by the police on the night of 22 January and interned in Tehri jail, where he continued his fast. Meanwhile, a reading of the Bhagavad Gita was started on the 26th. Even though Bahuguna had been forcebly removed. The villages continued their resistance. The contractor and forest officials had to admit defeat and abandon felling.

**Participation:** A feature of the andolan was the active participation of all social groups. This was explained by the evident fact that all were equally affected by deforestation. The Bajgis, a caste of musicians, were solicited to mobilize villagers through their *dholaks* (drums). Women played a prominent part, government servants and defence personnel, gave a big support. Being government servants however. They could not come out openly.

When police camped in Dhadi Ghandiyal High School, children went on strike in protest at the invasion of a 'temple of knowledge' (Vidya Mandir). This was their contribution to the fight for justice. While the strike itself lasted four days, all through the andolan students skipped school with the connivance of the teachers. As the principal recounted, he was placed in an awkward position, with the police harassing him on the one hand and, on the other, villagers imploring him to let his wards come to the forest. The schoolteacher, highly respected in Garhwal, symbolized in his person the conflict between government and people. As a figure of authority the state expected him to control the people, while the people wanted sanction for their acts by that very same authority.

**The Moral Content of Chipko:** The labour that had brought to fell trees was from Himachal. The contractor fed the scene. The labour was left unattended. They did not have anything to eat. The locals fed them from village ration shops and petitioned officials to alleviate their plight. Only with the arrival of the labour commissioner could the grievances be redressed and the labour sent home to Himachal.

The second incident relates to the wood felled prior to Chipko, which was not allowed to be carried away for conversion to sleepers. The Baḍyargarh Van Suraksha Samiti (BVSS) resolved to release the wood only after the local people had fulfilled their needs. This entailed that the first claim would be exercised by those individuals and villagers who had not been granted timber rights, following which the requirements of the other inhabitants of Badyargarh and its neighbouring pattis would be met on payment of nominal rates. It was proposed that the income so generated would be used to regenerate the deforested areas of Badyargarh. The BVSS stuck to their stand.[39]

### Chipko and Popular Consciousness

There are several important characteristics of Chipko as the movement relates to popular perceptions.

**The Link between Humans:** Forests and everyone I interviewed was aware of the importance of forest cover in regulating soil and water regimes. Chipko has contributed to a heightened awareness—the interesting question is the extent to which this ecological consciousness predates Chipko. Thus, in Badyar village no grass cutting has traditionally been allowed on the steep hill overlooking the settlement. The cliff has a thick crop of grass and shrubs, in the absence of which boulders would come tumbling down the hill during the monsoon—hence the ban. As I argued the link between humans and forests that existed before the inception of commercial forestry has been eroded by the loss of community control. Chipko movement aims at halting the growing alienation of humans from nature, this alienation if not checked in time in faught with potentially damaging consequences.

**Chipko and Community Solidarity:** The manifold benefits of forest cover to the hill economy (and ecology) and consciousness of ecosystem can explain Chipko's success in mobilizing all sections of hill society. In response to criticism that the andolan depended largely on Bahuguna's appeal, the BVSS pointed out that if the movement did not enjoy popular support it would have terminated with Sunderlal's arrest and removal. As villagers see it, efforts to put out forest fires, which they are obliged to do under the settlement, are made in the belief that their property was being destroyed. Thus, when the government started indiscriminate felling *(andhadhun katai)* it was keenly resented.

***Attitude towards officials:*** The lack of fulfillment of the basic needs of education, health and employment found the accumulated grievances being crystallized in Chipko. One BVSS activist put it thus:

> Humme thoda sa anaaz mila, jab usse bhi
> nahin paka sake, tho andolan karna pada.

The implacable hostility towards state officials, particularly those belonging to the forest department, can be read as a symbol of such disillusionment. Chipko participants expressed delight in recalling the impotence of high officials *(ucchadhikari)* in the face of the andolan. Senior officials of the civil and forest administration, as well as the police, arrived but were powerless to resume felling operations ('*Ucchadhikari pahunch gaye, lekin kuch nahi kar paye*').

**Women and Chipko:** It has been stressed that hill women have agricultural tasks. This situation is further aggravated, in Badyargarh and elsewhere, by the absence of adult males. Some analysts see a direct causal link here. According to Bahuguna himself,

> Due to washing away of fertile soil, the menfolk were compelled to leave their families and wander in search of employment, thus making the women bear all the responsibilities, collecting fodder, firewood and carrying water, which form the main chores besides farming.[41]

The post office economy has its impact. Make members are away. The basic needs have to be taken care of by women. The important economic role of women is culturally specific to the hill family and not merely a result of changed ecological or economic conditions. Can one then relate the subordinate position of women in Uttarakhand to the enthusiastic support given by them to the Chipko Andolan?

### The Simmering Conflict

This is a topic of general discussion among makes in the till area. There is a conflict simmering under the surface, which generally comes out in group discussions. One retired army man was strongly of the opinion that women's participation in Chipko was a consequence of their inferior position in hill society. Observing the men gathered around the shop, he asked rhetorically, 'We men are sitting drinking tea, but can we see any woman here? Why not?' A look at the far hillside, where women were gathering firewood, provided the answer: 'They are not here for they have work to do.' This feminist stand brought forth jeers from fellow villagers, who later advised me not to take him seriously.[42] Nevertheless, the local women's leader, Sulochana Devi, was emphatic that the success of Chipko depended on women. The movement, she argued, was only the first step; women needed to be educated and dowry banned in order that others did not fritter away women's wealth *('ladkiyon ka dhan na khoya jaye')*. That also shows resentment against make members of the society.

**Chipko in a History of Protest**

Elsewhere integration of the princely states with India was on the basis of a general policy put in place by Sardar Patel. In the case of Tehri state, it occurred because of the wide ranging peasant movement, which started in Badyagarh. Protesting against extortion of money by the king's officials, villagers gathered at a religious fair at Dhadi Ghandiyal, marched towards the capital, Tehri, capturing outposts on the way and symbolically replacing corrupt patwaris by their own men. The 1948 dhandak remains vividly in the collective memory of the peasants of Badyargarh and their heroism then was invoked by the Chipko leaders in 1979. Apart from the participation of many in both, the movement itself has strong similarities—such as the identification of officials as the main exploiters, the belief that justice was on their side, and the forms of protest itself. In both instances the act of protest was seen as having a moral-religious sanction. While in 1948 the peasantry was mobilized on the occasion of a religious fair held once in thirteen years, an important event in Chipko was the reading of the Gita. Camped in the forests, Chipko volunteers commenced the reading of the epic and the rendition of folk songs. The conservator of forests who opposed the ceremony was firmly told that all the Vedas were written in the forest. When the Patwari threatened one of the priests with arrest, the priest replied: 'Arrest me under any section of law, but what are the rules for the Nigam people?'

**Bahuguna and the Idiom of Protest:** The idiom of Chipko, then, can be understood in terms of the 'moral economy' of the Garhwal peasant, who could readily comprehend the tactics of the charismatic leader of the Badyargarh Andolan, Sunderlal Bahuguna. Bahuguna concentrates his fire on the officials of the forest department who, in league with contractors, 'do not leave a splinter of wood in the forests'.[43] The call to forest officers to change their ways and serve local communities evokes a positive reaction from a people exposed to extortion by officials during earlier regimes. Nowhere did he blame the government in power at the centre or at Lucknow.

Bahuguna's method of functioning is far removed from that of self-seeking politicians. A non-political person, he was able to strike a chord in the hearts of those disenchanted with the hypocrisy of politicians and the electoral process. Gandhian methods of non-violence and Bahuguna's personal asceticism were appreciatively responded to by the predominantly Hindu peasantry. The capacity for physical suffering (vide the hunger fast in the bitter cold) and spirit of sacrifice *(tyaga)* in an age of selfishness were constantly marvelled at by villagers who read into these acts the renunciation of worldly ambition as exhorted by Hindu scriptures. Sunderlal's charisma is undoubted and his deeds are still an object of wonder in Badyargarh. His success is clearly related to the distinctive character of social protest in Tehri Garhwal. The attacks on forest officials can be understood in the context of dhandaks aimed at the raja's minions. Sunderlal's remarkable physical endurance and sage-like appearance make him a natural leader whose followers look to him to restore a pristine state of harmony and just government.

In fact, Bahuguna records that his life was changed by a chance encounter with Sridev Suman when he was a schoolboy. He 'proudly refers to Sridev Suman as his guru in all respects'—a theme he stresses repeatedly in his speeches.[44] Here one finds a striking parallel with other agrarian movements, where too the invocation of the spirit and memory of peasant martyrs is a primary 'means by which a sense of the past is revived, codified, and used'. References to predecessors like Suman a notable ascetic of his time reinforce Bahuguna's own credentials, to be the undisputed leader of the peasantry of these districts. The Tehri Garhwal case provides yet another illustration of what is a much more pervasive phenomenon so far as lower-class movements are concerned, for, as Eugene Genovese has pointed out,

> from the peasant revolts of medieval Europe, to revolutionary Puritanism, to the early working class organizations, to the great revolutionary movements of our own time, asceticism has provided a decisive ingredient in the mobilization of popular risings.[45]

**Local Cultural Idiom**

Even as Bahuguna's own lifestyle evokes a sympathetic response among peasants, his message is conveyed through a local cultural idiom, both by his own acts and those of his followers—for example the noted folk-singer Ghanshyam Sailani, who has played a central role in the Chipko movements of Tehri Garhwal. For its practitioners, asceticism is a potent vehicle of cultural communication.

What is distinctive about Sunderlal Bahuguna's asceticism is that it is accompanied by a call to the higher authority to side with the suffering peasants. During the course of the Badyargarh Andolan, Sunderlal assured the villagers that even if the forest department was opposed to the movement, the Prime Minister Morarji Desai, and Lokanayak Jayaprakash Narayan were on their side. While breaking the fast he commenced in Badyargajh in Dehradun jail Bahuguna said he did so only due to a request from 'JP', whom he called his general *(senapathi)*. He recalled Suman's historic eighty-four-day fast in Tehri jail and also mentioned the support of Home Minister H.M. Patel for his *dharmayuddha* (holy war) to save the Himalayan forests.[46] After the victory of the Congress Party in the elections of 1980, he invoked the support of the Prime Minister, Indira Gandhi, citing her concern at the situation in the Himalaya.[47] In this invocation leading politicians assume a role not dissimilar to that of the Tehri Maharaja in earlier days. While their functionaries are viewed as being in league with corrupt contractors, those in power are believed to sympathize with the oppressed. Chipko then becomes, in a strikingly similar fashion to the dhandak, the only possible means to obtain justice by bringing the wrongdoings of officials to the notice of heads of government. It boiled down to one issue. There was nothing wrong with politician. Whatever was the problem was with forest official. They were the crllains. The fight was against them and the contractors.

**Custom and Confrontation in Chipko**

In this study, too, I have highlighted several classic themes in the literature: the pattern of leadership, the forms of mobilization, the emergence of a codified ideology, and the relationship between leader and led.[48] I would, however, stress that this analysis of the formal characteristics of Chipko as a social movement must be supplemented by a study of its less formal features. Moving away from the public arena of Chipko and its popular stereotypes, through a case study of the Badyargarh movement I have tried to understand the transformations of meaning it has brought in the lives of its participants. An exploration of the less structured aspects of the movement reveals the existence of certain tenaciously held values, adhered to by village participants. The ideology that can be inferred from peasant actions is not entirely consistent with the formal ideology of Chipko as presented to the outside world. Finally, one of Chipko's central features is its historicity—i.e., its relationship with past movements, which raised similar questions concerning the relationship between the state and the peasantry. Therefore, as an organized movement of both national and international significance, Chipko can be analysed from the perspective of the sociology of social movements.

Locating Chipko culturally and historically provides a long overdue corrective to the popular conception of Chipko, which is that of a romantic reunion of humans, especially women, with nature. The dramatic act—often threatened but rarely brought into play—of hugging the tree to save it from the contractor's axe is the chief characteristic with which the movement is identified. Some writers have seen Chipko as having its origins in an incident believed to have occurred in Rajasthan in 1763, when members of the Bishnoi sect laid down their lives to protect trees being felled under orders from the Maharaja of Jodhpur.[49] Within the movement, Sunderlal Bahuguna's writings and lectures have done much to propagate this view of Chipko.[50] Other writers have stressed the role of women, as the sex crucially affected by deforestation. It has even been suggested that Chipko is a 'feminist' movement.[51] It will be clear from our study that the above stereotypes are seriously inadequate in interpreting the origins, idiom and trajectory of the movement.

**The Most Organised Protest**

The analogy with the incident involving the Bishnoi community obscures Chipko's origins, which are specific to the conditions of Uttarakhand. Chipko is only one, though undoubtedly the most organized, in a series of protest movements against commercial forestry dating from the earliest days of state intervention. Different Chipko agitations have invoked the spirit and memory of past upsurges against the curtailment of customary rights. This continuity is also strikingly manifest in the moral idiom in which protest has been expressed. Similar notions of morality and justice, have permeated movements against the durbar and the colonial state as well as Chipko. As this case study of the Badyargarh Andolan reveals, the peasantry was protesting against the denial of subsistence rights, which state policy has wrought. Essentially, the movement was in response to a perceived breach of the informal code between the ruler and the ruled known as the 'moral economy' of the peasant.

Clearly, this continuity is more marked in the case of Tehri Garhwal. Here, Bahuguna's personal acquaintance with later movements against the durbar as well as the distinctive flavour of the dhandak has informed a movement whose contemporary character cannot be adequately grasped without reference to its historical context. The identification of officials as oppressors, the belief that Indira Gandhi or other high-level politicians—the contemporary equivalent of sovereigns—could intervene and dispense justice, and Bahuguna's own asceticism, which is reminiscent of Suman, all testify to this continuity. In so far as Chipko constitutes a part of an overall tradition of protest, this continuity is present, albeit in an attenuated form, in other parts of Uttarakhand as well.

Thus, certain variations in the different subcultures of Chipko can be explained with reference to the different socio-political structures in which they operate. Bhatt's identification of macro forces, such as overall state policy, as the major cause can perhaps be related to the rather different political history of the Alaknanda valley, where, much earlier, the rupture between the state and the people had occurred as a result of British colonialism. Similarly, the adherence of the USV to a more radical posture may in part be a consequence of the earlier, and deeper, penetration of 'modern' political ideologies into Kumaun.

**Anti-alcohol Protest**

In Uttarkhand Anti-alcohol agitation of 1960's was the first popular movement in which the women took active part. It was led by Sarvodaya workers. However, despite the important role played by women, it would be simplistic to characterize Chipko as a feminist movement. In several instances, especially the early mobilizations at Mandal and at Phata, it was men who took the initiative in protecting forests. Women came to the fore in Reni, when in the contrived absence of menfolk they unexpectedly came forward to thwart forest felling. In other agitations, such as Badyargarh, men, women and children have all participated equally. Dungri-Paintoli is the only instance of an overt conflict between men and women over the management and control of forest resources. As such, even at the level of participation Chipko can hardly be said to constitute a women's movement. Undoubtedly, the hill women have traditionally borne an extraordinarily high share of family labour—and their participation in Chipko may be read as an outcome of the increasing difficulty with which these tasks have been accomplished in the deteriorating environment.

Interestingly, Chandi Prasad Bhatt does believe that women are capable of playing a more dynamic role than the men who, in the face of growing commercialization, are apt to lose sight of the long-term interests of the village economy.[52] On the other hand, it has been suggested that while they are the beasts of burden as viewed through the prism of an outside observer, hill women are in fact aware that they are the repository of local tradition. In the orbit of the household, women often take decisions which are rarely challenged by the men. In the act of embracing the trees, therefore, they are acting not merely as women but as bearers of continuity with the past in a community threatened with fragmentation.[53] The conflict between men and women has surfaced much more sharply in other social movements in the hills, most notably in the anti-alcohol movement organized by the USV in 1984.[54]

**Role of Sarvodaya Movement**

Another possible source of confusion lies in the important role the leaders owing an allegiance to the Sarvodaya movement have played an important role in this agitation. Gandhian institutions have been quick to hail Chipko as a modern example of satyagraha, calling it 'direct action in the best Gandhian spirit'.[55] In so far as the personal commitment and personal lifestyle of activists like Bhatt and Bahuguna exemplify the highest traditions of Gandhian constructive work, the characterization is not altogether incorrect. However, both Bhatt and Bahuguna, like the Praja Mandal activists of an earlier era, are anything but alienated from the historical and contemporary specificities of village life in Garhwal. Their involvement in Chipko is crucially informed, albeit in quite different ways, by a sharp historical sense and the experience gleaned from years of social activism in the hills. At the level of popular participation the Gandhian label is even less appropriate. It seems clear from the description of different Chipko agitations that the role played by external ideologies is a severely limited one. Villagers see Chipko as a fight for basic subsistence denied to them by the institutions and policies of the state. Although Chipko, like many Gandhian movements, has an important ethical dimension, its underlying notions of morality and justice are intrinsic to a history of protest against state restrictions on peasant access to forest produce. Its 'non-violent' method being an inspired and highly original response to forest felling rather than ideologically motivated. The methods of protest bad one to delineate Chipko as a Gandhian movement, which in foul, nothing but a superficial similarity.

**Commercial Forestry**

Commercial forestry in the Himalayas was in fact on a rampage, when Chipko movement started. Another ten years and the hills of Uttarkhand would have been denided of whatever trees were left. Gandhian association may have helped Chipko. It is noteworthy, that while the last decade has seen the emergence of several forest-based movements in peninsular India, none of these movements has had a comparable success in attracting public support or influencing the direction of government policies.[68] Indeed, they have on occasion been crushed with a brutality that has been notably absent in the state's attempt to deal with Chipko. Several factors account for the relative lack of success which these movements have enjoyed. First, the regions in which they have arisen have undergone rapid economic differentiation; wracked by internal contradictions, these struggles are unable (unlike in single-class hill society) to present a united front in opposition to forest policies. These movements have also tended to be more violent. Second, the cultural composition of forest dwellers in peninsular India is overwhelmingly non-Hindu. Chipko, on the other hand, located as it is in an area of enormous religious significance for the majority Hindu community, has struck a sympathetic chord in the heart of the Indian public.

**Veneer of Gandhianism**

Finally, there is the veneer of Gandhianism with which Chipko is cloaked, a matter of some embarrassment for a state claiming to be the rightful successor of the freedom struggle and upholding Gandhi as the Father of the Nation. In this manner, Chipko has, knowingly or unknowingly, successfully exploited the ambiguities in the dominant ideology of the Indian state. While this ideology is avowedly non-religious in its actions, the state goes to considerable lengths not to offend the Hindu sentiments of the majority of its subjects; and while its development policies are a strong repudiation of Gandhian economics, by paying daily obeisance to the Mahatma in its official rituals the state tries to symbolically appropriate the enormous prestige associated with his name. Faced with a popular movement, which originated in the watershed of the holy Ganga, used techniques of non-violence and was led by Gandhians, even the state is grouping in the dark to find the ways to deal with the situation.[57]

**Chipko as an Environmental Movement**

Chipko in fact picked up the threads of earlier peasant struggles and jungle bachas movements in Uttarkhand. I have repeatedly emphasized the fact that Chipko lies in a path of continuity with earlier peasant struggles in Uttarkhand; At the same time, as an organized and sustained social movement it promises to go beyond them. Here it is useful to distinguish between the 'private' face of Chipko, which is that of a quintessential peasant movement, and its 'public' profile as one of the most celebrated environmental movements in the world. Thus, while the last Chipko agitation in Uttarakhand occurred in 1980, the movement's activists have since been tirelessly propagating its message. Within the Himalaya, foot-marches and environmental camps are organized at regular intervals. There has also been a significant attempt to contribute to the environment debate in India and abroad.

**The Widening of Chipko**

In April 1981, Sunderlal Bahuguna went on an indefinite fast, urging a total ban on green felling in the Himalaya above an altitude of 1000 metres. In response, the government constituted an eight-member 'expert' committee to prepare a comprehensive report on Himalayan forest policy. Although the thrust of the committee's report was to exonerate the forest department and 'sustained-yield' forestry, the government agreed to allow a fifteen-year moratorium on commercial felling in the Uttarakhand Himalaya.[58] Well before the moratorium, however, there was little doubt that the Chipko movement had significantly slowed the march of commercial forestry. Thus, the output of major forest produce from the eight hill districts had declined, in the decade 1971-81. Exact figures of the decline are not available but at an estimate production came down by 402.[59]

Chipko movement put brakes on commercial forestry in the Himalayas. But this not all the state forestry is by no means the only threat to the ecological and social stability of the hills, for the past decades have witnessed a rapid expansion in the scale of commercial penetration in Uttarakhand. This is exemplified by the location of large dams, increasing mining operations and the spread of alcoholism. This intensification of resource exploitation has been matched almost step by step with a sustained opposition, in which Chipko has played a crucial role, in catalysing and broadening the social consciousness of the Himalayan peasantry. Thus, movements against big dams, unregulated mining and the sale of illicit liquor have been organized by all three wings of the Chipko movement. While a detailed description of these ongoing struggles is beyond the scope of this study, in such a widening of the movement's horizons changes in forest policy are conceived of as only one element in an alternative development strategy. Moreover, despite insinuations that Chipko has a localized frame of reference, the bid to rescue hill society from the ravages of capitalist penetration does not call for a narrow 'regionalism'. The agriculture of the Indo-Gangetic plain depends heavily on an assured supply of water from the rivers that originate in the Himalaya. Therefore the stabilization of ecosystem of Uttarkhand has very wide ramfication covering the plains from hardware to Ganga Sagar.

## References

1. The narrative of social movements in Chapters 4 and 5 mentions women only in passing. This fact should be taken only as indicative of the biases of the sources used. It is very likely that women played a key supporting role in the peasant movements in both Tehri Garhwal and Kumaun divisions, by keeping the household and farm economy going in periods of social conflict with the state, and perhaps even by aiding rebel movements. The sources are obviously biased towards reporting the activities of men, who, unlike women, came into repeated contact with the state and its officials.
2. *The Report of the Kumaun Forest Facts Finding Committee* (Lucknow, 1960), esp. p. 26ff.
3. Speech by Ramachandra Uniyal in Vidhan Sabha, reported in *YV*, 3 *April* 1960.
4. See *YV*, 20 November 1966.
5. See Gopal Singh, 'WP for the Nainital For. Div., Kumaun Circle, 1968-69 to 1977-79', mimeo (Nainital, 1969).
6. *YV*, issues of 2 April and 9 July 1967, 22 May 1970, etc.
7. *YV*, issues of 14, 21 and 28 November 1971.
8. See *YV*, issues of 13 June, 15 July, 29 July, 5, 12, 19, 26 and 3 October 1971, 24 and 31 December 1972, and 28 January 1973.
9. C.P. Bhatt, *Eco system of the Central Himalayas and Chipko Movement* (Gopeshwar, 1980), pp. 11-13.
10. S. Bahuguna, 'Uttarakhand mein Mrityu aur Tabahi ki Janam key Liye Jangalon ka Janaja Zimmedar', *YV*, 4 October 1970.
11. C.P. Bhatt, 'Eco-development: People's Movement', in T.V. Singh and J. Kaur (ed), *Studies in Ecodevelopment: Himalaya: Mountains and Men* (Lucknow, 1983), p. 475.
12. *YV*, 31 October 1971; *Uttarakhand Observer* (in Hindi), 25 October 1971, in Chipko file, Centre for Science and Environment, New Delhi (hereafter CSE file). The DGSS is now known as DGSM (M for Mandal). However, I shall continue to refer to it as DGSS.
13. See *YV*, 24 June 1973.
14. This account is based on A. Mishra and S. Tripathi, *Chipko Movement* (Delhi, 1978), pp. 7-12, supplemented by S. Bahuguna, 'Uttarakhand ka Chipko Andolan', *YV*, 24 June 1973; news report in *YV*, 6 May 1973; interview with Alam Singh Bist (ex-Pradhan, Mandal village), Gopeshwar, May 1982.

15. The villagers rendered the firm's name as 'Simon Co.' Interestingly, the firm has been referred to as 'Simon Co.' in all subsequent literature on the Chipko Andolan:
16. Based on Mishra and Tripathi, 'Chipko', pp. 16-18, 21-30; JC. Das and RS. Negi, 'The Chipko Movement', in KS. Singh (ed.), *Tribal Movements in India*, volume (Delhi, 1983), pp. 383-92; poster issued by Zila Chamoli Sangharsh Samiti, Joshimath, in CSE file; interviews with CP. Bhatt. Gopeshwar, May 1982, and Pithoragarh, October 1983.
17. Das and Negi, 'Chipko', p. 390.
18. Interview with CP. Bhatt, Gopeshwar, May 1981.
19. *YV*, issues of 17 November 1974 and 7 August 1977; Bhatt, *Eco system*, p. 18.
20. V. PS. Venna, 'WP for the Tehri For. Div., Garhwal Circle, 1973-74 to 1982-83', mimeo (Nainital, 1973), p. 377.
21. B. Dogra, *Forest and People* (Delhi, 1983), pp. 38-40; S. Bahuguna, 'Let the Himalayan Forests Live', *Science Today*, March 1982, pp. 41-46.
22. File no. 15 (25), cellulose and paper branch, FRI, Dehradun.
23. See *YV*, 5 September 1976.
24. *YV*, issues of 20 October and 10 November 1974.
25. Dogra, *Forest and People*, pp. 46-47; Shekhar Pathak, 'Chipko Andolan ki Nayi Lahr', *Dharmayug*, August 1977.
26. Dogra, pp. 52-53; *YV*, issues of 14 August and 18 December 1977.
27. *YV*, issues of 13 and 27 August 1978.
28. *YV*, 8 October 1978.
29. *YV*, 17 December 1978; Dogra, *Forest and People*, pp. 53-54.
30. *YV*, 29 September 1974.
31. *Dinman*, issues of 23-29 October and 18-24 December 1977 (CSE file); interview with GB. Pant of the USV, Nainital, May 1983.
32. *Janpath*, 15 December 1977, CSE file.
33. Dogra, *Forest and People*, pp. 60-61.
34. Rosalyan Wilson, 'Phulon ki Ghati mein Chipko Andolan', *Dainik Nayi Duniya*, 1 March 1978, CSE file.
35. Gopa Joshi, 'Men Propose, Women Dispose', *Indian Express*, 14 January 1982.
36. Interview with CP. Bhatt, Gopeshwar, May 1982.
37. CP. Bhatt and SS. Kunwar, 'Hill Women and Their Involvement in Forestry', in SS. Kunwar (ed.), *Hugging the Himalayas: The Chipko Experience* (Gopeshwar, 1982), p. 84.
38. CP. Bhatt, 'Joshimath mein "Chipko" Andolan', CSE file.

31. *Dinman*, issues of 23-29 October and 18-24 December 1977 (GSE file); interview with GB. Pant of the USV, Nainital, May 1983.
32. *Janpath*, 15 December 1977, CSE file.
33. Dogra, *Forest and People*, pp. 60-61.
34. Rosalyan Wilson, 'Phulon ki Ghati mein Chipko Andolan', *Dainik Nayi Duniya*, 1 March 1978, CSE file.
39. *Chipko Samachar*, datelined Badyargarh, 4 February 1979, in file of the Badyargarh Van Suraksha Samiti (BVSS).
40. Freely translated: 'when we could not obtain the wood to cook even the little grain we get, we had to resort to a movement.'
41. S. Bahuguna, *Chipko* (Silyara, 1980), p. 5. Emphasis added.
42. This is in keeping with the tendency, often reported by anthropologists, to minimize internal criticism in the presence of outsiders.
43. S. Bahuguna, 'Her Story: Women's Non-violent Power in the Chipko Movement', *Manushi*, no. 6 (1980), p. 31.
44. Interview in *The Telegraph*, 6 August 1983; S. Bahuguna, *Van Shramik* (Silyara, 1977).
45. See Anne Walthall, 'Japanese *Gimin:* Peasant Martyrs in Popular Memory', *American Historical Review*, Vol. 91, No. 5, December 1986; Eugene Genovese, *Roll, Jordan, Roll: The World the Slaves Made* (New York, 1973), p. 276.
46. S. Bahuguna, 'Badyargarh mein Itihas Ban Raha Hai', *YV*, 7 January and 21 January 1979. Cf. also *YV*, 4 February 1979.
47. Cf. S. Bahuguna, *Walking with the Chipko Message* (Silyara, 1983).
48. Cf. JR. Gusfield, 'Social Movements and Social Change: Perspectives of Linearity and Fluidity', in Louis Kriesberg (ed.), *Research in Social Movements, Conflict and Change*, volume 4 (Greenwich, Conn., 1981); J.C. Jenkins, 'Resource Mobilization Theory and the Study of Social Movements', *Annual Review of Sociology*, No. 9, 1983.
49. Richard St Barbe Baker, 'Chipko—Hug to the Tree People', in S. Bahuguna, *Chipko* (Silyara, 1981), pp. 1-4.
50. See, for example, S. Bahuguna, *Paryavaran aur Chipko Yatra* (Silyara, 1983).
51. Centre for Science and Environment, *The State of the Environment: A Citizen's Report* (Delhi, 1982), pp. 42-43.
52. Speech at a village meeting at Bakarkhatia, district Pithoragarh, October 1983.
53. This is the position (as expressed in personal communications)
54. See Shekhar Pathak, 'Intoxication as a Social Evil: The Anti-Alcohol Movement in Uttarakhand', *Economic and Political Weekly*, July 1985.
55. Foreword by Radhakrishna of the Gandhi Peace Foundation, in A. Mishra and S. Tripathi, *Chipko Movement*.

56. For an analysis of these movements see, *inter alia*, Peoples Union for Democratic Rights, *Undeclared Civil War* (Delhi, 1982); Nirmal Sengupta (ed.), *Jhar-khand: Fourth World Dynamics* (Delhi, 1982); G. De Silva, *et al*, 'Bhomi Sena: A Struggle for People's Power', *Development Dialogue*, no. 2, 1979.

57. A relevant analogy within Uttarakhand is with the massive anti-alcohol campaigns organized by the Uttarakhand Sangharsh Vahini (USV) in 1984. Divorced from the Gandhian movement, the USV leaders do not enjoy the kind of access both Bhatt and Bahuguna have to several high officials. This element, and the more militant nature of their struggle, clearly played a role in the state's punitive response and its reluctance to concede the long-term demands of the movement.

58. 'Report of the Experts Committee to Look into the Policy Regarding Fellings and Protection of Trees and to Bring Improvement in the Maintenance of Environmental Balance in the Himalayan Region of U.P.', mimeo, Uttar Pradesh Forest Department, Lucknow, March 1982. In Uttarakhand proper, Bahuguna's fast marks an end to the activist phase of Chipko and its shift towards both publicity and reconstruction work. While Chipko-style movements (for example, the Appiko movement in Karnataka) have emerged in other parts of India, one must not make the mistake of seeing these movements as merely derivative of Ghipko. Appiko, like Chipko, must be studied in its local historical and cultural contexts; assimilating it to Chipko, as some writers have done, does it as much violence as assimilating Chipko itself to abstract ideas of feminism, environmentalism, Gandhianism, etc.

59. N.C. Saxena, 'Social Forestry in the Hill Districts of Uttar Pradesh', mimeo, ICIMOD (Kathmandu, 1987), Table 22.

# 7

# Development Project vis-a-vis Ethno-Religious Sentiments: The Rathong Chu Imbroglio in Sikkim

## Introduction

The development projects, as the term implies, are meant for the upliftment of society, or loosely one can say, for the material benefit of the common man there are also the mechanisms when any government ought to put in place. The spectrum of such projects include very basic to highly sophisticated infrastructural development. Unfortunately, such projects often create undue confusion among the hoi polloi, who become sceptical about the motive of the project planners. Issues produced by confused minds very often prove to be devoid of merit in the long run, but before fizzling out, they may cause imbroglios involving huge wastage of spirit, time and money. The issues raised by the critics of development projects may be as cognizable as conservation of environment and ecology, or as intangible as religious sentiment, tradition and culture.

Very recently, the Rathong Chu hydro-electric project in Sikkim generated much controversy among a section of Sikkimese people on the grounds of ethno-religious sentiments. This, project and the related controversy may be cited as a blazing example of development projects in the crucibles of ethno-religious rage.

## The Unneccessary Unrest

A few years back, some of the leading dailies of the country briefly mentioned some unrest among a section of people in Sikkim on the issue of a power project. The news item was overshadowed by similar, but, far graver concerns over the Tehri and Narmada Projects in Uttaranchal and Madhya Pradesh Gujarat, other parts of the country which involved large-scale submergence of land, rehabilitation of the displaced multitude and above all, the ecological issues. In comparison to the above two projects, the Rathong Chu hydro-electric project was miniscule; neither did it involve submergence of land, nor mass rehabilitation.[1] But what was unique, in the case of Rathong Chu project, was the fact that, unlike Tehri or Narmada projects the unrest in Sikkim involved religion, ethnicity and culture. Here, the agitators were mostly lamas, i.e., the Buddhist monks, representing the 'Sangha' or the Monks' body of Sikkim. All these lamas and their followers primarily belong to the ethnic Bhutia-Lepcha population of Sikkim. This particular ethnic group vehemently opposed the hydroelectric project on the Rathong Chu and brought allegations that the project had been undertaken in total disregard of the religious importance of the area. It was also alleged that the project was detrimental to the people of Buddhist faith and violated constitutional provisions. The tribal organisations of Sikkim, too, felt that the project may usher in alien culture to their homeland, thus leading their traditional culture towards extinction. So, in association with the monk's body, different tribal organisations of Sikkim raised their voice for the protection of their culture. The ethnic Bhutia-Lepcha population was so alarmed and motivated that writ petitions against the project were filed in the court of law. For centuries, Sikkim had been a peaceful state. This was the first instance that an agtation took place there. Development was bound to take a back seat.

## Why RATHONG Chu Hydel Project?

By virtue of Sikkim's location in one of the most humd tracts of the Himalaya, it has a vertiable reserve of water resource. The Hydro-electric power potential of this tiny Himalayan state is commendable. It is estimated that the total power potential of Sikkim's water resource is 8000 MW, out of which barely 20 MW is presently being tapped.[2] Economists are of the opinion that Sikkim has immense opportunity to mobilize its water resources for domestic as well as commercial purposes. Otherwise handicapped by a highly undulating terrain, hydel power generation is the only favourable aspect of the mountain topography of the state. Power being regarded as one of the most vital inputs of economic development, there is no alternative but to explore the water resources, which are abundant, renewable and pollution-free. However, keeping in mind the cost-effectiveness, actual volume of demand, feasibility, and the vulnerable eco-system of the region. Cast-effectiveness, actual volume of demand and vulnerability of the ecosystem were some of the issues to be pondered over.

In a bid to mobilise the indigenous resources of Sikkim the Rathong Chu Hydro-Electric Project with an installed capacity of 30 MW was conceived as early as 1977, i.e., two years after Sikkim's merger with the Union of India. It may be mentioned here that, at that time the State was producing only 3 MW[3] of electricity indigenously from three mini hydro-electric projects, providing the barest minimum the State. Rural electrification was almost unheard of while the State had to buy power from the neighbouring State to meet the institutional demands. Under such circumstance the need of the hour was to construct a full-fledged State-owned power project, which would not only meet the home demand but also earn some revenue to boost up the stagnant economy of the State. In that two years period, the planners had made the right assessment that the state of full of promise.

**The Project**

The site of the Rathong Chu Hydro-Electric Project (RHEP) is located at Yuksam on the left bank of the river Rathong. The gorge through which the river flows is very deep and several hundred metres below the built-up area of the Yuksam block. The total area involved in the construction of the project is 125 acres, of which 62.5 acres are cultivated land, 25 acres are cardamom plantations and 37.5 acres are forested land. An area of approximately 4 hectares in the outskirts of Yuksam would be used for project colony, offices, workshops, stores and storeyards.[4]

According to the Detailed project Report (WAPCOS),[5] the RHEP would have simple features comprising trench type diversion weir, power channel, forebay, penstocks and surface power station. The project has an estimated potential of contributing 30 MW of power per year. It would have three generating units, each of 10 MW capacity. The cost of the project, estimated on 1989 price level amounts to Rs. 53.10 crore, corresponding to a cost of Rs. 17.690 per KW of installation. It was also worked out that at 9 per cent discount rate, the cost of generation would be 37.10 paise per kwh. Transmission of power was planned at 132 KV to Gangtok, the State capital, and Geyzing, the headquarters of the West District of Sikkim. The project would be the first independent power plant of the State Government of Sikkim.

**Demand for Power**

According to XIII Power survey of the state, the peak demand of Sikkim is expected to grow to 84 MW by 1999-2000.[6] Hence, it is imminent for the State to take up a medium scheme to meet the immediate requirement of 40 MW. The RHEP is well suited to meet the immediate demand. There are several advantages of the RHEP. Firstly, it would be a run-of-the-river project which requires no reservoir. In absence of reservoir, the problems of submergence and subsequent evacuation-rehabilitation of people do not arise. Secondly, the requirement of land is minimum and there would be hardly any displacement of inhabitants or deforestation. Thirdly, the capacity of 30 MW matches with the volume of demand. On the whole, the RHEP is viable as well as attractive from the point of view of financial and technological aspects.[7]

The project was planned with a mind to sell the surplus electricity to the eastern grid[8] of the country, so that the under-nourished economy of the State would be benefited. The Detailed Project Report of the RHEP was prepared by the Water and Power Consultancy Services in 1989. The report was further examined by the Central Electricity Authority (CEA) and the Central Water Commission (CWC). The project was given techno-economic clearance by the government. of India in February 1990 at an estimated expenditure of Rs. 71.19. crore Thereafter, the clearance of the Ministry of Forest, Government of India was obtained in November 1991 and that of the Minister of Environment in December 1992. Finally, the State Government accorded administrative approval for its implementation in January 1993.[9]

It would be worthwhile to mention here, that the construction work of the project does not, by any means, encroach upon the spots significant from the point of view of religion, archaeology or otherwise, neither is it disturbing the bio-diversity of the nearby Kanchendzonga National Park. The private owners of 87.5 acres of land are well-compensated while the forested land of the government is proposed to be adjusted by way of exchange of land as well as replantation after the completion of the construction work. Since the project was first of its kind in the State. The economic, ecological and cultural aspects had all been considered before all the clearances were given.

**The Imbroglio**

The Rathong Chu Hydro-Electric Project, which was conceived in 1977,[10] took about fifteen years to cross all hindrances before the final taken off. During the long gestation period, the state witnessed several changes in the Governance, but the project proposal survived. The construction work of the project could finally start in the year 1993. But no one was aware of the impending setback arising from an altogether different quarters. As soon as the construction work started, a section of the Sikkimese people, especially the ethnic Bhutia-Lepcha population, demanded immediate closure of the project. Several, tribal associations and the Monk's association of Sikkim appealed to the State administration to take steps in this regard. The selection of the project site offended the people of Buddhist faith, who saw it as an encroachment upon their religious rights. The protestations took shape of agitation, followed by hunger strike, heated demonstrations and filing of writ petitions in the High Court of Sikkim. In August 1994, three tribal associations, namely, the Denzong Lho-Man Choda or the Bhutia-Lepcha Association, the Tribal Women's Association and the Sikkim Tribal Scheme Welfare Association, submitted a writ petition to the High Court.[11]

The petition was written on the matter of "Preservation and safeguard of Ancient Monuments, Holy and sacred places having Historical Significance". According to the petitioners, "The said power project would grossly infringe upon the *religious sentiments** and belief of the State of Sikkim professing Buddhist faith in-as-much-as the said power project

---

* Underlined by the author of the paper.

would destroy and defile the places of worship, pilgrimage and threaten the existence of very ancient monuments having historical and religious significance to the people of the state of Sikkim which are situated within the periphery of the area where the said project is to come up. The action amounts to gross violation and interference with the religious rights of the Buddhists of the State of Sikkim".

It is evident from the above statement that the whole argument is based on religious sentiments of the tribal Lepcha-Bhutias. The monks of Sikkim proclaim that the area on which the project is to be erected, is the abode of the protective deities of Sikkim. Hence, the area should be protected and kept out of touch of the outsiders even at the cost of development.

**The Sentiments**

Religion is intricately woven with their day to day life that an average Sikkimese Buddhist cannot think of living unguarded by his deity. Their religious sentiments are very deep-rooted. His belief in spirits makes him extremely vulnerable in the hands of evil power, and he is unable to draw a line of demarcation between myth and truth. There are numerous legends about the mountains, rivers and lakes of Sikkim and almost every landmark of nature is associated with certain religious rituals. The Rathong Chu and the Yuksam valley is no exception. The annual 'Bum Chu' ritual of Tashiding in Sikkim is one such event which involves the Rathong Chu.

The Rathong Chu is one of the sacred rivers to the Buddhists of Sikkim. The river is enlisted in the 'Nay sol' or the holy scripture which serves as a guidebook of the sacred places of Sikkim. According to legends, the river contains some holy spots where the Great Buddhist teacher, Guru Padma Sambhava concealed sacred treasures. The river is believed to be blessed by the Guru. Hence, the water of this river is used to refill the sacred vase of Tashiding Monastery during the annual 'Bum Chu' ritual.[12] According to the holy scripts, it is the bounden duty of each and every Buddhist to protect the sanctity of the Rathong Chu. Moreover, there are numerous holy places along the bank of the Rathong Chu which must be protected as per the instruction given in the 'Nay sol'. Apart the Buddhist community all over Sikkim, nature lovers also rever the river.

The valley of Yuksam through which the Rathong Chu flows is revered by all Buddhist Sikkimese. The valley is like a bowl or a plateau guarded by mountains on all sides. This was the seat of the first Chogyal of Sikkim. 'The Norbu Gang', i.e., the coronation throne on which the first Chogyal Phuntsog Namgyal was consecrated, is treated as a sacred spot by the Sikkimese. The Buddhists of Sikkim who are devout followers of the Guru's teachings, and tradition-bound to the core, revere the Rathong Chu as well as the 'Norbu-Gang' as the abodes of devine spirits.

The 'Bum Chu' ritual is one of the holiest rituals for the Buddhists of Sikkim. Every year, the 'Bum Chu', i.e., "Water of the sacred vase" ritual takes place at Tashiding in West Sikkim on the 14th day of the first month of the Tibetan calendar. The sacred vase is believed to be made of sacred soil, sacred water and five precious jewels collected from holy places by the legendary Guru Padma Sambhava. The vase contains the holy water of the Rathong Chu and is kept under strict vigil in the sanctum sanctorum of the Tashiding monastery. Every year, on a full moon day, the vase is opened and three cups of water is taken out of it. The first cup of the water goes to the royal family of Sikkim, the second cup to the lamas and the third cup of water is distributed among the common devotees who gather at Tashiding in large number to receive the holy water on that auspicious day. It is believed by the Sikkimese Buddhists that a drop of the Bum Chu water relieves the taker from all the distress, evil spirits and miseries of life. They also believe that if the level of water contained in the vase decreases, that is an indication of a bad year for their country. An increase in the level of water, however, symbolises prosperity and glory. If the water turns turbid, the country may witness untoward incidents, such as war and death. Every year, after the ceremonial distribution of holy water, the sacred vase is refilled with the water of holy Rathong Chu.

The Sikkimese people, particularly the Bhutias believe that, if the Rathong Chu is harnessed for power generation the river will lose its sanctity, the water will be polluted and can no longer be used for the 'Bum Chu' ritual.

The seed of the imbroglio over the Rathong Hydro Electricity project lie in the sentiments of a group of people for whom religiousness is second nature. For them it seems in possible to forsake their age-old tradition and belief, even though such practices border irrationality. Even the educated minds are not free from such sentiments It is rather surprising to note that the persons who took leadership for the cause are educated in the liberated West and belong to the elites of Sikkim.

**Ethno-Religious Backdrop**

A look at the ethno-religious background of the people of Sikkim is necessary to understand the problem. The population figures of Sikkim, if seen in the light of rational and religious affiliation, may produce a deceptive picture.

The ethnic mosaic of Sikkim shows the numerical dominance of Hindu Nepalese but does not necessarily reflects the dominance of Hindu culture. Sikkim inherited a predominantly Buddhist lamaistic culture from the theocratic Bhutia aristocrats who ruled the State for more than three centuries. Despite the diminutive percentage of the Lepcha -Bhutia population, Sikkim's cultural as well as religious scenes are overwhelmingly dominated by Bhutia tradition and Mahayana Buddhism.

Buddhism in Sikkim has developed some peculiarities of its own. It has deviated to a great extent from the other forms of Buddhism prevalent in India and elsewhere but has retained the basic traits of Mahayana Buddhism. Here, Buddhism is highly intermingled with animism. The fusion of animism and Buddhism took place slowly but steadily over the centuries and at the moment, it seems an arduous task to demarcate the two. The Sikkimese Buddhists worship the deities as well as the local spirits who are believed to be inherent in the mountains, rivers, lakes and even rocks, caves and trees of Sikkim. For example, 'pang Lhabsol', or the worship of Mount Kanchendzonga is one of the most important religious rituals of the Sikkimese Buddhists. Similarly, they also perform some religious rites with the water of Rathong Chu, which they regard as a holy -river.

The influence of the 'Sangha', the monks body is very great on the Sikkimese society as was the case in India, before the advent of Brahma Samaj in Bengal in the early nineteenth century or in Punjab in early twenteth centure before Arya Samaj movement took hold. So much so that it is mandatory to reserve one seat for the 'Sangha' in the State legislative assembly. The obligation of an average Sikkimese to the 'Sangha' is manifested in every aspect of his life from birth to death. Even the non-Buddhists of Sikkim are often found to be guided by the lamaistic rituals in their hours of distress. An average Sikkimese, irrespective of his religious affiliation, pays homage to the Buddhist deities as well as high priests. If the ethnic scene of Sikkim is dominated by the Nepalis the religious scene is undoubtedly dominated by the Bhutias, who still envisage themselves as superiors, standing higher than the rest of the society. In the last two centuries there has been an increasing in Nepali-speaking population. However, the Sangha and Lamaism region supreme over the Sikkimese society.

## The Stir

The motion against the project was first surfaced in 1994 when the Denzong Lhaday Yangki Chokchen (Association of Buddhist Monks of Sikkim) officially raised objection to the project by submitting a memorandum to the then Chief Minister of Sikkim, S. Limbo, during one of his visit to West Sikkim. The memorandum demanded immediate removal of the project from the Yuksam area. In the same year, several tribal associations took part in the stir and filed law suit in the High Court of Sikkim.

In 1995, a group of Bhutia activists under the banner of 'Concerned Citizens of Sikkim (CCS)'[14], appeared in the scene with the demand of immediate scrapping of the project. According to this group, "the environmental and socio-cultural costs of the project would be too high a price to pay for its hypothetical economic benefits."[15] Following the example of Medha Patkar on the Narmada issue, one of the leading members of the CCS, S. Denzongpa, began hunger strike. However after 28 days, the hunger strike was called off following the state government's decision to constitute a high level committee to look into their grievances. The CCS issued a press statement stressing, "The project will have to be reviewed in light of it being environmentally unsound, economically disastrous and imposed on the public as a 'fait accompli'. All this was due to the conspiracy of corrupted officials and well-connected commission agents and contractors whose greed proved no match for the negative environmental, historical, religious and socio-economic consequences the project will cause."[16]

Meanwhile the monks of Sikkim submitted another Memorandum[17] to the Chief Minister stating,

"Hon'ble Sir, 18 June 1995

The Buddhists of Sikkim hereby wish to express their objections regarding the proposed Rathong Chu hydel project..... the project will destroy the hearth of the most sacred area of Sikkim which has enormous historical and religious significance for our people. This issue is not a question of mere 'sentiments' or 'emotion' hindering progress and development as some non-Buddhists might have insinuated... It is unethnical to sacrifice the basic foundation of a vulnerable minority such as its history, culture, religion and environment for the benefit of others. By now, the authorities should have learned from the rise of fundamentalism in the rest of the country, that they should be more careful and avoid attacking people from a religious angle".

* * *

"......we would like to submit that from a religious point of view the proposed project is undesirable as it is located at the heart of our place of worship, that it will defile the most sacred region of Sikkim and that the Rathong Chu hydel project goes against the religious sentiments of the people.

"Thus, we request your Hon'ble Sir to intervene in the implementation of the Rathong Chu hydel project by stopping all work at the site"........

Buddhist Monks of Sikkim

In another memorandum, dated 2 9.7.95, the Sangha of Sikkim wrote,

"We, the monks of Sikkim hereby demand that the Rathong Chu hydro-electric project located at Yuksum be stopped immediately. We oppose the project because it will have severe negative consequences for the most sacred area of Sikkim ...

"We oppose the Rathong Chu project because it will........ defile the whole area which is sacred to us. *It is offensive to see outside labourers* *washing meat next to Chorten, dumping excavated* mud around the Kattok Lake, and to witness that the human waste of *these labourers are dumped into the sacred Rathong Chu and will end up in the Bum Chu of Tashiding*"*.......

"The Nay sol text is to the Sikkimese Buddhists what the Ramayana is to the Hindus, the Koran to the Muslims and the Bible to the Christians. If the Rathong Chuhydro-electric project is not stopped, and abandoned, we the Lamas of Sikkim are ready to burn our Nay sol texts as its meaning and purpose will be lost.....

"This time we hope that our voice will be loud enough so that it may not be ignored".[18] In retaliation, the lamas of Sikkim took to the street. Their year long agitation culminated in thronging the High Court premises as well as the State Secretariat. However, on the whole, the mob was not violent, no casualty was reported either.

Subsequently, another writ petition was submitted to the High Court by the President and members of the CCS in August 1995.[19] This time, to strengthen the cause, the petitioners mooted the question of conservation of environment along with conservation of their heritage.

All points against the project were found to be exagerated. On enquiry by different high level committees, it was proved that, the construction of the Rathong Chu Hydro-Electric Project does not involve mass deforestation, nor does it involve permanent evacuation of any family. The colony is situated in a barren land. It does not interfere with any religious or cultural or historical monuments.[20] The nearest religious-cum-historical monument, the 'Norbu Gang' lies at least two kilometres away and at a much higher altitude. The Dubdi monastery, which was repeatedly cited by the petitioners to be in danger, is several kilometres away from the project site.

Consequently, both the writ petitions were rejected by the court on the ground that they were devoid of merit.[21] Following the verdict, the agitation subsided but the under-current still persists.

## Conclusion

Two things are clear from the protestations. Just like in some other part of the country, the people of Sikkim are averse to part with their religious sentiments even at the cost of development and prosperity. The water of the Rathong Chu, which is believed to be so sacred, is being used day to day by the local inhabitants for centuries just the way the water of the holy Ganga is being used by people since time immemorial, although on different scales. If daily use by the local inhabitants does not alter the purity of water then it is irrational to think that the construction workers of the project will render it impure for domestic use.

---

* Underlined by the author of the paper.

Secondly, and more importantly, the ethnic Bhutia-Lepcha population of Buddhist belief are not so much worried about water pollution or environmental degradation as they are about immigration of outside labourers in a land which is a strong Bhutia enclave for centuries. Bhutas and Lepchas have been migrating and setting in Sikkim. Now that they are there, they do not want any other community to come, work and settle there which is bound to happen. There are precedences of similar mass immigration in the history of Sikkim. Way back in the 1880's, mass immigration, took place in Sikkim when the copper mines of East Sikkim were opened for the first time. Since superstition prevented the indigenous Sikkimese from mining activities, they hired mine workers from the neighbouring Nepal,[22] who, within decades, outnumbered the Bhutia-Lepcha. Another mass immigration, mainly of white-collared workers, took place in the wake of Sikkim's menger with India in 1975 and thereafter. By 1980, the tertiary sector of the state was visibly dominated by the plainsmen coming from the adjoining states of West Bengal, Bihar as well as from distant Punjab, Rajasthan, Haryana and even as far as Kerala. The Bhutia-Lechas who have already become ethnic minority in Sikkim are afraid of further submergence by people of alien culture.

## Acknowledgement

I am grateful to Hon'ble Justice M. Sengupta, High Court of Sikkim, and Mr. T. Bhutia, Engineer-in-charge, RHEP, Yuksam for providing me with necessary data and informations. I am indebted to Mr. T. Adhikary, field supervisor, RHEP for helping me in my fieldwork at Yuksam. I am also thankful to the Director, Centre for Himalayan Studies, North Bengal University for sponsoring my fieldwork.

## References

1. *WAPCOS: Rathong Chu Hydro-Electric Project, Sikkim, Detailed Project Report*, Vol. II Chapter 3, prepared by Water and Power Consultancy Services (India) Limited (WAPCOS). July 1989.
2. *Sikkim Express*: "Water Resources That Flow From Sikkim: An Economists, View", *Sikkim Express* 1st July-7th July 1995, Gangtok.
3. *Ibid.*
4. *Op. cit.*, 1.
5. *Op. cit.*, 1.
6. *Op. cit.*, 1.
7. *Op. cit.*, 1.
8. Manisha Aryal: "The vocabulary of Protest", *Himal*, July-August, 1995, Vol. 8, No. 4, pp. 11-21
9. *Sikkim Express:* "Rathong Chu Hydro-Electric Project Domestic Resource Mobilisation Effort of Sikkim, *Sikkim Express*, 1st and 7th July 1995. Gangtok.

10. L. Tiwari: "Affidavit-in-opposition in the High Court of Sikkim", 1.9.95.
11. Writ Petition No. 10 of 1994, in the High Court of Sikkim.
12. R.N. Dokhampa: "Origin of the Bum Chu of Dakkar Tashiding", *Bulletin of Tibetology*, SRIT, New Series, No. 3, 1992, Gangtok.
13. *Ibid.*
14. Ludwig Schaefer: "A Sikkim Awakening" p. 10, *Himal*, Sept-Oct. 1995, Kathmandu, Nepal.
15. *Ibid.*
16. Sikkim Express : "Hunger strike on Rathong Chu called off", *Sikkim Express*, July 15th to 21st, 1995, Gangtok.
17. Memorandum submitted by the Association of Buddhist Monks of Sikkim to the Chief Minister of Sikkim dated 18th June 1995.
18. Memorandum submitted by the Sangha of Sikkim, Dhotapo, Deorali to the Chief Minister of Sikkim dated 29th July 1995.
19. Writ Petition No. 25 of 1995, in the High Court of Sikkim, Gangtok.
20. Sikkim Express: "Compensatory Afforestation and non-interference of Religious Place" Sikkim Express, 1st July-7th July 1995, Gangtok.
21. Sikkim Express: "Sikkim High Court Quash writ petition on Rathong Chu", Sikkim Express, 22nd December 1995.
22. Risley, H.H : *Gazetteer of Sikkim*, Calcutta, Bengal Secretariat Press, 1894.

# 8
# Background to Political Unrest in Nepal

With Tibet in the north and India in the south, Nepal had for a long time pursued a destiny peculiarly her own. All along it has been a secluded pristine state. The inaccessibility of the region, intersected by mountainous passes, deep rivers and impenetrable forests, fostered a spirit of isolation and divided the country into small and mutually exclusive social units, whose divergences were accentuated by the infinite variety of local conditions. The difficulties of intercommunication among various districts and regions and the backward and static economy of the villages retarded the growth of a common national feeling among the people.

Further, Nepal's peculiar geographical position of being hemmed in by the two giant powers of Asia—India and China—dictated the policy of isolation which her rulers had followed until very recently. Prithvinarayan Shah, the founder of Nepal's present greatness, who laid the basis of this policy, pointed out that his kingdom was "sandwiched between two giant powers"[1] and advised his followers not to develop intimate relations with either of them.[2] Though this policy was not fully followed by the Rana rulers, on the whole, they also pursued a course which served to keep the country rigidly shut off from outside contacts. While this policy helped in preserving Nepal's independent entity, the forces of modernization, which became active in other parts of Asia, left her untouched until the middle of this century. The isolation as well as the fact of the slow political progress, economic immobility and social backwardness, all are the result of Nepal's having starneyed determindly isolated.

### The Making of Nepal: A Historical Outline

The foundation of the modern State of Nepal was laid by King Prithvinarayan Shah of Gorkha in A.D. 1769. Before the Gurkha conquest, the kingdom of Nepal consisted mainly of the Kathmandu valley which was ruled by three Malla kings with their respective capitals at Kathmandu, Bhatgaon and Patan.[3] Ippolito Desideri, a Jesuit missionary, who visited Nepal in A.D. 1721 wrote in his famous account:

> The Kingdom of Nepal is not large, one can go from one end to the other in a few days; part of it is flat, open country, but the principal part is mountainous; the mountains, however, are well wooded and pleasant. The chief products are wheat, rice, a certain black millet, vegetables, and various kinds of fruit such as prickly pears, pine-apples, lemons and oranges.[4]

Apart from that the riches of Kathmandu valleys and natural bounties of Nepal were templations enough for the Rajput chiefs to embark upon their minism of taking control of the valley. Malla kings minted coins for Tibet in return for a huge profit,[5] constituted a source of great temptation to the rugged hillmen of the small states which congregated in the western part of Nepal. The chiefs of some of these states were the descendants of the ruling families of Rajputana who had fled to Nepal at the time of the Muslim invasion. By the middle of the eighteenth century these states were roughly divided into two loose confederacies called the *Baisi* and the *Chaubisi,* according to their approximate number 22 and 24 respectively.[6] The rulers of the *Baisi* and *Chaubisi* states, especially those of Gurkha, Tanahu and Makwanpur, made several attempts to wrest the Nepal valley from the Malla rulers.[7] Later, the chaotic rule of the Malla kings and their continuous warfares created great dissatisfaction among various sections of the nobility, the merchant and priestly classes who sought the help of these adventurers from the hills to oust their rulers. It was at this time that Prithvinarayan Shah a Gurkha embarked on his scheme of conquering the valley and, after several abortive attempts, defeated the three Malla kingdoms in A.D. 1769.[8]

**Age of Gurkha Expansion**

With this the history of Nepal turned a new leaf. Kathmandu had been insular for centuries. With Prithvinarayan Singh at the helm, this gave way to the insatiable land-hunger of the Gurkha soldiery. The rabble which had gathered round Prithvinarayan Shah was organized into a regular army, which was sent to conquer new territories in all directions. By A.D. 1775 the Gurkhas overran the whole of the *Kiranti* land east of Kathmandu, Morang in Terai, and Ilam touching the border of Sikkim. After Prithvi-narayan's death, Gurkha conquest was pushed further by Bahadur Shah who acted as the Regent of his nephew, King Rana Bahadur Shah (A.D. 1777-99). After winning over the Rajah of Palpa by a marriage alliance, Bahadur brought under control the *Baisi* and *Chaubisi* states and sent his forces as far west as Kumayun. In the east Gurkha arms penetrated into Sikkim and even threatened Bhutan.[9] Emboldened by these victories, the Gurkhas began to cast a longing eye on Tibet.

The prospect of winning the rich lamaseries of Tibet itself constituted an inducement to the Nepalese army to move northward. Further, the refusal of the Tibetans to accept Gurkha coins on the same basis as that of the debased Malla coinage not only disrupted the old trade between Tibet and Nepal but deprived the new rulers of a lucrative source of income.[10] It was, therefore, partly to satisfy their avarice and partly to teach the Tibetans a lesson, that the Nepalese invaded Tibet in May 1788. The war, after a brief interval, continued till A.D. 1792 when the Tibetans with the help of a Chinese army defeated the Gurkhas and pursued them as far as Jeetpur Phedi inside the Nepalese territory.[11] Forced by this defeat, the Nepalese *Darbar* sued for peace which the Chinese granted on condition that Nepal would accept Chinese suzerainty and send presents to China every five years in token of "filial love."[12] The Nepalese, in their turn, got the right to carry on trade in Tibet and received an assurance from China that she would help them "if Nepal be ever invaded by a foreign power."[13] With the foregin power they meant the East India Co. The company by that time had taken full control of Bengal and has consolitating its position Bihar and Uttar Pradesh, just about knowing at the other periphery of Nepal.

### Setback to the Policy of Expansion

The humiliation which the Gurkhas suffered at the hands of the Tibetans caused a violent shake-up in their political set-up. A regime which squarely depended for its sustenance on an army, raised on a "war-footing,"[14] could not sit at rest until it found new avenues of territorial expansion. Hence, failing in the northern region, the army was sent to push the frontier further south—a policy which culminated in the Anglo-Nepalese War of A.D. 1814-16.[15] After a protracted period of mountain warfare in which the Nepalese "fought with the greatest gallantry,"[16] a treaty was signed at Segowli on 4 March 1816 by which Nepal lost her possessions in Sikkim, Kumaun and Garhwal. To the south Nepal was compelled to cede western Terai to the kingdom of Oudh, and eastern Terai to the British a portion of which was, however, returned to her in the same year.[17] By the same Treaty the Nepalese *Darbar* agreed to receive a British representative at Kathmandu. Thus, by 1816, the political boundaries of Nepal were finally settled which, with a few minor adjustments and alterations, have remained intact to the present day. That defeat however still rankles the valiant Nepalese.

## Politics during the Pre-Rana Period

### Hereditary Monarchy and the Nobility

The Shahs of Gurkha established a political system in Nepal, which was essentially military and despotic in character. They traced their origin from the royal family of Chittor.[18] As sovereign, the King wielded supreme authority in both civil and military affairs of the State. Monarchy was a hereditary institution and every Monarch, on his accession, assumed the title of *Sri Panch Maharajadhiraja.* For the purposes of administration, however, the King employed ministers and *Bharadars*[19] from higher caste noble families with whom he had intimate contacts. These ministers and *Bharadars* were given lands called *Jagirs* and *Birtas* in payment of the services they rendered to the King. The *Birta* lands were mostly granted in the form of reward to military chiefs and others who had distinguished themselves in war, and these lands were not taxed by the Government. As these grants, excepting a few cases, were granted to the chiefs and nobles on a hereditary basis, this system raised, in course of time, a feudal oligarchy which became the strongest political force in the country next only to the Monarch.

Again, among the nobility, some important families came to enjoy hereditary rights to the highest offices of the State even during the reign of Ram Shah (A.D. 1606-33), an illustrious ancestor of Prithvinarayan.[20] These families were the Pandes, the Aryyals, the Khanals, the Ranas and the Boharas who, according to the Gurkha *Vamsavali* had helped Ram Shah's predecessor, Drabya Shah, to capture Gurkha in A.D. 1559. Some of these families and the royal collaterals, called the *Chautarias,* played an important role during the campaign of Prithvinarayan Shah and, in recognition of their service, received further confirmation of their hereditary titles.[21] At the same time, Prithvinarayan acknowledged the supreme position of the Brahman in the social order. He declared Nepal to be the "true Hindustan with 4 castes and 36 varnas."[22] He distributed tax-free lands called *Birta* and the *Guthi* lands for exclusive religious purposes among the Brahmans and granted them total immunity from capital punishment. With the ascendancy of the Gurkhas in Nepal Brahmanic orthodoxy also took hold of the society which was otherwise also predominantly Hindu.[23]

The nobility in the meanwhile had become very powerful. They a parallel ruling class in the kindom. Differences were bound to occur. Groupism took hold. This brought new complications and tensions in Nepalese political life. While powerful feudal chiefs tried to outshine one another, other members of the nobility and *Bharadars* who did not enjoy hereditary rights constantly engaged themselves in intrigues to plan the destruction of the former. Often, when the King was a minor or proved to be a weakling the nobility grew too powerful. These tendencies were, however, kept in check so long as a strong personality like Prithvinarayan Shah ruled over them and the Gurkha flag of victory extended far and wide. But once his strong hand was removed, a showdown among the top noble families became not only immediate but unavoidable.

**Contest for Regency**

The contest began during the minority of King Rana Bahadur Shah. The Queen-Mother Rajendra Laxmi and his uncle and Bahadur Shah vied for the throne. As they clashed with one another, the nobles also got divided into two parties to the support of their respective leaders. But the untimely death of the queen in A.D. 1786 left Bahadur Shah" unchallenged in the field. With the help of his associates, Damodar Pande, Abhiman Singh and Gajraj Misra—a *Rajguru* (royal teacher), Bahadur Shah sought to become the actual ruler of Nepal. He treated the minor King with impunity, held back his regular allowance and, in the bargain, accumulated for himself "considerable treasures."[24] His plans were, however, frustrated when Rana Bahadur, coming of age, threw him out of power in A.D. 1795. The impetuous King, in turn, attempted to revive the personal despotism of the monarch in all state affairs. But his policy was stoutly resisted by the privileged nobility and the Brahman priestly families. At the end, he was forced to abdicate in favour of his infant son, Girvan Juddha Bikram Shah, and live in exile for some time. Later, when Rana Bahadur returned to Nepal to become the *Mukhtiyar* of his son, he used the support of the Thapas to fight the old aristocracy and replace it by a new one. It was to achieve this purpose that he also persecuted the Brahmans, confiscated their lands and proclaimed that the Brahmans had "forfeited the laws of their caste by the unworthiness of their conduct."[25] But this is as far as Rana Bahadur Shah could go, for in A.D. 1806 he was murdered and, from then on, there ensued a frantic struggle for power among various factions of the nobility led mainly by the Pandes and the Thapas.

**Rise of Bhimsen Thapa**

Finally Bhimsen Thapa emerged as the strongest man of the kingdom and dominated the arena of politics for the next thirty years (A.D. 1806-37) as *Mukhtiyar* (Prime Minister) of Nepal.

Bhimsen Thapa brought into force a scheme in which all important posts in civil and military administration were filled by members of the Thapa family and their kinsmen. The Pandes and their partisans were ruthlessly persecuted. They were deprived of their landed properties and even some Brahmans suffered humiliation.[26] At the same time, Bhimsen established a political system in which the Monarch was reduced into a figure-head while all real powers belonged to the Prime Minister. Fortunately for him both the Kings, Girvan Juddha Bikram Shah (A.D. 1799-1816) and Rajendra Bikram Shah (1816-47), were minors when they ascended the throne. In Queen Tripura Sundari Devi, who acted as the Regent during the minority of Rajendra Bikram Shah, Bhimsen also found a sympathetic friend who was willing to help him further his political designs.

How far Bhimsen succeeded in his designs can be seen from the following excerpts of a letter which Hodgson, the then British Resident at Kathmandu, wrote to the Governor General of India:

> ...almost every office is filled with Bhimsen's creatures; he and his family monopolise all the loaves and fishes. Mere children of his kindred hold high commands. The ancient families of the Pandes and others who, by the constitution of this State, are entitled to share its counsels and exercise its highest offices, are excluded almost wholly from the one and other, besides being treated with habitual contumely by Matabar Singh, Bhimsen's overbearing and heedless nephew.
>
> The Raja is hemmed into his palace, beyond which he cannot stir unaccompanied by the Minister, and then only to the extent of a short ride or drive. Even within the walls of his palace, the Minister and his brother both reside, the latter in the special capacity of a "dry nurse" to His Highness.[27]

By his acts Bhimsen did not make himself popular. There were several serious flaws in Bhimsen's new arrangement. In the first place, his powers of an absolute despot alienated other sections of the nobility. Secondly, though the Pandes and their supporters were driven out of power, they still constituted, as Hodgson wrote, "a weight of adverse rights which needs only to be put into motion to crush him [Bhimsen] and his family to pieces."[28] Thirdly, the presence of the British Resident in Nepal created new difficulties for Bhimsen. Eager to build direct contact with the ruler, the Resident was as much interested in breaking Bhimsen's monopoly over the royal palace as were the Pandes and their allies. This brought the Resident in close contact with Bhimsen's enemies and made the British Residency a *nucleus* of nefarious intrigues. Finally, a section of the army and even certain members of the Thapa family got dissatisfied with the manner in which Bhimsen conducted his office. The combined efforts of all these factions and parties led to the downfall of Bhimsen in A.D. 1837.[29] But thirty years was a long time. They damage had been immense to the kingdom.

**Disintegration and Anarchy**

Bhimsen's fall only set in motion the forces of political disintegration. Almost immediately old family disputes, dissensions and violence returned to politics. In view of the ambitions of rival factions of the nobility, King Rajendra Bikram Shah failed to reassert the authority of the Crown. On the other hand, none of the families or their chiefs proved strong enough to restore stability in the administration. As a result, for the next eight years, "the people let the rival nobles kill each other, and obeyed whichever faction for the time being spoke in the name of royalty."[30]

For a time though the process of disintegration was checked by Matabar Singh Thapa, Bhimsen's nephew, who was made *Mukhtiyar* and Commander-in-Chief by the King in November 1843.[31] But the ruthless manner in which Matabar settled old scores with the Pande faction fanned, instead of subduing, the clan warfare. He also lost favour with the *Chautarias* by confiscating the property of Fateh Jang, their leader. Even the King, who watched with alarm Matabar's growing influence, became suspicious and uneasy. The end came soon when on the night of 17 May 1845 Matabar Singh was treacherously murdered by his nephew, Jang Bahadur.[32]

After the death of Matabar Singh, a coalition ministry was formed with Fateh Jang Chautaria at the head. But the petty intrigues among the various factions in the ministry made the administration totally ineffective. Taking advantage of the unsettled conditions, Jang Bahadur quietly laid his plans to oust the *junta* which ruled in the name of the King. On 14 September 1846, Gagan Singh, one of the ministers and a favourite of the younger Queen, was found murdered. The next day Jang Bahadur and his brothers slaughtered at the *Kot* all the leading chiefs and *Bharadars* belonging to the camp of the *Chautarias,* the Pandes, the Basniats, the Thapas, etc. Thus, the house of Jang Bahadur, later known as the Ranas, replaced the noble families of old.

## Politics and Political System under the Ranas

### Jang Bahadur's Policies

Jang Bahadur also proceeded to crush his opponents at the very beginning. By massacring, hounding and exiling them out of the country he crushed for all time their chances of recovery. At the same time, Jang Bahadur realized that without securing the goodwill of the British Government of India, it would not be possible for him to consolidate his position. To this end he applied himself with the thoroughgoing *finesse* of a diplomat and soon secured British recognition of the new arrangement he had effected after the *Kot* massacre. Another event favoured Jang's fortune at this stage.

In 1847, he forced King Rajendra Bikram Shah to abdicate in favour of his son, Surendra Bikram Shah—a fact which was endorsed by 370 officers and *Bharadars* created by Jang Bahadur himself.[33]

The two important objectives with which Jang Bahadur began his office were, first, to entrench himself in power as permanently as possible and, second, to pass on the Prime Ministership as well as other important offices of the State to his brothers and descendants in perpetuity. In order to achieve these goals, he forced the Monarch to retire into his palace and take as little part in the administration as possible. Secondly, he procured, from King Surendra Bikram Shah, in 1856, a *Lal Mohar* (royal order) granting him the title of the *Maharaja* and the rulership of Kaski and Lumjung, which was to pass from him "to his offspring to offspring."[34] He was further invested with powers to exercise rights over life and death of the Nepalese subjects throughout the domain, to appoint or dismiss all public servants, to declare war or conclude peace or sign treaty with foreign powers, to inflict punishments on offenders and to repeal or amend or frame laws of the country.[35]

By the same *Lal Mohar* it was fixed that the succession to *Mukhtiyari* would pass from Jang Bahadur to his brothers and then to his son Jagat Jang.[36] These extraordinary powers were reaffirmed, in 1857, by another *Lal Mohar* and a copy of it, attested by four brothers of Jang Bahadur, was sent to the Governor-General of India.[37] Thus, by obtaining the highest legal sanction of the country, Jang Bahadur avoided the mistake which had cost Bhimsen Thapa his life. He also raised the social status of his family by securing from the King the elevated "caste of the Ranas"[38] and, later, he began the policy of contracting marriages with the members of the royal family which none of his predecessors had thought of doing.[39] These marriages, as his own son suggests, "were downright political treaties"[40] which raised the social standing of the Ranas on par with the members of the Shah family. Again, knowing well the immense political influence of the Brahmans and the position they held in society, Jang Bahadur bestowed liberal favours on them. He preserved their ancient rights, granted them lands and Birtas and, in general, promoted their economic interests. Similarly, though he advocated certain reforms like abolition of the *Sati* and slavery, he left untouched the civil and criminal laws based on the Hindu *Dharmashastras* (religious code).

**Upsetting the Existing System**

This attitude reflected Jang Bahadur's anxiety to show, notwithstanding the violence which attended his rise to power, that he was not unwilling to follow the rules and precepts of caste and society as laid down by the Brahmans. It was the same motive which prevented Jang Bahadur from upsetting the existing system on land or the essentially military structure of the Government.[41] The only change that occurred was that now the lands granted to the rival families of the nobles changed hands and became the sole possession of Jang Bahadur's brothers, kinsmen and supporters. The previous basis of granting *Birta* lands as part of a feudal contract between the King and his servants, however, dwindled during the long period of Rana rule as, in later times, lands were bestowed to the Ranas and their descendants as a privilege, and not as an obligation. In other matters, the Ranas continued to preserve older institutions like the granting of *Jagirs* and the practice of *Pajani* by which the services of all officers of the State from the top downward were reviewed, renewed or terminated. Kirkpatrick has made a mention of the grand council or Bharadari. Jang Bahadur did not ban the Bharadari but no many oneetings of Bharadari took place. Its use to the despot was at best nominal.[42]

## The Rana Hierarchy

The advent of the Rana regime did not usher in an era of revolutionary change in the social and political life of the country. What it actually did was to eliminate the great families of old and to replace them by a new one. The administration was made hereditary property of the Ranas whose ranks and positions were determined on the basis of their seniority of birth. At the head of the family was the *Maharaja, the* Prime Minister, who centralized in himself all civil and military powers. The scope of his jurisdiction, executive or legislative, remained mostly undefined and he ruled the country more or less like an absolute despot.

The Commander-in-Chief was the next seniormost member of the Rana family after the Prime Minister. Then followed the four Commanding Generals of the army holding both civil and military authority in four different parts of the country. The appointments to other successive posts were made on the same basis of seniority among the various families of the Ranas. In the army, also, top offices were filled by the Ranas who held military titles from the very moment of their birth. Apart from getting their regular salaries, the Ranas also received grants of *Birtas,* commissions on revenue collection, *Nazarana,*[43] and other feudal dues from their tenants.

## Over-Centralization of Power

The new system brought in a long period of peace and stability in the Government. The centralization of power in a single man succeeded in checking, to a large extent, the dangerous drift towards disintegration caused by endless warfare among the older families. Secondly, by keeping friendly relations with the British Government of India, the Ranas also preserved Nepal's political independence. But the dangers of over-centralization cannot be over-emphasized. Ranging from all policy matters, administrative, fiscal and judicial, the Prime Minister kept control over every branch of administration.[44] The overall effect of such a system, though it proved conducive to the personal despotism of the *Maharaja,* was to kill trust and initiative in the lower echelons of the administration. On the other hand, the burden of daily work of the Prime Minister increased so enormously that it became almost impossible for a single man to tackle it efficiently. He became overburdened. The decision making became erratic, impulsive. There was no claim of command in sight.

The highly personalized character of the rule also made top officials, *Bada Hakims* (district governors), army generals and others throng to Kathmandu to crave for pleasures of the Prime Minister and of those Ranas who mattered in the Government. Even the four Commanding Generals who were supposed to attend duties at their regional headquarters spent the greater part of the year at the capital. As a result, the rest of the country, especially the Terai and the Hills, was left to suffer its own fate and bear the worst exploitation of the regime. Kathmandu, on the other hand, came to represent the seat of power, filled with the hubbub of intense lobbying among the Ranas and such intrigues and rumours as are commonly associated with the court politics of a feudal potentate. The city became a centre of intrigues rumours and court gossips.

**Dissensions in the Rana Family**

But the greater evil of the system was in the kind of politics, personal jealousies and perpetual tensions which it germinated within the Rana family itself. Jang Bahadur himself was not unaware of this danger as twice during his own life-time attempts were made by his brothers to kill him.[45] For all practical purposes the *roll of succession* which he had prepared in 1856 proved useless. Immediately after his death, two factions arose in the Rana family—one headed by his brothers and the other by his sons. The squabble proved to be fatal.

Despite the *roll*, the next Prime Minister, Ranoddip Singh, was murdered in 1885 by his own nephews.[46] The succession was rearranged by Bir Shamsher (A.D. 1885-1901) but, in spite of it, his successor Dev Shamsher was deposed by Chandra Shamsher only three months after his accession. It was during the Prime Ministership of Chandra Shamsher (A.D. 1901-29) that another elaborate succession *roll* was prepared and the Rana families were divided into 'A', 'B' and 'C' classes.[47] Later, in 1935, the names of the 'C' class Ranas were struck off from the succession *roll* because they were considered to be illegitimate by birth. This gave rise to resentment and conspiracies.

**Results of the Rana Rule**

When pepole at the top quarrel the populace become confused. These dissensions and incessant struggles for power among important Ranas reduced the Government to a state of perpetual flux and anxiety. In view of the uncertainty about the future, every person, from the *Maharaja* to the petty officers, got busy in accumulating for himself as much wealth as he could. As a result, in its later stages, the Rana administration became an instrument of systematic loot and oppression. It did little in the way of improving the basic amenities of life and lost every initiative to absorb new ideas from outside.

The system of granting *Birtas* to the Ranas and their dependants, on the other hand, raised a class of big landowners who represented the ruling aristocracy of the country. Between them and the masses, consisting mainly of the peasantry, there was hardly anything in common. The only intermediary class which grew up under the Ranas consisted of merchants, *Zamindars*, small Birta owners,48 priests and petty officials who remained completely dependent on their feudal benefactors. As servants of the Ranas, the fate of these men was closely interlinked with that of their patrons. As such they adopted in politics an attitude which only helped in preserving the Rana rule.

Its prevalence the ruling hierarchy was feudial and lord-and-servant relationship prevented the growth of an independent middle class which, in the long run, might have exerted its influence against the continuation of an autocratic regime. During the later phases of the Rana rule, it became an article of faith with the rulers to suppress the growth of an educated intelligentsia. The right to higher education was strictly limited to the members of the ruling family, while the acquisition of knowledge by ordinary citizens was regarded as an act of sedition.[49] Further, in order to prevent the growth of new ideas among the people, the Ranas kept the country rigidly shut off from all outside contacts. Those of the non-ruling families who dared to leave for education and business were frowned upon by the rulers. Their properties were confiscated and if they were persecuted.

As has been happening every monarchy, the survival of the Rana rule mainly depended on its capacity to suppress the growth of political awakening in the country. Yet, notwithstanding the oppressive character of the regime and social and economic backwardness of the country, the urge for change began to gain momentum in a section of the people. Some families in Nepal Terai, who came in greater contact with India than with Kathmandu, got imbued with the ideas of social and political reforms as generated by the Indian nationalist movement. Similarly, some members of the lower class civil servants left Kathmandu to settle permanently in India. At a still later stage, some 'C' class Ranas migrated to India where they received higher education and such knowledge as could allow them to participate in commercial enterprises. It was from these three types of emigre Nepalese families that opposition to the Rana rule came in the shape of political movements. As these movements culminated in the armed revolt of 1950-51 and as the nature and scope of that struggle determined, to a large extent, subsequent political developments of Nepal, the genesis of the revolt and its various phases form the subject matter of the next chapter.

## Origins of Anti-Rana Movements and Fall of the Ranas

### Origin and Evolution of the Anti-Rana Movement

Right from the beginning, Ranas had been very careful. More than administering the country, their resources were diverted towards consolidating their own rule. The Rana Government took enough precaution to prevent the outbreak of any organized movement in the country. At first, the only form of opposition which it faced came from among the members of the old nobility—the Thapas and the Basniats, who wanted to avenge the wrongs done to them and to their ancestors. Sometimes, the *Chautarias,* the non-Rana *Bharadars* and even the King himself joined these men to conspire against the Rana Prime Minister. In the prevailing conditions of factional intrigue among the ruling Ranas, the formation of such secret plots became not only easy but frequent. But, more often than not, these conspiracies were motivated by the urge for simple blood-revenge which had nothing to do with the idea of better government or popular rule. These abortive attempts to overthrow the Rana regime set the stage for the development of later popular movements in Nepal. Commoners also took ideas from these internecise plots. The stage was getting sel for popular revolt against the Ranas.

Around that ensued a movement for religious and social reforms which threatened to impair the hegemony of the Brahmans and the priestly groups who also formed a section of the landowning classes in Nepal. It was inevitable Great changes were taking place at the time. Reseatment against the British were mounting. Nepal could not stay immune to all. Nepalese expats living in India starling have their ideas. Though this movement was speedily suppressed, it broadened the social basis of opposition to the Rana rule. By the thirties, some young men who drew inspiration from the activities of terrorist groups in India began to form secret political societies in Nepal. Like the earlier family plots of the nineteenth century, these societies also aimed at the physical extermination of the Ranas, but they seemed to have also developed some vague ideas about democratic and popular rule. When these secret societies failed, the Nepalese residing in India began to make preparation for fighting the Ranas from outside.

**Non-violent Movement**

In 1947, they launched an organized non-violent movement in Nepal Terai which forced the Rana ruler to declare a limited measure of constitutional and political reforms. But in view of the growing popular disaffection against the rule, and especially in the context or great political changes in India, these reforms failed to make any impression. Finally, the anti-Rana forces led by the Nepali Congress decided to enter their country with a liberation army which culminated in the revolt of 1950 and the fall of the Ranas.

Thus the origins and development of the anti-Rana movement can be studied in four stages: first, the court intrigues of the non-Rana nobility and *Bharadars* in the nineteenth century; second, the beginning of social and religious reforms; third, the secret clubs of the thirties of which the *Praja Parishad* was the most famous and, last, the anti-Rana agitation organized from India.

**Court Intrigues of the Non-Rana families**

All the powers rested with Jang Bahadur. He had the king to a figure head. Thus, he laid the foundation of 104 years of Rana rule.

Intreques however continued. These in any case can never be eraducated. Some survivors of the ousted Thapa and Basniat families and their supporters continued to lay plots against him. Thus, in 1847, when the deposed King, Rajendra Bikram Shah, made a futile attempt to invade Nepal, a large number of exiled Thapas and Basniats joined him.[50] Later, a younger generation of the Thapas came of age and waited for their opportuing. They wanted average the death of Matabar Singh at Jang's hands."[51] Among the *Chautarias* (royal collaterals), Guru Prasad Shah made several attempts on the life of Jang Bahadur but, failing in all these attempts, he finally reconciled himself to his fate.[52] In 1851 the King's brother, Upendra Bikram Shah, conspired with Badri Nara Singh, Jang Bahadur's brother, but before any plan could mature, he and his associates were rounded up and sent to Allahabad to be kept in the custody of the British Government.[53] Mercifully, they for put to death.

Plotting against the Prine Minister had become a way of life for the conspirators. Though, in this manner, more than half a dozen plots were made against the life of Jang Bahadur none of them succeeded. Nevertheless, they showed that neither the Shah rulers nor the non-Rana families of old had reconciled themselves to the rule of the usurper. This was proved again when, on the death of Jang Bahadur, Crown Prince Trailokya Bikram Shah (A.D. 1848-78) formed a close group of conspirators and enlisted the support of his brother-in-law, Jagat Jang,[54] who in his turn was trying to oust his uncle Ranoddip Singh from Prime Ministership.[55] But Trailokya Bikram's untimely death and Jagat Jang's subsequent humiliation caused the dissolution of this group.

**non-Rana Factor**

The non-Rana factor was never idle. They were always plotting. The next concerted attempt by the "non-Rana elements of [the]- nobility"[56] was made under the active direction of Narendra Bikram Shah, the uncle of King Prithvi Bir Bikram Shah (A.D. 1881-1911). Narendra actually wanted to replace his minor nephew and rule the kingdom with the help of a new set of ministers.[57] His two close associates were Bikram Singh Thapa and Sangram Sur who enjoyed the support of a large number of officers in the Rana army. Together they laid a plot to assemble all the prominent Ranas at a fixed place and slaughter them at a single stroke. Accordingly, 6 January 1881 was fixed as the appointed date. But again, at this stage, the plot was unearthed by secret informers of Dhir Shamsher, the Commander-in-Chief. As a result, all the ring-leaders, including Narendra Bikram Shah, were arrested and about twenty young men of the group were immediately put to death.[58] After that the non-Rana factions were in a limbo for quite some time.

The main reason why such attempts failed to succeed was the lack of a common objective among the conspirators themselves. Some of them joined hands only to take revenge upon the Ranas, some wanted to set up their own rule, while there were still others for whom such plots were a necessary part of their every day court life. As a result, it was not difficult for the Rana police to unearth such plots by planting secret informers among the conspirators. Secondly, on the whole, the state army, barring a handful of officers and their men, remained loyal to the regime. Lastly, these plots had no popular basis so as to start any organized revolt which could have upset the political hegemony of the Rana family. All the members and their associates were arrested. Some of them were killed, others were jailed. With that the resistance ended.

**Beginning of Social and Religious Reform Movement**

Winds of change had sweeping across India. Religio-social movements had taken hold. Gandhiji had become active in Africa. Gopal Krishan Gokhale Dadabhay Naoroji and others had started how-key movements against the British. At the close of the nineteenth century, some enlightened Nepalese came to be drawn towards these movements. A lew of them embraced the teachings of the *Arya Samaj,* founded by Swami Dayanand Saraswati, and one of them, Madhav Raj Joshi,[59] returned to Nepal to begin a series of discourses on the Hindu *sastras.* In 1896 he started an office of the *Arya Samaj* at Kathmandu. His preaching soon attracted wide attention and it was said that even *Maharaja* Mohan Shamsher once invited him to listen to his lecture. But Madhav Raj's popularity became an eye-sore to the *Rajgurus* and priestly classes who regarded him as an intruder in their sacred field and, hence, they pressed the *Maharaja* to take action against him. As a result of their concerted attempts and malicious advice, Madhav Raj was finally disgraced and sent out of the country. In 1905 he left for India and made his permanent home at Darjeeling.

**Arya Samaj**

*Arya Samaj* had taken roots in Nepal the beginning made by Madhav Raj Joshi did not prove completely futile. The threads of his teachings were picked up by a younger generation of the *Arya Samajists* who began to spread them among different sections of the people. In 1920, these *Samajists* came under fire for the second time, when their leaders, Tulsi Meher, Chakra Bahadur and Amar Raj Joshi, were arrested and thrown into prison. But, though the movement suffered a temporary eclipse, the *Samajists* carried on their work under different names. At this stage, the non-cooperation movement of Gandhi also began to make its influence felt upon a section of the Nepalese people. A few educated Nepalese in India openly joined Gandhi's movement. On the other hand, among the returning Nepalese soldiers who had fought in the Great War, there were many who got dissatisfied with home conditions and began spreading their new ideas among their fellowmen.

Thus, by the twenties, a new social consciousness began to develop in Nepal under the guidance of a new set of leaders among whom Subba Devi Prasad Sapkota, Krishna Prasad Koirala and Dharani Diar Sharma were the most outstanding. Subba Devi Prasad, who was an officer in the Foreign Department of the Rana Government, left his service to come to Banaras and start a weekly called the *Gorkhali* which, for the first time, wrote boldly about the conditions prevailing in Nepal under the Ranas.[60] Krishna Prasad Koirala of Birat-nagar was deeply influenced by the teachings of Gandhi and he began to express his liberal ideas through his poetical com positions in the Nepali language.[61] In 1926, Tulsi Meher who was released from prison, began to propagate the importance of the *Charkha* which soon led him back to prison. Later, again influenced by the teachings of Gandhi, another group of young men began to propagate against the practice of untouchability, of meat-eating, cruelty to animals and so on. Gandhiji had greatly influenced the younger generation of Nepalese. The cultural thread also had a very big impression.

By this time, the ideas of nationalism also began to spread in Nepal. The writings of Krishna Prasad Koirala and Dharanidhar Sharma's *Naivadhya* which "ushered in the twilight of modernity,"[62] the revival of historical interest through the works of Surya Bikram Gyavali and Lekhnath Paudiyal's forceful novel *Pinjda ko Suga*[64] helped the process of development of nationalist sentiments among the new generation of literate Nepalese. Inspired by the same sentiment, Subba Krishna Lal wrote a line on the virtues of native dogs as against the European ones in his little book named *Makaii Ka Khetti* which immediately brought upon him the ire of Chandra Shamsher.[64] The unfortunate writer had to spend the remaining days of his life in prison where he ultimately died.

**Awakening of Educated Class**

The awakening the educated class of Nepalese through slow, was sure. The impact of new ideas was making itself felt more and more. A number of young men who had smuggled to India to receive higher education returned to Nepal by the end of the 'thirties and began starting social and educational movements on new lines. Among a section of the lower official classes mostly belonging to the Newar community, who specially suffered social degradation under the Ranas, a rumbling discontent was fast growing up. In 1937, some of these men started a school at Kathmandu to impart education on modern lines. But, fearful of such a venture, the Rana Government ordered the closure of the school and sentenced about 28 teachers to long terms of imprisonment.[65] The rumblings however could not suppressed.

During the thirties, a new organization called the *Nepali Nagarik Adhikar Samiti* was started at Kathmandu with Pandit Sukra Raj Sastri, son of Madhav Raj Joshi, as its central figure. The *Samiti* worked on a purely socio-religious plane. It engaged Pandit Muralidhar to interpret the teachings of the *Puranas,* employed Kedarman "Byathith" to organize relief work and sent Sankar Prasad to India to rally public opinion in support of its activities. Though the meetings which the *Samiti* held at Kathmandu were purely religious in character, their impact on the minds of the people was tremendous.[66] Recalling these days in his reminiscences, Pandit Muralidhar explains why the *Samiti* worked on a purely religious basis :

> We decided to impart political consciousness through the medium of the *Mahabharata* stories. Lessons were drawn through citing examples from current life. It was no small act to try even that at a time when tongues were cut off even for mere blabbing.[67]

But the *Samiti's* exclusive concern with spiritual aspects of life made some of its younger members very restive. Finally, at a big meeting held under its auspices, a Newari youth named Gangalal started hurling abuses on the Rana rulers which produced a great sensation in the city.[68] This was perhaps the first political speech ever delivered in Kathmandu. The Ranas could digest all this Both Sastri and Ganga Lal were arrested and put in jail for some time the Samiti's work came to lalt. There was no leader to run it.

### Secret Clubs and the Praja Parishad

Extreme action became invertable open protest, meeting and other activities unfavourable to the regime were not possible. The impracticability of organizing even normal social activities brought home the conviction to a section of the Nepalese that only underground terrorist activities could succeed in Nepal. Hence, as early as 1931, a handful of men founded a secret society called the *Prachanda Gurkha* which aimed to establish democratic rule by ending the Rana system. But even before this club could begin functioning its members were arrested and thrown into prison. But the sense of utter frustration and urge for revenge drove another extremist group to found, in 1935, under a thick cloak of secrecy, the *Praja Parishad,* in the very heart of Kathmandu. Some leading members of the Parishad were Tanka Prasad Acharya, Dasarath Chandra, Ram Hari Sharma and the physical instructor of the King, Dharma Bhakta. It was even reported that the King was secretly associated with it. The Parishad's aim was to end the Rana *Sirkar* (Government) and establish a democratic government under the aegis of the monarch.[69] In 1937-38 Tanka Prasad and a few others visited India, Burma and some other places to learn more about the methods of secret terrorist activities. After their return the Parishad decided to function on two levels, first, to educate the people in political movements and, second, to assassinate some important Ranas to bring a swift change in the Government.[70] From Banaras, Tanka Prasad also brought a printing machine to print handbills and leaflets whose circulation created a new sensation in Kathmandu. The Praja Parishad, however, could not work for a long time. In 1940, through betrayal or vigorous police investigation, the Ranas came to know the names of its organizers. By October 1940, about 500 persons were arrested and after a brief trial Dharma Bhakta, Dasarath Chandra, Gangalal and Sukra Raj Sastri were executed. Tanka Prasad Acharya, Ramhari Sharma, Chuda Prasad, Ganeshman Singh, Hari Krishna, Govinda Prasad Sharma, Puskarnath and Bal Chandra were awarded long terms of imprisonment.[71] A few workers of the Parishad, managed to escape to India there they were to draw the attention of media. Thus, the India's came to know of the persecutions and execation of pobtical opponents in Nepal.

The fate of the Praja Parishad was sealed. Under the conditions then existing in Nepal, it was not possible for it to carry unsustained political agitation without attracting the notice of the Rana rulers. Secondly, the fear of the Government was so deeply ingrained in the minds of the people that it was too much to expect any open response from them through the distribution of a few leaflets. Finally, the membership of the Parishad had grown far too numerous to be kept any more a secret. But, in spite of its failure, the importance of the Praja Parishad movement cannot be minimized. It infused new courage and confidence in the anti-Rana elements. Successive struggles that followed had emanated from this movement. This movement made a Nepalese in the street aware of what was on at upper level of society. Resentment against the Ranas was growing. Above all, its activities became a part of the modern Nepalese movement liberation.

**Anti-Rana Movement in India**

For a long time, some groups of exiled Nepalese had carried on a kind of anti-Rana agitation in India, but due to the over-zealous watch maintained over them by the British Government they could not build up any active movement. In 1921, however, a beginning was made when Thakur Chandan Singh, a retired soldier, founded the *Gurkha League* and a weekly paper called the *Gurkha Sansar* which was later renamed the *Tarun Gurkha.* On the political plane, Chandan Singh had no definite views, but his angry outbursts through the columns of his weekly created a stir among the literate sections of the Nepalese then living in India. After a few years, however, Chandan Singh was forced to stop his activities "as a result of [the] betrayal practised by his associates who walked into the Rana's parlour."[72] That always happens when a society is in turmoil.

By this time, a growing number of educated Nepalese came in closer contact with the Indian freedom movement. During the 'Quit India' movement in 1942, some of them were arrested among whom were B.P. Koirala, K.P. Upadhyay and D.R. Regmi. In the same year the people of Saptari in Eastern Terai broke open the gates of Hanuman Nagar jail where the revolutionary socialist leaders of India, Jayaprakash Narayan, Dr. Rammanohar Lohia and others were interned by the Rana Government when they escaped into Nepal to seek political asylum. As a result, a reign of terror was let loose in that district and some 22 arrests were made.[73] These incidents and close association with the Indian national movement made a large number of the Nepalese realize that until British colonial rule was brought to an end in India, it would not be possible for them to fight against the Ranas.

**The Indian Influence**

When, therefore, in 1946 the Interim Government was formed in India, as a prelude to India's achievement of freedom, a new wave of enthusiasm flooded them. In January 1947, the exiled Nepalese, especially youth and students, gathered together to form the *Nepali Rashtriya Congress* at Calcutta.[74] At the same time, the first rumbling of discontent among the people of the Terai, where a serious famine was raging, began to be heard.[75] On 4 March 1947, the mill workers of Biratnagar struck work and began the first organized strike in Nepal. In response to their call, B.P. Koirala and other leaders of the Rashtriya Congress joined the strike which turned from a small scale employer-employee conflict into a full-fledged political battle. The Rana Government sent an armed contingent to suppress the strike. It resorted to firing which resulted in the killing of several unarmed men and women.[76] On 24 March, B.P. Koirala, G.P. Koirala, Balchandra Sharma and other leaders of the strike were rounded up and sent to Kathmandu. At Calcutta the Nepali Rashtriya Congress held an emergency meeting and sent an ultimatum to the Rana Government asking it to put an end to its policy of coercion.[77]

When the latter did not respond to this call, a general conference of Congress workers was held at Jogbani (North Bihar) where it was decided to launch a Civil Disobedience movement in Nepal from 13 April 1947.[78] The movement which was first launched at Biratnagar, in the way of individual *Satyagraha,* soon spread to other districts. At Birganj students of a local school brought out a long procession which was also joined by a few civil servants. On 6 May 1947, the students of Kathmandu organized a big demonstration demanding the end of Rana regime. In other parts of the Terai like Janakpur, Ilam, etc., popular-response to the *Satyagraha* was so widespread and spontaneous that it appeared as it, for the first time, a mass movement was in the making in Nepal.[79]

As a sequel to the movement, Prime Minister Padma Shamsher announced on 16 May 1947 that he would be willing to introduce far-reaching political reforms provided the Rashtriya Congress agreed to withdraw the *Satyagraha.* On 2 June, after a long and heated discussion among the ranks, the Rashtriya Congress decided to call off the movement. It did so because of two reasons. First, the offer seemed to give it a partial victory over the Ranas. Secondly, it also found out that as yet its organizational resources were not enough to give a call for a nationwide movement. Hence a settlement through compromise appeared to be most expedient under the circumstances.[80] As the latter events, it turned out to be beneificial.

**Reforms of Padma Shamsher: 1947-48**

According to his proclamation of 16 May 1947, *Maharaja* Padma Shamsher declared that he would form a Reform Committee to suggest changes in the administration so that it could be carried on by "an assembly of elected and nominated members."[81] As first step, he suggested that elections to local *Panchayats* (village councils), municipalities and district boards would be held within a year. He also gave the assurance to establish an independent judicial system, to publish annual budget, to give grants-in-aid to private schools and establish Consular Offices both in India and in other countries.[82] To help the Reform Committee, he also invited a panel of Indian legal experts to visit Nepal in June 1947.[83]

Meanwhile, to try the reform scheme in part, an election to the Kathmandu Municipality, described as a "provisional autonomous local council,"[84] was held in the month of June. For the purpose of election, the city was divided into 21 wards each of which was asked to send the name of four candidates to the Municipal *Goswara* (office).[85] Each candidate was required to collect signatures of 15 prominent citizens from his ward in order to make his nomination paper valid. There was to be one member from each ward and it was laid down that the candidate receiving highest number of votes would be declared elected.[86] This election was the first experiment in democratic methods in Nepalese history.[87] Its significance is yet more heightened when it is noted that, in spite of official control, some independents and sympathisers of the Nepali Rashtriya Congress were elected to the Kathmandu Municipality.

The writing was on the wall now. the Maharaja was loosened his control. He could not help doing it. This limited freedom for political activities in Nepal as granted during the election, gave new courage to Kathmandu's citizens. In July 1947, students of the Sanskrit College broke out into a strike and demanded introduction of new subjects in their curriculum, amenities in their hostel life and enhanced salary for their teachers.[88] As the movement gained considerable public sympathy, Padma

Shamsher was obliged to make an announcement to the effect that he would fulfil the demands of the students. But this ready submission on his part made conservative sections of the Ranas more hostile. They began accusing him of surrendering old rights and of mismanaging the entire administration. As these die-hard Ranas under Mohan Shamsher grew bolder and threatened to depose him, Padma Shamsher announced his desire to retire from active political life on grounds of ill-health.[89] But before doing so, Padma Shamsher promulgated on 26 January 1948 the Government of Nepal Act, 2004 (1948 A.D.) This was the first written Constitution of Nepal.

## The Rana Constitution or the Government of Nepal Act, 2004 V.S. (A.D. 1948)

Amongst Ranas, fissures had started. Systematic agitation by intellectuals influenced some of them. In many ways the constitutional Act of 1948 represented a compromise between two groups of the Ranas, viz., the one trying to liberalize the administration and the other resisting all kinds of innovation. In essence, this Act did not contemplate any change in the prerogative rights of the Prime Minister as "vested through the instruments of their sacred *Panjapatras* by *Sree Panch Maharajadhiraja* of Nepal."[90] Article 3 of the Act[91] laid down that the law governing the succession of *Sri 5 Maharajadhiraja* (King) and *Sri 3 Maharaja* (Prime Minister), "shall for all time be inalienable and unalterable." Thus the old order of family rule was kept intact. But, in another sense, by regularizing the structure of the Government under various heads and departments, the Act, as Padma Shamsher observed, "translated into action the deep aspirations I have entertained for such a long time to bring about an improvement in the administration of the country."[92] These aspirations were, as the Preamble stated, first, to bring Nepal in line with the advanced nations of the world and, second, to provide for "closer association of our dear people in every branch of administration and thus bring about enhanced prosperity and happiness to our people." Nepal had taken its first step to usher in a change.

### Features of the Rana Constitution

This Act was set to make far-reaching changes in the governance of Nepal. The most important features of the Act were the provisions for the establishment of a Council of Ministers, a bi-cameral Legislature and a Judiciary under a *Pradhan Nyayalaya* (High Court). The executive authority, as in the past, was to be exercised by the *Maharaja* either directly or through officers subordinate to him. He was, however, to be assisted by a Council of Ministers of at least five members, two of whom were to be chosen from among the elected members of the Legislature [Article 7b]. The Council was to transact all executive business and

> to lay down the general policy of the State, scrutinize the budget of the various departments, to give final consideration to the government bills to be placed before the Legislature, and to bring about co-ordination and co-operation between the various departments of administration [Article 11a].

Though the Prime Minister kept every thing under him he had to loosen his grip on the administration of the country. Administrative committees were appointed from among members of the legislature to deal with "all matters of administrative policies and measures pertaining to the subjects allotted to them" [Articles 13 and 14]. The Ministers were to hold office for a term of four years but they could be dismissed if they ceased to command the confidence of the *Maharaja* Prime Minister [Article 9]. The Act also provided for the appointment of an Advocate General to give legal advice to the Government [Article 9].

The Act envisaged the establishment of a comprehensive legislative structure beginning from the *Gram Panchayat* (village council), as the lowest unit, to a Central Legislature containing two Houses—the *Bharadari Sabha* and the *Rashtra Sabha.* The *Gram Panchayat* representing a village or a group of villages, was to consist of 5 to 15 members to be elected by adult franchise. The *Nagar Panchayat* representing a town or city was to contain 10 to 50 elected members. *The Pradhan Panchas* (Heads of the Councils) of several *Gram* and *Nagar Panchayats* were to elect from among themselves 15 to 20 members to form the *Zila Panchayat* (district council). The *Panchayats* of all these categories were to work within their areas and to look after education, health, transport, bridges, and public buildings etc. [Articles 16, 17, 18 and 19]. These were quite different from what the Nepalese had been experiencing for generations.

**Rashtra Sabha**

The *Rashtra Sabha* at the centre was to contain 42 elected and 28 nominated members [Schedule A]. Among the elected members 32 were to be *Pradhan Panchas* of the *Zilla Panchayats,* the 4 *Pradhan Panchas* of Kathmandu, Patan, Bhaktapuv and Birganj, and the remaining 6 representing different sectional groups and classes.[93] The *Bharadari Sabha* was to comprise between 20 to 30 members to be nominated by the *Maharaja* "to represent as far as possible the chief national interests and activities" [Article 22c].

The Legislature was to be a permanent body with one-fourth of its members retiring at the end of every year. The two Chambers were given equal status, though demands for grants were to be submitted first in the *Rashtra Sabha* and then to the *Bharadari Sabha* [Article 39c].

The jurisdiction of the Legislature was, however, severely limited. The list of expenditure charged upon the revenues of the State[94] could not be discussed, nor could a demand for grant be made without the recommendation of the *Maharaja* [Articles 38d and 39d]. Nothing could be said or done in the Legislature so as to interfere with

> the succession, position, rights, and privileges of His Majesty *Sree 5 Maharajadhiraj* or His Highness *Sree 3 Maharaja* as by ancient law, custom and usages established [Article 34b].

Further, the Prime Minister was empowered to promulgate emergency regulations which were to have the force of law for six months [Article 46]. He could, at any time,

(i) assume to himself all and any of the powers vested by this Act upon any body or authority.

(ii) declare that such questions as are defined in this Act shall be conducted in the manner prescribed by him in his discretion [Article 47a].

Part V of the Act relating to the administration of justice stated that "justice shall be cheap and speedy" [Article 48]. It was provided that the *Maharaja* should appoint a Judicial Committee[95] to act as the Supreme Court of Appeal in special cases, to frame rules and regulations for the administration of justice, and to resolve any difference arising out of the interpretation of any provision of the Act [Articles 52 and 67]. Article 53 provided for the establishment of a *Pradhan Nyayalaya* (High Court), consisting of a Chief Justice and other judges not exceeding 12, to be appointed by the Prime Minister. It was to work as a Court of Records and was given jurisdiction to supervise the lower courts, to issue general rules and to prescribe forms "in which books, entries and accounts shall be kept by the officers of any such courts" [Articles 55 and 56].

The Act empowered the Prime Minister to remove a judge on grounds of "gross misbehaviour or infirmity, physical or mental" on the recommendation of the Judicial Committee to be set up by him [Articles 54c]. Moreover, his rights to grant pardon, reprieve, respite or remission of punishments were guaranteed. Thus, on the whole, the *Government of Nepal Act of 2004 V.S.* preserved all the traditional rights which belonged to the *Maharaja* Prime Minister since the days of Jang Bahadur. The Central Legislature, in spite of its elected members, was so circumscribed in its rights and jurisdiction that it could not work better than the *Bharadar Sabha* of earlier times. The Judiciary as envisaged by the Act was to exist only in form, as an adjunct of the family despotism.

**Constitutional Act**

At that time, it seemed to be a drama, a sort of farce played on the people of Nepal. This however proved otherwise. The passing of the Constitutional Act turned out an important landmark in the history of modern Nepal. By regularizing the system of government in which the personal wishes, likes and dislikes of a single individual had so long wielded the force of law, Padma Shamsher laid down constitutional checks on the Rana rule. Secondly, by admitting two elected members to the Council of Ministers, the Act recognized that henceforward even the non-Rana members had a right, howsoever limited, to participate in official transactions. Thirdly, the principle of representative rule was incorporated so far as elections to *Gram* and *Nagar Panchayats* were concerned. Fourthly, certain fundamental rights, at least in form, were granted to the people.[96] Again, by guaranteeing freedom of speech and immunity from arrest to the members of the Legislature during its sessions, the Act provided certain democratic rights where there had been none. Fifthly, the mention of an Auditor General "to examine and audit the accounts of the State" [Article 62a], and a Public Service Commission "for the purpose of selecting qualified candidates to all civil posts under the Government" [Articles 65a] indicated, in theory, that new ideas had begun making inroads into the forbidden land of the Ranas.

This fact is made more evident from the objective of the Government as laid down by Article 60,

> As soon after the commencement of this Act as expedient, the Government shall provide for universal, free compulsory elementary education, and technical and higher education will be provided by the State to the extent necessary to prepare candidates for wider opportunities of service of the people of Nepal...

Five years back, to say even a part of this would have meant an act of treason. Hence, on the whole, the Act of 1948 marked an important advance upon the previous state of affairs. But before the Act could be implemented, Padma Shamsher left for India from where he sent his letter of abdication on 26 April 1948. He might have thinking of abdicating earlier but he could not implement. India was then under British rule. He abdicated when India was free and he did not any feare of reprisal.

## Revolt of 1950-51: End of the Rana System

*Maharaja* Mohan Shamsher, the new Prime Minister negated everything that his predecessor had done. He stood for everything that ran contrary to the liberal views of Padma Shamsher. In his first public speech he declared that he had come to bear the responsibility of ruling the country "in accordance with the traditional usages and custom of the forefathers."[97] As if to prove this, he issued a proclamation banning the Nepali Rashtriya Congress throughout the kingdom.[98] Even the limited autonomy which was conferred on the Kathmandu Municipality was withdrawn. Similarly, the new *Ains* (laws) which Mohan Shamsher promulgated in 1949 relating to freedom of person, of expression and of association, made a mockery of the fundamental rights as mentioned in the Government of Nepal Act. In brief, these *Ains* categorically laid down that any expression, speech or assembly against the interests of the regime would be considered as a cognizable offence.[99] Thus, for all practical purposes, the brief era of reform as initiated by Padma Shamsher came to a close. Nepal was where it been before Padma Shamsher had brought in his token reforms.

**Birth of the Praja Panchayat**

As hopes about the immediate realization of reforms began to recede, in October 1948 a group of young men led by Tripubar Singh, Gopal Prasad Rimal and Bijay Bahadur Malla founded, the *Nepal Praja Panchayat* at Kathmandu. This organization proposed to work entirely in accordance with the spirit of the Rana Constitution and demanded its immediate implementation.[100] At this time, a contingent of Rashtriya Congress workers led by B.P. Koirala reached Kathmandu to lay the foundation of a network of underground activities in Nepal. B.P. Koirala and other leaders of the Praja Panchayat were arrested.

As news about these arrests reached India, the Congress ranks decided to wage a second round of non-violent movement in Nepal. They received further impetus when B.P. Koirala and his associates began a historic hunger strike in jail which lasted for 21 days.[101] Finally, bowing under pressure, Mohan Shamsher released B.P. Koirala and assured him that his Government would carry out the promised reforms.[102] On the basis of this assurance, B.P. Koirala advised his followers to stay the proposed *Satyagraha* for a while. But soon it became clear that the Rana Government was not eager to fulfill its promises. All hopes about reforms turned out to be mere delusion and the Rashtriya Congress organ, the *Nepal Today,* bitterly commented:

> Hoping for reforms from the selfish Ranas is like hoping for milk from a dry cow. The salvation of the Nepalese lies in struggle, not in compromisory attitude. Too much of this attitude has already been exhibited, further exhibition will be dangerous and possibly suicidal.[103]

B.P. Koirala had shipted base to Patna. From there he issued a statement accusing Mohan Shamsher of "going back" on his promise and of "pursuing ruthless policy of repression."[104] Thus the prospect of a peaceful change-over from Rana despotism to popular democratic rule came to an end for all time.

**Politics of Cold War in Nepal**

Mohan Shamsher did not badge. He stuck fast to the policy of maintaining the *status quo* as long as possible. When coercion and force did not suffice to achieve this end, he began a two-fold policy of dubbing the Rashtriya Congress as anti-national and of seeking closer links with

America and Great Britain. He propagated the view that the pro-Congress elements in India were trying to subvert Nepal's independence. Even India was accused, though indirectly, of encouraging anti-national elements in order to impose her control over Nepalese affairs.[105]

It is Indian government was also disturbed at the unrest that was disturbing peace at the country's northern border. It is also true that the Indian Government advised the Rana Government at this time "to make an effort to keep pace with"[106] the rapidly changing world. But Mohan Shamsher completely misunderstood this advice. On the one hand, he came to believe that India was anxious about her own security and wanted Nepal's assistance to deal with threats from Pakistan and China.[107] On the other, considering India's interest in Nepal's internal conditions as undue interference, the *Maharaja* made overtures to the Western powers to keep Nepal's former position intact. Both the United States and Great Britain responded to his call because it did not conflict with the general objectives of their foreign policies.[108]

All this dragged Nepal into the midst of cold-war politics and made India anxious about her own security in the northern region. Broadly speaking, India's policy towards Nepal was guided by three main considerations—first, to keep Nepal away from cold-war tensions; secondly, to strengthen her northern border against Communist China's expansionist policy in Tibet, and, thirdly, to help Nepal achieve political and economic stability which alone could have been her best guarantee against foreign intervention under the circumstances.

These objectives were explained by Nehru in the Indian Parliament on 17 March 1950 when he declared that it was not possible for the Indian Government "to tolerate an invasion of Nepal from anywhere"[109] and that, owing to geographical and other intimate ties, the interests of the two countries were identical. He added:

> Freedom interests us in the abstract as well as in the guise of a practical and, in the context of Asia, a necessary step. If it does not come, forces that will ultimately disrupt freedom itself will be created and encouraged. We have accordingly advised the Government of Nepal, in all earnestness, to bring themselves into line with democratic forces that are stirring in the world today. Not to do so is not only wrong but also unwise from the point of view of what is happening in the world today.[110]

### Convening the Rana Parliament

Seemingly it was under the pressure of the Government of India, that Mohan Shamsher made, at least, a fake attempt to introduce some reforms. On 22 September 1950, he convened a Legislative Assembly which he described as the "Parliament of Nepal."[111] In taking this step perhaps he was anxious to impress public opinion abroad that his regime actually enjoyed support of his subjects. Moreover, the signs of disaffection among a section of the Ranas grew so alarming that it became imperative for him to announce some reforms. Hence he also declared that he had co-opted two elected members of the Assembly in his Council of Ministers in accordance with the provisions of Padma Shamsher's Constitution.[112] Further, his Government also claimed that it had set up about 158 *Gram Panchayats* during the year on the basis of adult franchise.'[113]

Similarly, he reported that the *Nagar Panchayats* of Bhaktapur, Lalitpur and Birganj had begun functioning, though he admitted that out of 21 elected members of the Kathmandu Municipality, 11 had resigned on the plea that it would not be possible for them to exercise their functions smoothly. If anything, these measures reflected a very poor attempt on the part of the Prime Minister to carry out the promised reforms.

They failed to satisfy the pro-reform elements, and the prevailing mood of the time was aptly expressed by the *Nepal Today* from Calcutta:

> What can be more ridiculous than the set-up of Parliament in a country where elementary civil rights are denied, where people demanding the implementation of the Constitution, now supposed to be introduced by the *Maharaja* are still rotting behind the prison bars? The age of befooling the world by such self-exposing assertions is long past. The feudal autocrats of Nepal are befooling themselves by such ridiculous announcements.[114]

**The King's Flight and the Revolt of November 1950**

Had Mohan Shamsher declared his reforms some years earlier there would have been some possibilities of avoiding the catastrophe which now confronted him. The anti-Rana movement took a sharp turn when the Nepali Rashtriya Congress merged with another party, the *Nepal Prajatantrik Congress,* in April 1950 to form the Nepali Congress.[115] In September 1950, the Nepali Congress took a historic decision at its Bairgania Conference to launch a liberation campaign in Nepal. At Kathmandu, trouble brewed to boiling point when a new conspiracy was unearthed involving some top-ranking Ranas.[116] It was even alleged that King Tribhuvan was secretly in contact with the conspirators.[117] This incident made the Rana Government more watchful about the movements of the King. The latter, on the other hand, fearing harm to his personal safety, began to lay plans to escape from the palace where he was virtually kept a prisoner.

Finally, on 6 November 1950, the King and his family left the palace and took refuge in the Indian Embassy at Kathmandu. Four days later, a special plane brought the King and his family to India. It was an unheard of event in Nepalese history. It focussed the attention of the entire world on the developments in this little kingdom. Instead of a mere family feud, the insurrection which followed the King's daring escape changed the whole course of politics in Nepal. As soon as the King reached India, the Nepali Congress launched its liberation struggle. "An unauthorized aircraft"[118] dropped Nepali Congress leaflets on Birganj and Kathmandu and about 300 armed men of the Congress "made a surprise attack on Birganj and captured the Governor and other officials."[119] After a brief scuffle with the Rana troops they set up a parallel Government at Birganj. Simultaneously, the Congress liberation force called the *Mukti Sena* struck at other places. In Eastern Terai, an assault on Biratnagar failed due to the stiff resistance of the state troops. A similar attempt to penetrate Amlekhganj, an important oil and railway centre, proved unsuccessful as a reinforcement of the Rana army reached there in time.

In Western Terai, the rebels under Dr. K.I. Singh captured Parasi, a small town 9 miles off Bhairawa, on 13 November 1950. But their attempt to march on Bhairawa failed after a short skirmish with the state troops. Undaunted by this reverse, Singh reorganized his *Mukti Sena* to resort to a kind of guerilla warfare which succeeded in completely disrupting administration in the entire Butwal district. Meanwhile, the rebellion spread from village to village in the form of loot, arson and stray murder of *Zamindars* and money lenders.[121] By January 1951, the rebel forces captured Dang, Deokhuri, Kailali Kanchanpur and Palpa in Western Terai. In the east, however, Birganj fell to the advancing Rana army on 20 November after two days of bitter fighting. With its loss, the fate of the *Mukti Sena* followed, more or less, an indifferent course.

The government forces had sufficient men and armaments. Mukti Sena was no match for them. In the first place, the *Mukti Sena* was not an organized army; it represented a motley organization of students, ex-soldiers and mere mercenaries. Secondly, its operations and campaigns were conducted in a very uncertain manner. There was little co-ordination or co-operation among the various divisions of the liberation army. Even the Congress leaders were not united in their objectives and the opposite directions towards which they pulled their ranks made military campaigns mostly ineffectual.[122] Thirdly, the supply of arms and ammunition to the *Mukti Sena* was too insufficient to conduct a protracted warfare. Finally, contrary to the presumption of the *Mukti Sena,* the state troops remained staunchly loyal to the regime. As the Rana Government boasted:

> The Army of Nepal is a jewel of the State, and our gallant soldiers have ever displayed and are displaying now unexampled heroism and promptitude when they fight the enemies of the country.[123]

### The Delhi Settlement of 1951

On the contrary, Nepali Congress had a clear cum. The leadership know that they could not achieve by taking on the Nepalise army. They were boanking on the popular upsurge. It followed in the wake of the insurrection scared the Rana circles. Even the people of Kathmandu broke out into spontaneous demonstrations which the Rana police failed to suppress.[124]

The two other factors which helped the liberation movement were, first, the moral support it received from the fugitive King and, second, the firm attitude which the Indian Government adopted towards the Ranas at this time. King Tribhuvan's negotiations with the Government of India through Bijay Shamsher and Narendra Mani Dixit. The talks concluded on 1 January 1951 and a week later, the Nepalese "Parliament" and the *Bharadari* adopted in substance all the suggestions made by the Government of India. According to the fresh decision, the Government of Nepal agreed to recognize King Tribhuvan as King of Nepal, to form an interim cabinet of 14 members half of whom would be popular representatives, to hold elections to a constituent assembly by 1952, to give legal sanction to political parties functioning within or outside Nepal and to proclaim a general amnesty "after arms taken up since November last are laid down, violence abjured, and a ceasefire effected."[125]

Explaining this changed attitude Mohan Shamsher stated in a public declaration of 8 January:

> The circumstances in which His Majesty King Gyanendra Bir Bikram Shah Deva was installed on the throne have been known to all. But as no friendly country, having diplomatic relations with us, has recognized the new King and as it has been seen that there is suspense and unrest among the people pending the settlement of this question, and seeing how mischief monagers have used the name of [the] King in the perpetration of disturbances, looting, arson, indignity over women, culminating in the taking of many innocent lives, and as according to the friendly suggestions made during discussions by the Government of India that His Majesty King Tribhuvan should continue to be King of Nepal, ... I have now to announce that the Government of Nepal consider the decision of Parliament and *Bharadari* a wise one and endorse it.[126]

**King Tribhuvan's Appeal**

Both the Government of India and King Tribhuvan welcomed the announcement. The latter in a statement of 10 January 1951 appealed to the liberation army to put down arms in the interest of the country.[127] After slight vacillation, the Nepali Congress also declared a ceasefire on 16 January. The tripartite talks between the King, the Ranas and the Nepali Congress commenced in New Delhi in the first week of February 1951. At the Conference, the Nepali Congress placed the following four demands as basis for discussion: (i) that all the seven popular representatives in the interim cabinet should be the nominees of the Nepali Congress; (ii) that the key portfolios should be allotted to the popular represen-tatives so that they could be in control of the administration of the State; (iii) that the cabinet should be responsible to the King so long as a duly elected Parliament was not set up and (iv) that reforms should be proclaimed by the King.[128]

As discussions continued, K.I. Singh with his 300 armed men embarked on a course of indiscriminate violence in Western Terai. As a result, the Rana Government was forced to come to an early decision. On 12 February a settlement was finally reached to the satisfaction of all the parties. According to the terms of the agreement, the number of ministers in the proposed interim council was brought down from 14 to 10 of whom half were to be Congress nominees and other half the Ranas. Three days later King Tribhuvan returned to Kathmandu amidst scenes of great popular festivity. On 18 February 1951, a new Government was installed by a royal proclamation. The long family rule of the Ranas came to an end that day. They had ruled the country with an iron land making the king just a figure head.

**Causes of Failure of the Ranas**

The factors which led to the failure of Mohan Shamsher were partly internal and partly external. In the first place, in spite of the over-centralization of power in the hands of the Prime Minister, the Rana state machinery was too weak to meet the new challenge. Its survival had depended on the submission of the subjects to medieval methods of oppression. But once the idea of defiance entered the public mind, the Rana system collapsed like a house of cards. Its authority ceased to exist beyond the capital while in the districts the local officials began to act on their own in total disregard of their higher authorities. Again, the divisions among the important families of the Ranas created new problems for the Prime Minister. His inability to enforce his decisions showed that he had lost the powers of a despot.

As a result, chaos reigned at all levels of the administration. But the greatest shock to to the Rana Government came from a totally unsuspected quarter. The sudden flight of the King threw it into a state of panic and disorder while it drew the attention of the world to the events happening in Nepal. The King's moral support to the revolt as started by the Nepali Congress gave it the shape of a national liberation movement. At the same time the stand taken by the Indian Government in favour of King Tribhuvan shook the foundations of the Rana regime. It signified a radical departure from the old British policy of stabilizing the Rana misrule at the cost of the people. Finally, Mohan Shamsher failed to appreciate far reaching significance of the Asian nationalist movement. He could not believe that the newly awakened aspirations for democratic rule and national independence could also overtake his country. Padma Samsher understood the mood of the people and what was going on in world more so in India. Had Mohan Shamsher carried on with what Padma Samsher had started he could have weathered the storm. But when this happened, he proved unequal to meet the challenge. Hence, the old order collapsed.

## Reference

1. Yogi Naraharinath and Baburam Acharya, ed., *Rashtrapita Sri 5 Bada Maharaja Prithvinarayan Shah Dev Ko Divviya Upadesh* (Kathmandu, 1953) 15.
2. *Ibid.*, 18-19.
3. For the early history of the Malla dynasties of Nepal, see Luciano Petech, *Medieval History of Nepal* (c. 750-1480) (Rome, 1958); for later history see Baburam Acharya, "Sri Jai Prakash Malla," *Pragati* (Kathmandu), 3 (n.d.), 35-85.
4. Sir E. Dension Ross and Eileen Power ed., *An Account of Tibet : The Travels of Ippolito Desideri of Pistoia, S.J.* 1712-27 (London, 1937) 317.
5. The Malla kings had minted coins for the Tibetans since the reign of Mahindra Malla, Raja of Kathmandu in the sixteenth century. According to Kirkpatrick minting of coin was first the monopoly of Kathmandu. Later the Rajas of Patan and Bhatgaon also sent silver coins to Tibet. He estimated that the annual profits on silver coinage had yielded Nepal, before the Gurkha conquest, over 100,000 rupees. See Colonel Kirkpatrick, *An Account of the Kingdom of Nepal* (London, 1811) 211, 217.
6. The history of the *Baisi* and the *Chaubisi* states can be found in D.R. Regmi, *Modern Nepal* (Calcutta, 1961) 1-42, and Balchandra Sharma, *Nepal ko Aithasik Ruprekha* (Banaras, 1951), 197-213.
7. Acharya, n. 3, 39.
8. For details see Regmi, n. 6, 52-103.
9. See Sylvain Levi, *Le Nepal, Etude Historique D'un Royaume Hindon* (Annales du Musee Guimet, Bibliotheque D'etudes, Tomes. 3 vols. Paris, 1905-08) (Typewritten translation, Indian Council of World Affairs Library, Delhi) II, 313-14.
10. Bogle who visited Tibet in 1774 A.D., as the Agent of the East India Company, reported that the currency question had become the bone of contention between Nepal and Tibet. See Clements R. Markham, *Narratives of the Mission of George Bogle to Tibet and of the Journey of Thomas Manning to Tibet* (London, 1876, 2nd edition, 1879) Ch. XV.
11. The Gurkha-Tibetan war is discussed in Schuyler Cammann, *Trade Through the Himalayas — Early British Attempts to Open Tibet* (Princeton, 1950); D.B. Diskalkar, "Tibeto-Nepalese War, 1788-93," *Journal of the Bihar and Orissa Research Society* (Patna), 19 (December 1933) 355-98, and

Alistair Lamb, "Tibet in Anglo-Chinese Relations 1767-1842," *Journal of the Royal Asiatic Society of Great Britain and Ireland* (London), 34 (October 1957) 161-76. For Nepalese source see Baburam Acharya, "Nepal-Chin Yuddha Sambandhi Smaranpatra," *Nepal Sanskritik Parishad Patrika* (Kathmandu), 3 (Baisakh 2011) Vikram Samvat [V.S.], 1-28.

12. For text of the Treaty see General Pudma Jung Bahadur Rana, *Life of Maharaja Sir Jung Bahadur of Nepal* (Allahabad, 1909), 7-8. However, some authorities consider this text to be fictitious.
13. *Ibid.*
14. Levi, n. 9, I, 39.
15. For a discussion of the War see R. Hunter, *Military Sketches of the Gurkha War in India, in the years 1814, 1815, and 1816* (London, 1822); Henry T. Prinsep, *History of the Political and Military Trans- action in India during the Administration of the Marquess of Hastings* 1813-23 (London, 1825) I, 54-213; and H.H. Wilson, *The History of British India from* 1805 to 1835 (London, 1858) II, 1-60, 419-28.
16. Major W. Brook Northey, *The Land of the Gurkhas or the Himalayan Kingdom of Nepal* (Cambridge, 1937), 58.
17. *Ibid.*, 59. For text of the Treaty see C.U. Aitchison, *A Collection of Treaties, Engagements, and Sunnuds Relating to India and Neighbouring Countries* (Calcutta, 1929) XIV, 35-69.
18. Dhundi Raj Bhandari *Nepal ko Aitihasik Vivechana* (Banaras, 1959) 155-57.
19. The meaning of the term *Bharadar* is not clear. Sometimes they worked as important state officials, at other times as feudal chiefs who helped the King in various state business. Together they formed the *Bharadari* or the Council which Kirkpatrick describes as follows:

    "This Council is composed of the principal ministers of government, and of such other persons as the Prince or Regent thinks proper to entitle to it, and its business is to examine the conduct of all public officers during the preceding year, to degrade, punish, and reward them, according to their merits, and to bestow governments, military commands, and *jaghire* lands for the ensuing year in all which it is the policy of the court to make frequent changes. ..." Kirkpatrick, n. 5, 87.
20. Regmi, n. 6, 20.
21. By a *Sanad* of Prithvinarayan Shah, the chief offices of the State were distributed among the noble families in the following manner — *Kappardari* to Kalu Pande's decendants; *Kaziship* to the Basniats; foreign affairs in regard to southern countries to the sons of Shivaram Basniat and affairs regarding Tibet to the Pandes; the Panthas, the Magars and the Chautarias were to serve as commanders of the armed forces.
22. Naraharinath and Acharya, n. 1, 20.
23. Levi, n. 9, I, 33.
24. Kirkpatrick, n. 5, 213.

25. Levi, n. 9, II, 320.
26. *Itihas Prakash* (Itihas Prakash Mandal, Kathmandu, 1951) I, 119-20.
27. Quoted in W.W. Hunter, *Life of Brian Houghton Hodgson, British Resident at the Court of Nepal* (London, 1896), 132-37.
28. *Ibid.*, 135.
29. Later he committed suicide in prison. For details see Baburam Acharya, "Bhimsen Thapa Ko Patan," *Pragati*, 2 (n.d.), 1-8; and Chittaranjan Nepali, *General Bhimsen Thapa* ra *Tatkalin Nepal* (Kathmandu, 1956).
30. Hunter, n. 27, 157.
31. For Matabar Singh Thapa and his time see H.B. Edwardes and H. Merivale, *Life of Sir Henry Lawrence* (London, 1873) I, Ch. XI, and J.T. Wheeler, *Diary of Events in Nepal 1841 to 1846* (Calcutta, 1878).
32. See Pudma Jung, n. 12, 49-58.
33. Sharma, n. 6, 311.
34. For English translation of the *Lal Mohar* see Satish Kumar Agarwal, *Political System under the Ranas*, 1846-1901 (Thesis, Indian School of International Studies, New Delhi, 1961), 236-38.
35. *Ibid.*, 237.
36. *Ibid.*, 238.
37. *Ibid.*, 238.
38. *Lal Mohal* granted by Surendra Bikram Shah on 5 May 1949, *ibid.*, 233-35.
39. In 1854, Jang Bahadur's eldest son, Jagat Jang, was married to the eldest daughter of the King. In the same year he himself married the sister of Fateh Jang Chautaria. Later his second son, Jeet Jang, was married to another daughter of the King.
40. Pudma Jang, n. 12, 171.
41. See Captain Orfeur Cavenagh, *Rough Notes on the State of Nepal: Its Government, Army and Resources* (Calcutta, 1851), 7.
42. The three important occasions when the *Bharadari* was called to endorse the decision of the Prime Ministers were: (1) in 1847 when Jang Bahadur declared the abdication of Rajendra Bikram Shah, (2) in 1885 when Ranoddip Singh was killed and Bir Shamsher proclaimed himself the Prime Minister, and (3) in 1950 when Mohan .Shamsher declared the abdication of King Tribhuvan Bikram Shah.
43. The practice of making presents on the landlord on such occasions as festivals or marriages in the latters house.
44. It is said that Jang Bahadur carried the practice to such extremes as to decide even the leave application of every soldier in the army. See Cavenagh, n. 41, 57.
45. Pudma Jang, n. 12, 155-59.
46. For an account of the assassination of Ranoddip Singh see William Digby, 1857 *A Friend in Need:* 1887 *Friendship Forgotten (An Episode in Indian Foreign Office Administration)* London, 1890) 75-81.

47. See Pereival Landon, *Nepal* (London, 1928) I, 248-49.
48. *Birtas* were, again, divided into several categories, e.g., *Kusha Birta* (given to the Brahman), *Pota Birta* (liable to pay the tax called *Pota), Sewa Birta* (given in the form of emoluments to government servants), and *Tiruwa Birta* which paid a nominal tax. See Mahesh Chandra Regmi, *Some Aspects of Land Reform in Nepal* (Kathmandu, 1960) 2-4.
49. Throughout the Rana period only one College and four High Schools were started. Admission to the Tri-Chandra College at Kathmandu was limited to the Rana and some other higher caste families. See D. R. Regmi, *Vartman Nepal aur Jana-Andolan ka Uddeshya* (Banaras, 1948) 3.
50. On 25 March 1847, at the head of a small army, King Rajendra Bikram reached Segowli. There his men began to desert him. After a brief skirmish, the King was captured in July and sent to Kath-mandu. For full details see General Pudma Jang Bahadur Rana, *Life of Maharaja Sir Jung Bahadur of Nepal* (Allahabad, 1909), 91-99.
51. Percival Landon, *Nepal* (London, 1928) II, 56.
52. By marrying Guru Prasad's sister, Jang Bahadur secured his neutrality. See Pudma Jung, n. 1, 97-100.
53. *Ibid.*, 155-61.
54. Trailokya Bikram's two sisters were married to Jang Bahadur's two sons—Jagat Jang and Jeet Jang.
55. For details of the conspiracy see Baburam Acharya, "Rana Shahi ra Sada Yantra," *Sarada* (Kathmandu), 21 (Chait, 2013, *Vikram Samvat* [V.S.] 1-8.
56. D.R. Regmi, *A Century of Family Autocracy in Nepal* (Banaras, 1950) 136.
57. Landon, n. 2, II, 59.
58. According to Acharya these were the first martyrs of the Rana rule. Among those executed were Col. Bikram Singh Thapa, Col. Amar Bikram Singh, Captain Shamsher Jang and his brother, six Thapas, Major Sangram Sur and his brothers, 5 Bisth, Ensign Ranadal, Subedar Pahalvan, 2 Karkis, Col. Indra Singh Tandon, Adjutant Banka Adhikari, Capt. Faud Singh Gurung, Subedar Jog Bikram Pande, Capt. Bhaktarwar Shahi, Lt. Chattra Dvaj Shahi and another person. Acharya, n. 6, 7.
59. By caste, *a Newari Brahman.*
60. It was closed in 1922 under the pressure of the British Government. See Ramji Upadhyay, *Nepal Ko Itihas arthat Digadarsan* (Banaras, 1950) 75.
61. Father of M.P. Koirala and B.P. Koirala. He was known as "Nepal's Gandhi." His free thinking made him so obnoxious to the rule that he and his family members were banished from Nepal. His later sufferings are described by B.P. Koirala in "Mero Jeevan Katha," *Pragati* (Kathmandu), 2 (Asadh-Sravana, 2011 V.S.), 123-32.
62. Krishna Chandra Singh Pradhan, "Trends in Modern Nepali Poetry," *United Asia* (Bombay), 12 (1960), 155.
63. Balchandra Sharma, *Nepal Ko Aitihasik Ruprekha* (Banaras, 1951), 430.

64. The exact line which he wrote runs as follows: "We care more for the foreign dog than for the native one, but when it comes to guard ourselves against thieves and robbers, it is the native dog and not the foreign one, sleeping in the sofa, that proves more useful." Quoted in *ibid.*, 355.

65. *Ibid.*, 391.

66. Recounting his reminiscences, Ganeshman Singh told this writer:

    At these meetings Muralidhar Pandit began teaching, through the medium of the *Puranas*, the qualities and duties of an ideal ruler. Sometimes he contrasted Rama with the Rana rulers and the meaning of his subtle lessons did not escape the grasp of the listeners. These meetings drew a great number of people, including even the scions of the Rana family. It was rumoured that even the King attended these meetings *incognito*. These meetings greatly alarmed the Rana Prime Minister, but he left them undisturbed because of the fear of infringing religious sentiments of the people.

67. Muralidhar Bhattarai, *Nepal Kranti Va Mera Jail Jeevana*, (Kathmandu, 1953), 3.

68. To reproduce what Ganeshman Singh said about this incident: Then one day a great religious procession was taken out from *Asantol* to *Indra Chowk* [Bazar places in Kathmandu]. It was an unprecedented event in our history. The entire route of the procession was packed with crowds, and from windows and verandahs women threw flowers and vermilion.

    At the end, a mass meeting was held at *Indra Chowk* where Sukra Raj Sastri gave his *Gitapravachan*. He discussed only spiritual matters which disgusted some members of the younger blood, like Gangalal and others. They demanded to speak at the meeting and, forgetting the time and place, they told their listeners that they were worse than dogs since they allowed the Ranas to kick them without even protesting. The police were only waiting for such an occasion and they jumped into the crowd. Somehow, the people managed to save Gangalal, but Sukra Raj was arrested. Later, Gangalal was also apprehended.

    See also, Dharma Ratna Yemi, *Nepal Ko Kura* (Kathmandu, 1956) 194.

69. See Jagat Bahadur Singh, *Nepal Praja Parishad Ko Samksipta Itihas* (Lucknow, n.d.), 4.

70. *Ibid.*, 5.

71. Sharma, n. 14, 365-66. Another event of importance was the revolt of the Gurkha soldiers at Almora who were about to be sent abroad for war duties. The issue was a small one, but the Gurkha Subedar who had led the revolt was taken to Nepal and hanged.

    See "Nepal's Fight for Freedom," *India Today* (Allahabad), 1 (June 1952) 23.

72. Regmi, n. 7, 227. Others, however, hold the view that Chandan Singh himself deserted the cause in return for Rana money. See Sharma, n. 14, 355, and Narendra Kumar, "Dehradun and Nepal Movement," *Nepal Today* (Calcutta), 6th issue (August 1949), 8-9.

73. Sharma, n. 14, 392.

74. For details see Chapter Six.
75. *Gorkhapatra* (Kathmandu), 46 (4 Asvin 2003 V.S.), 2.
76. For details see *Nepal Aur Uska Navajagaran* (Nepali Rashtriya Congress, Banaras, 1948), 48-49.
77. *Ibid.*, 53-54.
78. The Conference was attended by 125 delegates. Dr. Lohia was also present. At this time, however, the Rashtriya Congress decided that only Nepalese should participate in the *Satyagraha. Ibid.*, 55.
79. *Ibid.*, 58-68.
80. Some sources state that the *Satyagraha* was suspended because Nehru personally asked the Congress leaders to do so. See *ibid.*, 73, and *Nepal Today,* 1st issue (25 July 1947), 9-11.

    The Rana Government also quoted Nehru while asking the Rashtriya Congress to suspend the movement. *Gorkhapatra,* 47 (17 Jaith 2004 V.S.), 1.

    When interviewed by this writer, K.P. Upadhyay who was at that time the General Secretary of the Congress, stated that the movement was withdrawn because of Nehru's personal intervention.
81. *Gorkhapatra,* 47 (4 Jaith 2004 V.S.), 1, 4.
82. *Ibid.*, 4.
83. The experts were Sri Prakash, Raghunath Singh and R.U. Singh.
84. See "Report Read by Colonel Subarna Shamsher J.B.R. on the Work of the Constitution Office at the Inaugural Session of the First Legislature of Nepal on 22 September 1950." *Nepal News Bulletin* (Kathmandu), No. 24 (September 1950) (typescript). Henceforth referred to as Subarna Shamsher's Report.
85. *Gorkhapatra,* 47 (24 Jaith 2004 V.S.), 1.
86. *Ibid.*
87. In his speech of 26 January 1948 Padma Shamsher stated that even in 1851 a "parliamentary *cutchery*" [Court] was established at Basantpur, but due to popular disapproval, the experiment was dropped. Again in 1918 an attempt was made in the same direction with the introduction of an elective system in the municipality of the capital. "But there was much disorder in the city during the election, and communal quarrels and breaches of the peace occurred among the city dwellers, who had been living heretofore in peace and mutual co-operation, and so the election had to be abandoned..." *Maharaja Padma Shamsher's Inaugural Speech of 26 January 1948 Inaugurating the Government of Nepal Act, 2004 Samvat* (Free English rendering issued by the Law Ministry, Kathmandu, 1948) (typescript).
88. See Dilliram Tunsina Darṣhanacharya, "2004 Sal Nepal Sankritik Sanskrita Chhattra Andolan Ko Ek Jhalak," *Chhattra Doot* (Banaras), 2 (2012 V.S.), 34-36.

89. See Dhundi Raj Bhandari, *Nepal Ko Aithiasik Vivechana* (Banaras, 1959), 325.

90. Preamble, *Government of Nepal Act, 2004 Samvat* (A.D. 1948) (Law Ministry, Kathmandu, 1948) (typescript).

91. Since the Act was given the status of a constitution, the term Article instead of Section has been used throughout.

92. Padma Shamsher's Speech, n. 38, 1.

93.

| | *No. of seats* |
|---|---|
| Merchants and traders | 1 |
| *Zamindars* and *Birta*-holders | 2 |
| Intelligentsia (only a graduate or Acharya) | 2 |
| Government Servants | 1 |
| Labour | 1 |

94. Article 38(c) enumerated the following expenditure charged upon the revenues of the State—

*(i)* Civil Lists of the *Maharajadhiraja* and of the *Maharaja*,
*(ii)* expenditure on the armed forces,
*(iii)* pay, pension and allowances of public servants employed by the Maharaja,
*(iv)* expenditure on foreign affairs,
*(v)* expenditure for maintaining peace and order in the country and items classified for being spent at the exclusive discretion of the Maharaja,
*(vi)* salaries and allowances of the Ministers, the Advocate-General and the Auditor-General,
*(vii)* expenditure on religious *Guthis* and Trusts,
*(viii)* interests on loans and charges on account of Sinking Fund,
*(ix)* Any other expenditure declared by the Act or any other law to be so charged.

95. To be appointed from among members of the Legislature, consisting of not more than 12 members including two members from outside the Legislature.

96. Such as freedom of person, freedom of speech, liberty of the press, freedom of assembly and discussion, etc. were granted by Article 4. These appeared, however, too sweeping to be true.

97. *Gorkhapatra*, 48 (18 Baisakh 2005 V.S.), 13.

98. *Gorkhapatra*, 47 (31 Chait 2004 V.S.), 1.

99. See *Maulik-Hak-Sambandhi-Ain* (Gorkhapatra Press, Kathmandu, 1949), 1-4.

100. Regmi, n. 7, 303-04. The author suggests that the Praja Panchayat had nothing to do with the Rashtriya Congress.

101. Sharma, n. 14, 399.

102. In a press conference, Koirala stated: "After my release I had a long- talk with the *Maharaja* and on my presentation of the people's point of view to him, he seemed to be genuinely anxious to do something — to ease the

situation. . . .He left me in no doubt that [the] Government would concede them if they got a breathing space." See *Nepal Today,* 5 issue (July 1949), 7.

103. *Nepal Today,* 7 issue (September 1949), 3.

104. *Ibid.,* 1.

105. In an editorial comment, the *Gorkhapatra* wrote that anti-Rana elements were gathering arms in India with the full knowledge of the Indian Government. *Gorkhapatra,* 51 (16 Asvin 2007 V.S.), 2.

106. *Jawaharlal Nehru's Speeches,* 1949-53 (Publication Division, Delhi, 1954), 175.

107. During his visit to India in early 1950, Mohan Shamsher declared at Banaras, "We shall give assistance to India whenever she needs it and come to her succour when she is in danger." *The Hindu* (Madras), 16 February 1950.

108. The British policy was guided by the traditional understanding that the Ranas had been always faithful to British interests, and secondly, it wanted a continuous flow of Gurkha soldiers to fight the rebels in Malaya. The American attitude was mainly guided by the British policy. America was also keen to recognize Nepal's importance as a strategic location. For further study on the subject see Werner Levy, "Government and Politics in Nepal," *Far Eastern Survey* (FES) (New York), 21 (December, 1952), 5-9; Girja Shankar Bajpai, "Nepal and Indo-Nepalese Relations," in *Indian Yearbook of International Affairs* (Madras, 1954) 3-8; K.P. Karunakaran, *India in World Affairs* 1950-53 (Oxford University Press, London, 1958), Chapter VIII, 189-200, and Girilal Jain, *India Meets China in Nepal* (Bombay, 1959), 7-26.

109. *Jawaharlal Nehru's Speeches,* n. 57, 147.

110. *Ibid.,* 147.

111. "Speech of His Highness the Maharaja on the occasion of the inauguration of the Legislative Assembly of Nepal, Singh Durbar, Kathmandu, 22 September 1950," *Nepal New Bulletin* (Department of Publicity, HM Government, Kathmandu), No. 24 (1950) 1, (typescript).

112. *Ibid.*

113. Colonel Subarna Shamsher's Report, n. 35, 3-4.

114. *Nepal Today,* 7 issue (November 1950), 4.

115. The formation of the Nepali Congress has been fully discussed in Chapter VI.

116. The revelation followed the arrest of Sunder Raj Chalise who was a prominent worker of the Nepali Congress. His connections with ex-Commanding General Hiranya Shamsher were well-known. Later the ex-Commander's son-in-law, Captain Pratap Bikram Shah, was also arrested. See *Gorkhapatra,* 51 (20 Asvin, 2007 V.S.), 1.

117. See Sharma, n. 14, 383.

118. "Press Note of the Government of Nepal issued through the Indian Embassy on the recent events in Nepal, dated 11 November 1950," *Nepalese News Bulletin,* No. 28 (1950), 1, (typescript).

119. Press Communique through the Delhi Embassy on Insurgent Activities on 12 November 1950. *Ibid.*, 1.
120. Detailed accounts of the armed insurrection can be found in Sharma, n. 14, 404-16; Ram Hari Joshi, *Nepal Ko November Kranti* (Patna, 1952) ; Nirmal Lama, *Birganj Akraman ra Budhsingh Gurung* (Kathmandu, n.d.) and D.R. Regmi, *Whither Nepal* (Kathmandu, 1952), 107-15.
121. For details see Kashi Prasad Srivastava, *Nepal Ki Kahani* (Delhi, 1955), 148-63. The writer of this book himself took an active part in the insurrection.
122. In the west, differences between K.I. Singh and Gopal Shamsher caused enough trouble among the ranks. Singh's grievance against some of the top Congress leaders was responsible for his rebellion in 1951.
123. *Nepalese News Bulletin*, n. 69, 5.
124. Sharma, n. 14, 414-16.
125. "His Highness the Maharaja summons special sitting of the Parliament and Bharadari to consider Constitutional Reforms," *ibid.*, 2.
126. Declaration by His Highness the Maharaja on 8 January 1951, *ibid.*, 3.
127. *The Hindu*, 11 January 1951.
128. *Ibid.*, 29 January 1951.

# 9

# Security and Political Environment: A Nepalese Perspective

King Prithivi Narayan Shah, the founder of modern Nepal, emphasised that Nepal's territorial integrity can be preserved only through a defensive strategy by maintaining good neighbourly relations between the two giant neighbours. Nepal was "a Yam between two boulbers". He was right this dictum remains the reference point of Nepal's security policy even at present. During the period of rising British power, the Rana family oligarchy tailored a foreign policy favourable to British interests primarily to maintain their oligarchy, while preserving national independence and security.

## No War

The country has not fought any war since 1916. Even now the dynamics of relations between India and China constitute the basic ingredient of Nepal's geo-strategic thinking, and maintaining good neighbourly relations between the two remains the core strategy of Nepal's security policy. This policy was conditioned by Nepal's geo-strategic setting constituting the 1590 kilometre-long border with India and the 1414 kilometre-long border with China. The country's location bordering the Gangetic belt where an enormous share of its human and natural resource base is concentrated makes it critically important from the perspective of India's security and stability. Furthermore, Nepal's social-cultural ties with and economic interdependence on India are extensive and deep, and it is dependent on the latter's seaports for trade. For China, the possibility of Nepal acting as a springboard for Khampa like anti-Chinese activities in Tibet that continued until the mid-1970s is the most paramount and sensitive issue.[1] Nepal's geo-strategic setting renders it impossible to allow the use of its territory for any subversive or hostile activity aimed at either of its neighbours.

Balancing and responding to legitimate interests of these neighbours and not offending their sensibilities is critically important for its survival and security. Ultimately, it is successful diplomacy and not military buildup which can guarantee the security of small states. Nepal's reliance on diplomacy has been successful not only in ensuring its independence, security and achieving international status, but also for extracting development assistance for the country. The end of the British Empire in India and the end of Rana oligarchy in Nepal contributed to Nepal's expanding relations with the outside world. The expansion and diversification of Nepal's participation in the global system got further impetus under subsequent phases of political development. At present, the country has diplomatic relations with 113 countries and is represented in all major international organizations and forums.

**Broader Concept of Security**

The basic concept of security has undergone a profound change in recent years. The traditional concept with focus on military and strategic consideration is no longer sufficient; security of the people has assumed centre-stage. National security is still important, but its attainment is linked increasingly to human security. Security of the national border is not sufficient to guarantee the security and welfare of the people living within. The Human Development Report, South Asia, says[2] that national security cannot be achieved in a situation where people starve and arms accumulate; where social expenditure falls and military expenditure rises. Like the concept of development, the concept of security has increasingly become people-centred.

South Asia today is the most militarized region of the world, but that does not make the region any more secure. The mighty Soviet Union crumbled, despite its having nuclear arsenal capable of destroying the entire world ten times, when human aspirations for more freedom, better jobs and economic well-being could not be met. More human lives are lost every day due to malnutrition, hunger, disease and natural calamities than from armed conflicts. Even when lives are lost due to armed conflicts, such conflicts have been largely internal. Insecurity emanates from vulnerabilities which need not necessarily be inter-state; they could be intra-state with the potential to weaken and destroy state institutions, political order and even national sovereignty. Viewed against this backdrop, it is important to ponder about Nepal's vulnerabilities.

**Reasons for Vulnerability**

What are the sources of Nepalese vulnerability? Is Nepal's insecurity more due to our military weakness, small size, land-lockedness, a location which is sandwiched between two nuclear powers, or the open border with India which could be misused against either country, or due to poverty, economic deprivation, poor governance, exclusion of large proportion of the population from the basic needs of human life, or failure to meet the rising aspirations of the people? The vulnerability of a nation state like Nepal arises from internal problems—failure of the state, slow development, rampant corruption, erosion of institutions, crisis of leadership, aberrations within the system and the failure of the leadership to correct them, and influence gained by external powers and international institutions over the decisions of the government.[3]

The events of September 11 show that terrorism can pose a security threat even to the most affluent and militarily mightiest power on the globe. Maoist violence and terror has already taken a death toll of about 8000 lives in the last seven years. The experience of many other countries indicates that ethnicity, language, and religion could represent other sources of insecurity. Nepal could fall victim to this problem, unless appropriate interventions are made to assure adequate space to all disadvantaged communities of our national life. The presence of about 100,000 refugees coming from Bhutan for more than a decade could be another source of insecurity, unless appropriate action is agreed upon for their early repatriation.

The following four issues are required to be given a serious thought.

- Governance
- Political Stability
- Terrorism
- Ethnicity

**Governance and Delivery**

Governance addresses the peoples aspirations. How people are looked after how they meet thir daily needs. Their children's education, this is the concerns of the people who occupy high positions in government in executive and the judiciary, the arms of government. It involves the functioning of institutions, processes and relationships in the exercise of power, and through which citizens articulate their interest, exercise their rights and obligations. It is also linked with the degree of efficiency with which resources are managed in response to critical needs of the society. People are now questioning the degree of accountability of their rulers towards the ruled, the transparency process, and their own participation in decision-making. Good governance ensures equitable access to resources without regard to gender, class, ethnic or religious affiliation. The hallmark of good democratic governance is its ability to secure freedom from discrimination, want, injustice and fear.[4] Therefore, the manner and mode of governance is closely linked with the notion of security.

Human feelings suppressed under thirty years of the Panchayat regime suddenly erupted in the wake of the successful People's Movement of 1990. Expectations from subsequent elected governments were naturally very high. This period also coincided with the time when the communication revolution throughout the globe brought the country's poverty into sharp focus vis-a-vis the situation in other fast growing economies. Unrealistic expectations were further pushed by frequently-held elections in keeping with the worldwide trend and based on own experience with the performance of the general command and control economic policy adopted by the Panchayat regime. Nepal moved towards a market-friendly economic policy with reduced state role in business activities and the social sector where more space was left to private and non-government sectors.

### State's Role

The state's role became more pronounced in such activities as the creation of enabling atmosphere for market forces, building up infrastructure, expansion of education and health services, preservation of environment, poverty alleviation and decentralization of power. Nation building requires a coalition and creative partnership among the state, private sector and the civil society, for which the state must take a lead role with appropriate national and local level development policies. Naturally, in such a situation, people are closely watching the functioning of the state institutions which are responsible for delivering services, and showing results, and bringing about socio-economic transformation.

Let us briefly summarize the gains made in the decade of the 1990s under the democratic dispensation.[5]

Progress in the social sector includes:

- Improvement in Nepal's global ranking of human development from 152nd to 129th position;
- Human Development Index up from .0416 to .0490;
- Average life expectancy at birth up from 49.5 to 58.6;
- Literacy rate rose from 40 to 58 per cent;
- Net enrolment in primary education increased from 64 to 72 per cent;
- Girls to boys ratio in primary education from 56 to 78;
- Infant mortality from 102 per 1000 live births to 60;
- Contraceptive Prevalence Rate (CPR) from 24 to 39 per cent and
- Decline in percentage of population without access to safe drinking water from 54 to 20 per cent.

A review of statistics on infrastructure shows:

- Total length of roads increased from 6,700 kilometres to 15,200 kilometres;
- Electricity generation from 201 megawatts to 520 megawatts (including Kaligandaki A commissioned in 2002);
- Telephone line distribution from 57,000 to 256,000;
- Number of hotel beds from 10,300 to 35,000; and
- Additional 332,000 hectares of land under irrigation.

The indicators on macro economy show:

- An average growth of 5 per cent, with per capita income growth of 2.7 per cent, annual growth in non-agricultural sector being 7 per cent.
- Annual export growth of 18 per cent in dollar terms, and generally favourable balance of payment throughout. Foreign exchange reserves sufficient to cover eleven months' imports.
- Revenue/GDP ratio from 9 per cent to 12 per cent.
- Inflation stabilized at less than 5 per cent for the last several years.

Despite the general scepticism and all- pervasive negativism that one finds in the Nepalese society, the poverty level has gone down from 49 per cent in 1991, to 38 per cent estimated for 2000.[6] The economy has witnessed some structural changes. Agriculture's contribution to GDP has now come down to about 40 per cent from a level of 50 per cent, thanks to the rapid expansion of non-agricultural modern sectors, propelled largely by private sector initiatives. But now because of Maoist insurgency and other political developments the performance of the economy has not been very robust.

These achievements may not be spectacular or even comparable to high performances of East Asian, and South East Asian countries. Nevertheless, they are not far different from the South Asian norms, and adequate to prove wrong the often-mentioned "failure on all fronts" criticism. At the same time, these gains give ground neither for satisfaction nor complacency; nor do they provide justification for poor governance under successive governments. Economic growth has not been sufficiently broad-based to make a meaningful impact on the economy. The economic structure has diversified but new employment opportunities fall far short in proportion to the additional labour force entering the labour market each year. Performance of agriculture has fallen below expectations. Growth largely derived from the non-agricultural sector has benefited urban centres, thereby widening income disparities. Concerted efforts are required in agriculture sector to give it a puch.

**Politicisation**

Administration and executive has created some further problems. The already prevailing problems of inefficient civil administration, and weak public institutions have worsened with excessive politicisation under successive governments. Charges of nepotism and corruption, both real and perceived, are widespread. Public institutions do not properly deliver services to the people. Public sector enterprises suffer from excessive political interference and control. They already represent a huge financial liability to the government which is adding up each day. Public investment in the social sector such as education and health services has led to quantitative expansion, but this is accompanied by deteriorating quality. Increasing disparity in quality between public and private education has brought up social contradictions. The country does not lack good policies and innovative programmes for poverty reduction, but there is an implementation crisis due to poor governance, ineffective institutions and weak sustainability. The popular perception about the functioning of national institutions, including government ministries, cabinet, Parliament and judiciary, is not favourable. All these point out to weak governance which has been a subject of much public discussion in Nepal. This is time the politician give a thought to this.

**Politics, Leadership and Stability**

For the last twelve years governments in Nepal have been very weak and unstable. Although elected for a period of five years, no House of Representatives (*Pratinidhi Sabha*) has completed its full term. All general elections conducted or announced but not held have been of mid-term nature. It has become almost a practice to recommend the dissolution of the House whenever the prime minister senses a threat to his government. During this period, practically every prime minister has recommended the dissolution of the House, and called for mid-term election. G.R. Koirala did it twice. The first one was challenged in the Supreme Court but was upheld; the second was done with the consensus of all political parties, therefore, never questioned. Man Mohan Adhikary dissolved the House when a vote of no-confidence was registered against him; therefore the recommendation was overturned by the court. Surya Bahadur Thapa's recommendation to dissolve the House was not accepted by the King on judicial advice; Sher Bahadur Deuba's recommendation was challenged but was upheld by the court. However, he himself could not hold the general election and was subsequently sacked by the King under a questionable constitutional move.

The first government elected in 1991 saw only one prime minister. This was unusual for Nepal. Despite serious internal problems within the ruling Nepali Congress (NC), it completed its full tirm. Making and unmaking of the government became very frequent from the second Pratinidhi Sabha which produced five prime ministers with five cabinets under various set-ups. In the process of cabinet-making, practically all parties, except for some small radical left parties, have been parts of the government. In the third Pratinidhi Sabha, the NC had a comfortable majority; but even this period saw the making and unmaking of government with three cabinets under three prime ministers due to serious infighting within the ruling party, which culminated in its official split in June 2001. Naturally, changes in government produced not only more prime ministers, but also a large number of ministers.

**Excess of Ministers**

During the second Pratinidhi Sabha out of the 265 Members of Parliament (MPs) (including both Houses), 121 (45.7 per cent) became ministers. Within this review period, 55 (65.5 per cent) of the 84 NC legislators, 26 (29.2 per cent) of the 89 Communist Party of Nepal-United-Marxist-Leninist (CPN-UML or UML) legislators, 20 (100 per cent) of the Rashtriya Prajatantra Party (RPP) legislators and 3 (100 per cent) from the Nepal Sadbhavana Party (NSP) have become ministers, along with 3 (100 per cent) independent legislators. Between 1996 and 1997, Nepal had the largest cabinet of 48 ministers.[7] Even the third Pratinidhi Sabha dominated by the NC saw the making of some 79 ministers out of its 112 members in the Pratinidhi Sabha under three prime ministers, not counting the ministerial status enjoyed by more than half a dozen other MPs as committee chairmen and party whips. This was a record of sorts.

Another important political behaviour witnessed during this period is the resort to extra constitutional methods that the opposition parties started used in the sabha the wishes of the opposition. This practice started from the very beginning of the first Parliament when the opposition parties started physically blocking Parliamentary proceedings, and reached a climax in the wake of the Tanakpur agreement; they demanded the prime minister's resignation on the alleged "sell-out of national interest". This became very frequent in the second Parliament. The most notable instance of blockade of Parliamentary business through gherao of the Speaker's chair by slogan-shouting opposition members was in 2002 for 57 days, rendering the entire winter session of Parliament futile. Interestingly, this exercise against alleged corruption involving the prime minister in the infamous Lauda deal was taking place at a time when the Commission of Investigation against the Abuse of Authority (CIAA) was seriously investigating the case. When the commission was looking into the deal the opposition should not have raised this issue. The matter was sub-judice. This was very Lam-handed way of influencing public opinion.

### The Turmoils

Then there was another kind of furore and upheaval. Practically every major political party went through a period of serious internal turmoil. The Communist Party of Nepal (CPN) which split into UML and ML over the Mahakali Treaty have now reunified. Similarly, RPP and NSP, which were once divided during the second Pratinidhi Sabha, have also reunited. Internal problems, however, remain. The NC has now been divided in the wake of Deuba's untimely recommendation of the dissolution of the Pratinidhi Sabha. Such periods of political turmoil and uncertainty, marked by frequent government changes and untimely elections, tend to provide fertile ground for malpractice, populist policies and corruption. Naturally, allegations of corruption, scandals and malpractice involving ministers, MPs and politicians became frequent newspaper headlines, shaking the people's faith in their representatives. Increasing perks and privileges of MPs, like the import of duty-free cars and the pension scheme, became subjects of wide public criticism. These privileges were subsequently withdrawn. The politician however resented this withdrawn. They aired their views openly.

Such behaviour and political conduct naturally reduces the credibility of the leadership and erodes political values and ethos which do not contribute to the process of strengthening democracy. Government instability takes its own toll in civil administration, development policy and programmes and overall governance. However, one also needs to acknowledge that such behaviour is not uncommon in a nascent democracy of developing societies. While some may accuse Nepal's Parliament of being a problem for democratic consolidation and a challenge to governance,[8] it is also the only legitimate and effective institution for voicing people's grievances, articulating their interest and legislating reforms. Despite criticisms, 275 bills were passed in a period of 12 years, some of them of landmark nature.

The last Pratinidhi Sabha saw the passing of some anti-corruption laws which included the empowering of the CIAA with draconian power, which has perhaps no parallel in South Asia. The Act provides the CIAA with sweeping power to search, confiscate, seal and arrest anybody on charges of corruption. A corruption case can be registered against anybody who is alleged to hold property disproportionate to his known source of income, and the burden of proof lies on the accused. A high-level judicial commission was formed to look into the assets of all those who have held political, administrative and other positions since 1990. Parliament has also passed a historic bill guaranteeing women's right on parental property. The passage of the Local Self-Governance Act represented another milestone in the history of decentralization of power to local bodies. As a result of this administration at the grass-roots level will become efficient involving the least previledged also.

**Violence and Terror**

Now, terrorism and unrest have struck this pristine land. The biggest sources of insecurity to the Nepalese society at present remain terrorism and violence unleashed by the Maoists. In the name of "People's War" they have used murder, abduction, extortion, intimidation and all such methods for the last seven years, since 1996. Ambush and mining, raids and commando attacks, various types of sabotage and selective annihilation are the acknowledged methods used by them. Army barracks, police posts, banks and government offices have been targets of their attacks to acquire arms, ammunition and money, inflict casualty and cause damage to security forces and demoralize them. Political activists and local leaders in rural areas are selectively targeted for physical liquidation, abduction, and physical cruelties and other punishments in the name of "Janakarbahi" (People's Action).

This has forced a large number of social workers, school teachers and other local leaders to leave the countryside and migrate to secure urban centres, creating a serious problem of "internally displaced" people. Those who remain in the villages are forced to pay protection money. The leadership vacuum thus created in the rural community, particularly in hilly areas, is filled up by armed gangs of Maoist workers. Under threat and pressed for extortion money, many private schools in rural areas have closed down. In the wake of the Maoists killing large numbers of policemen, most rural police posts have now been withdrawn and confined to the district headquarters. Banks and other offices have similarly been relocated. Innocent civilians and children are used as human shields during clashes. Official figures released by the Royal Nepal Army on the cumulative combat casualties as of December 20, 2002 included a total of 7,730 deaths, of which 951 were civilian police, 102 were armed police and 238 soldiers. The rest were Maoists, suspected Maoists or civilians.[9] These figures do not include the killings of civilians by Maoists in the name of "Janakarbahi".

Despite terrorist methods used by the Maoists, their objective remains political. The result of the 1991 general election clearly showed that it was not possible for them to capture state power through electoral means. The radical communists who had put up candidates under the banner of the United People's Front could win only nine seats in a House of 205 members. Obviously, this led the Babu Ram Bhattarai group in the UPF to boycott the 1994 mid-term election and choose the armed movement to push their agenda. Some of their frequently mentioned political demands include a republican state, abrogation of the present constitution, electing a constituent assembly to prepare a new constitution, placing the army and police under people's control, abolition of privileges and special rights of the King and Royal Family and formulation of an all-party interim government.

**Raw over Foreign Policy**

Their demands relating to foreign policy include abrogation of all "unequal" treaties with India, including the 1950 Treaty of Peace and Friendship, Mahakali Agreement and withdrawal of Indian troops from Kalapani, etc. Their original 40-point charter of demands and those presented during the negotiations under the Deuba Government also included other socio-economic agendas. The Maoists have drawn most of their cadres from poverty-stricken rural areas, targeting communities and ethnic groups which are traditionally disadvantaged and oppressed and whose political space in national life is limited. When young people both boys and girls see no future in the society. They are easy targets of ertremist and other and social organisation.

Wherever insurgency and terrorism raise their ugly head, they their toll. The impact of insurgency on the economy has been enormous. It has drained away state resources; development activities in rural areas have practically stopped; and industry, commerce and the export sector have badly suffered. The thriving tourism business has nosedived. Consequently, the economy which had been registering an average growth of 5 per cent in the last decade, has slowed down to negative growth in the fiscal year 2001/02 when the Maoist violence intensified. The security budget which had stagnated for over a decade to less than 10 per cent of the total budget is likely to jump to 18 per cent (including army and police budget) during this fiscal year (2003-04). In addition to the 16 per cent budgeted, extra budgetary demand may be around 2 per cent of the total budget. This does not include the external assistance received from friendly countries like India, the UK and the USA. The soaring financial liability of expanding and the strengthening the army, the civilian police and the newly created armed police is reaching an unsustainable level.

If things continue like this, not only money meant for development will be spent on insurgency there may not be enough to meet current account liabilities. The Deuba Government held three rounds of peace talks during August-September 2001 but the Maoists broke the talks unilaterally and attacked the army barrack in Dang on November 23, 2001. This was setback to offorts for a perceful seltment. This led the Government to declare an emergency, officially describe them as "terrorists" and mobilize the army in a nation wide anti-terrorist operation. The rebels have launched major offensives against security forces even after the mobilization of the army. In a dramatic development, a ceasefire between the Government and the Maoists was declared again on January 30, 2003. Curiously, this happened immediately after the killing of the Inspector General of Armed Police, Krishna Mohan Shrestha, and his wife by suspected Maoists. According to the Maoists' preconditions for talks, the government agreed to withdraw the INTERPOL red corner notice and price tags on the heads of some of their leaders, and revoke the previous government's decision declaring them terrorists, as well as set free the five detained Central Committee members.

**Optimism**

Political forces within the country and international community, including the UN, have welcomed the move with cautious optimism. What ultimately triggered this dramatic development and whether this truce will lead to a long-term peaceful solution to the country's protracted problem is now a matter of much debate and speculation. However, there were compelling factors which must have conditioned this decision. The Maoists' side was feeling the pressure from the beefed-up army which was being fully equipped with sophisticated weapons and communication systems, night vision helicopters and other logistics rendering it now almost impossible for the Maoists to repeat the type of attack on army barracks they indulged in previously without massive losses on their part. They were also feeling the squeeze from the Indian side against using Indian territory as a safe haven.

Material support from external sources, particularly India, the USA and the UK, was pouring in to strengthen security agencies to fight the battle against terrorism. Meanwhile, new recruitment into their cadres was getting difficult with a large number of youth leaving the countryside for fear of being conscripted. This had led them to kidnap school children en masse. Maoist cadres on the ground were getting out of control and indulging in petty crimes. On the other side, the King's action of October 4, 2002, had created a serious cleavage vis-a-vis political parties, which blamed him for encroaching upon the constitution and siding with regressive elements. A four-party meeting including, among others, NC and CPN-UML representatives agreed to launch a joint agitation against the King's move. Even with the strengthened army and other security forces, the insurgency was assuming the character of protracted warfare. The economy was gelthing a beating. One bading newspaper reported: "the king needed a peace dividend to bolster his own legitimacy and that of a government he appointed ... after sacking an elected Prime Minister, the King had staked everything on the October 4 move, and needed to pull this rabbit out of his hat".[10]

**Ethnicity**

The diversity is reflected in ethnicity, languages, cultures, religions and costumes. It is believed that there are well over 100 ethnic and caste groups, and well over 100 languages and dialects.[11] Despite religious and cultural harmony subsisting for centuries, the disproportionate domination of limited caste groups, particularly Brahmin, Chhetri and Newar in politics, administration and education has been a subject of much debate and controversy. Accounting for about 37.5 per cent of the total population, these groups' share in integrated national governance is 81.7 per cent.[12] The Brahmin-Chhetri-Newar domination is strong in all segments of national governance including judiciary and constitutional bodies, cabinet and Parliament, political party leadership, local government and public administration, industry and education system, science and technology and culture and civil society leadership. Therefore, the constitution of the Kingdom of Nepal (1990) recognizes Nepal as a multi-ethnic and multi-lingual Hindu Kingdom. Nepal is a country of great diversity not just in ecological terms.

The most conspicuous case of non-representation in governance is that of the Dalits who constitute about 9 per cent of the total population, but have no representation in any of the institutions, except in Parliament and education in a token form. Their share in the integrated national governance is 0.3 per cent. The extreme exclusion can be gauged from the fact that there has been no Dalit minister since the restoration of democracy in 1990. Their position is nil in almost all influential spheres of Nepalese society. The Brahmin-Chhetri-Newar combination controls over 80 per cent of leadership positions in important areas of governance. The other unrepresented communities are the Madhesis and the Janajatis. Madhesis are indigenous people living in the southern plains of the Tarai who constitute 31 per cent of the total population but account for only 11 per cent share in the integrated national governance. Their share in primary national governance (including cabinet, judiciary and Parliament) is 17 per cent. Within the Madhesi community, the exclusion of Dalits and Janjatis is even more serious. Janjatis are indigenous people accounting for 22 per cent of the total population with control over only 7 per cent in the national governance. Their share in the primary index of governance improves to 13 per cent.[13]

The wide disparity and discrimination is apparent in their access to state resources. Dominant groups have disproportionate access to public goods and services, the labour market, and credit institutions; Dalits and other disadvantaged groups benefit much less from public services. The continuous deprivation and marginalization of the disadvantaged groups who constitute large segments of the Nepalese population could result in a problem of alienation creating an environment conducive to civil strife and insurgency movements. Radical movements grow out of extreme deprivation and exclusion. The Maoists are already using this soft spot of the Nepalese state to their advantage. They are mobilizing the Dalits and ethnic groups in the hills to their cause by promising distribution of political power along ethnic lines. Their slranle hold on there communication is becoming story day by day. Many of the youth from these faryatis have alredy prned thir sanks.

## Looking Ahead

Nepal does not face any threat from its neighbours be it Bhutan, China or India. It's vulnerabilities internal, which call for timely interventions. Despite problems and weaknesses, there is no alternative to democratic polity. Democracy is the best political system, but also difficult to administer. It calls for continuous hard work, nurturing and care to succeed. It grows and matures with trial and error through constant reforms and refinements. Nepal's future as a functioning democracy is clearly linked with effective functioning of governance institutions, efficiency in public resource management, effective delivery of services to the people, particularly the poor, disadvantaged and the excluded, and how far the economic and development agenda, rather than politics, will form the principal political agenda.

Democracy cannot survive without a high degree of social discipline; there is an urgent need for Nepal to shed the characteristics of a "soft state". It is easy to bring new laws and regulations, but equally important is commitment to their implementation. Democracy also entails certain duties and obligations on the part of its citizens and the civil society which must be fulfilled. The last few years have seen increasing strength of public opinion against political indiscipline, abuse of authority, malpractice and corruption.

This has helped in enacting stronger legislation and building institutions against corruption and abuse of authority. Consequently, corruption cases have been filed in the special court against former ministers, public figures and civil servants. The World Bank's recent decision to upgrade Nepal's low case status to base case in its lending operation was, in large measure, the result of reform measures undertaken during these years. The problem of the disadvantaged communities like the Dalits, Janajatis and Madhises with narrow space in national life and limited access to governance institutions should be taken up as an agenda of priority.

Addressing the problem of mismanagement of resources and leakage in public and public sector institutions is of critical importance to increase public faith in democracy. Delivery of services can be improved through involvement of local institutions and stakeholders in the management of resources. Nepal has already enacted the landmark Local Self-Governance Act to guarantee a strong role for local bodies in the management of public services. In order for this Act to come into full force, more than a dozen existing laws which contradict this legislation will need to be amended, and commensurate regulations put into place. This also requires building of capacity, a strong monitoring and supervision system and a clear demarcation of functions and responsibilities between local and national governments.

**A Fresh Review**

There is also need for a fresh review of the present structure of local bodies, particularly the Village Development Councils (VDCs) and District Development Councils (DDCs). These bodies as they exist now are not financially, administratively and functionally viable. Therefore, a fresh restructuring is called for. The royal action of October 4 seems to have cashed in on the popular disenchantment with the behaviour of political parties and their leadership. Some sections have tried to justify the action on grounds of "failed political leadership" and "misrule" under multiparty democracy. The royal action also seems to have undermined the basic feature of the present constitution which recognized the Nepalese people as the ultimate source of national sovereignty. Cabinet formation since then has bypassed the constitutional provisions. This, together with the hasty promulgation of new ordinances and various regulations to strengthen royal power on financial matters, civil administration, foreign affairs, army and police, would appear to strengthen the suspicion that efforts are being made to move in the direction of executive monarchy. The King has repeated his commitment to the constitution, multi-party system and constitutional monarchy; however this has yet to be matched with concrete action.

There is no commitment to a time-frame to hold Parliamentary elections nor is there willingness to accept the demand to restore Parliament which was prematurely dissolved. In the absence of the House of Representatives, the normal Parliamentary functions are being performed by the Upper House of Parliament which is a permanent body. But the present government is not ready to call the meeting of this body for fear of being outvoted, as the Upper House is heavily dominated by UML and NC members. These developments have now encouraged major political parties, particularly the NC, UML and other left parties, to opt for mass agitation. They have presently confined their action to mass meetings, mobilization of party cadres and processions. If public participation in the mass meetings organized by the NC and UML is any indication, their popular base remains intact. It any man movement has a popular base. That is the time when people at the helm of affairs should take note. In Nepal this is being ignored by the king.

Amid these developments, which indicate an increasing belligerence of main political parties against the royal move on the one hand, and the intensifying of Maoist violence on the other, which threatened to create chaos and anarchy in the country, the cease fire declaration came as a respite. Everything culminated after more than a month of secret parleys, obviously at the King's initiative. However, the initial relief and hope for peace is giving way to fear and apprehension. The government met with several pre-conditions that the Maoists had set to attend peace talks. They have also demanded the release of their comrades facing trial under various charges, restricting/limiting the movement of army personnel to within five kilometres of their barracks, repealing of the Anti-Subversion and Terrorism Act, greater access to government-owned media, greater freedom for their mass activities, etc.[14]

**Relaxion of Control**

The government has already relaxed controls on security checking. Curfews in district towns have been lifted. Scepticism is already being voiced about the Maoists' seriousness for lasting peace unless it is on their own terms. There is suspicion that they will use the opportunity to consolidate their position as they did in the past. The rebels' chief, Pushpa Kamal Dahal "Prachanda", is already threatening an unprecedented bloodbath in case of failure to reach an agreement.[15] With their "terrorist" tag removed, the Maoists are coming overground to "peacefully" mobilise the masses for the attainment of their basic strategic objectives.[16] As other political parties may not be venturing to go to the countryside as long as the rebels continue to hold arms, the present situation will give the Maoists tremendous opportunities to openly build and expand their organization under the shadow of guns.

The rebels hold enormous fire power which is spread throughout the countryside. In addition to arms procured in the private market and robbed from private households throughout the country, arms snatched and looted from government forces comprise about 1,600 .303 rifles and a large number of .22 magnum rifles, pistols, shotguns, sten-guns, 7.62 rifles, SLRs, 9 mm SMGs, 7.62 LMGs, rocket launchers, mortar bombs, explosives, a huge quantity of ammunition and other accessories. Only a tiny fraction (about 15 per cent) of the arms looted from the security forces has been recovered so far. Unless and until fool-proof demobilisation of armed Maoist cadres, and surrender of arms takes place, Nepalese society will never be free from the spectre of violence and terror; therefore this consideration should be the principal part of any peace package.

The rebels have been steadfast. On their part, they have not given up anything, not even a commitment to renounce violence. Even if and when such a commitment is made, agreement will have to be reached over various demands. It seems, during the behind-the-scene confabulations the government agreed to have discussions with the constituent assembly, while the Maoists accepted the monarchy within the constituent assembly.[17] Besides, the Maoists might seek the integration of their rebel force into the national security system in some form. The most interesting part of the new development is the complete absence of any role for the political parties. The refusal of major political parties to join the Lokendra Bahadur Chand government and their belligerent mood against the royal action of October 4, which they termed as unconstitutional, must have prompted the King to go his way.

It is, however, just a question of weeks, if not days, before political parties are invited for talks to find a solution. A round-table conference already forms one of the Maoist demands. Notwithstanding their respective positions at the moment, major political parties like the NC and the UML are not likely to oppose the proposal of the constituent assembly, if this is the only way to bring about peace, as long as there is commitment from the concerned parties to accept multi-party democracy, constitutional monarchy, human rights and sovereignty vested in Parliament which already remain the basic features of the present Constitution.

## Constitutional Amendments

However, if the constituent assembly is to retain the basic features of the present Constitution in the new set-up, the demand for the constituent assembly loses justification, because Parliament can, under the present

Constitution, make any other constitutional amendments. So far the Maoists have not spelt out the content of their proposed Constitution. If the substance and end-product may be the same, the process (constituent assembly or constitutional amendments) becomes irrelevant. One school of opinion believes that the process of the constituent assembly will ensure the recognition of people's sovereign right and may resolve the issue of legitimacy. It is for this reason that the NC has already opened the debate on the constituent assembly, and the UML kept the option open. However, there is another school of thought which believes that the constituent assembly could be used to strengthen the role of the Monarchy; hence the scepticism about this demand. Obviously, the demand for the constituent assembly is more of strategic significance than of substance for the Maoists. Should the demand for the constituent assembly be agreed upon, the rebels will be seen as victorious and the legitimacy of their violent method established. Such a scenario will give them tremendous psychological advantage in national politics, almost similar to the situation in 1990 following the successful People's Movement when the NC and the left front took over the reigns of power. In fact, Babu Ram Bhattarai, the head of the Maoists' parallel government, has been demanding the formation of an interim government in which clearly the Maoists would emerge as the leading members. If he is able to western interim government, this will clearly be a victory for his political movement.

**Fate of he Constitution**

Under the existing circumstances is of paramount importance the fate of the present Constitution. The Maoists want the abrogation of the present Constitution. As for the Monarch, his recent actions have already gone beyond the constitutional ambit. Regarding the constitutional forces, despite their commitment to the present Constitution, positions taken by parties like the UML and RPP are not in keeping with constitutional provisions. The RPP supports the Chand government. The UML is not averse to the idea of another interim government without Parliament. Only the NC and insignificant leftist parties like the Jana Morcha Nepal and Nepal Peasants and Workers Party are insisting on strict adherence to the present Constitution. The Constitution does not envisage a situation of Parliamentary hiatus beyond a period of six months. This period has already expired since the last Pratinidhi Sabha was dissolved to seek a fresh mandate which did not materialize.

This view has strong merit even in the context of the peace process: The legitimacy of any future arrangement to be negotiated with the Masoists can be provided only by a functioning legislature. The dynamics of Nepal's political scene is undergoing rapid change. If the newly initiated peace process moves forward, the scenario of the last decade—dominated by two or three constitutional parties—with the King as a constitutional head is giving way to triangular power centres: the monarch, constitutional parties and the Maoists. Any future political arrangement will be determined by the respective strength and negotiating skills of these forces. The Maoists who have drawn strength so far from the politics of violence and terror have yet to prove their popular base without arms. Used to violence they may find it very difficult. In that case, they have their cadre. Who may easily surrender their arms.

## References


1. For an analytical discussion on the subject, see Dev Raj Dahal, "Geopolitics of Nepal", *The Political Economy of Small States*, Anand Aditya ed., Kathmandu: Nepal Foundation for Advanced Studies, 1997.
2. Mahbub ul Haq, *Human Development in South Asia*, 1997.
3. See Lok Raj Baral, 'Governance and Security in Plural Society: The Case of Nepal,' *Security and Governance in South Asia*, P.R. Chari ed., Colombo: Regional Centre for Strategic Studies, 2001.
4. Human Development Report 2001, UNDP-Nepal.
5. Data sources include: *UNDP Human Development Reports, Nepal Millennium Development Goals, Progress Report, 2002, HMG: Economic Survey Reports.* Also see Statement by Ram Sharan Mahat at the Nepal Development Forum Meeting, 2002.
6. See publications from the National Planning Commission, Nepal, particularly the chapter on Poverty Alleviation of the Eighth Plan (1992-97) and Mid-term Evaluation of the Tenth Plan, 2001.
7. Dhurba Kumar, "Trends in Security Studies in Nepal", *Security Studies in South Asia*, Dipankar Banerjee ed., Colombo: Regional Centre for Strategic Studies, 2000 pp. 170-77.
8. *Ibid.*
9. See www.kantipuronline.com, December 26, 2002.
10. Kunda Dixit, *Nepali Times*, January 31-February 6, 2003.
11. See Krishna B. Bhattachan, "Challenges of Ethnonationalism in South Asia," *Nepal Journal of Contemporary Studies*, Vol. I, No. 2, September 2001.
12. See Mahendra Lawati, "Defining Minorities in Nepal", *Nepal Journal of Contemporary Studies*, Vol. II, No. 1, March 2.
13. *Ibid.*
14. See *Nepal Samachar Patra*, February 8, 2003.
15. See Prachanda's statement in *The Himalayan*, February 9, 2003.
16. See Prachanda's statement, *The Kathmandu Post*, January 30, 2003.
17. *The Himalayan*, February 1, 2003.

# 10

# Nepal: Quest for Elusive Peace

Recent developments have, reconfirmed that while the Maoists have been successful in gradually pushing their agenda through violence and intimidation, the four-party coalition government led by Sher Bahadur Deuba is increasingly finding it difficult to evolve a coherent strategy to counter it. Infact, ever since his reinstatement on June 2, 2004, Deuba has been trying to work out a framework to deal with the eight-year old insurgency, which has claimed approximately 10,000 lives. However, the limited success of counter-insurgency operations, the government's inability to forge consensus on the peace process, the continued opposition by the Nepali Congress-led political front, the emerging differences within the government, the withdrawal/collapse of state institutions and a sustained Maoist offensive have made the government increasingly vulnerable and catapulted the Maoists into the political centrestage. Amidst the continuously expanding sphere of Maoist influence, political uncertainties and growing international interest, Nepal continues to remain one of the most volatile countries in South Asia.

Deuba had no way out. He had been outflanhed. He visited India in September from 8 to 12. His effort was to strengthen his regime both militarily and politically. According to the joint statement issued on September 12, 2004, both the countries viewed the Maoist insurgency as a common threat and agreed to further intensify cooperation in curbing their activities. India reassured more assistance to Nepal's security forces in addition to existing support in terms of arms, ammunition, helicopters, intelligence sharing and training. At the same time, India also reportedly pointed out that there is no military solution to the Maoist problem and the government should initiate a meaningful dialogue process. However, Deuba's success on this front will be determined, to a great extent, by his ability to retain the legitimacy of his regime and strike a balance between the key players in Nepal's politics—the King, the political parties and the Maoists.

**Basic Problems**

If basic problems like as poverty, underdevelopment and discriminatory social order had been addressed earlier thing would not have come to this pass. Maoists could get an upper hand in Nepali politics only because of this. A fractured polity, the absence of an elected government and continuous power struggle between the King and the major political parties have provided the Maoists with an opportunity to control approximately half of the territory. Besides, the near collapse of development work and civil governance in violence-affected areas, breakdown of the rule of law, and lack of democratisation at the grassroots level sustain the Maoist activities.

**Maoist Influence**

The Maoists have been able to exert considerable influence in urban centres for example, the week-long blockade of the Kathmandu Valley imposed on August 18, 2004. They have also set up parallel structures of governance in many parts of the country. Though the visible impact of the blockade was not significant because the Maoists 'suspended it for one month' on August 24, 2004, they were, nonetheless, able to gain significant psychological advantage particularly the capability to cut off links to the capital city at will. The deteriorating situation was further aggravated when the Maoist-affiliated All Nepal Trade Union Federation (ANTUF) enforced indefinite closure of 47 industrial establishments, hotels and transport services to press for their demands, which include among others, making public the whereabouts of its workers and leaders who have allegedly disappeared from government custody, compensation to the families of those killed by the state, removal of the terrorist tag slapped on them and increased wages and facilities to workers.

Though the ANTUF agreed to withdraw its call on September 15, 2004, after the government agreed to release two of its detained leaders and make available information on the whereabouts of people 'disappeared' from custody within one month beginning September 22, 2004, it is unlikely to restore the confidence of the business community due to continued threat of extortion and the government's inability to provide protection to industries. Simultaneously, the Maoists continued with their violent campaign, attacking district headquarters, government infrastructure, security forces and civilian population. On September 10, 2004, the Maoists were reported to have exploded two bombs at the American Information Center at Gyaneshwar in Kathmandu. No one was injured in the incident after which the US government decided to suspend all Peace Corps activities. Development activities suddenly came to a halt.

**Lack of Counter-Insurgency**

Another factor that helped the Maoists the absence of counter-insurgency measures. That helped them grow from strength to strength The main thrust of counter-insurgency operations has been the excessive use of force and towards that end the government has worked on a policy of strengthening the Royal Nepal Army (RNA) with sophisticated weapons from India, the US, the UK, Belgium and other countries. It is estimated that approximately 25 per cent of the total national budget is now allocated to security. However, despite considerable augmentation of the strength of the RNA, the situation on the ground remains alarming. Though the security forces have achieved some success in counter-insurgency operations, the task is becoming difficult due to lack of adequate state presence in the violence-affected areas. As a result, the government has not been able to supplement the success of counter-insurgency in one area with strengthening/restoration of civil governance, institutions of law enforcement and democratic process.

The experience of the counter-insurgency operation has, therefore, necessitated all assessment of the broad direction of government policy and implications of continuous strengthening of the RNA. There is an apprehension that while the continuation of this approach may not be able to contain the Maoists militarily, it might catapult the RNA into an important player in Nepali politics with its own stake. It might further strengthen the King and weaken the democratic government and its ability to pursue a meaningful peace process. The impetus to the peace process is being reinforced by the realisation that there cannot be a purely military solution to the problem. The Maoists are in a stronger position as is evident from their tough stand on talks. Reports in the first week of September 2004 said, the Maoists have ruled out the possibility of dialogue with the Deuba government favouring instead direct negotiations with King Gyanendra and have reiterated their demand for a Constituent Assembly election under the aegis of the UN.

**Maoist Demand**

It is clear that the present Maoist demand will further strengthen the King and reinforce the perception that the government is not in a position to play a decisive role. Consequently, the role of the monarchy becomes important. When King Gyanendra appointed Deuba in June 2004, he had spelt out three tasks before him: to take on board all major political parties on important national issues, find ways to deal with the Maoist insurgency and prepare the nation for elections. If Deuba fails to deliver on these counts, the King might be compelled to remove him from office. Given the fact that an extreme Right Wing opinion within the political spectrum wants the King to play a more active role, the success of the present government will depend largely on the King whose inflexible approach has thus far only complicated the problem. The differences within the mainstream political formations have only added to the complications.

While Deuba has been able to form a coalition government with the help of the Communist Party of Nepal-United Marxist-Leninist (CPN-

UML), he has failed to evolve a consensus even within the ruling coalition on issues such as ceasefire, external mediation and elections to the Constituent Assembly. The UML reportedly favours unilateral ceasefire by the government as a prelude to the resumption of negotiations while Deuba insists that unless the Maoists show any sincere commitment towards a result oriented peace process; declaration of a unilateral ceasefire would be meaningless.

On the question of the Constituent Assembly, the UML has hinted that the issue is not closed and could be addressed during the peace talks. In January 2004, the UML presented a nine-point roadmap favouring either amendments to the new Constitution or the preparation by the House of Representative. On the question of external mediation involving the UN, Deuba has rejected the idea on the ground that the issue was an internal one; the UML, on the other hand, incorporated a possible UN role in its nine-point roadmap. However, it has yet to expand on the type of role it envisages for the UN in the conflict. Outside the government, the four-party alliance led by the Nepali Congress has refused to participate in the peace process and has announced fresh agitation against what they call 'regression'. Members of this alliance have been pressing for the restoration of Parliament and a consensus government that should initiate dialogue with the rebels. They argue that the new government will command more credibility and legitimacy, and certainly strengthen the government at the time of the talks with the Maoists. Nepali Congress Chief G.P. Koirala has refused to participate or nominate a representative for the high-level peace committee formed on August 12, 2004, under the leadership of the Prime Minister.

**Peace Process**

The objective of the committee is to coordinate the peace process and finalise the political agendas for negotiations. Reports suggest that he is holding a parallel dialogue with the Maoists in order to bring them to the political mainstream. While there appears to be a broad consensus on negotiating with the Maoists, it, however, cannot be achieved until the political parties bridge their own political differences and evolve an effective negotiating strategy. In the light of this, a pertinent question emerges: does Nepal need external mediation to break the deadlock. Those who favour external mediation argue that despite two rounds of ceasefire and negotiations in 2001 and 2003, the government and the Maoists failed to reach a minimum consensus, hence an impartial body like the UN could play a vital role in facilitating the peace talks.

The UN system has, on a number of occasions, expressed its desire facilitate peace talks and has sent special emissaries to explore the possibilities of securing a role. But the government has shown little inclination for any external mediation.

Does India have a role to play in breaking the deadlock? India's concerns at the stalemate between the Nepalese government and the Maoists insurgents are growing. The geo-strategic position, the open-border policy and a history of amicable relations make Nepal important in India's strategic calculus. The unbridled use of India-Nepal open border by the Maoists for shelter, training, supplies and arms smuggling, their deepening linkages with the Indian left-wing extremist groups such as the Communist Party of India Marxist-Leninist (People's War), the Maoist Communist Centre of India (MCCI) and the Northeast insurgent groups pose serious security threats to India.

Further, there is apprehension that Pakistan's Inter Services Intelligence (1SI), active in border areas, could forge links with the Maoists to destabilise the region. India needs to be watchful so that its core interests are not hurt in the confrontation between the Deuba government and the Maoists. India has been providing military assistance to Nepal and has also taken a number of steps to contain the Maoist activities on its soil as well as coordinating security strategies on both sides of the border. While it might not be possible to defeat the Maoists militarily, it is, however, critical to India's interest in ensuring that the Maoists are unsuccessful in exploiting a divided Nepalese polity. India has repeatedly emphasised that only the monarchy and Nepal's democratically elected parties can solve the Maoist problem, provided they work in unison.

Ways now have to be found to facilitate a peace process with an aim to restore and strengthen a viable and sustainable democratic government in Nepal. The onus for this falls on India.

# 11

# The Roots and the Emergence of the Maoists

The Maoist insurgency has emerged as one of the most serious political and security challenge in Nepal, with its disturbing implications for the adjoining regions in India. The rise of the dates had to Feb. 1996 insurgency is dated to February 19 per cent. It has, by now, taken a toll of some 7500 lives with many more casualties. The numbers of these casualties and deaths have swelled rather significantly after November 2001 when an open confrontation, almost a civil war, broke out between the Royal Nepal Army (RNA) and the Maoists. After about fourteen months of this civil war, the Maoists and the Nepalese government, now led by the King with a puppet government, agreed on 29 January 2003, to agree to a ceasefire and start negotiations; thus going back to the situation that existed before the outbreak of the civil war. In this paper, we propose to look at the nature of the insurgency and the prospects of its solution.

The Maoists took birth in India in 1949 with the aim of actively participating in the anti-Rana struggle of 1950-51. When the first general elections of Nepal were held in 1959, under a Constitution to establish democracy with Constitutional Monarchy the communists were still very weak and isolated. They won barely four seats in the elections and did not count for much political influence. The Communists got split on the question of support to King Mahendra's takeover in December 1960, from the then elected government of the Nepali Congress, led by the charismatic leader B.P. Koirala, barely after it had been in office for 18 months. The faction of the Communist Party that sided with the palace got support and encouragement since the King wanted to use the Communists for countering the Nepali Congress and all other democratic forces opposing his direct rule, which was subsequently protected under the Panchayat System.

### Evolution of Communist Movement

The evolution of the Communist Movement in Nepal was also influenced by developments in the International Communist Movement, particularly the Sino-Soviet split, but it may be a digression to go into the details of those developments here. It is pertinent here to note that at least until the latter half of the 1960s, both the pro-Soviet and the pro-Chinese Communist factions operating within Nepal supported the King and his Panchayat System. The only exception was the Communist faction led by Pushpalal, who still operated from his base in India and worked along with the Nepali Congress to oppose the King and his system. The interests of the Nepal-based Communist groups converged on opposing the Nepali Congress led democratic resistance to the King, as that was seen to be receiving support and sustenance from India.

The so-called anti-India nationalism was whipped up by King Mahendra and his associates and made a binding thread between the King and the divergent Communist factions. Towards the latter half of the 1960s and early 1970s, the Communist Movement in Nepal also developed its extremist sections. Their rise was influenced by the Chinese cultural revolution and the rise of Maoists in India who came to be known as the Naxalites, because of the area of Naxal Bari in West Bengal where they started their early operations. Following the footsteps of the Indian Naxalites, the Nepali Communist Party (Marxist-Leninist) also carried out killings of the local feudals in the Jhapa area of eastern Nepal during the early 1970s. This is known in Nepal's contemporary history as the Jhapali uprising. Nirmal Lama and Mohan Bikram Singh led different Maoists factions of the Nepal Communist Parties between the early 1970s and the Peoples' Revolution *(Jan Andolan)* of 1989-90. The areas of their ideological and military operations were located mainly in the western and central-western hills as well as eastern Nepal.

**Extremist Groups**

Around the 1980s, these extremist groups had been joined by young, well educated and ideologically motivated leaders like Dr Baburam Bhattarai and Pushpa Kamal Dahal-Prachanda.[1] The factional divisions among the extremist communist groups in Nepal from whom the Maoists emerged have been identified in the chart attached at the end as Annexure-I. The Maoists and other extremist Communist groups played an active role in the Peoples' Movement of 1989-90. They did not join the United Left Front, formed under the leadership of the mainstream Communist parties. Instead, they operated under their own umbrella organization called United National People's Movement (UNPM). It must be borne in mind that even during this movement, they were clearly and assertively demanding for the abolition of monarchy and the declaration of Nepal as a Republic. They were not happy with the compromise on a multi-party democratic system under Constitutional Monarchy that ended the Peoples' Movement against the partyless panchayat system in May 1990. They stood for a Constituent Assembly to draft a national democratic constitution. They were forced to accept the 1990 compromise as a 'first step'—'the necessary capitalist revolution coming before the revolution and the final establishment of the true democracy in Nepal'.[2] In pursuance of this demand, they were not initially inclined to participate in the general elections of May 1991 for a multi-party Parliament under the new Constitution of November 1990. However, they changed their position, perhaps with a view to changing the system by working from within. For this, they formed a two-tiered organization, of a revolutionary and a political front, known as Communist Party of Nepal-Unity Centre and the United People's Front of Nepal (UPFN), respectively. An analyst summarising the tactical shift on elections made by the UPFN said that the Front was "willing to contest elections in order to gain a platform to 'expose' the inadequacy of the parliamentary system but rejects the goal of securing a parliamentary majority".[3] Realistically, it was not even possible for the Maoists to secure a majority and capture power through a democratic electoral process.

The political front, i.e., the UPFN, participated in the elections of 1991. They put up 69 candidates and won nine seats, polling 4.83 per cent of the votes cast. Of these nine seats, they won four in the Western region (three in the two districts of Rolpa and Rukum), two in Kathmandu, two in the Terai and one in the Central region.[4] They emerged as the third largest group after the Nepali Congress and the Communist Party of Nepal (UML). The UPFN also performed impressively in the local bodies elections of 1992 by capturing a number of seats in various Village and District Development Committees. However, the UPFN did not prove to be a cohesive front. After the 1992 local bodies elections and in the course of functioning within the Parliament, the egos and ideologies of the leaders clashed.

There were attempts on the part of factions to dominate the organization, the Unity Centre disintegrated and the UPFN got split into two factions led by Nirmal Lama and Niranjan Govind Vaidya on the one hand and Dr Baburam Bhattarai and Pushpa Kamal Dahal-Prachanda on the other. It is the latter group that represents the Maoist insurgency in Nepal.[5] The UPFN led by Lama and Vaidya succeeded in securing recognition of the election commission for the 1994 election and also participated in those elections, but the other group led by Baburam and Prachanda was not recognised as a separate party. Baburam took the case to the Supreme Court where the judgment took time until the completion of the mid-term poll. The Baburam group, being not qualified to participate in the elections, boycotted them "as a face saving" response and also gave a call to all others to do so.[6] In 1995, this group called itself as Communist Party of Nepal (Maoist) and went underground.

### Maoist Attacks

However, this Maoist group did not stop at boycotting the elections: in the areas of their influence and dominance, like Rolpa, Rukum, Jajarkot and Salyan, they started attacking landlords and government functionaries as also those voters and political activists who had taken part in the election process. The unleashing of violence by the Maoists was also a retaliation against the severe police action against their activities under a military operation code named 'Romeo' during 1994-95. On 13 February 1996, the Maoists declared their People's War (PW) in Nepal by attacking and looting a bank in Gurkha and three police posts in Rolpa and Rukum.[7] This background to the rise of Maoists insurgency raises one question, i.e., was it possible to keep the Maoists functioning within the system as a mainstream political formation? There is no doubt that the Baburam and Prachanda group had committed itself to the extreme left ideological position including the "new democracy" of Maoist thought, but they could be pursuaded to carry on their ideological programme within the democratic and peaceful framework. They had did participate in the 1991 elections and were inclined to do so in 1994 as well.

Reiterating his faith in democratic ideals and peaceful methods, Baburam said:

> We want real new democracy which gives power to the oppressed, the peasantry and the poorest of the poor living in the villages. How, then, can people say that we are against democracy and that we are terrorists? Only if the government tries to resist democracy with arms we are duty-bound to do the same. We don't use arms on our own but we do retaliate. Terrorist are those who do not believe in the people's power.[8]

**Maoist Claims**

The claims of Maoists are exaggerated and diversionary. The fact however remains that the other group of the UPFN, led by Lama and Vaidya, which got recognition in 1994 to participate in the elections, has continued to remain within the confines of the post-1990 Constitutional and political system. Unintentionally, perhaps the system created conditions for the marginalization of Baburam and Prachanda group and forced them to work from outside the system. Earlier in 1992, when they were a part of the larger UPFN and were represented in the Parliament, they had submitted demands to the government and also carried out a Nepal bandh (country-wide strike) in April 1992. This strike precipitated a crisis for the government as a result of the killing of 16 people by the police while resisting the demonstrations. The resignations of Prime Minister Koirala and Home Minister Sher Bahadur Deuba were demanded during the strike. The government diffused the crisis by reaching a negotiated settlement with the CPN-UML, the main opposition party, but without any talks with the UPFN leaders.

This kind of political marginalisation was not desirable in a multi-party democratic system. The Maoists also felt that the elected governments were using the state machinery, including the police force, to harass them and contain them politically, particularly between 1991-94. We have mentioned the "Operation Romeo" against the Maoists in 1994-95, which had the support of both mainstream parties, the Nepali Congress and the CPN-UML. An international report on Nepal underlining the harshness of the "Operation Romeo" says:

> ... efforts directed by the Congress Party leadership to suppress leftist political activity in the mountainous West, including through violent means such as the police-led Operation Romeo, only galvanized both the Maoists and a rising tide of localized resentment. An international official noted, "the police reverted to the way they had behaved during the *panchayat* era because they had no other framework of experience", and even a senior Nepalese government official agreed that Operation Romeo was little more 'than the use of police for looting'. These heavy handed police operations are widely seen in retrospect as a disaster that provided vital fuel for the insurgency movement.[9]

**Support Base and Political Goals**

Anti-feudal sentiment has been strongest in western region region because of its political economy. As a support base of Maoists, this region become very significant. This region is poorest and most underdeveloped, and is also inhabited by tribal and backward social groups who have felt exploited and discriminated against at the hands of the upper castes. Extremist Marxists like Mohan Bikram Singh and young rebels like Dr Baburam Bhattarai come from this region. Baburam's Ph.D. dissertation on 'Regional Development in Nepal' also made him conscious of the poor living conditions of this region. Kathmandu-based think-tanks have produced studies that show that the Western districts are "the worst in terms of child literacy, child labour, landless households and per capita food production".[10]

A large section of these people also go as migratory labourers to India and the economy of the region is sustained by the remittances sent by them. The Maoists' roots have been in the Western mid-hilly region but in the course of the past few years, these roots have expanded fairly, speedily to other areas in the central and eastern regions of Nepal, particularly in the mid-hills. At the time of their first attacks on the army in November 2001, it was estimated that the Maoists had strong support in about 44 of the 75 districts, particularly in the rural areas. Nearly 40 districts are shown as 'highly affected'. The districts where more than 50 deaths were recorded as a result of the Maoists' activities were Rolpa,

Rukum, Jajarkot, Salyan and Kalikot, all in the Western mid-hills and Sindhuli and Kabre in the Eastern mid-hills.

**Rise of Maoist Violence**

We have noted earlier that the eastern region witnessed the rise of Maoists violence, of the *Jhapali* group, during the early 1970s. The headquarters of the 'Maoist government', established in November 2001, is in Rolpa. The social groups that constitute the bulk of the Maoist support are from the Magurali combination of indigenous people *(janjatis)*, i.e., Magars, Gurungs, Rais and Limbus. Besides them, the Kiratis, other Dalit groups and the Tharus of Terai have also joined the Maoists. Most of the tribals and Dalits are non-Hindus (Buddhists, atheists or animists) as well as non-Nepali speaking groups. They have their indigenous culture and want to preserve it rather than being dominated by the majority Hindu community. They approximately constitute 35 per cent of the kingdom's total population.

Drawing attention to these people, the Maoist leader Baburam Bhatarai says:

> The oppressed regions within the country are primarily the regions inhabited by the indigenous people since time immemorial. These indigenous people dominated regions that were independent tribal states prior to the formation of the centralized state in the later half of the eighteenth century, have been reduced to the present most backward and oppressed condition due to the internal feudal exploitation and the external semi-colonial oppression. They have been left behind by the historical development process.... Thus it is quite natural that the question of regional oppression of Mongol dominated eastern, central and western hilly regions or the Austro-Dravid dominated Inner Terai and Terai regions are manifested in the form of national oppression. There the regional and the national questions have intertwined with one another. Besides this, the problem of the Khas dominated far western Karnali region can occur as regional question, instead of a nationality question, and it will have to be tackled accordingly. Thus, according to the concrete situation, it is necessary to solve the problem of oppressed regions and nationalities by granting regional and national autonomy.[11]

This is endorsed and reinforced by the top Maoist leader Prachanda who says:

> Along with the developments of the people's war, a new consciousness fighting for their own rights and liberation is spreading amongst many oppressed nationalities of the country such as Magars, Gurungs, Tamangs, Newars, Tharus, Rais, Limbus and Madhesies. People's War has speeded up the formation of

> various national liberation fronts and expansion of nationality organizations. Similarly today, along with the development of People's War, a wave of organization and struggle has been created among Dalit castes at a great speed and a wider scale. Dalits are today rebelling against inhuman tyranny perpetrated upon them by the feudal state of high caste Hindus.[12]

However, this support is not spontaneous. While Prachanda's statement clearly underlines the organised support of tribal and Dalit groups, some observers contend that tribal and Dalit support to the Maoists is on voluntary and individual basis. The organizations officially representing the nationalities, and so recognised by the government of Nepal, have not publicly and politically identified themselves with the Maoist movement, particularly because its leadership is with the upper castes, as both Baburam and Prachanda are Brahmins. Underlining this aspect, Deepak Thapa contends:

> ... after initially flirting with the Maoists, the leadership of many ethnic groups has begun to argue that Nepali Maoism may not be the answer to the challenge of communal discrimination, for the state power will likely remain with the upper castes, no matter how the contest ends. In this reading, the Magars of western hills who have died in disproportionate numbers in the People's War are no more than cannon fodder.[13]

**Caste Distinctions**

There may be a point in the caste distinctions between the top Maoist leaders and other cadres. This has been highlighted recently in what appears to be officially sponsored mobilisation of indigenous communities and Dalits asking for redressal of their victimisation in Maoists' violence when the Maoists negotiating team had already arrived in Kathmandu in April 2003. But it should not be stretched too far because indigenous and backward people are also adequately represented, and are in the forefront of the movement at every level of the organization including the Central Committee and the Politburo. The Maoist leadership has consistently and quite forcefully emphasised the question of the rights of the indigenous people and the backward castes, and consciously mobilised them as the solid support base of their movement.[14] The nationalist organizations continue to make their demands and agitate against the government of the day.

The post-4 October, 2002 government of the King, headed by Lokendra Bahadur Chand as Prime Minister, has claimed to have made attempts to woo some of the organizations representing backward castes and 'nationalities' in the hope of depriving the Maoists of their support.[15] This indirectly underlines the fact that nationality and backward groups are indeed under the Maoist's influence. Without this support the Maoists could not expand so fast in the areas dominated by these social groups. The professional groups that are the backbone of the Maoist Movement are teachers and students both in the rural as well as urban areas. They not only propagate the Maoists programme and agenda, but also actively participate in the strikes. The All Nepal National Independent Student's Union (Revolutionary), popularly known a ANNISU, which is supportive of the Maoists' claims membership of 600,000 ranging from school children of age 9 and above.[16]

**Intellectual Dimension**

Both the students and the teachers add an intellectual dimension to the movement and provide an 'effective network and communication link between the leadership and the masses. The women's cadres constitute another significant dimension of the support base of the Maoists. Women also occupy important places of leadership in the military wing of the movement and they have helped the movement gather strong support from women in general.[17] In addition to those living in Nepal, the Maoists also look towards the persons of Nepali origin living in India as one of the most important source of support for them. Dr Baburam Bhattarai, during his education in India, had worked with Nepali students and Nepali expatriates in India and had helped organise them. The All India Nepalese Students Association (AINSA) is a very active organization working in India under the influence of the Maoists.

In his report to the Second National Conference of the CPN (Maoist) in February 2001, the Secretary General of the Party Com. Prachanda said:

> The Party has assumed the expatriation of millions of Nepalese in search of jobs in India as a significant characteristic of Nepalese society. In fact, the success of Nepalese People's War and revolution cannot be imagined if Nepalese dwelling in India are separated from it.... Nepalese front located in India has been playing a role of far reaching importance in the process of historic initiative of People's War and afterwards in its total development process.[18]

While landless peasants, workers and poor farmers have been the mainstay of the movement, the Maoists haven identified lower middle classes like school and college teachers, doctors, engineers, white collar employees, small traders and artisans also as their natural sympathisers and supporters. Even rich peasants and the national bourgeoisie have also been seen as potential, though undependable, sources of support to the movement.[19] The Maoists have systematically structured, ideologically cultivated and consistently mobilised this diversified social support.

**Ideological Programme**

Like every disgrintled, and anti-government movement, the ideological programme of "new democracy" adopted by the Maoists and the demands made by them to the government reflect the concerns of their support base. Initially the UPFN made an eight-point demand in February 1992, which was enlarged to 14 points within a month. While formally launching the movement in February 1996, the Maoists presented to the government a charter of 40 demands. This charter of demands cover three areas, i.e., demands related to nationalism, welfare of the people and the basic living conditions of the people. The demands related to nationalism are mostly concerned with Nepal's relations with India. The Maoists ask for abrogation of the 1950 Treaty and the Mahakali (1996) Treaty. They want Gurkha recruitment in foreign armies to stop. In the area of domestic governance closely related to the people's welfare, they ask for a Constituent Assembly to draft a new Constitution for removal of Monarchy and the special rights and privileges of the King and the royal family of the Royal Nepal Army to be placed under the people's control and for Nepal being declared a secular, not a Hindu, State.

As a means of improving the lives of the ordinary people, the Maoists have demanded that the land should go to the cultivator, there should be right to work, minimum wages for the industrial, agricultural and service sector workers, free education, control of corruption and all other requirements of good governance. (For the full list of these forty demands, see Annexure II, Section 3). Of these demands, the Maoists underlined two or three as critical ones, namely: making Nepal a republic, i.e., the abolition of the monarchy; establishment of an interim government to hold elections for a Constituent Assembly, in order to draft a new Constitution. They dropped the demand for abolition of the Monarchy in the course of three rounds of talks with the Deuba government in November 2001. But that was a tactical move to get the government to accept other demands of an interim government and an elected Constituent Assembly. They calculated that the objectives of abolition of the monarchy and Nepal being declared a republican and a secular state could be pursued through the Constituent Assembly.

**Design to Form Government**

Though it has not been specifically stated, there are firm indications that the Maoists want to head the interim government themselves, and do not want to leave these vital questions to be decided in the king's or the political parties' discretion. They suggest that the interim government should be headed by the people's forces, as was done during the 1990 revolution. Since this time the Maoists are in the forefront of the people's forces, they should take control of the interim government. Whether such government will have representatives of the political parties and monarchy is not made clear, but in their subsequence reformulation of demands, they have asked for a round table conference of the 'old' and the 'new' powers, i.e., the king and the political parties as 'old' powers and themselves as 'new' powers. This means that the representatives of political parties, or even of the king could be a part of the interim government. But Maoists wanted to be the dominant faction in the government. They wanted to run the country in their own way.

External influence and of China under Mao and naxalite movement of India has played a big role in the making of the Maoists. As noted earlier, the Chinese cultural revolution of the mid-1960s and the consequent Naxalite movement in India during the late 1960s and the early 1970s provided strong initial stimulation in the evolution of Maoist movement in Nepal. Com. Prachand and his associates also recall the 'positive' contribution made by Pushpa Lal and his faction of the Communist Party Nepal in the growth of the movement. In the Party documents, the influence and continued relevance of the 'Great Proletarian Cultural Revolution' (GPCR), launched in China under the leadership of Mao is underlined with respect and admiration, but it is emphasised that the party was "moving further ahead from Maoism and the GPCR".[20] The international contacts of the Nepali Maoists expanded during the 1980s when they became a founding member of the 'Revolutionary International Movement' (RIM), along with the comrades from the US, Latin America and other parts of the world. The RIM has been a competitor of the Comintern (Communist International).

***Prachanda Path***

The evolution and naming of the Nepali version of Maoism as *Prachanda Path* (Prachanda's Way) may have been inspired by Peru's *Sendero Luminoso* (Shining Path). Experiences of other Communist movements in Asia have also enriched the Maoist's ideological formulations and approach. Explaining this Com. Prachanda says:

> In this context, RIM committee kept on playing important role in synthesising experiences of the world .... Among all of them, those of People's War in Peru, initiated by Communist Party of Peru led by Com. Gonzalo had been the highest and most important. Also, the documents and articles written by the Revolutionary Communist Party, the USA and its Chairman Bob Avakin played an important role in lifting the debate to a new height. At the same time, positive and negative experiences of armed struggles in various countries including Turkey, India, the Philippines, Bangladesh, Iran had been the agenda for direct debates and interactions.[21]

**International Influence on Movement**

These Indian movement have also some extent bolstered Maoists in Nepal. People's War Group (PWG) and the Maoist Communist Centre (MCC), are specifically mentioned.[22] The Maoists of South Asia have tried to institutionalise their contacts developed through RIM. In June 2001, 10 Maoist parties and organizations namely Purba Bangla Sarbahara Party (CC), Purba Bangla Sarbahara Party (Maoist Punerghatan Kendra), Bangladesh Samyabad Dal (ML), Communist Party of Ceylon (Maoist), Communist Party of India (M-L) (Naxalbari), Communist Party of India (M-L) (PW), Maoist Communist Centre, Revolutionary Communist Centre of India (MLM), Revolutionary Communist Centre of India (Maoist) and Communist Party of Nepal (Maoist), got together to form a Co-ordination Committee of Maoist Parties and Organizations of South Asia (CCOMPOSA). The stated objective of this organization is to "Unify and co-ordinate the activities of the Maoist parties and organizations in South Asia". This organization has hailed the People's War led by the CPN (Maoist), and attacked "US imperialism in Afghanistan", "Hindu fascit BJP in India", and "threats posed by Indian expansionists to Bhutan and Bangladesh".[23]

The CCOMPOSA also aims at establishing a 'Compact Revolutionary Zone' (CRZ) that will join Nepal with the parts of India in Bihar, Jharkhand and stretching up to Andhra Pradesh to link up the areas under the influence of the PWG. This zone, if established, can become the base for launching a people's war in the whole of India and even South Asia. This networking with other South Asian Maoist Parties, particularly those in India, have surely provided required support to the Nepal Maoists in their current People's War. While it is necessary to identify and understand the external ideological and organizational links of the Nepalese Maoists, we must clearly keep in mind that the Nepalese uprising is largely and authentically nationalist and the Nepalese Maoists are the most motivated, organised and powerful among their fraternal groups in South Asia.

For instance, a number of Maoist groups in India have been operating for more than two decades in various parts, but there is no indication of their emerging as a system-threatening force. There is no evidence available that shows that the Maoists have either been prompted, encouraged or funded by any outside forces. Their external links do not make them dependent in their activities in Nepal though they may use their fraternal links outside Nepal, in India and elsewhere, to seek shelter, medical help, supply of arms and ammunition, publicity and even financial support. Their funding has come mostly from exactions, looting of Nepalese banks and contributions from Nepalese diaspora in places like Hong Kong and the US.

**Funds**

According to one estimate, there collections through these sources may add up to somewhere between $64 million to 128 million.[24] There are reports of the Maoists of Nepal procuring arms through some of the insurgents groups of India and South Asia like the PWG, MCC, ULFA, BODO, KLO (Kamtapur Liberation Organization) and LTTE, though hard evidence in such case is difficult to come by. Most of the money and arms use by the Nepal Maoists so far seem to have come from the looting of Nepalese banks and police and army's store. They have also collected money through extortions and other coercive methods within Nepal. Some report emanating in the Indian media also link the ISI of Pakistan with the Maoists, but in that regard too, there is a dependable evidence.

The ISI may as well try and explore the Maoists' violence to their advantage as it hurts India but the Maoists are aware that their association with the India can prove counter-productive and suicidal for them. The political goal of the Maoists is therefore very clear viz., to capture power in the name of establishing 'new democracy'. The parameters of "new democracy" have been explained in the ideological programme, emphasizing the justice and equality for the backward, indigenous and suffering people of Nepal. These parameters are constantly being refined and articulated as the movement evolve but the bottom line is that the "new democracy" will have any room for the dominance of feudal forces, and capitalist' democratic parties.[25] The Maoists are conscious of the fact that it may not be possible for them to capture total power and establish 'new democracy' in one go, even through the people's war, launched by them since 1996.

Tactically, therefore, they are willing to move in stages and accept to work within the 'capitalist democratic' framework but not under the monarchy. As such they are willing to have a multiparty system. In one of his interviews to an Indian English daily, Com. Prachanda, the supremo of the Maoists said: "We are definitely against one-party dictatorship. There will be full freedom to all the anti-feudal and anti-imperialist political parties in New Democracy".[26] The people's war has been launched by the Maoists since February 1996 to capture power and create conditions for "new democracy".

**Seven Years of Insurgency**

It is for the last seven years, that the Maoists are waging a violent struggle in the name of 'People's War' (PW) for advancing their political goals. Two critical aspects of the PW deserve careful understanding, viz., its 'military line and its strategy of forging a 'united front'. On the military line, the PW is envisaged as a 'total war'. This 'total war' is defined by the Maoist leadership as:

> Stress on rural works, but do not leave the urban ones, too; stress on the illegal works but don't give up legal possibilities, too; stress on certain strategic areas, but do not leave other areas, too; stress on the works of war, but don't leave the mass movements, too; stress on the underground works, but do not leave the over ground ones, too; stress on the rural class-struggle but don't leave the countrywide struggles, too; stress on the guerrilla warfare but do not leave the political propaganda and exposure, too; stress on the dissemination inside the country but don't leave the worldwide publicity, too; stress on the works of the formation of army, but don't leave the works of the formation of fronts organizations, too; stress on depending upon your organizations and forces, but don't give up actional (sick, operational/practical) unitv and taking support, co-operation from international community, too.[27]

Nepal has no direct access to the sea. The Maoists are aware of this geographical limitation. If they try to establish their base in India bordering Nepal or in Bhutan, these two governments will permit this. However, the western and eastern hilly regions have been considered as providing ideal theatre. Accordingly, the PW and the regional military commands have been organize to be compatible with the east-west hilly region with their 'north-south flows'. The work on the strategy of waging war with the 'storm of the armed masses', and for this three-tiered military formations have been built up. They are: the militants or the main military force, which can be called the hardcore fighter force; the defence or the supporting and reserve force, and lastly; the volunteer groups, i.e., people's militia. There is a clear emphasis in raising a Peoples' Liberation Army (PLA), comprising of a permanent hardcore fighting force. Besides, there is also clear emphasis in building a 'base area', i.e., control of territory along with the guerrilla zone. The base area and the guerrilla zones have to be the 'areas of general action' and then the 'cities, including the capital, for propaganda zone'. The attempt of the leadership is to keep a harmony among these formations through the evolution of a synthesis between the controlled 'centralised planning and decentralized action' on the one hand and between political and military action on the other.[28] It is difficult to make an approximate assessment of the armed strength of the Maoists. Speculative assessments range from 5000 to 8000 hardcore fighters, but they can even be more.

**Strength and Support Base**

After their latest effective operations in Jumla and Gurkha in the month of November 2002, Baburam Bhattarai answering a question on their army's strength and funding support, told *Washington Times* in an interview on 14 December 2002:

> We have in recent months carried out highly successful military raids at district and zonal headquarters simultaneously in the Western and Eastern regions by brigade level formations of the People's Liberation Army. At the same time, we have conducted smaller raids, ambushes, sabotages, etc. in all the 75 districts of the country. We hope this will help you to make an intelligent guess about the strength and logistics of the PLA.
>
> Since ours is a genuine People's War, the people themselves are the real source of our finances. We also collect taxes from businessmen and industrialists, and occasionally seize from banks. As regards the sources of weapons, it is an open secret that our enemy is the greatest source so far. As Mao said, even the foreign powers may supply us via our enemy.

Accordingly to Maoists they have kept their political moves flexible to isolate their worst adversary at a given point of time by joining hands with all possible other forces. Such alliances are changed when the main challenge to them shifts. Their flexibility is also reflected in their demands, such as the dropping of the demand for Republic, and also the occasional offer of ceasefire and negotiations. It must, however, be noticed that this flexibility is tactical to serve the interest of their basic goals. It helps them to regroup, project the image of being a reasonable and politically oriented organization and keep the initiative with them when conditions do not seem to be favourable. Two instances may be recalled to illustrate the point. While launching the PW, the Maoists faced greatest challenge from the Nepalese governments headed by the mainstream political parties like the Nepalese Congress and the CPN-UML. Accordingly, during the period between February 1996 to June 2001, the main targets of the Maoists' violence were the NC and the UML cadres and political activists and supporters along with the key state functionaries.

**Police Operations**

This was because the police operations against them were directed by the government headed by the political parties. During this period, they had a tactical understanding and tacit co-operation with King Birendra, who on his part, might not have been averse to let the Bhattarai Maoists weaken and discredit the political parties. Baburam has admitted of having a "working unity" and understanding on some principles with King Birendra.[29] An advantage of this working unity to the Maoists was that King Birendra dilly dallied the Koirala government's requests for the use of army against the Maoists, and also, the King did not approve, until 2001, the government's proposal for raising a new armed police force to fight the Maoists.

The Maoists have changed their tracks after the massacre of king Birendra and his family in June 2001, which led them to launch their first direct attacks on the Royal Nepalese army in November 2001.

In the aftermath of the massacre of the Royal family, the Maoists described the new King as a 'murderer' and identified themselves openly with the slain King Birendra in order to harness popular support and sympathy. Particularly after King Gyanendra's take over on 4 October 2002, the Maoists have established contacts with the political parties and are now insisting on having a round table with the King, along with the political parties in pursuance of their objective of forming an interim government to hold elections for a Constituent Assembly.[30] The Maoists are also in continuous touch with the various political parties to mobilize their support in driving hard bargain with the King. The resilience in their approach is also evident with respect to the external dimension of their 'revolution'. For instance, two countries singled out for the strongest criticism in their debates and programme are the US and India.

**Seeking India's Help**

Soon after their attacks on the army pockets in November 2001, that escalated the civil war, the Maoist leadership has tried to reach the Government of India to seek India's help, atleast by way of non-interference against their activities, in their struggle. They are conscious and politically sensitive to the fact that India is a critical factor not only in winning their struggle but also afterwards. Any substantial Indian intervention against their People's War (PW) can frustrate their goal of capturing power in Nepal and even after their capture of power, they may not be able to either stabilize themselves or carry out their political and economic programme without India's co-operation.

For this tactical reason, the Maoists have also been sending messages to the US not to treat them as terrorists. They are also not averse to the possibility of external 'mediation or facilitation' by a 'truly independent and impartial force or organization', 'if necessary'.[31] With the combination of their military line and political strategy, the Maoists have waged a ferocious war for the past seven years. Their violent campaign started systematically after the formal announcement of the People's War in 1996.

Within two years, they establish their military credibility, and their political influence and control grew in leaps and bounds. Even after absorbing massive police onslaught through Operation 'Kilo-Sierra' 1998, they carried out successful raids in Dhanusha, Rolpo and Salyan districts. A major Maoist operation occurred in September 2000 in Dolpa district headquarters Dune Bazar which shook the confidence of the government forces. Until November 2001, all these operations were targeted againt the armed police of Nepal. It is interesting to note that Maoists did not attack the army, and moreover the RN did not come to the rescue and protection of the police, in Dune Bazar, it had been stationed at a distance they would barely take a 40 minutes'[32] drive. This was the gain resulting from their tacit understanding with the King Birendra.

**First Attack**

The first Maoist attack on the army came on 23 November 2001. Much had changed in Nepalese political situation since the Dolpa operations of the Maoists in September 2000. King Birendra and his family were assassinated in June 2001 in a ghastly incident in the Palace at the hand of Crown prince, who was himself killed by a bullet at the end of the drama. Gyanendra, King Birendra's brother became the new King. This was followed by the changing Deuba, leading a breakaway faction of the Nepali Congress displaced G.P. Koirala as Prime Minister. The Maoist termed the Royal Palace massacre as a conspiracy involving the new King, the US and India.[33]

The new Deuba government initiated talks with the Maoists in August 2001, which had its third round in November. Soon after the third round, the Maoists walked out of the talks and launched widespread attacks on army and police posts in Dang, Pyuthan, Syangja and Surkhet districts causing extensive damage. They declared the setting up of a 37-member United Revolutionary Peoples' Council headed by Dr Bhattarai, with headquarters in Rolpa. These attacks also came after September 11, when almost the whole world had committed itself to fighting terrorism and the US bombing of Afghanistan was still in progress. The question that is generally asked is why the Maoists walked out of talks and escalated violence when international atmosphere was not favourable. One explanation offered in media circles widely in Nepal was that there were serious disagreements between the political and the military leadership of the rebels on the issue of talks with the government.

**Counter-Attack**

Accordingly, the military wing, supposedly headed by Col. Ram Bahadur Thapa *a.k.a.* Com. Badal, launched the attacks on his own initiative to force the withdrawal of political leadership from talks.[34] The explanation sounds plausible, but one must keep in mind that Prachanda was the institutional head of both the political and military wings of the party. Further, even if there were differences, they did not affect the subsequent military operations and the political line, because soon after these attacks, the political leaders issued several statements to justify their violation of ceasefire, withdrawal from talks and resort to military action.

Their contention was that the government side was not willing, or even in a position to make a compromise for peaceful resolution of the problem. Instead, there were preparations by the army to launch their operations against the Maoists as there was no let-up in the government's harassment of the Maoists' cadres in villages and no releasing of those who were in prisons.

According to Prachanda:

> The Deuba government not only made nationwide preparations for military offensive but even banned the peaceful mass rallies. Even then we exercised maximum patience and proposed the convening of constituent assembly which was proclaimed even by King Tribhuwan after the Delhi Agreement of 1951, but never implemented.
>
> The government not only rejected it but intensified the preparations of military offensive by procuring arms and ultra modern military helicopters from the US. In this situation of closing down of all political avenues, we had no alternative but to continue with the people's armed resistance.[35]

The Maoists therefore, took the advantage of a pre-emptive action and surprise. They were also feeling confident that they could now graduate from fighting the police to fighting the army after their battlefield experience of the past five years. There were reports of sophisticated automatic weapons being procured by the Maoists just a couple of weeks before the November 2001 attack took place.[36] Earlier, by February 2001, they had reformulated and streamlined their military and political strategy to raise the PW to a higher level during the Party's second general conference.

**Maoists Become Bold**

The Maoists inflicted another serious blow to the army in mid-February 2002 in Achem district. They suffered some set-backs in July, but then had again reinforced their prowess by the November 2002 operations in Jumla and Gurkha simultaneously. The early impressions and claims of the army that the Maoists will be soon subdued were subsequently being replaced by nervousness and a sense of despair. After the November operations, it became clear to everyone that the Maoists had an upper hand, militarily speaking. Politically also, they launched near-total strikes throughout the country and threatened to disrupt King Gyanendra's public reception in Biratnagar in January 2003. They did not actually carry out the threat, perhaps as a gesture to the government to lure them towards ceasefire and talks.

This was a clear indication also of the fact that contacts had been established between the King's emissaries and those of the Maoists. The merciless killing of the Chief of the Armed Police Force, Krishna Mohan Shrestha and his wife days before announcement of the ceasefire, perhaps was an indication that key personalities were now on their target besides armed operations. As subsequent ceasefire announcement underlined, this killing could as well be aimed at hastening rather than to stalling the beginning of ceasefire and talk. In these seven-year long operations, the Maoists lost until February 2001, some 1500 hardcore and other cadres. Included among them were the members of the Party Politburo and Central Committee, high-ranking women cadres and even children.[37]

**State of Civil War**

After their first attack on army in November 2001, Nepal has virtually been in state of civil war. According to official estimates, in the last one year of this civil war, out of a total number of 4,300 persons killed, 4,050 have been Maoists. The Maoists assert that many of these people are civilians, killed indiscriminately by the army. There were reports that in some cases, the Maoists beheaded their slain leaders in areas of operations to avoid their identification by government forces. The killings were brutal and carried out without any consideration for human rights. The Party also faced considerable internal debate and bickering various stages of military operations and on political issue but the leadership claims that eventually these differences were resolved. In the course of the PW, women cadres have been repeatedly sexually exploited by their male colleagues.[38]

During the past one year of civil war, the Maoists have also attacked infrastructure like roads, bridges, power stations and even drinking water plants. In some cases, the Maoists have apologised for these attacks and promised not to target such facilities in future. They have also kidnapped school children, sometimes for forcible recruitment. Thus, the insurgency and the civil war have inflicted the worst kind of violence and disruption in Nepal, on a scale unprecedented in its history.

The Maoists have always been proposing talks and ceasefire as a part of their flexible strategy. The present round of ceasefire (2002-03) also serves their purpose as it will give them much needed time to regroup and recoup. This is necessitated by the fact that the RNA is not only being expanded but is also getting training and large arms supplies. The guns received from the US and in the pipeline from Belgium have been taken note of by the Maoists. Arms supplies have also gone from India in considerable quantities.

**Problems in Recruitment**

As against this accretion of strength to the RNA, the Maoists have been facing problems in recruitment and ammunition supplies. There have also been signs of erosion in their support base due to continued and ruthless violence for more than two years.

Commenting on the possible compulsions on the Maoists to ceasefire and start political negotiations, a former Maoist says:

> The logistical challenge of managing its wildfire growth, supporting a brigade-strength fighting force on looted cash, the handicap of antiquated weaponry, the steady erosion of support from an intimidated countryside, and the possibility that the law of diminishing returns may have begun to set in with cadres getting restive over the failures in converting night time strike missions into actual territorial ganis—all these would have influenced the decision to engage in serious peace talks.[39]

The Maoists also perhaps have been approached by international agencies like the Red Cross, Amnesty and Norwegian and other western governments to stop violence. They even feel politically better placed to keep initiative with them with the differences between the king and the political parties sharpening since the king's 4 October 2002 take-over. And also at a time, when militarily they had a upper edge.

Contrary to its tall claims that it will curb the insurgency in no time, the RNA has miserably failed to bring a semblance of order in the areas of its operations. The government of Nepal needs ceasefire. The RNA has also failed in clearing areas of Maoist domination or snatch military initiative from them. In private conversations, it is admitted by the American officials and other independent observers that the RNA is ill-equipped to take on the Maoists effectively, and would take another year or so to reach that status of preparedness through the induction of new recruitments, more weapons and proper training.[40] The RNA is notorious for ruthless violation of human rights and indiscriminate killings and arrests. Politically, having taken over power himself, the King is under pressure to show results. The peace process can bring back the political initiative to him and help him rebuild his fractured legitimacy with the ordinary people who need peace and stability.

**Peace Process**

Through peace process with the Maoists, the King can also keep the political parties at bay from seeking power again through the restoration of 1990 Constitution and of the dissolved Parliament, the latter demand being specifically made by the Nepali Congress. It is important to note in this respect that the government has yielded tactical ground to the Maoists in obtaining ceasefire by agreeing to withdraw the label of 'terrorists' from them, repeal the Act to combat and contain terrorism, cancel the red line notices for the arrests of Maoists leaders and cadres from the Interpol, to release some of their cadres, relax security checks and restrictions on their movements and withdraw the army and police force to their respective barracks."[41] There are indications that informally, the government is inclined to have a round table discussion for the formation of an interim government as demanded by the Maoists though the government stoutly denies that they have agreed to any pre-conditions for ceasefire and talks with the Maoists.[42] The only agreement between the two sides was on protection of 'sovereignty and nationalism' according to Col. Narayan Singh Pun, the Minister for Works and Physical Planning, who negotiated ceasefire with the Maoists.[43]

On their part, the Maoists have agreed to call off their planned programmes of strikes and bandhs and stop attacking government installations. Whether Chief of Armed Police Force Krishna Mohan Shrestha's murder and attacks on customs department just before the announcement of ceasefire were planned as a signal to force the government in accepting the ceasefire were the results of differences within the Maoists on ceasefire, will remain a subject of debate and speculation. There could also be the possibility of a communication gap between the top leadership and local operatives in this regard. The leadership took time—about 10 days to own IGP Shrestha's killing.[44] That is the sign that the government is bucking under pressure.

**Response of the Nepal Government**

The Nepal government has acted with tardy in this crises. Their response was inconsistent and far from being effective. Under the system of constitutional monarchy adopted in 1990, the palace and the political parties are the two main political centres of decision-making. Both have adopted short-sighted approaches to serve their respective narrow political vested interests, thus creating conditions for Maoists to build themselves as a formidable political force. Looking at the monarchy's approach, the contrast is clearly evident in pre-July 2001 and post-July 2001 situations. King Birendra, as claimed by the Maoists had an understanding with them and was instrumental in restraining the use of army against them. King Gyanendra unleashed the full force of the Nepalese state in suppressing the Maoist challenge, without desirable results. However, the possibility of the palace now trying to use (successfully or otherwise) the Maoists to discredit its political party detractors and to retain as much power and influence as possible in any new political arrangement, cannot be ruled out.

There are sharp differences within the King's cabinet on how to deal with the Maoists, but these are not very critical as the King's direction will prevail. In a cabinet reshuffle on 11 April 2003, the King removed his Home Minister D.B. Thapa who was critical of ceasefire and talks with the Maoists. The sensitive portfolio of Home is now being handled by Prime Minister Chand himself, at least temporarily.[45] The Nepalese governments led by the political parties over the past seven years have been equally erratic in dealing with the Maoists. The Nepali Congress has projected itself as a deeply divided organization where clash of personalities and conflict of sectional interests have defined policy approaches rather than the enlightened interests of either the organization, the democratic system, or the nation as a whole.

**Internal Differences**

The factions led by the veteran leaders G.P. Koirala and Krishna Prasad Bhattarai have torn apart internally the very organization that twice led struggle for democracy in Nepal and made innumerable sacrifices. G.P. Koirala when in power has preferred a law and order approach to counter the Maoists by force. And when he was doing so, his youger aspirant rival Sher Bahadur Deuba with the backing of Krishna Prasad Bhattarai had argued for a peaceful negotiated approach towards the Maoists. However, when in power, Deuba could not carry the process of negotiations to a logical conclusion and instead, called them 'terrorists' and vowed, "they need to be stamped out with all the might at our command. We will crush them, whatever it takes; we will defeat them wherever they are".[46] He was probably led by the post-September 11 anti-terrorism context of international and regional situation. He was also constrained by the role of the palace under the new monarch, King Gyanendra, who, at least initially, wanted to deal with the Maoists firmly.

The other mainstream parties like the CPN-UML and the royalist Rastriya Prajatantra Party (RPP) have also not been much different from the Nepali Congress. Whenever in government, or even in the Opposition, they have failed to project any viable alternative approach for dealing with Nepal's most serious security and political challenge during all these years. The broad thrust of the government's approach to the Maoists was to treat them as a national security and a law and order problem and deal with the use of force. We have mentioned about the two major security operations of 'Romeo' and 'Kilo-Sierra-2' conducted by the police forces in 1995 and 1998. They were very harsh and ruthless operations with no respect for human rights. They managed to physically eliminate a good number of Maoist cadres but contributed to the strength and spread of the Maoist movement. People in the areas of operation lost faith in the government and developed sympathy for the Maoists who were seen as victims of repression.

**Retaliation to Operation Romeo**

In a very significant way, the Maoists' formal launching of the people's war was in retaliation to 'Operation Romeo'. These operations however, could not dent the rise of the Maoists as they were not adequate even in military terms, being launched by the police force. They led to a serious debate and tension within the government, between the elected government and the King in particular, on the use of army against the Maoists.

We have mentioned earlier that the King did not favour the use of the armed forces as he thought that the army was not ready for it or that its long-term consequences were not desirable for the country. The fact of King Birendra's tacit sympathies for the Maoists influencing his views in this regard cannot be ruled out. In a tension between the Prime Minister and the King on the question of using the Army, the decision-making structure also favoured the King. This decision could be taken only by the King on the recommendation of the National Security Council, which is constituted by the Prime Minister, Defence Minister and the Chief of the Army. Since G.P. Koirala was also his own Defence Minister, and the Chief of the Army Staff was directly loyal to the King, the National Security Council had a split vote and the King could have a decisive and final say in the matter. The King was forced to accept a parliamentary decision initiated by the Koirala government to raise additional armed police forces, but on the use of army he did not relent. The RNA did not enjoy a harmonious relationship with the police force and this continues to affect the overall efficiency of the Nepalese security forces in dealing with the Maoists.[47]

**Change in Situation**

This situation changed only under the new monarch, King Gyanendra and that too because the Maoists had opened their operations against the army in November 2001. In the post-November 2001 phase, the army initially claimed that it would blunt the Maoist challenge in a short time. It achieved some successes in Dolpa during April-July, but they were not lasting or adequate. The Maoists felt the pressure but they held on to their ground and soon took an edge over the army, as became clearly evident during the Jumla and Gorkha operations in mid-November 2002. The army ruthlessly violated human rights, raped women, carried out fake encounters, and killed the Maoist suspects held in captivity to show their success in operations so as to boost the morale of the forces, but the leadership knew that they were not getting anywhere.[48] The army claims to have recovered some of the money and property looted by the Maoists but this is in no way a dent in the Maoists operational capabilities. Accordingly, the army started blaming the political leadership, particularly the Opposition, for their own failures. They also put pressure on the government to postpone elections because they realized that almost 60-70 per cent of the rural areas were still under the control of the Maoists.

**RNA**

The RNA has had some skirmishes and minor brush with insurgency and guerrilla operations during the 1960s, early 1970s and the late 1980s. But these were brief and sporadic encounters. They had no sustained experience of fighting either a regular war or motivated and determined guerrilla operations. The army's strength was also not adequate with only 55,000 men and officers. The Maoists, mostly of the same ethnic composition as the lower rungs of the army, had spread widely in difficult terrain which army had never had a chance to map out earlier. They also did not have adequate and modern weapons or training to match the challenge.[49]

**Ceasfire and Negotiations**

The King's moves towards ceasefire and negotiations are a clear reflection of his government's realisation that the Maoists cannot be tamed militarily, certainly not yet. The Maoists, as we noted earlier, have been consciously and consistently synchronising their military operations with political moves. No such organized thinking or planning is evident on the government side. There have been occasional references to the issues of economic under development and ethnic discrimination that lie at the root of the Maoist problem, but no concrete action has been taken on that count. In the past couple of months, the King's government has planned relief and rehabilitation programme at a cost of 500 million rupees in the Maoist-affected areas to erode the social base of the Maoists but this plan is still in the process of finalization. For funding this programme, the government has been appealing to its bilateral and multilateral donors for help.[50]

Giving some details of this plan, Minister of Physical Planning and Works, Narayan Singh Pun said in January 2003:

> The government has finalized Disarm, Demobilize, Rehabilitate and Reintegrate (DDRR) programme and this will soon get Cabinet approval. The objective of the programme is to make the misguided Maoists realize that there is an alternative to war. Under this programme, to be supported by a number of donors, five camps—one each in five development regions—will be set up .... People who will give up insurgency will remain in the camps for six to eight months. They will receive training and other income generating skills so as to wipe out their war mindset, making them fit to return to their previous life.[51] The Asian Development Bank has now announced a concessional loan of $321 million over three years to support developmental projects in the conflict affected areas.[52]

**Maoists Demand**

Maoists had demanded free education. The Chand government had also promised to make made it so. This however did not invoke a positive response from the 'rebel students'.[53] In fact, the political record of the governments in Nepal, elected or otherwise, over the past four decades, has been so poor on governance and concern for the common man and the Maoist as well as royalists' propaganda against the corruption, inefficiency and misgovernance of the political leaders has been so effective that the credibility of government to meet socio-economic needs of the Nepalese people is extremely shaky.

The government has either not been able to start serious negotiations with the Maoists as in November 2000,[54] or it is just not in a position to show meaningful accommodation towards the political agenda of the Maoists, as during August-November 2001 parleys.

The government's, rather the King's most significant response to the Moaists has been the establishment of back channel contacts with the Maoists soon after the 4 October 2002, take over of power. These back channels in which King seems to have directly authorized one of the hand picked Ministers, Col. Narayan Singh Pun, without taking the Cabinet into full confidence, have yielded the ceasefire and promise of talks between the King and the Maoists of 29 January 2003. Since the declaration of ceasefire, two other related developments have taken place, namely, the 'Code of Conduct' (See Annexures), between the two sides to be implemented during the negotiations signed on 12 March 2003, and the first goodwill meeting between the two sides in Kathmandu on 13 April 2003. How these talks will proceed and what will they produce, remains to be seen.

**International Responses**

September 11, 2001 was the turning point when world powers took notice of Nepal. Prior to that the outside world did not really bother much about the Maoist insurgency in Nepal until November 2001 escalation of conflict. It was the world got out of the shock of demise of twin towers in New York that the world woke up to Nepal. To a large extent, the attention of the US and other external forces to Nepal was the result of post-9/11 context in South and Central Asia. It is difficult to say if the international attention would have been drawn to Nepalese Maoists at all, even after the November 2001 if September 11 had not occurred. In many significant ways, the Maoists are not terrorists to be covered under the 'war against global terrorism'. They have had no links with Osama bin Laden and the Taliban. They have a specific political agenda and the PW, under which the armed rebellion is being carried out, is a part of their ideological struggle. Such rebellions have existed both before and after 9/11.

The Maoists can be seen as international rebels in their approach since they seek to coordinate their activities with like minded ideological groups and they indeed claim to have a programme to liberate the poor and suppressed peoples all over the world. Their Programme in South Asia, particularly involving Nepal, India, Bangladesh and Sri Lanka has been clearly defined as noted earlier. They also have international links in other countries including America and Europe. And yet, the post-9/11 framework of 'war against global terrorism' would not justifiably apply to them.

**Support to the King**

Soon after the November 2001 escalation of PW, support started pouring in to the government of Nepal in its fight against the Maoists from various countries. Looking at the regional and strategic context of Nepal, support from three sources, viz., China, the US, UK and their Western allies, and India, matter most.

The Chinese government had, even before the present escalation, distanced itself from the Maoists saying that they were neither following Chairman Mao's ideology and philosophy nor the Beijing government have any sympathy for them. In view of the Chinese government, Mao's thought was China-specific and had no relevance to Nepal. The Chinese government expressed its concern at the sudden escalation of violence in the country and pledged all its support to the government of Nepal in dealing with the Maoists' activities.[55] China, however, did not label the Maoists as terrorists but called them 'revolutionaries' and has been periodically cautioning the Nepalese government not to seek external involvement in dealing with them. This caution is in reaction to the growing US presence in the Kingdom that the Chinese do not see as desirable either for Nepal or compatible with their interests in Nepal. The most notable aspect of external support to the Nepalese government has come from the US, the UK and some of the European countries.

**Workshop on Conflict Management**

The Swiss government was sponsoring a workshop on 'conflict management', which was expected to be attended by representatives of the Maoists, political parties and the King's government.[56] Among the international organizations, the UN, UNHCR and the ICRC (International Committee for Reel Cross) have actively got involved in the peace related activities between the Maoists and the government. The ICRC wanted to have a dialogue with the two sides to improve living conditions of the ordinary people—"restore freedom of movement for people and goods and improving civilian security"—in the conflict zones.[57]

The UNHCR intervened with the Government of India on the question of deportation of a Nepalese Maoist to the Nepalese government from India.[58] The UN, through its Resident Representative in Nepal, Dr Henning Karcher, directly and publicly offered to 'broker peace' between the government and the Maoists, as early as in October 2002. This was the first time an international organization had done so after the King's takeover of power.[59] Though donors pleaded for peace, they also pledged support to the Nepalese government in fighting insurgency. All the donors of Nepal held a conference in London in 2002, where it was decided to pool joint efforts to help Nepal get out of the current crisis. The US and the UK have been the driving force behind this conference.

**Multilateral Committees**

They have established at least three multilateral committees of defence and security, political issues, and economic and developmental issues to fund and monitor these areas. It may, however, be noted here that the European donors always emphasized the peace and humanitarian aspects. Norway also expressed strong concern on the destruction of infrastructure and even threatened to discontinue assistance if violation of human rights was not stopped and the democratic process was not resumed.[60] The US and UK were comparatively more emphatic on combating insurgency, and they seem to be working in tandem. Senior Foreign Ministry officials have visited Nepal to take cognizance of the situation directly. This included the US Secretary of States Gen. Colin Powell (February 2002) and the British Under Secretary of State in the Foreign and Commonwealth Office Michael Jay (December 2002). These visits were the first visits in many decades at such high levels. Both Powell and Jay pledged strong military and economic support of their governments to Nepal in fighting the Maoists.

The UK, due to its sizeable influence in the Nepalese army and the retired British Gurkha troops, has also been believed to be behind the peace moves in Nepal. The government of the United Kingdom also appointed a special representative, Sir Jeffrey James, to facilitate the proposed peace talks between the Maoists and the government. This was done, according to British diplomats in Kathmandu, at the initiative of Prime Minister Tony Blair and not on the request of the Nepalese government.[61] The Maoists on the other hand may be to secure international legitimacy for themselves wanted a third party involvement in the peace process.

**US Position**

The US position two on Nepal was different. It was more active, visible and unprecedented. The Assistant Secretary of State Miss Christina Rocca has visited Nepal thrice in 2002, and has been in direct contact with the King and the armed forces. In her last visit, she reiterated the US government's resolve: "We are committed to help Nepal combat the insurgency by providing security assistance to the Nepalese government. Assistance will be provided in the form of a package including equipment, supplies and training for the Nepalese security forces".[62] It may useful to keep in mind that this visit took place after the Maoists had killed two of the Nepalese security guards of American Embassy alleging them of indulging in espionage and they had also threatened attacks on the Embassy.

Reacting strongly to such threats, the US issued a travel advisory for the Americans against visiting to or moving freely in Nepal. The US has, however, not yet formally designated the Maoists as terrorists. Answering a question on the issue, Ms Rocca said: "... this step may be taken in consideration if their violence continues unabated".[63] This also indicates that the US, while helping the King's regime militarily, was also trying to explore the possibility of opening negotiations with the Maoists.

A junior State Department official, Donald Camp, claimed that ceasefire and proposed talks between the King and the Maoists announced in January 2003, were "a success of the US policy" and that the US will not allow the Maoists to prevail".[64] This US position has again been reiterated by Camp's boss Ms Rocca again recently when in a statement before the US Senate Committee on Foreign Relations in Washington, she said:

> We believe the parties have come this far only because the RNA was able to make an effective stand—a goal which US security assistance aims to bolster ... In co-ordination with Great Britain, India and other partners, our security assistance will provide directly needed arms, equipments and training to enable the Royal Nepal Army (RNA) to counter the Maoist military threat... (the US) also support efforts to bolster government control in areas vulnerable to Maoist influence by funding high-impact rural infrastructure and employment projects.[65]

The notable aspect of the US position on the Maoists question is that there is a great deal of backing provided to the RNA and the King's post-4 October 2002, notwithstanding occasional reference to democracy.

**King takes over direct power**

The US neither disapproved of the King's take over of direct power in violation of the 1990 Constitution, nor has the US asked the King to carry Nepalese political parties with him so as to effectively and politically deal with the Maoists. It may be of interest to note here that after the early 1960s, direct military assistance by the US to Nepal has transpired for the first time. The arms supplied by the US include MI-16 AZ rifles, helicopters, twin engine STOL aircraft, ammunition and other non-lethal weapons. The quantum of military assistance actually received was reduced from $20 million initially promised during the then Prime Minister Deuba's visit to the US in May 2002, to $12 million. This has naturally disappointed the Nepalese security forces. The reasons advanced for this reduction are "budget stringencies and shifting priorities in the war on terrorism".[66]

Perhaps the indications of the coming ceasefire and caution sounded by other donors, as well as India, regarding not strengthening Royal Nepal Army, and hence monarchy, against other democratic forces might also have weighed on the US administration. The possibility of the US having long-term interests of a strategic nature in Nepal cannot be ruled out. There were reports of the seeking Nepal's co-operation in setting up a military observation post in northern areas, possibly in the Mustang region bordering Tibet, where the US intelligence agencies had trained and used Khampa tribals for organising raids in Tibet between 1960-74. Speculation in this respect was raised during Deuba's visit to the US, but the reports were strongly denied by the US Ambassador in Kathmandu Michael Malinowski, saying that such reports were "erroneous, uninformed and foolish".[67]

**America Military Assessment Mission**

The Defence Ministry, however, separately disclosed that an American military assessment mission was invited to Nepal to assess military requirements in the context of Maoists' threat.[68] This team of about a dozen experts and officers came in April 2002, and visited the areas affected by the Maoists insurgency, including the parts of northern region. It is believed in Kathmandu's media circles that Nepal has developed cold feet on this proposal of setting up a military post, under the Chinese pressure. There may also be strong reservations on any such proposals. The Maoist leader Baburam Bhattarai comments that the growing US military presence in Nepal is in the long-term interest aimed at encircling China and containing India is significant.[69]

**Establishment of a Siesmic Centre**

Some corroboration of speculation in this respect was evident in Nepal government's recent decision to establish a siesmic centre to monitor possible nuclear explosions in the region under Comprehensive Test Ban Treaty (CTBT) regime[70]. Nepal is not even a member of the International Atomic Energy Agency as yet and its limited capabilities in respect of monitoring nuclear tests will allow this centre to be manned and managed by foreigners.

This has in fact a different motive. The countries that this centre will keep an eye on are China, India and Pakistan. Besides supply of arms, the US has also started training Nepalese forces. The US military team visiting Nepal had suggested augmentation and upgrading of the Royal Nepal Army.[71] Along the US lines, the RNA has raised a "Rangers Battalian" of up to 1000 soldiers for commando type operation.[72] An estimated 40-member US training team from the Pacific Command has had a joint military exercise with the RNA. The stated purpose of this exercise was to "enhance operational capability, inter-operability with other forces and tactical efficiency of the host nation". But these US soldiers were working with the RNA in the Maoist affected areas.[73] The US has also extended a grant of Nepali Rs 390 million to strengthen human rights cell in the army. There is a reason for that. The human rights violation in RNA are becoming serious by the day. Increasing international concerns have been raised on this issue.[74]

**India and the Maoist Challenge**

India woke up to the Maoists' challenge in Nepal only after the escalation of violence in November 2001. Until then, for nearly six years since the February 1996 declaration of the PW by the Maoists, the Government of India's approach to the possible threat arising from this insurgency was casual. Law and order being treated as a state subject, the Central government in India absolved itself of any responsibility in restraining and containing the activities of the Maoists along the Indo-Nepal border. A Co-ordination committee of the South Asian Maoists was established in June 2001, Indian intelligence agencies did not take a serious note of it.

Even before the Nepalese government react, India did, declared the Maoists as terrorists and promised all possible support to the government in Kathmandu. It was infact a reaction to November escalation of violent activities. However, the actual delivery of the military assistance was allowed to be processed leisurely under the consideration that military support was likely to strengthen the RNA and hence, indirectly the monarchy at the cost of democratic institutions. Not much effective steps were also taken to restrict the free movement of the Maoists across the Indo-Nepal border. Nepalese and Indian army chiefs and officers exchanged visits and assurances of support, but military hardware moved slowly. All this changed only when pressure started building from the Nepalese side through allegations that India was indirectly supportive of the Maoists, by letting them use Indian territory for shelter, sanctuaries and logistic help. King Gyanendra's visit to India in July 2002 was significant in this respect.

**Rise of US and British Presence**

By then, India was also getting concerned about the steady rise in the US and British military presence in Nepal. India had a written understanding with Nepal concluded in 1965, that Nepal could procure arms from third countries such as the United States and the United Kingdom, if India could not supply its requirements. Slowly, it started dawning on Indian policy-makers that the gradual spread and consolidation of the American and British military and political presence in Nepal was not a very desirable development in India's own long-term interests. India's Foreign Secretary Kanwal Sibal in his speech at the French Institute of International Relations in Paris on 17 December 2002, hinting at this concern said with regard to Nepal that: "Western countries should also be careful about extending excessive military assistance to Nepal in order to avoid increase in the lethality of internal conflict and leakage of arms to the Maoists."[75]

India's reservations on the western donors' approach to the question of insurgency in Nepal became evident when it refused to join multilateral committees to monitor developmental, political and security issues in Nepal. India also showed its displeasure with the flow of third country arms into Nepal by delaying the over-flight permission to the American and Belgian guns. India also inspected these arms cargos to make sure that they did not pose any long-term threat to India's internal stability and security by these arms falling eventually into wrong hands. Indian policy received a further set-back when a whispering campaign was let loose in Nepal blaming India of sheltering the Maoists, contrary to all that it was doing, including providing military assistance to Nepal government. Then came on 4 October 2002, the dismissal of the Deuba government and the takeover of direct power by the King. The puppet government installed by the King was seen as a breach of the principles of Constitutional Monarchy and the multi-party democracy, the two pillars of India's basic approach in Nepal.

**India Sidelined**

Subsequently, India also felt left out when suddenly on 29 January 2003, the King's government and the Maoists announced ceasefire and agreed to hold talks to resolve the problem of insurgency. Expressing resentment at this marginalisation of India, Foreign Secretary Kanwal Sibal said at a Track-II meeting of Indian and Nepalese participants where Nepal's Ambassador in India Dr B.B. Thapa was also present, that India was not taken into confidence and that there was no consultation from the Nepalese side on vital issues affecting bilateral relations between the two countries. He asked as to what was India expected to do in relation to the Nepalese Maoists: stop monitoring their movements across the borders and stop giving military support to the Nepalese government since ceasefire and talks have been announced?[76] India's displeasure was shown in no uncertain terms.

India cannot be absolved from its own responsibility in bringing itself to this state of marginalisation with regard to its concerns in Nepal. There are two serious problems with India's Nepal policy. One is that it does not recognise the fallacy of its two-pillar approach. There is a serious inherent conflict between the interests of multi-party democracy based on the concept of popular sovereignty and the King's political aspirations and self-perceived divine role to rule. Even in 1990, the co-existence between the King and the political parties was neither natural, nor sincere nor honest. A former Chief Justice of Nepal's Supreme Court and a member of the Constitution drafting Committee in 1990, Mr Vishwambhar Nath Upadhyaya opined that from the first day, the palace had not cooperated in proper execution of the 1990 Constitution. The two pillars of India's Nepal policy, the King and the political parties, have on various occasions found it difficult to work in harmony with each other, more so since Gyanendra's coining to power and particularly after the King's take over of October 2002.

**Internal Conflicts**

It also be not out of place to mention here that political parties are fraught with internal conflicts, lack of credible leadership, failure on account of governance and erosion of ideological and political integrity to lead Nepal out of the present crisis. The monarchy on its part, since the first political coup by King Mahendra against the representative government in December I960, built its political base by pursuing policies that have been incompatible with India's legitimate and enlightened interests in Nepal. The contribution of monarchy in shaping Nepalese nationalism along anti-Indian lines has been the single largest. It is unrealistic on India's part to continue to harp on the two pillar policy under these circumstances. This basic incompatibility of interests between India and the Nepalese monarchy had brought them into direct clashes not only during the periods of Nehru and Indira Gandhi's rule but also during Rajiv Gandhi's period, during 1988-89, which in a significant way, contributed towards the success of the people's revolution and anti-Panchayat movement of 1989-90.[77] There are, no doubt, socio-cultural and emotional constituencies in India that hold the Hindu monarch of Nepal in high esteem and there is also an intricate web of family ties at the elite level in India that the King nurses to ensure support for him. However, the monarchy as an institution has done precious little in accommodating India's legitimate security and economic concerns and interests in Nepal. Even within the Constitutional framework and as a symbol of stability, India need not rely so much on the monarchy in Nepal.

**Dispassionate Assessment**

The other problem of India's Nepal policy in the present context is that it has failed to make a balanced and dispassionate assessment of the Maoists. The Maoists have been seen by the Government of India as a serious security challenge to India's interests in more than one ways, viz.:

- Genera ting instability in Nepal and creating conditions for intervention from outside powers.
- Networking with other insurgent groups in India and South Asia to create instability in the region. The establishment of a Coordinating Committee of Maoists Groups in South Asia in June 2001 provides an institutional structure for this purpose.
- Possible and potential links of Maoists with ISI, North-east insurgent groups, the LITE, etc.

- The Maoists' use of violent and terrorist methods to capture power at the cost of democratic institutions and governance.[78]
- Demanding a restructuring of India-Nepal relations, through revision or abrogation of some of the important bilateral treaties like the Treaty of Peace and Friendship of 1950, and the Mahakali treaty of 1996, and projecting India as an exploitative and hegemonic power in the region.

On the face of it, these issues may seam reasonable but they need to be looked into. To begin with, there is no hard evidence to suggest that the Maoists are either inspired, funded or influenced by any of the foreign interests. The Maoists' violence has certainly facilitated the US and the UK to expand their respective strategic interests and presence in Nepal, but that could have happened even otherwise in the aftermath of 9/11 events under the impact of which strategic interests of the Western powers in Asia have been redefined, reinforced and vigorously pursued. Further, the credit for the consolidation of the Western presence should go to the King and the governments in Nepal, who have always looked with favour at any opportunity to encourage outside powers to counteract India's stakes in Nepal.

**Maoists Demand**

Maoists are demanding too much. They are asking for all the treaties with India including the one 1950 and Mahakali treaty to be abrogated. But then, Maoists are not the only or even the first to raise these issues in India-Nepal relations. Almost every political party in Nepal as also the King have done so on may occasions and at times, consistently in the post-Rana Nepal. The review and revision of the 1950 Treaty is almost a national demand of Nepal. It is unfair to credit or blame only the Maoists for this demand. The other insurgent groups in India and South Asia particularly the PWG, the MCC and some of the Northeast-tribal and ethnic insurgents, have been operating much earlier than the Maoists came on the scene. Somehow the Government of India has evolved a pattern of its own to deal with these internal insurgencies and the Maoists can hardly make any significant difference to their activities.

**Procuring Arms**

The possibility of the Maoists using these groups for procuring arms and other logistic support in their activities exists and has certainly been harnessed, and this is a cause of security concern for India as the arms may flow to Indian groups through these channels as well. However, the extent of security threat posed by this to India should not be unduly exaggerated to rationalise India's hostility to the Maoists. If this threat was so serious, why India took the emergence of the Maoists casually between February 1996 and November 2001. It also needs to be stated here that the spread and success of the Maoists in Nepal should be seen as a reflection of the political and socio-economic context there. The Naxalites, the MCC and the People's War Group can never attain comparable success in a democratically resilient and developmentally dynamic India that can keep ideologically inspired insurgencies contained. Last but not the least, the Maoists, as any other political force in Nepal, realise that India is crucial for their struggle, victory or survival in power, if ever they were to come to power.

Their anti-India rhetoric notwithstanding, they have tried to establish contacts and understanding with India, but without any response. There were also indications that the Maoists moderated and diluted their anti-India rhetoric between November 2001 and January 2003. India has refused to touch them with a barge pole, ignoring the fact they have emerged as a powerful player in the Nepalese political context and represent support of a large section of its poor and oppressed masses in the mid-hill regions. After all, even the King whose abolition is the principal goal of the Maoists has agreed to deal with them, and the Maoists on their part, have shown a remarkable flexibility and pragmatism in their approach to monarchy. This possibility existed, and does exist even now, between India and Maoists as well, if the former sees this as worth exploring, in its own policy calculations.

**India's Engagement with Maoists**

In fact, a practical engagement with the Maoists in Nepal cannot be avoided if India wants to see Nepal stabilized, its monarchy democratized and its internal autonomy preserved from the growing Western and other undesirable influences. There is a pressing need for Indian policy-makers to reassess the Maoists and recast their whole approach to the emerging situation in Nepal. There are too many cooks and diverse social and political interests in India's Nepal policy-making process to let a sincere and dispassionate reassessment take place, though the need for such a reassessment is deeply felt in some foreign policy establishments. A more realistic alternative for the Indian policy in Nepal is to alter its two-pillar policy of supporting the King and the democratic parties. Nepal stands at a junction where it could launch itself on the way to the evolution of a true democracy. India needs to get engaged with the ongoing peace process and help Nepal take a direction towards reinforcing democratic forces and institutions reflecting aspirations of the ordinary Nepalese. India cannot meaningfully get engaged with the peace process unless it gets constructively engaged with the Maoists. India's image in Nepal today is that it is an ally and supporter of monarchy. India needs to bring the Maoists and the political parties together which, in the process will also moderate the Maoists' extremist stance and use of violent methods.

It is this combination of the mainstream political parties and the Maoists which can contain monarchy's powers, help India emerge as a people-friendly neighbour and reduce the excessive influence and strategic presence of the Western powers. This will also help India assume greater political initiative in Nepal during this sensitive and delicate peace process. An improvement in the rapport between India and the Maoists may be helpful in moderating the activities of the left extremist forces within India.

**Prospects**

The compulsions that drove the King and the Maoists to ceasefire and negotiations have been identified earlier. The indications are that the process of negotiations will move rather slowly, with tough bargaining inevitable at almost every stage. This is evident in the fact that within days of the signing of the mutually agreed 'Code of Conduct', each side is accusing the other of violating this code. Members of the Maoist negotiating team in the course of their public meetings all over the kingdom have repeatedly blamed the King for not adhering to the 'Code of Conduct' regarding releasing the central level Maoist leaders, and Minister Pun has accused the Maoists of 'increasing their demands' adding that the government is not bound to agree to all their demands'.[79] Chief of the Maoist negotiating team Dr Bhattarai has directly blamed the King for blocking the peace process.

While the Maoist negotiating team was announced in the very first statement of the Maoists leader Prachanda on the ceasefire, the official negotiating team from the King's side was announced only on 16 April 2003, after considerable delay and speculation. As noted earlier, the first contacts, for the 'good will' talks, between the Maoist negotiators led by Baburam, and the King's side, represented by Minister Pun, took place on 13 April 2003. The government negotiating team is headed by the Deputy Prime Minister Badri Prasad Mandal. This team includes Col. Pun and four other ministers, including a woman minister Ms Anuradha Koirala. This indicates the direct involvement of the Cabinet in the peace process, that had not been the case thus far. This is not yet clear as to what brief, if any, the King has given to this team but Col. Pun's presence on the government side underlines that these talks will have some sort of continuity with the earlier contacts and the King will keep in touch with the pace and content of negotiations. The first contacts could be established only after the King's side had partially accommodated the Maoists' pre-condition of the release of five Maoists leaders, including the party's Central Committee members. The peace process in Nepal is a delicate and complex one, but everyone seems to be having stakes in sustaining it, at least for the present. There are three possible directions that this peace process may take place. One is based on what has been termed as a 'strategic pause'.[80]

**Strategi Needs**

Accordingly, either side will sustain the talks and the ceasefire as long as its strategic needs so demand. Here, the strategic needs would depend upon completing arms acquisition and training programmes, and making adequate recruitments by the RNA and the Maoists. Both the combatants would also like to reinforce and expand their political constituencies and ensure continued help and co-operation from the international community for their respective positions. The extensive tours and public meeting addressed both by the King as well as the Maoist negotiating team during March and April 2003, may be taken note of in this respect.

It is interesting that the King in his addresses to the people of the western region, the stronghold of the Maoists, emphasised the centrality of monarchy in Nepal's history and the bond of affection existing between the Kins and the people. He said in Dhangarhi on 3 April 2003:

> The quintessence of our Nepal identity is the strong bond between the institution of monarchy and the people nurtured by mutual affection and confidence. Nepal has been able to maintain her independent identity and self-respect throughout her history only because of the peoples' unwavering trust in the institution of monarchy and the monarchy's unqualified dedication towards the people...
>
> It is but natural to have differences of opinion and competition in a multi-party democracy. However, the converging point of all these different opinions must be patriotism. A monarchy ever devoted towards the country and the people and a people with an innate love for their land is the glorious past of Nepal history, its present and also its future.[81]

**US Backing**

The King seems to be assured by the US that he will be backed up to the hilt and the RNA's preparations and training programmes have only been stepped up. If the purpose of ceasefire and talks on both sides is to use it as a 'strategic pause', then no substantive issues are expected to be brought on the table and no compromises and mutual accommodations are to be sought or extended. Talks will continue to take place slowly, in one form or the other, as long as either or both the parties are not prepared to get back to the conflict with greater confidence. The second possibility is that the 'strategic pause' is used by either side to out-manoeuvre the other politically. The King's side may over-stretch the negotiations without conceding anything substantially to the Maoists to encourage cleavages and divisions among the Maoists leaders as also between the leadership and the cadres. It may also try and lure the sections of the more pliable leadership through offers of money, office and other material or political advantages to break the leadership and disintegrate the movement. If that becomes possible, the RNA would find it easy to deal militarily with the sections isolated through this selective process of co-option.

Perhaps, such fears have prompted the Maoists for postponing the talks indefinitely on 19 April 2003. To them, the delayed constitution and the composition of the King's official negotiating team shows the lack of seriousness on the part of the King. According to one assessment, the RNA is hopeful that once it has acquired sufficient quantities of modern weapons and reached a force strength of 70,000 men, it would be able to defeat the Maoists militarily.[82] Others speculate that the RNA will have to raise its manpower threefold, at least 150,000, before it can be confident of taking on the Maoists.[83]

**Kings briefing to Indian**

It is believed that the King was briefing his Indian interlocutors along the lines that nothing much may come out of the talks and that the Maoists may not be able to sustain the process of negotiations, during his recent visit to India in March 2003. Sections of Kathmandu elites also suspect this to be the King's game plan. They seem to be in sympathy with the mainstream political parties' allegations that the King has been instigating splits and divisions in their ranks and files in order to weaken them and co-opt the pliable sections.[84] The only flaw in the King's strategy in this respect appears to be that he is not cultivating the mainstream political parties which is a necessary condition for isolating the Maoists in a triangular balance of power. The Maoists on their part are mobilising support from the mainstream political parties and are also trying to establish their credentials with international community to isolate the King.

The Maoist negotiating team had talks has with the leaders of all the mainstream political parties and sought meetings with the representatives of the EU, the US, the UK, China and India to explain their point of view. If the Maoists and the mainstream political parties decide to build a peoples' movement on the lines of 1990, the King can surely be outmanoeuvred. There are indications that both the Nepali Congress and the UML are getting round to this point of view, but reservations and opposition from within the ranks in each of the parties exist. They are preparing to launch a movement on these lines as they continue to be neglected by the King. The core of the mainstream political parties' approach may be to use the Maoists' pressures in forcing the King to restore multi-party constitution and hand over power to them. The Nepali Congress leader, Koirala said in his many public meetings that "the time has come for the King to choose between constitutional monarchy within multi-party set-up or republican setup under the current circumstances".[85]

**The Dilemma**

The dilemma of the political parties lies in their neglect by the King and their fear of the Maoists who have a formidable armed strength and do not have faith in parliamentary and democratic institutions. The Maoists, on their own, are also keeping their agitational mode infact to maintain pressure on the King. This is evident since the first half of April 2003, when student agitation flared up on the question of death of a Maoist sympathizer student-leader in Butwal in police firing. The firing was resorted to disperse students protest demonstrations on economic demands of rise in the prices of petroleum products, etc.[86] The students are also agitating on the question of elections in the University. This agitation continues and it threatens to have country-wide strikes on 27, 28 April.

The international community also does not seem to be very responsive to the Maoists. The US and UK have refused to meet the Maoist representatives. Justifying his negative response to the Maoists, the US Ambassador in Kathmandu Malinowski said: "Given their violent history of destroying infrastructure projects, does any one take the Maoists seriously" .[87] The British Ambassador has avoided meeting the Maoists by forwarding their request to London for instructions, but he has stated in Kathmandu that the root causes of the Maoists' uprising will have to be addressed seriously.[88] The EU Representative has met the Maoists but Indian and Chinese representatives in Kathmandu are still to be approached.

**Indian's Reachions**

The Indian Ambassador in Kathmandu has come out with a statement saying that if the Maoists are willing to function democratically then they will not be treated as terrorists. It may, however, be noted here that the general public opinion thinks that the Maoists are serious in their peace talks this time than on the earlier occasion in August 2001. The Maoists' Central Committee's decision, in its first statement ore ceasefire and talks in February 2003 (19 *Magh 2059,* Nepali calendar) to involve intellectuals and eminent public figures as facilitators in the talks with the King, was also an indication of their seriousness. The third possibility is that the King and the Maoists may strike a deal, leaving the political parties on the fringe.[89] The basis of a deal between these two fundamentally conflicting groups lie in the fact that the King is willing to talk to them, even accommodate some of their critical demands such as the release of their leaders and not recognising them as terrorists. The King has also invoked the concept of 'patriotism' in his addresses to underline a possible common point between him and the Maoists. The Maoists have dropped their demand of a republican State and are willing to adjust with a monarchy with reduced role in any new future set-up. They have also indicated their willingness to give up the demand of Constituent Assembly, since considerable reservations on this demand have been expressed by the political parties.

**Maoists Rescheme**

We have earlier noted that the Maoists have often shown the resilience on their stated demands in order to achieve their desired goal of getting closer to power. Underlining the flexibility in their approach in the forthcoming negotiations, Baburam Bhattarai said recently:

> The current politics is a conflict between two regimes and three political forces. For the strategic balance no party side can lead the country alone. As such we are advocating for a progressive solution. The major agenda of the talks is for all the three forces—pro-monarchist, parliamentary parties and us—to come out with a solution from give and take. The new system would not be like Panchayat or the current parliamentary system. How far we will achieve it depends on the negotiation.... Every one has to show certain flexibility. The bottom line should be the interest of the general public.[90]

The Maoists and the King also had some rapport and understanding between them during King Birendra's regime the ground reality was identical his regime. They have also come to accept the continuing role of monarchy, but without any effective power or any guarantee for hereditary rule of succession. That is why the Maoists leader Baburam Bhattarai has proposed Cambodian King Sihanouk like status for the Nepali monarch in a new political order.[91]

**King's Dilemma**

It may be extremely difficult for the King to accept such a status, particularly for a power conscious and ambitious King like Gyanendra, unless forced beyond his capacity. The monarchy's mind-set, since the coming to power of King Mahendra in 1995, is such that it may not accept a truncated status, shorn of any residual or potential power for itself. The King may also not be willing to risk the future of his family by accepting the Cambodian model. The basic positions of the King and the Maoists are such that for any deal between them substantial compromises will have to be made by both the sides.

Their common interest lies in keeping the political parties marginalized. No wonder then, the King has not involved the parties in the process of negotiations. The only accommodation gestured to the political parties in this respect is by the Deputy Prime Minister and the head of the King's negotiating team, to ask political parties if they want to join the Committee proposed to be set-up to give direction to the negotiating team. The parties have rejected this offer. The Maoists are also not asking for or insisting on the political parties' presence on the negotiating table.

All they keep repeating is that the political parties and other political and civil society representatives should be involved in the proposed 'Round Table' discussions that no one know when will be launched, if at all. Though it is not stated clearly, even the King and the Maoists also share their views of Nepal's relations with India where the former should have greater degree of freedom and autonomy in dealing with the latter. The Maoists would also like to see the reduced US influence in the kingdom that may not be compatible with the King's preferences.

**Deal, no deal**

Thus in totality, a deal between the king and the Maoists may also be easier said than done, but possibility exists. The political parties are weak and directionless at the moment but they have the potential to vitiate any such deal worked out between the King and the Maoists. Similarly, India will also not let its stakes eroded in Nepal. The US has already made it clear that they would not allow the Maoists to prevail even in a negotiated resolution of the problem. Of the three possible scenarios, Nepal cannot afford to see itself plunged into violence and anarchy once again. The economic and social costs of the collapse of negotiations and resumption of hostilities will be enormous. This is some thing that no one should allow to happen. In fact, the international community, including the donor group and multilateral financial institutions, are offering substantia_economic incentives to encourage the combatants to work for a resolution of the conflict. The best course will be the evolution of a package of political reforms in Nepal that accommodates constructive concerns of all the three principal forces in Nepal, viz. the Maoists, the king and the political parties. One can only wish and hope that this happens. If it does not then Nepal will be plunged into a deep crisis for years to come.

## Annexure I
## Origin and Development of the Communist Party of Nepal (Maoist)

**Key to Chart Overleaf**

*ULF: United Left Fronts*

1. NL=Nirmal Lama NCP Fourth Convention
2. Rohit=Narayan Man Bijkchhe Nepal Workers and Peasant' Party
3. V=Krishna Das Verma, NCP
4. A=Tulsi Lal Amatya, NCP
5. M=Bishnu Bahadur Manandhan, NCP
6. MX=NCP Marxist, Sahana Pradhan
7. ML=NCP Marxist and Leninist
8. Ind=Independent (Padma Ratna Tuladhar)

*UPNM: United National People's Movement*

1. MB=Mohan Bikram Singh, NCP-Masal
2. PR=Prachanda-Pushpa Kamat Dahal, NCP Mashal
3. RL=Rup Lat Bishworkarma, NCP-People Oriented
4. SR=Shambhu Ram Shrestha, NCP League
5. KD=Krishna Das Shrestha, NCP-Marxist Leninist Maoists.

Bidari=NCP-People Oriented (Ramnarayan Bidan-rebelled from Ruper Bista)

* BB=Baburam Bhattarat joined Unity Centre informally for functional before leaving his party-Masal. Actually he was in position for party or Due to this reason he left his party and joined Unity Centre.

UPFN (Vaidya)=Niranjan Gevinda Vaidya

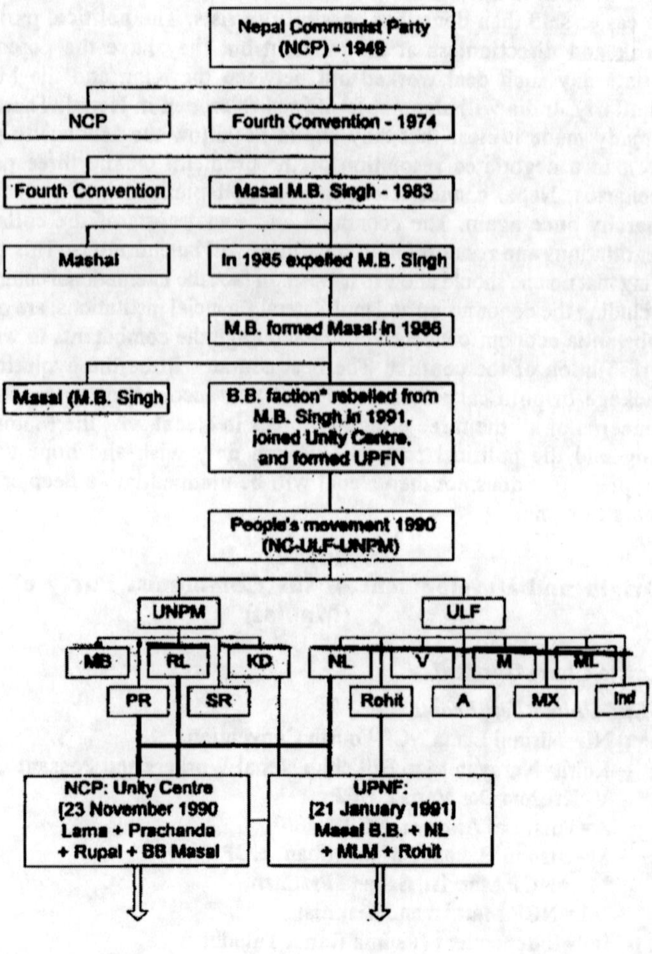

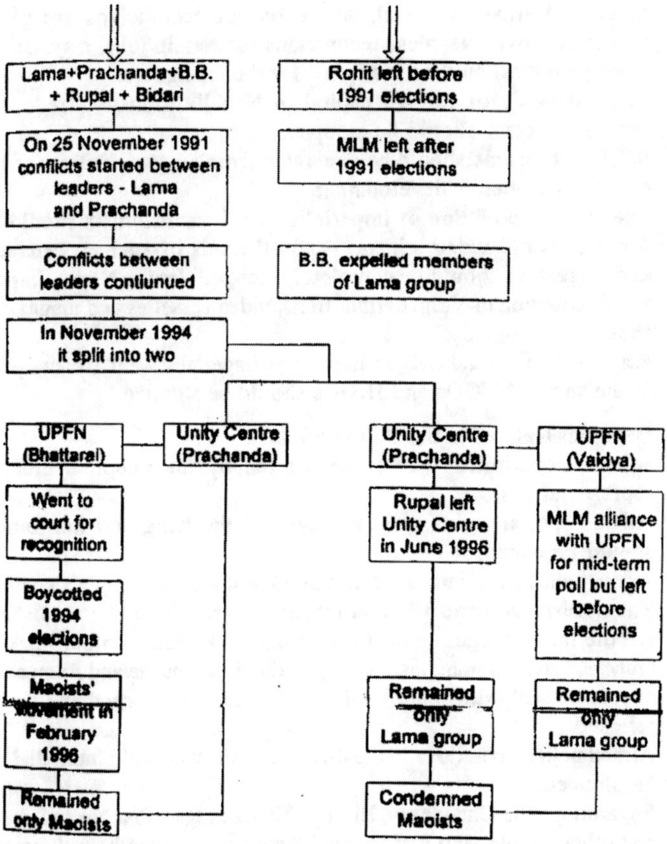


## Annexiure II
## 40-Point Demand of the Maoists

**1. Demands Related to Nationalism**

1. Regarding the 1950 Treaty between India and Nepal, all unequal stipulations and agreements should be removed.
2. HMG should admit that the anti-nationalist Tanakpur agreement was wrong, and the Mahakali Treaty, incorporating it, should be nullified.
3. The entire Nepal-India border should be controlled and systematized. Cars with Indian numberplates, plying the roads of Nepal, should not be allowed.
4. Gurkha recruiting centres should be closed and decent jobs should be arranged for the recruits.

5. In several areas of Nepal, where foreign technicians are given precedence over Nepalese technicians for certain jobs, a system of work permits should be instituted for the foreigners.
6. The monopoly of foreign capital in Nepal's industry, trade and economic sector should be stopped.
7. Sufficient income should be generated from customs duties for the country's economic development.
8. The cultural pollution of imperialists and expansionists should be stopped. Hindi video, cinema, and all kinds of such newspapers and magazines should be completely stopped. Inside Nepal, import and distribution of Vulgar Hindi films, video cassettes and magazines should be stopped.
9. Regarding NGOs and INGOs. Bribing by imperialists and expansionists in the name of NGOs and INGOs should be stopped.

**2. Demands Related to the Public Welfare**

10. A new Constitution has to be drafted by the people's elected representatives.
11. All the special rights and privileges of the King and his family should be ended.
12. Army, police and administration should be under the people's control.
13. The Security Act and all other repressive acts should be abolished.
14. All the false charges against the people of Rukum, Rolpa, Jajrkot, Gurkha, Kavre, Sindhuphalchowk, Sindhuli, Dhanusha and Remechap should be withdrawn and all the people falsely charged should be released.
15. Armed police operations in the different districts should immediately be stopped.
16. Regarding Dilip Chaudhary, Bhuvan Thapa Magar, Prabhakar Subedi and other people who disappeared from police custody at different times, the government should constitute a special investigating committee to look into these crimes and the culprits should be punished and appropriate compensation given to their families.
17. People, who died during the time of the movement, should be declared as martyrs and their families, and those who have been wounded and disabled should be given proper compensation. Strong action should be taken against the killers.
18. Nepal should be declared a secular state.
19. Girls should be given equal property rights to those of their brothers.
20. All kinds of exploitation and prejudice based on caste should be ended. In areas having a majority of one ethnic group, that group should have autonomy over that area.
21. The status of dalits as untouchables should be ended and the system of untouchability should be ended once and for all.

22. All languages should be given equal status. Up until middle-high school level (uccha-madyamic) arrangements should be made for education to be given in the children's mother tongue.
23. There should be guarantee of free speech and free Press. The communications media should be completely autonomous.
24. Intellectuals, historians, artists and academicians engaged in other cultural activities should be guaranteed intel lectual freedom.
25. In both the tarai and hilly regions there is prejudice and misunderstanding in backward areas. This should be ended and the backward areas should be assisted. Good relations should be established between the villages and the city.
26. Decentralization in real terms should be applied to local areas which should have local rights, autonomy and control over their own resources.

3. **Demands Related to the People's Living**

27. Those who cultivate the land should own it. (The tiller would have right to the soil he/she tills.) The land of rich landlords should be confiscated and distributed to the homeless and others who have no land.
28. Brokers and commission agents should have their property confiscated and that money should be invested in industry.
29. All should be guaranteed work and should be given stipend until jobs are found for them.
30. HMG should pass strong laws ensuring that people involved in industry and agriculture should receive minimum wages.
31. The homeless should be given suitable accommodation. Until HMG can provide such accommodation they should not be removed from where they are squatting.
32. Poor farmers should be completely freed from debt. Loans from the Agricultural Development Bank by poor farmers should be completely written off. Small industries should be given loans.
33. Fertilizer and seeds should be easily and cheaply available, and the farmers should be given a proper market price for their production.
34. Flood and drought victims should be given all necessary help.
35. All should be given free and scientific medical service and education and education for profit (private schools?) should be completely stopped.
36. Inflation should be controlled and labourers' salaries should be raised in direct ratio with the rise in prices. Daily essential goods should be made cheap and easily available.
37. Arrangement should be made for drinking water, good roads, and electricity in the villages.
38. Cottage and other small industries should be granted special facilities and protection.

39. Corruption, black marketeering, smuggling, bribing, the taking of commission, etc., should all be stopped.
40. Orphans, the disabled, the elderly and children should be given help and protection.

We offer a heartfelt request to the present coalition government that they should fulfill the above demands, which are essential for Nepal's existence and for the people's daily lives as soon as possible. If the government does not show any interest by 5 Falgun 2052,17 (February 1996) we will be compelled to launch a movement against the government. The above demands put forth by the Samyukta Jana Morcha, led by Dr Bhattarai, were handed over to the then prime minister Sher Bahadur Deuba.

The government showed no interest in fulfilling any or the above demands, or even taking these seriously. After a cruel government crackdown on members of the Samyukta Jana Morcha (which previously held nine seats in the parliament), in Rukum, and Rolpa, Dr Bhattarai declared the 'Jana Yudha.'

## References

1. For Prachanda's early life and political career, see Pratik Pradhan and Ameet Dhakal, "Uncovering Prachanda...", *Kathmandu Post,* 8 April 2003.
2. As told by Dr Baburam Bhattarai, to William Raeper and Martin Hoftun, *Spring Awakening: An Account of the 1990 Revolution in Nepal,* Viking, New Delhi, 1992, p. 34.
3. John Welpton, "The General Elections of May 1991", in Michael Hutt (ed.), *Nepal in the Nineties: Versions of the Past, Visions of the Future,* Oxford University Press, New Delhi, 1994, pp. 58-59.
4. Election Commission, *Pratinidhi Sabha Nirvachan, 2048,* (Election for the House of Representatives, 1991), Kathmandu, 1991.
5. The account of the early stages of the Maoists evolution is based on; R.S. Chauhan, *The Political Development in Nepal 1950-70,* Associated Publishing House, New Delhi, 1971; R.S. Chauhan, *Society and State Building in Nepal,* Sterling Publishers, New Delhi, 1989; Bhim B. Rawal, *Nepal Ma Samyabadi Andolam: Uddhav Ra Bikas (Communist Movement in Nepal; Emergence and Development),* Pairabi Prakashan, Kathmandu, 1991; Sridhar K. Khatri, et. al., *Political Parties and Parliamentary Process in Nepal: A Study of the Transitional Phase,* Political Science Association of Nepal, Kathmandu, 1992; Pancha N. Maharajan, "Role of the Extra-parliamentary Political Party in Multi-party Democracy: A case Study of the CPN-Unity Centre", *Contributions to Nepalese Studies,* Vol. 20, No. 2, Kathmandu, July 1993; Pancha N. Mahajan, "The Maoist Insurgency and the Crisis of Governability in Nepal" in Dhriba Kumar (ed.), *Domestic Conflict And Crisis of Governability In Nepal,* CNAS, Centre for Nepal and Asian Studies, Tribhuwan University, Kathmandu, 2000, pp. 163-87; Krishna P. Khanal et al., *Nepal: People, Polity and Governance: A Survey Analysis of*

*People's Response to the Democratic Experiment (1991-95)*, Kathmandu, 1996; Krishna Hachhsthu, *Party Building in Nepal*, Mandala Book Point, Kathmandu, 2002.

6. Maharajan in Druba Kumar volume, *op. cit.* n. 3, p. 168.
7. Anand Swaroop Varma, *Rolpn sc Dolpa Tak* (From Rolpa to Dolpa: Nepal's Maoist Movement), Contemporary Third World, NOIDA, India, February 2001.
8. As quoted in Raeper and Hoftun, *Spring Awakening, op.cit*, p. 34.
9. *Nepal Backgrounder: Ceasefire — Soft Landing or Strategic Pause?* International Crisis Group (ICG), ICG Asia Report No. 50, Kathmandu Brussels, 10 April 2003, p. 4.
10. Bertil Lintner, "Nepal struggles to cope with the diehard Maoist violence", *Jane's Defence Weekly*, June 1999, p. 43.
11. Dr Baburam Bhattarai, *Politico-Economic Rationale of People's War in Nepal*, Monograph, 1998, www.icpnm.org. This monograph was also published in Kathmandu by Utprerak Publications Pvt. Ltd.
12. As quoted in Krishna B. Bhattachan, "Possible Ethnic Revolution or Insurgency In A Predatory Unitary Hindu State, Nepal", in Dhruba Kumar volume, pp. 135-62. Also see "Great Leap Forward", *The Hindustan Times*, 21 April 2001.
13. Deepak Thapa, "Day of the Maoist", in *Himal-South Asian*, Kathmandu, August 2000.
14. See, for instance, the documents of the National Convention of United Revolutionary People's Council (UPRC), held in September 2001 which underlines the representation of "oppressed nationalities, depressed regions, depressed castes and mass organizations" in the 37 member Executive Committee of the UPRC, *The Worker*, Organ of the CPN (Maoist), No. 7, January 2002, p. 10.
15. Speaking at a programme of Tharu Students Society and the Tharu Kalyankarini Sabha, Prime Minister Chand said that the "development of all nationalities is the prime need of the day". In that meeting the Tharu leaders demanded the establishment of Indigenous Nationalities Academy and introduce Indigenous Decade (1994-2004), "in order to rehabilitate the freed Kamaiyas and stop the Tharus from falling prey to both the security forces and the Maoists". The Tharus have been the original inhabitatnts of 22 districts from the east to the west of the country. *The Rising Nepal*, 16 January 2003.
16. Paul Harris, "Riots, bombs and strikes hit Nepal as Maoists' step in People's War", *Jane's Intelligence Review*, February 2001, p. 45.
17. Verma, *Rolpa se Dolpa Tak, op.cit*, n. 6, p. 31. Also Com. Parvati, "The Question of Women's Leadership in People's War in Nepal", *The Worker*, No. 8, January 2003.
18. *The Worker*, (Organ of the CPN-Maoist), No. 7, January 2002, pp. 60-61.
19. Documents adopted at the Third Plenum of the Central Committee of the CPN (Maoist) in March 1995, as quoted in Verma, *ibid.*, pp. 44-45.

20. Com. Prachanda's Report at the Second National Conference of the CPN-Maoist. *The Worker,* January 2002, *op.cit,* p. 52.
21. *ibid.,* p. 44.
22. Deepak Thapa, on Maoists Indian connection, in *Nepal Times* (Weekly) Kathmandu, 14-20 December 2001. On the Maoists with the fraternal groups in India, in the provinces of Bihar, UP, Jharkhand, Bengal and Sikkim, also see, Sanjay K. Jha, "The Maoist Maze", *South Asia Intelligence Review,* Vol. 1, No. 14, 21 October 2002, pp. 4-6. www.satp.org
23. Deepak Thapa, *Nepal Times,* see also his, "Day of the Maoists" in *Himal-South Asia,* Kathmandu, August 2000 and Sanjay Jha, 2002.
24. Bertin Lintener, "Nepal's Maoists Prepare for Final Offensive", *Intelligence Review,* October 2002. Also his, "Maoist Moneybags", *Eastern Economic Review,* 24 October 2002.
25. An outline of the economic policy, programme and process of the "New Democratic Revolution" can be found in Dr Baburam Bhattarai's article on "Politico-Economic Rationale of People's War in Nepal", *op. cit.*
26. Interview to Aunohita Mazumdar. *The Sunday Times of India,* New Delhi, 2 December 2001, p. 13.
27. Prachanda's Report at the Second National Conference, February 2001, *The Worker,* January 2002. *op. cit,* p. 55.
28. These components of the Maoists military line have been developed through four extended meeting of the party where experiences gathered in the field have been integrated to develop new concepts and approaches. *ibid.* pp. 54-56.
29. Prachanda's latest interview to *Janadharana Weekly,* (Nepalese) 19 December 2002.
30. *Ibid.,* see also his article "Nepal: Triangular balance of Forces", in *Economic and Political Weekly,* (Bombay), 16 November 2002. His article "*Nepali janakranti ka kehi tatkalin prashna-haru* (Some Contemporary Questions of Nepalese People's Revolution", *Third World (Committed to the Oppressed Nations & People),* Yr. 2, No. 2, May 30, 2002, pp. 5-8.
31. Dr. Bhattarai's interview to *Janadharana* (Nepalese) Weekly, 19 December 2002.
32. Verma, *Rolpa se Dolpa Tak, op. cit.,* pp. 22-33.
33. Baburam Bhattarai's statement soon after the Palace events. Also see, ICG Asia Report No. 50, *op. cit,* p. 5.
34. See *Indian Express,* 2 December 2002.
35. Interview in *The Sunday Times of India,* 2 December 2002.
36. Bertil Lintener, "Nepal Maoists Prepare For Final Offensive", *Janes Intelligence Review,* October 2002.
37. Com. Prachanda paid tributes to these martyrs in his report to Second National Conference, *The Worker,* January 2002, *op. cit.*

38. This has been brought out in a recent study conducted by Nepal Women's Council on request from Maoist Women's group, *Kathmnndu Post,* 7 February 2003.
39. Pushkar Gautam, "The King's Ceasefire", *Himal* (Kathmandu), Vol. 1, No. 2, February 2003, p. 10. A detailed discussion of the Maoists compulsions, for talks can also be found in, ICG Asia Report No. 5. *op.cit.*, pp. 10-12.
40. Personal interviews.
41. See Baburam Bhattarai's article in *Nepal Samacharpatra,* 8 February 2003.
42. Prime Minister Chand's assurances on this count to the CPN-UML leader Madhav Kumar Nepal. <nepalnews.com> 8 February 2003.
43. *Kathmandu Post,* 30 January 2003.
44. Baburam Bhattarai has owned it in his statement in *Nepal Samacharpatra* on 8 February 2003.
45. *The Himalayan* (Kathmandu), 12 April 2003; also *The Rising Nepal,* (Kathmandu), 12 April 2003.
46. *Indian Express,* 1 December 2001. On Koirala and Deuba approaches to the Maoists, also see, Deepak Thapa, "Maoist Insurgency in Nepal", *Dialogue* (A journal of Astha Bharati), Vol. 4, No. 2, October-December 2002, pp. 89-100.
47. ICG Asia Report No. 50, pp. 20-21, International Crisis Group.
48. "Nepal: A Deepening Human Rights Crisis", London, December 2002, Amnesty International.
49. Deepak Thapa, "Erosion of the Nepali World", *Himal-South Asia,* April 2002. Some observations on Nepalese army can also be found in Gen. Ashok K. Mehta, "The Maoist Insurgency in Nepal", *Dialogue,* Vol. 4, No. 2, Oct-Dec, 2002. pp. 101-109.
50. *Kathmandu Post,* 12 November 2002.
51. *Kathmandu Post,* 9 January 2003.
52. *Kathmandu Post,* 11 April 2003.
53. *Kathmandu Post,* 7 and 8 December 2002.
54. Verma, *op. cit,* see "The Story of a Failed negotiation", pp. 51-55.
55. Statements of the Chinese Ambassador in Kathmandu, *The Rising Nepal,* 30 November and 20 December 2001; *Kathmandu Post,* 3 September 1999. Also <www.nepalnews.com> 29 November, 11 and 19 December 2001.
56. <http://www.nepalnews.com>, 10 February 2003.
57. <nepalnews.com>, 16 January 2003.
58. *Kathmandu Post,* 8 November and 8 December 2002. Also <nepalnews.com>., 11 November 2002.
59. <kantipuronline.com>, 23 October 2002.
60. *Kathmandu Post,* 6 December 2002; also 28 January 2003.
61. *Kathmandu Post,* 1 March 2003.
62. For reports of her last visit in December 2002, see, *Kathmandu Post,* 14 and 15 December 2002.

63. *Ibid.*
64. For Deputy Assistant Secretary Scott Camp's statement at Heritage Foundation, see <nepalnews.com>, 4 March 2003. Also see the report on this subject in *Nepali Times,* No. 135, 7-13 March 2003.
65. *Kathmandu Post,* 28 March 2003.
66. *Kathmandu Post,* 2 January 2003.
67. <nepalnews.com br> 4 May 2002; *The Hindustan Times,* 5 May 2002.
68. <nepalnews.com br> 4 May 2002.
69. See Dr Bhattarai's article, "Some Current Issues of Nepali People'[5] Revolution", in *Third World,* Yr. 2, No. 2, 30 May 2002.
70. Suvecha Pant, "Seismic Station to be setup", *Kathmandu Post,* 4 March 2003.
71. General Ashok Mehta, in *Dialogue,* October-December 2002, *op. cit.* p. 104.
72. *Kathmandu Post,* 12 February 2003.
73 *Kathmandu Post,* 14 January 2003.
74. <nepalnews.com>, 7 January 2003.
75. The Indian Express (New Delhi), 3 January 2003.
76. For his statement see *The Hindu,* 17 February 2003.
77. For further details of these events see S.D. Muni, *India and Nepal: A Changing Relationslip,* Konark Publishers, New Delhi, 1993.
78. See for instance, two USI Journal articles, Shri Nishchal Nath Pandey, "Nepal's Maoist Movement and Implications for India", and Major General Ashok K. Mehta, AVSM (Retd.), "The Maoist Insurgency In Nepal: Implications for India", *Journal of the United Service Institution of India,* Vol. CXXXII, No. 550, October-December 2002, New Delhi, pp. 558-579. Also see, Puskar Gautam, "The King's Ceasefire", *Himal,* Vol. 16, No. 2, February 2003, Kathmandu, pp. 9-13.
79. Ghanshyam Ojha, "Seeds of doubt begin to sprout about peace process", *Kathmandu Post,* 8 April 2003.
80. The ICG Asia Report No. 50 of 10 April 2003, (*op.cit.*) on Nepal describes it as such.
81. www.kantipuronline.org
82. *Ibid.*, p. 20.
83. Major General Ashok K. Mehta in *USI Journal,* October-December 2002, *op. cit.*
84. The latest of such allegations has been made by the UML leader Madhav Kumar Nepal saying that the King is trying to instigate splits within the parties because they have decided to launch a decisive movement against hxim for democracy. <nepalnews.com> am 19 April 2003.
85. *Kathmandu Post,* 7 April 2003.
86. *The Kathmandu Post,* 11, 12 and 13 April 2003.
87. *The Himalayan Times* (Kathmandu), 3 April 2003.

88. <nepalnews.com> 16 April 2003.
89. For views expressed in Nepal to this effect see "Maoists need to clarify certain pertinent questions", in *The Telegraph,* (Weekly), Kathmandu 2 April 2003. Also Ram. S. Mahat, "Government - Maoist meeting of minds", *The Kathmandu Post,* 10 April 2003.
90. Interview given to Prateek Pradhan and Guna Raj Luitel, *The Kathmandu Post,* 2 April 2003.
91. Keshav Pradhan, "Nepal Maoists offer Sihanouk-like role to monarch", *The Hindustan Times* (New Delhi), 13 April 2003.

# 12
# The End of Shangri-La

### A Political Vacuum and Government Incompetence are Weakening Resistance to the Longstanding Insurgency

An enormous bomb blast ripped through a downtown government building still under construction. The residents of Kathmandu were jarringly reminded that their nation is not the idyllic redoubt it used to be. Apparently planted by Maoist rebels, the blast injured 38 people, the highest number of casualties recorded in a single day in the Kathmandu Valley. The bombing wasn't an isolated incident: over the course of a month, beginning in mid-August, rebels bombed two luxury hotels, forced a month-long shutdown of more than 35 businesses, announced plans to blockade the Kathmandu Valley (forcing the Army to help shuttle food and supplies into Nepal's capital for a week) and bombed the American Center—their first direct attack on a western diplomatic target. Officials in Nepal have finally woken up to the fact that the Maoist insurgency that began nearly nine years ago poses a genuine threat to the government. "Over the past two years the Maoists have obtained the ability to roam much more broadly through the country," says a Western diplomat in Kathmandu. "We are much closer to that which seemed almost laughable two years ago; a Maoist takeover has become possible. It has to be taken very seriously."

**Rebellion and Democratic Government**

It did not happen in a day. The rebellion has been growing in strength just as the democratically elected governments have been weakening. Since elections were introduced 14 years ago, Nepal has had 14 different governments. In the last two years the Parliament has been dissolved and King Gyanendra, an unpopular figure only raised to the throne after most of his family was killed in a palace massacre, has hired and fired three prime ministers. One of them, Sher Bahadur Deuba, who'd been sacked for "incompetence," is now once again running the country. Ordinary Nepalis are frustrated. On September 1 riots broke out in the capital after 12 Nepalese citizens were killed in Iraq. The government's response to that crisis was slow and telling. "There is no security in this country," says Tulsi Tladhar, 38, a motorcycle-parts dealer whose business was destroyed by the mob.

**Maoists Base**

In the hinterland of the country, the Maoists rule the roost. With upwards of 5,000 hard core combatants, they now exert some degree of control over two-thirds of the countryside. Many villages in Nepal's far western region stand deserted owing to Maoist threats of violence and forced enlistment, as well as the lack of a reliable food supply. The Geneva-based Global IDP Project estimates that between 100,000 and 200,000 people have been displaced as a result of the conflict, and more than 10,000 people have lost their lives. In addition, an estimated 700 schools across the country have been closed owing to the insurgency. The rebels have destroyed government buildings, airports, bridges, power plants and telecommunications systems. Nepal's GDP will grow at an estimated 3.7 per cent this year—but that's about half of what could be achieved, say experts, if the rebels could be defeated. The Royal Nepalese Army is stretched thin coping with the Maoist threat. The RNA has 78,000 troops now, but about two-thirds of them have been hired in the last few years. It's not exactly a battle-hardened force; the Army was a largely ceremonial organization before democracy was restored to the Himalayan kingdom in 1990. While the military budget has increased 150 per cent in the past four years (from $ 80 million to $ 204 million), Army officials say they still need more soldiers and weapons.

The United States—which has provided $ 22 million in military aid and, along with India, is one of Nepal's biggest aid donors—has promised 20,000 M16 rifles, but sources say only 17,000 have been delivered. Washington has put additional funding requests on hold, citing possible human rights abuses by the Army.

One of the world's largest per capita recipients of foreign aid, Nepal now has serious problems delivering aid to rural residents. Many development projects have been delayed. The latest casualty is the 70 megawatt Middle Marsyangdi hydropower project. Valued at $165 million and largely funded by Germany, it was one of the country's largest infrastructure projects until it was shutdown by Maoists last week—the third work stoppage at the site since construction began in 2001. When he appointed Deuba as prime minister five months ago, the king gave him two priorities—hold elections as soon as possible and start peace talks with the rebels. Neither is imminent, though Deuba saysi he's determined to have elections by April.

On the other hand analysts apine that the polls are crucial, given that there has been no popular representation in more than two years. The prime minister says that restoring peace is a priority but cautions: "One cannot make miracles in 14 years. People's expectations were very high after democracy. In a poor country like Nepal, it's very difficult." He admits that "Nepal won't remain the same, but a new Nepal will emerge." What kind of country will it be? The prime minister couldn't say.

# 13
# Tibetan Legend

### The Magic Word is Dalai Lama

For many westerners, Tibet is only a vague geographical conception. For some it breathes mystery and magic. But Tibet moved into the bright light of the present when insistent forces in the Indian continent and later in China brought about a reorganization of their states. Then Tibet too was caught up by the tide of political reorientation.

For Tibetans themselves, is the centre of the earth and the earthly reflection of the all-embracing cosmos. Kailash mountain is in Tibet, which is also home to the lake Mansrovar. After Chinese byted restrictions for those who wanted to go, it has become a place of pilgrimage. In Hindu mythology, it is the abode of Lord Shiva. Tibet is the 'navel of the earth', as the Tibetans call it, *Ssa ji lTa ba.* Between the glaciers of the Himalayas in the south, and the steppes and inhospitable desert lands of the north, stretches the high plateau, into which the great river valleys are carved: those valleys that form green oases in summer and have become the homes of most of the population. The great rivers of eastern and southern Asia flow from the land of Tibet or have their source in the border territory of this 'navel of the earth'.

### Springs of Tibet

From the Indus to the Brahmaputra, from the Irawadi, Salween, Mekong and Yang-tse Kiang to the Hwang-ho, the springs of Tibet or of the Sino-Tibetan frontier zone water the soil of the Indian, Indo-chinese and Chinese countryside. Thus Tibet, with a present population of three or four millions, about a third of whose men live as Lamas in the many monasteries of the country, has in past centuries almost always lived on the edge of events. The world of its people was different from that of neighbouring races. Therefore the neighbours were moulders of Tibet's fate to a greater extent than her own sons were.

In the seventh century A.D., the first historical character of this Central Asian area made himself the sole ruler of the whole of Tibet. He came Yarlung region which is the eastern part of Tibet, to the south of Brahmaputra. This was Sron bTsan sgam po. His battles with Nepal and China were so successful that he was able to begin a great game of world politics and make an alliance with the Arabs. In about 715 the two allies, Tibet and Arabia, even jointly established a king in Iranian Ferghana, who served as a link between the Tibetan king and the Arab caliphs.

**Harun al Rashid**

Harun al Rashid, the most popular of all the Abbassid caliphs in Bagdad was not interested in Asia. His eyes were looking at the West. West rather than to the East, and neglected the Tibetan alliance. Militarily, of course, he relied upon Iranian troops from Khorasan and Ferghana in modern Turkestan. The uncertainty of aim as between military and political goals hastened the dissolution of the Arabian empire. In Morocco the Idrisids made themselves independent, as did the Aghlawids in Tunisian Kairwan. At the same time Charlemagne sent an embassy from Aix-la-Chapelle to Bagdad. The western part of Islam, which received political preference from Bagdad, showed its gratitude for this preference by political decay. The eastern part—Khorasan—although it still took the lead, especially in military matters, replied in a military manner by a revolt which Harun himself had to set out to quell. He died on this punitive expedition in the town of Tus. The Tibetan flank, where the neglected former allies of the Arabians were passively watching the rebellion in Khorasan, was exposed, and therefore the question of Turkestan could not be decided. Then in 810 A.D. Harun's successor, Al-Maimun, remembered the Tibetans and asked for renewal of all the treaties. In 822 a 'Stele' was erected, which still stands in the Potala palace and on which the first Sino-Tibetan treaty was chiselled. The monolith informs us:

> The Lord of Tibet, the divine King, full of wonderful strength, and the great King of China, Hwang Te, nephew and uncle on the maternal side, have agreed to unite their kingdoms. This great agreement was made that it may always be faithfully kept and never changed. All gods and men were called upon to be witnesses of the sacred oath. That this may always be so from generation to generation, the terms of our alliance have been cut here in stone.
>
> The King of wonderful strength, Ti-de-Tsen, and the Chinese King Bun Pu He-u Tig Hwang Te, nephew and uncle, united their kingdoms, confident that it would further the mutual well-being of Tibet and China, and that all men would receive much happiness, within and without, and that each and every one would be happy and prosperous for a long time.

It was always difficult for the Chinese to rule in Tibet. History induates that it was easy for the Chinese to rule Tibet. At every opportunity the people of Tibet revolted.

Tibet remained a part of the East Asian world, and the unique opportunity of playing a part in world politics could not be used. In the place of external successes, internal inconsistencies suddenly made thdmselves felt. Through them the Tibetans experienced religious wars for the first time. Missionaries of Buddhism had crossed the Himalayas again and again, but King gLan dar Mar persecuted them between 836 and 842 by all possible means. To this end he favoured the *Bon* faith. This was a religion strongly permeated with magic and Shamanism. Bon priests have the reputation of being powerful magicians. They are said to conjure up demons, to rule over nature—especially hail—to heal the sick, and to be able to make astrological forecasts.

The *Bon-po*—the adherents of the Bon religion—often make inquiries into the fate of their relations in the other world through these priest-magicians, by sending them on a 'reconnaissance after souls'. To do this the priests, clothed in blue and black garments, like the Shamans of eastern Siberia, go into a state of trance. Today much of the Christian inheritance lies dormant in the Bon religion. Manichaeans and Nestorians have greatly changed its character, which was originally purely Shamanistic. Buddhism brought about something else, after the discussions throughout the centuries ended in the adoption of some doctrines from Buddha's teaching. The Bon are still partly represented in Tibet proper, but they have the largest number of adherents in the Tibetan provinces of the North and South which were not under the jurisdiction of the Dalai Lama.

**The Land of Bod**

A German research worker, Matthias Hermanns, believed that the very heart of Tibetan nationhood lay in one of these Tibetan frontier lands. In his work, *The Nomads of Tibet,* he writes of the Amdo, who are known elsewhere in European literature as Tunguts and dwell in the Koko Nor province, that they are the actual bearers of *Bod yul,* the land of Bod, as the Tibetans call their home. Hermanns rejects the view that this Bod signifies Buddha. According to him, Bod is the tribal ancestor of this race. However, Buddhism became known in the capital at the time of the first Tibetan king. Sron bTsan sgam po had two wives, princesses from China and Nepal. But in the times which followed there were again and again difficulties for the teaching of Buddha. It is true that in the tenth and eleventh centuries an intensified missionary drive established his doctrine in the minds of the people, but it soon led to dissensions.

**Tson K'a pa**

The reformer Tson K'a pa (1357-1419) called forth a great movement towards unity. He came from the region of the afore-mentioned Amdo Tibetans, and wanted to give priority above other sects to his own lamaistic interpretation of Buddha's teaching, in a Tibet which in the course of the centuries had become completely Buddhist—apart from the few remaining Bon.

Ever since this time only two sects have actually played a part amongst the Tibetans: the sect called Tson K'a po of the' Yellow Ones'—or *dge Lugspa,* which means 'virtuous sect'—and that of the' 'Red Ones', whose significance is fading steadily. The 'Yellow Ones' are predominant, and the great Lamas who attained world fame belong to this sect. The successors of the first pupil of Tson K'a pa since about 1470 have been held to be the incarnation of Bodhisattva Avalokitesvara. *Bodhisattva* is a person who has been called to highest perfection, that is to say, somebody who is close to attainment of Buddha-dom, but renounces it out of pity for other creatures and in order to smooth their road to perfection. Whilst the Dalai Lama is considered to be the earthly embodiment of the Bodhisattva Avalokitesvara, whereas is represented by Panchen Lama Buddha Amitibha.

In Mongols were on a rampage in Central Asia in the thirteenth century. After the proclamation of the Mongolian Qubilai (Kubla Khan) as Great Khan and simultaneously as Emperor of the Chinese, Tibet became politically part of Mongolian China, whose dynasty took the name Yuan. In past centuries the Chinese emperors had only now and then entered into brief political relationships with Tibet, which, in spite of vows of eternal loyalty, can count only as interludes. Following the union with the Mongolian rulers of China, there began the dependence upon the 'Middle Kingdom', which was stressed again and again from the Chinese side, but which was generally only nominal. The Mongolians who, soon after the death of Genghis Khan, had come under the influence of Buddhism, ruled mildly in Tibet in the subsequent years. There came about a kind of community of fate between Tibetans and Mongolians, especially after the sons of Genghis Khan bowed before Buddha and his teaching, and honoured as their spiritual leader, Ganden-Truppa, the Grand Lama of Tibet, who was a follower of Tson K'a pa. The first pupil of Ganden-Truppa (1391-1474) is reckoned as the first in the succession of the Grand Lamas who later received the title of Dalai Lama (that is, 'Ocean-wide Lama').

**Religious Activities of the Mongols**

In order to direct the religious activities of the Mongols the third grand Lama, Grand Lama Sonam Gyatso, in 1580 went to Mongolia, where Lamaism had been accepted as the official religion. Eversince the Western historians came across this word, it has been fasunation then. Some where around the last years of the eighteenth century the British nicknamed Tibet as "Middle Kingdom. When he died Tibetan-Mongolian relationships were deepened still further, because his rebirth was discovered in the Mongolian royal family. This fourth Grand Lama, bSod-nam-srgyam-tso, was the first to bear officially the name of Dalai Lama, a designation in which a Mongolian word was combined with a Tibetan one, thus announcing the future spiritual community of Mongolians and Tibetans. The Mongolian fourth Dalai Lama gave a special gift to his countrymen: in 1602 he confirmed a Mongolian reincarnation of another *Bodhisattva* near Urga: Maidari Khutuktu.

In 1924 the last in the succession of these three greatest Buddhist incarnations, Je-tsun tam-pa, died as head of state in Outer Mongolia, Outer Mongolia had by then become a communist-stat. Buddhism was no more the stae religion. The re-incarnation was no onger continued because of communism.

The sovereignty of China, which Tibet had always felt to be nominal, was forgotten for a time when the Manchus ascended the imperial throne of Peking. However, the Manchus did not forget Tibet. They invited the fifth Dalai Lama to Peking, where an unwritten concordat controlled their relations from that time onwards: the Chinese governed Tibet and respected the Dalai Lama as politically highest amongst the Lamas, but he was allowed to speak only as a spiritual authority. It is curious that the Panchen Lama (or Tashi Lama) yielded place more and more to the Dalai Lama, although the former was intended to be a 'higher embodiment' and actually also higher ranking. The political situation in Tibet remained unchanged. The Dalai Lamas continued to summon the faithful to worship by means of mussel shells, as they had done for centuries—the sixth, it is true, also found time to write really profane love songs, which are still sung today by young Tibetans—and, seen from Peking, their country was nothing but an inhospitable land. It was a punishment post.

### The British Interest

Tibet just about existed for the outside world, until the European powers—Russia and England—appeared on the scene. The British first took an interest in Tibet in 1768, when the Court of Directors of the East India Company decided to seek out possibilities of trading in the land of the Dalai Lama and in western China. However, no economic or political relations developed between India and Tibet until the Gurkhas of Nepal were suddenly involved in a war with the Chinese. At this juncture the Nepalese quickly made a commercial treaty with the British, although until then they had adopted a very hostile attitude towards them. During the war between Nepal and China, Lord Cornwallis, the Governor-General of Calcutta, received a letter from the Chinese commander-in-chief, Marshal Fu-K'ang-an, dated 31st March 1792, asking for the support of the British against the Nepalese troops. Similarly the Dalai Lama and the Panchen Lama wrote to him, the former in Tibetan, the latter in Persian.

In spite of these beginnings of diplomatic correspondence, Tibet remained closed, even though individual Britons attempted to cross the Himalayas, as, for example, Thomas Manning, who in 1811 was the first

Englishman to reach the court of Lhasa. Tibet had as a matter of fact been the goal of other Europeans for long enough, and here it was especially a question of Christian missionaries. The Jesuits tried often enough to penetrate into Tibet from India. In the years between 1603 and 1607 Benedict Goes undertook a dangerous journey from Agra, which in fact took him more to the north, to Khotan and Turfan. Desiderius visited Tibet between 1714 and 1722. At the same time the Italian Capucins had begun their Tibetan mission (1713).

### Christian Mission in Tibet

From 1625 to 1640 there was already a Christian mission to Tibet in Tsaparang, which today is unfortunately almost forgotten. At that time the ruler of Guge was about to be converted to Christianity in the mission founded by Father Andrade, but a war with Ladakh lost him the throne and his plan could not be carried out. The inhabitants of Guge, who had become Christians, were taken away as slaves. The vision of a Catholic Himalayan empire vanished. In the Treaty of Nanking, concluded in 1842 between the British and Chinese, which opened five treaty ports to the British, there were no clauses providing for trade with Tibet. This situation lasted until 1876 when, in the Convention of Ch'i-fu (concluded on 13th September), England reserved the right to carry out negotiations for British trade missions in Tibet also.

By the Convention of Ch'i-fu China established diplomatic foreign embassies, first in London, then in Berlin (1877), Paris, Washington, Tokyo (1878), St Petersburg and Madrid (1879). In the past decades the British had striven to improve their position in Nepal, Sikkim and Bhutan, and, since the two latter in particular had long-standing connections with Tibet, they had at the same time to come to terms with this country. It was not until 17th March 1890, in an agreement signed in Calcutta by the Governor-General of India, Lord Lansdowne, and the Chinese governor in Lhasa, Sheng-t'ai, that the British succeeded in separating Sikkim politically from Tibet and placing it under British protection. The Tibetans showed no inclination to keep this convention. Their words to the British and Chinese were the same: 'We are not parties to the convention and do not feel ourselves bound.' In recent years the Chinese themselves had suffered one reverse after another, in both diplomatic and military affairs: Korea, Annam and Burma renounced their loyalty to Peking. At this favourable moment the British tried to start conversations with Lhasa, so as to gain for themselves influence and opportunities for trade in Tibet.

### Russia Enters

At that point of time, Russia became a force to be reckoned with. The warm relationship between Tibetans and Mongolians has already been mentioned. The Russians, who knew of this connection, secured Mongolian agents in order to gain influence over the Tibetans. It was the time when the thirteenth Dalai Lama played a skilful part in world politics. Of course the spiritual diplomat from the roof of the world was waging an unequal struggle. He had to deal with world powers. That is when he started playing off the British against Russia.

Mongolians being next door, in their treatment of the Mongolians, the Russians always showed good psychological insight. After the long-standing remembrance, mingled with fear and terror, of the Mongolian-Tartar period of their history, there came in the nineteenth century an intellectual literary reaction, in which a new interpretation of their relationship to the Mongolians began. The Russians rediscovered amongst the Mongolians the dynamic strength, the action, which is necessary if a fresh wind is to blow through the landscape of ageing civilizations.

**Russia's Aversion**

It was the period when Russia felt an aversion to Europe and a corresponding inclination towards Asia. It was at one and the same time the intellectual under-pinning and the justification of the tsarist Asian policy, carried forward more and more ruthlessly. In his *Dnevnik pisatelya* (the 'Diary of a Writer'), Dostoyevsky had already challenged the Russians to take up a positive attitude towards Asia. 'We must free ourselves from the slavish fear of being called "Asiatic barbarians", more Asian than European, by Europe.' The Orthodox religious philosopher, N.F. Fyodorov, looked to the Himalayas, to Pamir, and challenged the Tsar to assume the title 'Pamirski', in order to indicate that the area where lay the grave of the first man, Adam, had come under the protection of Russia. It was Russia's task to be the guardian of this grave, and also of that of the second Adam, Christ—in the latter case in succession to the Emperor of the Second Rome. From these heralds of Asia, the intellectual path of the Russians turned towards Asia and passed by way of the Pan-Mongolianism of Solovyev, who out of his Christian chiliastic longing greets the rise of Asia as the end of history, to Alexander Blok, who amidst the turmoil of the revolution announced his 'Scythian Ideas' in verse:

> '. . . Yes, Scythians, we are Asiatics!
> We gaze greedily out of our slit-shaped eyes . . .'

**Asiatic Mongols**

It is no wonder that amongst the lamaistic Buryat and Kalmuck subjects of the Tsar, some regarded Russia as their fate. These Asiatic Mongolian friends of Russia identified the great future kingdom of eternity, Shambhala, the land of the North, with the state of the tsars. In 1893 a memorandum by the politically interested Doctor Badmaiev was laid upon

Alexander III's desk in which he indicated that lamaistic ideas must be given more attention in Russia. That was a prerequisite of an increase in the power of the Tsar over these regions. The Lamas desired it. Tibet must be the immediate goal of Russian endeavours.

In order to attain a successful Asian policy, Russia started training diplomats who were not influenced by Europe. Under the thirteenth Dalai Lama, Ngag-dbang Lo-bzang Thub-Idan, an experienced Buryat-Mongolian played an important part. He was Agran Doryiyev, whose Tibetan name was Nag-dban-rDo-rJe. Twice, in October 1900 and July 1901, the latter was sent by the spiritual and political leader of Tibet to St Petersburg, where he was received in audience by the Tsar Nicholas II. At the second visit he was able to present himself as Ambassador Extraordinary of Tibet. Doryiyev made to the ruler of all the Russians a proposition no less than that he should declare himself the protector of Buddhism and should see it as Russia's task to be a liberator of the Asiatic peoples. The appearance of Doryiyev on the Neva quickly put Great Britain on the alert.

A month after the last audience of Doryiyev, in August 1901, the British Foreign Minister, Lord Lansdowne, instructed his ambassador in St Petersburg to inform the Russian Foreign Minister, Count Lamsdorf, that the Government of His Britannic Majesty would not remain indifferent if an attempt was made from any direction to change the present status of Tibet. Another empire's attention was roused: the State of the Tenno. And it is remarkable that in the same year both island states set about defending themselves against the continental power of Russia. Japan saw the Tsar's influence growing fatefully in that area which she claimed as her sphere of interest in the Far East.

**British Efforts**

However, the Great Britain wanted to steal a march upon Russia, so as to remove Tibet from tsarist influence. Therefore in the year 1904 a British expeditionary force under Younghusband marched to Lhasa in order to open the trade route from India to China. A convention with the Tibetans gave the British the right to set up three trading stations on Tibetan soil: Gyantse, Gartok and Yatung. The convention was extended in 1906 to China, who then accepted the conditions. However, in 1910 the Manchu emperors sent troops into the country to reinforce their rule over the land of the Dalai Lama. The spiritual lord of the Potala palace fled to Darjeeling. Meanwhile the Chinese emphasized that Nepal and Bhutan were vassal states of China and Tibet.

It is true that a treaty between England and Bhutan had helped to hinder this development, but Chinese disturbances intervened. They were the starting signal for the first great October Revolution of modern times, when, on the tenth day of the tenth month in the year 1911, the Middle

Kingdom lost its imperial and monarchic character and became a republic. Whilst the Manchu emperors were being obliged to yield to the republican revolutionaries, the Dalai Lama proclaimed the independence of Tibet, which lasted from 1911 to 1949. In 1912 Tibet issued the first postage stamps. The stamps which appeared until 1950 are not exactly beautiful, to be sure, but they are nevertheless small paper witnesses of a modern expression of the sovereignty which before 1911 was just Chinese suzerainty, an iridescent word for the status of a country which, internally autonomous, has handed over its foreign policy to the government of another state.

**Chinese Efforts**

There has been no lack of Chinese attempts to change circumstances in Tibet once more; since about 1933, after the death of the thirteenth Dalai Lama, there have been some Tibetans who tried of their own accord to find means of reunion with China. But the majority was against it, and therefore the regent Ra-dreng Hutukhtu, abbot of the Ra-dreng monastery, who was friendly to China, came to grief. Yet there was no more good fortune in the choice of his successor, who drew up a rigorous system of government. In the course of the internal struggles and intrigues, the Panchen Lama went to China, and when he died his reincarnation soon came likewise under Chinese influence. When the Communist government of Mao Tse-tung was proclaimed in 1949, the claim to Tibet was immediately re-established. India was interested at once, and the developments in the neighbouring country were closely observed. On 25th October 1950 the troops of Red China moved into Tibet; on 26th October 1950 they occupied Lhasa. The 'agreement on measures for the peaceful liberation of Tibet' was signed on 23rd May 1951 in Peking.

The Dalai Lama had in fact appealed to international public opinion, but protests were of no avail. The Austrian Heinrich Harrer lived in Tibet for seven years before the Communist entry and was witness of the events which took place on the 'roof to the world' shortly before the *Anschluss*. He reported on these events in detail in his book *Seven Years in Tibet*. The Dalai Lama's protest against the entry of Red China into his country had been unavailing. He soon returned home from his brief flight from the soldiers of Peking, stripped, it is true, of all political power. Those nearest to him advised a policy of 'Wait and see'.

**Buddhism and Marxism**

Today both Tibetan Grand Lamas are pretty, decorative pawns in Peking's Buddhist game, a wonderful opportunity of showing that Buddhism and Marxism are not incompatible. The Buddhist card is one of the many which are intermingled in the game of world politics in Tien An Men, the old imperial city in northern China. The 'Case of Tibet', moreover, was to enrich the political 'double talk' of today by a treaty. In it the 'five principles' were formulated for the first time. This Tibetan Treaty, concluded between India and China on 29th April 1954, brought to an end the special status of the land of the Dalai Lama and recognized it as an autonomous region within the Chinese People's Republic.

Thereby, for the first time, the following general principles were established, which were to regulate the relationship of the states with each other:

1. Mutual respect for the state of possession and sovereignty.
2. Disavowal of all acts of aggression.
3. Non-interference in the internal affairs of the other country.
4. Equality of rights and preservation of mutual advantages.
5. Peaceful co-existence.

**Visit to India**

In 1956, on the occasion of the two thousand five hundredth anniversary of the death of Buddha, the Dalai Lama and the Panchen Lama Ngoerhtehni visited India also. It was the first time that these two supreme dignitaries had made a state visit to a foreign country. It is strange how far the two neighbouring countries of Tibet and India are removed from each other intellectually. What worlds divide the countries on both sides of the Himalayas! And how moved the spectator is during such a visit. A breath of far-off exotic distance touches us at the sound of the Dalai Lama's name.

The institution of this priest-ruler over the people of Tibet is unique. He lives far away in the mysterious city of Lhasa, in the fairy-tale Potala palace, and myth and legend have helped to spread around him the magic of the unapproachable and divinely distant. Then suddenly one is face to face with a laughing, black-spectacled young man who today embodies the tradition of the Dalai Lama. People of his race, living as merchants or shepherds anywhere along the southern slopes of the Himalayas, from Bhutan, Sikkim, Nepal or Ladakh in Kashmir, have travelled hundreds and hundreds of miles to do honour to the head of lamaistic Buddhism.

**Buddhist Tree Ceremony**

On 22nd December 1956, I was witness lo a Buddhist tree Ceremony. In the Buddha-Vihara in Mehrauli, outside the gates of Delhi, there stood a young shoot of the pipala or Bo-tree from Budh-Gaya. Once under the fig-tree of Budh-Gaya the monk Gautama, the 'enlightened one', had become the Buddha. Since that time Buddhists all over the world have tried to obtain a cutting from this tree which is sacred to them. Thus Asoka's son, who was already active as a Buddhist missionary, brought such a cutting to the royal city of Ceylon, Anuradhapura. Because of the two thousand five hundredth anniversary of the entry of Buddha into

Nirvana, the year 1956 saw in India one Buddhist celebration after another. Scholars from all over the world, whose field of research is Buddhism, had hastened to a Buddhist symposium, in order to pay their tribute in New Delhi to India's greatest son.

This tribute was scientific in that an attempt was made to assess the intellectual position of Buddhism. Nothing is more difficult than that, for there can scarcely be a greater difference than there is between the Hinayana Buddhism of Ceylon and south-eastern Asia, and the Mahayana of the Far East. In-between are the adherents of the lamaistic groups of the Himalayan countries and the Tibetan-Mongolian regions. Here magic has replaced the ethical discipline which was Buddha's aim. For the first time an attempt was made in New Delhi to find a formula uniting all the adherents of Buddhism. But it was only a polite discussion over and around the matter. How could there be a unity between those people who on the one hand see in the Buddha absorption in the Absolute, a state of happiness without feeling and suffering, and those who on the other hand believe him to be ever born anew in one of the lamaistic leaders of Tibet?

**Unity**

How is a magic formula of unity possible where on the one side cold reason denies almost everything metaphysical, whilst on the other, the mere simple recitation of magic formulae and the primitive technique of a prayer mill are supposed to translate one to the region of metaphysics ? Nevertheless there remains a certain demonstration of pan-Buddhism running through this first all-Buddhist symposium on the soil of India, which has long ceased to be Buddhist. Mahatheras from Hinayana-Buddhism, that is to say, the heads of the Buddhist monasteries in Ceylon, Burma, Thailand and Cambodia, sat at the same table with lamas from Mongolia, Tibet and Sikkim and with Buddhist priests from Japan, China and Vietnam.

The most impressive event was, however, the arrival of the Tibetan Buddhist leaders—the Dalai Lama and the Panchen Lama, The Dalai Lama had been invited to India several times, but the answer was always: He cannot come. And then he was there. He climbed down from the roof of the world, accompanied by a staff of the highest officials, the so-called 'Lotus-footed ones'. When one sees the smiling, youthful Dalai Lama, one is transferred to a primeval age of magic, when kings still walked upon the earth as the sons of god. The Panchen Lama always sits motionless; his smile gives the impression of a statue. One believes that Asia's mistrust lies hidden behind this frozen smile. On the other hand, the Dalai Lama has lively eyes, glancing hither and thither. Sometimes one sees a roguish wrinkle in the corners of his eyes. Nevertheless one dreams of the age of magic.

**Shadow of th Bo-tree**

Suddenly a camera is drawn out. A flash-light flares up. It does not disturb the Panchen Lama. But the Dalai Lama (shall I meanwhile reveal his full name? He is called Geston Ngwang Lbsang Tengin Gyapso Sisunwanggyur Tschungpa Mapai Dhepal Sangpo—that is to say: 'the only holy one, the tender glory, powerful of word, pure in spirit, of divine wisdom, preserver of the faith, ocean-wide'), the Dalai Lama, the fourteenth of a long succession, has bent forward in a way quite unlike a Dalai Lama. He follows closely every movement of the amateur photographer. One sees that he would now like to leave his throne with its golden brocade canopy in order to ask with interest about the make, the price, black-and-white or colour films and such like, as all inquiring students do here. He looked a ordinary, curious youngman, anyone who would be curious about any new gadget.

As I was coming away from the short tree ceremony, one of the Sikkimese princes smiled at me. I asked him what was amusing him so much. Amusing him? Had I not felt that the sacred shadow of the Bo-tree, of the tree of illumination, had fallen upon me? It was as holy as the tree. Of course I could not feel this, poor sceptical son of distant Europe that I was. The holy tree seemed to me a tree like any other, and the Dalai Lama—a nice boy. It is of such scenes taken from the picturesque course of the now vanished Tibetan legend that one must inevitably think in order to escape from the terrifying spectacle now offered by the contemporary history of Tibet, for who now will venture to deny that a frightful conclusion is being attempted through the forced absorption of the Tibetan people into the Communist society of the People's Republic of China?

**Flight to India**

The struggle in Tibet reached its height in the dramatic flight of the Dalai Lama to India in March 1959. Shortly after his arrival on Indian soil, a high Tibetan official announced from Tezpur in the North-Eastern Frontier Agency that he had fled from Tibet of his own free will. What the Chinese headquarters in Lhasa described as an 'invitation' to visit them constituted a danger to the Dalai Lama being held as a hostage in Communist hands or suffering some worse fate. The people in Lhasa knew very well that this sort of thing had gone on in Hungary in 1956, and they knew too how the will of the people was suppressed in 1953 both in East Berlin and in East Germany. Popular feeling was particularly roused in India by the flight of the Dalai Lama.

**India or Edge**

The foreign observer in India was able to sense during those years how political feeling and popular influence ran in relation to foreign affairs. Such an attitude had never become noticeable since the rising in Hungary. India was on edge during that period.

When he had reached India and Settled there, the normally retrient Dalai Lama became vocal about the tragIn order to direet the religious activities of the Mongols the third grand Lama.ic events in his home country, but he was forbidden to establish a government in exile in India. Nevertheless, contrary to the advice of the Indian Government, he determined to request the United Nations to mediate between China and Tibet.

The brother of the High Lama, Gyalo Thondup, whom correspondents delighted to call 'foreign minister of the exiled Tibetan Government' (which was never formed), travelled to New York, and got the U.N.O. delegates of Ireland and Malaya to listen to him and bring the case of his people before the world forum. They proposed a debate which lasted for two days, and ended on 21st October in a resolution deploring the events in Tibet and calling for respect for the fundamental human rights of the Tibetan people. For his part the Dalai Lama expounded the plight of his people in courageous and determined fashion from his successive places of refuge at Mussoorie and Dharamsala. On 7th August 1960 the International Commission of Jurists at Geneva had published a report running to 343 pages under the title *Tibet and the Chinese People's Republic,* in which this acknowledged aggression by the Chinese in Tibet was characterized as genocide, and further proved that Peking was trying to breakdown the social and religious structure of Tibet, that it had outraged most of the human rights formulated in U.N.O. declarations and that finally Tibet had been an independent state, *de facto,* previous to 1951.

One the other hand, the Panchen Lama found himself forced to play a degrading part in the tragedy of Tibet by declaring, on 24th October 1960, that he condemned the inclusion of Tibetan affairs in the agenda of the United Nations Organization, since it interfered in the internal affairs of China. But still the misery of Tibet remains unrelieved, an immediate fact about a country that once seemed to us dim with the mists of legend. In the meantime the battle for a 'progressive' development goes on in Tibet. The case of Tibet does not concern China alone. That is what the Chinese Tieh-Tseng Li expressed in his book, *The Historical Status of Tibet,* which appeared in 1956:

> Whatever the world situation may be, the author believes that an understanding between India and China such as exists between the United States and Canada, with an agreement on the demilitarization of the Himalayas, which are the decisive element of both Indian and Chinese geography, offers not only a guarantee of the autonomous state of Tibet, but is also a stabilizing factor for world peace.

# 14

# Political, Economic and Religious Relations Between Mongolia and Tibet

All along in history of Central Asia, Mongolia has had political, economic and religio-cultural connections with the lands of China, Tibet, Russia, Manchuria, Korea and other countries in the region. The Mongols have had ancient and deep connections with Tibet, the "Country of the Snows", dating back to the 1 century A.D. In the historical record, we have some evidence of this. The chiefs of ancient Mongol tribes, such as Tamachi and Horicher Mergen, are known to have invited Tibetan monks ot then methods Buddhist worship.

The beginnings of deep relationships date back to Chingis Khaan's time; during Khubilai Khaan's reign these were consolidated. In 1212 the Tanguts repealed their concordat not to attack each other; they started to assist the Mongols from 1213.[1] When the Mongols attacked the Tangut Xi-xia state, they never touched the Tibetan monasteries and monks who were part of this Xi-xia state.[2]

**Racial Affinity**

Concerning this matter, Rinchen Lhamo has commented that probably the racial affinity of Mongols and Tibetans contributed to this. Very likely there were Tibetans among the Mongol hosts. And the religious connection might perhaps, even at this early time, have already commenced. Around the XIII century A.D., when he was living in Khokhnuur, Lord Goodon, a son of Guyug Khaan, invited Saja bandida Gungaajaltsan to join him; Gungaajaltsan composed a new grammar for written Mongol script, which was very important in the formation of the Mongol written language.[4]

At that time Gungaajaltsan's nephew Lodoijaltsan. who was 10 years old, accompanied him. In 1260 Pagva lama was invited to the court of Khubilai Khaan and given the title of state teacher. Pagya Lama played an important role in establishing the two ruling systems of religion and state. The Mongols decided to adopt Buddhism as state religion. By order of Khubilai Khaan, Pagva Lama devised a new script in, square characters; the shape was akin to Tibetan, while the writing style was like Mongol script. Tibetans called it *hor-yig*. Khubilai Khan, eclectic in religion and sensitive like the Roman magistracy, to the use of the Church in temporal affairs, invited the then leading priest of Tibetan Buddhism, the abbot of the great Sakya monastery to his Court to give the blessing of the greatest Church in Asia to the widest Empire then known to man.

During the Mongol Empire, Tibetan monks had powerful rights: they could travel by relay services as state delegations. By this time the development of the Buddhist monastery in that country into a temporal power had progressed so far that the clerical princes were as numerous and as powerful as the lay, and the Sakya hierarch was himself the most important individual prince in the country.[5] When the Mongol Empire collapsed, relations between Mongol kings and lords and Tibetan monks were almost severed. This time was called "The nadir of religion" in the historical sources. So it is likely that the relations between the Mongol and Tibetan countries were not extensive. However, beginning once more in the XVIth century and lasting until the beginning of the XVIII century, there was once again a flowering of relations whose extent and depth had very important consequences in the history of the two countries.

**Political Fragmentation**

By the beginning of the XVI century, Mongolia had undergone political disintegration and was divided into fragments—Khalkh Mongolia, Inner Mongolia and Oirad Mongolia. The Mongol aristocracy desired this separation. China, Russia, Manchuria, Tibet and Central Asian neighbours likewise counted them as three different countries, and formally referred to them as the "Oirad State, Khalkh State" etc. It was also clear that the powerful neighbouring countries, Russia and China were keen to exploit this situation for their political advantage. Of course, the transmission of Buddhism to Mongolia was directly from Tibet; there was no need to receive it from other countries.

Tibet was the heartland of the Buddhist religion, the holy place to which all believers naturally gravitated. Thus the Mongol aristocracy supported Tibetan Buddhism, while by doing so they increased their prestige in both countries. They maintained this as a policy which enabled them to play a leading role in Central Asian relations. Hence it was a matter of historical necessity that relations between Tibet and Mongolia should be restored. Adoplion of Buddhism by Mongols filled this gap.

Many sects in the meanwhile had arisen in Tibet. More most of them was Gelugpa. By the start of the XVI century, in Tibet a political and religious crisis had arisen as a result of conflict between these sects. This had its ultimate origin in the conflict between the new Gelugpa sect founded by Tsongkapa (1357-1419) and the old established sects. At that time, the Pagro held the reins of state power in Tibet. This politico-religious group crushed the power of the Sakyapa in 1354 and from that time hence ruled for over 260 years.[6] So other groups were pressing to unseat them from government.

**Gelugpa Sect**

Out of all Tibet's religious and political groupings, only the new Gelugpa sect founded by Tsongkapa supported the Pagro government. The Gelugpa sect was opposed by three other sects; the Garjudva of Karmapa, the Garjudva or Beringanga, and a powerful politico-religious body grouped around Zambaa Khaan, the then ruler of Southern Tibet. Monkh Khaan, the ruler of Mongolia, bestowed the Black Hat on the Karmapa who was of the second generation of the Black Hat Garjudva sect. Meanwhile, a *khutugtu* of the Karmapa's Garjudva sect was bestowed with a red hat with a golden rim by the Yuan dynasty monarch. Thenceforth they were known as the Red Hats; gradually their power increased and they developed into a distinct sect in their own right.

Together, the Black and Red Hat sects made contact with Zamba Khaan, the leader of the influential group in Southern Tibet, and they formed a single entity that led all the separate groups which opposed the Gelugpa sect. In this struggle they sought a powerful outside ally. Such an ally was to be found in the Mongol aristocracy, with whom traditional ties, dating from the Yuan period, had never been fully broken and indeed were beginning to revive.

The Mongols were experienced in war; both sides had an interest in reviving relations, they were comparable in size and had the same lifestyle and aspirations, as a result of which it was possible for them to become of one accord. Some scholars have noted that certain Tibetans Lamas wished to pre-empt attack from Mongolia; they were exhausted by many years of warfare, and hoped that they would be able to derive economic advantage from Mongolia, which held them in such reverence.[7]

**Re-establishment of Relation**

By the second half of the XVI century it was possible for Tibet and Mongolia to *re-establish relations* on the basis of historical necessities. At the start of this century, Altan Gegeen Khaan (also named Ananda) (1502-1582), one of the lords of Mongolia, who was head of the Tumed tribe, established for the first time a contact with Tibet and with the Yellow sects. Both Altan Khaan's foreign and domestic policies were directed at enhancing his own political influence and personal reputation. Altan Khaan combated the efforts of the Ming dynasty to block off trade and other ties between Mongolia and China. He supported border trade that was mutually advantageous. He and the rest of the Mongol lords considered that if they had consolidated relations with Tibet and the countries of Central Asia, they would be able to make friends with the Ming on a more equal basis and would no longer be so subject to Ming economic domination. Altan Khaan established relations with China. In addition he attacked Khukhnuur, Tibet and Central Asian countries, and levied taxes from them.

He first made contact with the monks of the yellow sect who were working in the palaces of State of the Ming. He invited them to his court and received texts and sutras. Thereupon he adopted the precepts of the yellow sect. His attempt to worship in this way was not merely an act of devotion: it was politically motivated. Altan Khaan was better able than other Mongol lords to promote Buddhism in Mongolia and to increase his power in so doing. His territory bordered directly on Tibet after he annexed Khukhnuur at the start of the XVII century. Khukhnuur was a strategic region between several lands, a well-favoured spot for the massing of herds, and the crossroads—for several races the Mongols, Tibetans, Khoton and Uighur among them.

Altan Khaan was thus in astrategic position to develop the Mongol-Tibetan relationship. The leaders of Tibet were looking for outside allies. They had an interest in establishing relations with Altan Khaan, whose troops had already penetrated Tibet's borders. For the first time the high lamas of the Gelugpa sect made contact with Altan Khaan when he captured Khukhnuur in 1566, the Khutagtai Setsen Khun Taiji of the Ordos attacked Northeast Tibet at Altan Khaan's orders. The Taiji told the Tibetans that if they allied themselves to him, his people would adopt their religion. The Tibetans discussed his suggestion and sent delegations led by the Darkhan Lama, who held negotiations at the triple river junction at Shilimj.

### First Official Meeting

This was the *first official meeting between Mongols and Tibetans* in the course of the XVI century. When the Taiji returned from Tibet, he took several monks back with him to Mongolia and bestowed titles on them. In one source it is recorded that in 1570 Altan Khaan attacked Tibet, fighting with many merchants and saving the lives of many monks.[9] In 1571 he conveyed Ashin, Gummu sokho and many other monks of the Gelugpa sect to Mongolia.

### Meeting between Mongols and Tibetans

This Ashin Lama was one of the first to teach the Yellow sect's religion in Mongolia.[10] He also informed Altan Khaan clearly about Sodnamjamts, the head Lama of the Baraivan Temple in Tibet, and suggested that it would be useful to establish relations with him. Three dignatories of Altan Khan's court, Taglin Nanso, Lizeen Zaisan, Dain Khia and Bonbo Sandig were seat to invite Sodnamjamts to pass an invitation to Sodnamjamts, head of the Gelugpa sect. to meet him. After travelling for ten months they reached Tibet where they gave presents to three Gelugpa monasteries, (Galdan, Sera and Baraivan), and also gave gifts of food and money to the monks while explaining their purpose.

The high lamas of the Gelugpa sect and the local lords who supported them met in secret to discuss this invitation. They decided to accept. Then Sodnamjamts explained to the delegation that he wished to meet Altan Khaan near the Mongol-Tibet border, the timing of the meeting would be for further discussion. Altan Khaan also discussed the matter with lords of the Baruun Tumen; they chose a place called Tsavchaal in Khukhnuur the Tegchenchoinkhorlin Monastery was built for the meeting p;ace to known the head of the Gelugpa sect.

In 1577 Altan Khaan went to Tsavchaal and appointed three delegations who each in their turn would meet the Tibetan delegation. The first meeting was to take place in Ulaan Murun in the south of Khukhnuur. Yunshiobugin Barhuu Daichin grandson of Bujidara Otgon Taiji, a younger brother of Altan Khaan, and Khatanbaatar of the Ordos, with Magachin Bagshi of the Tumned, led the first delegation; they gave treasures, gifts, camels and oxen to Sodnamjamts. At the second meeting Chinbaatar of the Ordos and Zorigt Tumen Noyon of the Tumned headed the delegation; they also gave many gifts.

On the third occasion the Khutagtai Setsen Khun Taiji of the Ordos and, Dayan Noyon of the Tumned headed the delegation. They gave many treasures, gifts of gold and silver, fine knives, bear's gallbladders, camels with fine silk trappings and horses with golden saddles and bridles to Sodnamjamts. Sodnamjamts came to the Tegchenchoinkhorlin Monastery on 15 May 1578. Altan Khaan met him accompanied by his wife and lords, wearing a white robe and riding a white horse. In some sources it is said that Sodnamjamts came to Khukhnuur in 1577, but Yu. N. Roerich worked out from Tibetan sources that in fact he had left Lhasa in the autumn of 1577, but reached Khukhnuur in 1578. In the Monastery, over 10,000 Mongol, Chinese, Tibetans and Uighur monks and lay people crowded together.

### White History of the Ten Sacred Texts

At that meeting the two sides discussed Khubilai Khaan's law called the "White History of the Ten Sacred Texts" *(arvan buyant nomiyn tsagaan tuukh)* edited by the Setsen khun Taiji. On the basis of this law, the Mongol side formally vowed to adopt the Buddhist faith. At the meeting Altan Khaan bestowed the title of "Dalai Lama" on Sodnamjamts. Concerning this matter, Zava Damdin Gavch in his work the Golden Book (Altan devter) records that Altan Khaan gave to Sodnamjamts a golden seal with Mongol inscriptions, pearls, an outer robe made of ermine and a sable sleeveless jacket, a sitting mat made of felted birds' down and other treasures, as well as livestock. He also hounered him asking him to be free to travel in his territory.

At the same time the Khaan bestowed titles and gifts on the other monks who accompanied Sodnamjamts. Then Sodnamjamts. Manzushri and Maidar Khutugtu gave to Altan Khaan ritual scarves tied five-fold in a special charm and one precious bowl full of medicinal pills; they bestowed on him the title of Powerful Chakravartin king of the Dharma, as well as presenting a silver seal. They gave presents to his wife and the other lords in Altan Khaan's entourage. The meaning of the word "Dalai" is an assemblage of many waters collected in a mass. There was a reason for Altan Khaan to choose it. The idea was that it would imply that Sodnamjamits was to be the single leader of all the disparate Tibetan sects. He wished in this way to pursue his political aims through Sodnamjamts. Since this time until the Manchu occupation of Mongolia aristocracy, there can be no discussion of central Asian relations that does not take account of the figure of the Dalai Lama.

When Altan Khaan held his meeting with the new Dalai Lama in Khukhnuur, he handed over to be students 108 children who were sons of Bayagud Taiji and other nobles. The aim was both to create a cadre of monks and to guarantee that the lords would support the religion. The lords of Baruun Tumen gave different kinds of rich gifts to Sodnamjamts including 1,000 livestock. Sodnamjamts's reason for going to the meeting was to halt Altan Khaan's attack on Tibet and on the Ming. The Ming had asked him to persuade Altan Khaan to withdraw his forces. Sodnamjamts acted to resolve this grave issue, and thereby his name and reputation became greatly enhanced. The relationship thus established between Altan Khaan and Sodnamjamts did much to consolidate the influence of the Gelugspa sect and to cement relations between Tibet and Mongolia.

**Difference amongst Mongols**

Among the Mongol aristocracy there were some who did not welcome the establishment of ties between Mongolia and Tibet. Altan Khaan and Manzushri Khutugtu collected the lords of twelve *tumen* and together with the Setsen Khun Taiji, obliged them to abjure resistance to the monks. Then they passed an additional law to further legitimise the formal adoption of Buddhism. The new (but also formally Third) Dalai Lama did not go back directly to Lhasa; he made visits to the local lords in Amdo, Ningxia, and Khukhnuur. This was because there was a great crisis in Tibet and power rested with the Garjidva sects of the Karmapa. In (1581) Altan Khaan died suddenly, and it was vital to reinforce relations. In the next generation, Altan Khaan's son Sengeduuren adhered to his fathers policy. In 1582 he sent information to the Dalai Lama (who was then at the Kumbum Monastery) reporting his father's death and asking him to perform an obsequy. The Dalai Lama came in 1586. He established the relationship between Tibet and Mongolia through aristocracy of the Baruun Tumen and through Altan Khaan.

**The Mongol Lama**

During the XVII century an important development in the history of Tibeto-Mongol relations was the fact that the next, the Fourth Lama, was from Mongolia. In 1589, students of Sodnamjamts chose some a Mongolian boy to be his successor in the next generation. from the three main temples, delegations were sent to check the incarnation in 1592. They accepted it. This was vital to the development of Mongolia's relations with Tibet, and for the development of Buddhism on Mongol soil.

Till the age of 14, the Fourth Dalai Lama, Yondonjamts. (1588-1616) lived in Mongolia. After that he was invited to Tibet to receive teaching from the high-ranked monks. Among believers, the reputation of the Mongol Dalai Lama became high, and the power of Gelugpa sect grew greatly. Opponent sects were active against this. In 1960, at the age of 47, Yondonjamts suddenly died. As a consequence of his death a conflict began in Tibet between the Red and yellow sects, at which time 2000 Mongol soldiers moved to defend the Dalai Lama; they fought the soldiers of the Zamba Khaan, and were victorious.

From the beginning of the XVII century, relations between the states of Central Asia and the northern region of modern west and east China were in turmoil, with shortlived federations arising and fighting each other. In 1604, Ligden Khaan of the Tsakhar became ruler of Mongolia. He wanted to unite the Mongols by peaceful means, through the use of religion, and so made contact with the lamas of Tibet. By his orders many, temples were built. Between 1628 and 1639 he assembled 30 translators who started work on a great project—the 108 volume Ganjur. Some chieftains of Mongol tribes sided with the Manchus. Danger from the Manchu was acute at this time. Danzanbamba, the Tibetan Zamba Khaan, sent a delegation to Ligden Khaan suggesting that they might fight together against the Yellow sect. Ligden agreed and lent his support to the Red sect; he also invited Tsogt Khun Taiji of the Khaïkha, Donyed of Beriaimag in Kham and others who set up a new resistance against the Yellow sect. In 1634 Tsogt Taiji captured Khukhnuur and Amdo. Ligden Khaan died in that same year.

**Avtai Sain Khaan**

Another important figure is *Avtai Sain Khaan*. He met with Sodnamjamts in 1585 and gave him many gifts. When he returned to his homeland, he had the great temple of Erdene Zuu built. After him, relations between Tibet and Mongolia expanded greatly. Another key figure is the first Javzundamba, Zanabazar. In 1639 a ceremony was held to award this title. From Tibet, Yonsa Khutugtu Luvsandanzanjamts attended. He was one of Zanabazar's first religious tutors. The Fifth Dalai Lama sent lamas to Zanabazar to teach him. Between 1649 and 1651, Zanabazar visited Tibet and learned much from the Dalai Lama and from the Panchen Lama.

The lords of the Dorbon Oirad ("Four Oirad") from the XV century had invited Tibetan monks to their entourage, as is recorded in the Ming History. Therefore relations were very close between the Oirad and Tibet. During the reign of the Oirad ruler Baibagas, official relations were established. In 1636, Turbaikh of the Khoshuud people, with a great army defeated Tsogt Taiji when he was in Khukhnuur. Then he captured the whole of Tibet. Turbaikh assumed state and military control over Khukhnuur and Tibet, leaving religious control in the hands of the Fifth Dalai Lama and the Panchen Lama. Thus the Fifth Dalai Lama and the Gelugpa sect made contact with Turbaikh and the Khoshuud lords, and they unified the whole of Tibet after many centuries of regional in-fighting; they created a strong, centralised religion in the heart of Asia.

**Lavzan Khaan**

Later, *Lavzan Khaan*, himself of Khoshuud origin, supported the Red sect and Sanjaajamts sought to drive him out of Tibet; he fought but was defeated and killed. A well-known figure in 'Tibetan history Sanjaajamts died tragically young, fighting for his nation. In 1770, Tserendondov of Zuun Gar (Dzungaria) captured the Potala Palace; he ended the power of the Khoshuud that had lasted for more than 70 years. Then Mongolia and Tibet were both taken by the Manchus and remained under Manchu control until 1911. After the Nationalist revolution, in 1914 Mongolia and Tibet formally agreed to recognise each other's independence, but at this time, the international context made it impossible for this to be accepted by all other world states.

Since the time of the Third Bogd Gegeen Javzundamba all Bogds have been born in Tibet, but they have contributed greatly to Mongolia's culture and relations. They developed the corpus of Oriental science and knowledge. Nowadays in Mongolia the Mongol people honour Tibetans as persons living in the heartland of Buddha's faith.

**The Ernst-Schaefer-Tibet-Expedition (1938-1939): New Light on the Political History of Tibet in the First Half of the 20th Century**

> "When the Russians entered Berlin, they found among the corpses a thousand volunteers for death in German uniform without any papers or badges, of Himalayan origin. As soon as the [Nazi] movement began to acquire extensive funds, it organised a number of expeditions to Tibet, which succeeded one another practically without interruption until 1943'.[11] "The German expeditions to Tibet in 1937 and 1943 had as their

mission the discovery of a connection between lost Atlantis and the first civilisation of Central Asia[12]." "Schaefer believed that Tibet was the cradle of mankind, a refuge of an 'Aryan root race, where a caste of priests had created a mysterious empire of knowledge, called 'Shambhala" adorned with the Buddhist symbol of the wheel of life, swastika[13]'. These SS-men "were the warrior elite of a new civilisation, immeasurably superior to the old, the high priesthood of the New Age, the standard bearer of the coming Superman. Their leaders were magicians, who had formed alliances with the mystic Tibetan cities of Agarthi and Schamballah and had mastered the forces of the living universe[14]." They had "to measure Tibetan head sizes and ascertain that the Tibetans were not Jews but true Aryans. Hitler even is reputed to have brought a group of monks back to Germany, instructing them to perform special chants to alter weather patterns in preparation for his ill-fated Russian invasion[15]."

**The Schaefer Expedition**

These quotations refer to one of the most controversial expeditions to Tibet during the 20th century, the so-called *Schaefer expedition* of 1938/39 carried out by the German scientist Ernst Schaefer. Because the members of the expedition all belonged to the SS, a great deal of Nazi ideology, esotericism and occultism has been attributed to it. Because Schaefer's accounts of this expedition have never been translated into English, public opinion in the English-speaking world has been mainly formed by the available sources in the India Office in London.

This may account for the doubtful legacy of the expedition in the English-speaking world. In Germany this mission has nearly been forgotten. Also forgotten is the fact that the Schaefer expedition collected an amazing amount of scientific material about Tibet, material that continues to be of great value even today. What little is recalled concerns the potential political, ideological, esoteric and occultistic aspects of the expedition. this paper might contribute to the demystification of this expedition'[16]. Primary sources are the voluminous handwritten expedition diaries of Schaefer, the records of the interrogations of Schaefer, the SS Ahnenerbe files, as well as Tibetan documents.

For comparative purposes, the British sources have also been examined. They consist mainly of confidential reports and letters of British officials. That a relationship was successfully established between Reting Rinpoche and the members of the German expedition in Lhasa is quite well-known, but information hitherto available as to the nature of this relationship ultimately led to the distorted view of German-Tibetan relations in the 1940s. Today's Neo Nazi propaganda, however, still relies on the alleged "Nazi friendliness" of the Tibetans. Therefore one particular purpose of my paper is to correct this distorted view.

Schaefer graduated in 1929 from high school in Mannheim, he studied zoology and geology in Goettingen, Hannover and Philadelphia. In 1930 Brooke-Dolan, a rich young American, came to Germany to recruit scientists for his zoological expedition. Schaefer participated in this first Brooke-Dolan expedition to West China and Tibet, despite being only twenty years old at the time. In 1932 he returned to Germany to resume his studies. In 1934 he followed the advice of the Lord Major of Goettingen to enter the SS. From 1934-36 he took part in another scientific expedition with Brooke Dolan to Eastern Tibet and China. Schaefer returned with Dolan to the United States in January 1936.

**Praise from German Government**

In Philadelphia he received a telegram from the German government congratulating him on his successes and indicating that his return to Germany was desired. Shortly thereafter, a second cable arrived, informing him that in recognition of the success of his expedition he had been nominated SS Untersturmfuehrer (SS Second Lt.). The short obituary of Schaefer in 1992 of the Academy of Natural Sciences. Philadelphia, mentions that Schaefer and Dolan "collected scientific data and specimens of the region's birds and mammals that have never been equalled in size and importance. In recognition of his many scientific contributions Dr. Schaefer was elected to life membership in the Academy in 1932." Schaefer had done some real poineerig work in this field.

After his return to Germany, Schaefer continued his studies in Berlin and received his doctoral degree in Zoology in 1937. The "Reichsfuehrer-SS" Himmler was at that time already trying to avail for himself of Schaefer's reputation for Nazi propaganda proposes and he was summoned by Himmler, who inquired about his future plans. Schaefer told him of his wish to lead yet a further expedition to Tibet. Himmler, who believed in Karma and who was fascinated by somewhat crude and fantastic ideas about Asian mysticism, was immediately keen on sending this expedition to Tibet under the auspices of the "SS Ahnenerbe" (SS Ancestral Heritage Society). He wanted Schaefer also to carry out research based on the so-called "Glacial Cosmogony" theory of Hoerbiger.

**Legitimate Scientific Purposes**

While Himmler intended to use the expedition as a tool for those esoteric pseudo-sciences, which the "Ahnenerbe" wanted to promote, Schaefer, as a scientist, had more legitimate scientific purposes in mind and he declined to include Edmund Kiss, a representative of himmur's doctrine, on his team. Though Himmler did not like it, still he thought he could use Schaefer's findings for his own propaganda purposes. Thus

Schaefer, in order to obtain the scientific freedom he needed, asked for the acceptance of twelve conditions, all of which were granted by Himmler himself. However, Sievers, the head of the "Ahnenerbe", declared in January 1938, "The task of the expedition in the meantime had diverged too far from the targets of the Reichsfuehrer-SS and does not serve his ideas of cultural studies." Thus, in the end, the expedition was not sponsored by the "Ahnenerbe".

Himmler, nevertheless, only gave his consent to the expedition on the condition that all of its members join the SS. Schaefer understood that in order for the expedition to succeed, he needed Himmler's support to obtain foreign currency (extremely difficult during the Nazi period). He therefore had to compromise on some points. In preparation for the expedition he had "Schaefer Expedition 1938/39" letterhead printed and applied for sponsorship from businessmen. The expedition's name, however, had to be changed on the order of the "Ahnenerbe" to "German Tibet-Expedition Ernst Schaefer (in big letters), tunder the patronage of the Reichsfuehrer-SS Himmler and in connection with the Ahnenerbe" (in small letters).

**Difficulties from British Authorities**

By the time, Schaefer arrived in India with his expedition on way to Tibet, he faced difficulties from British authorities in India. Schaefer actually raised the funds of his expedition by himself. 80 per cent of the cost of the expedition was financed by the "Werberat der deutschen Wirtschaft" (Public Relations and Advertising Council of German Business) together with large German business enterprises, Deutsche Forschungsgemeinschaft (the Reich Research Council) and Brooke Dolan. The rest was provided by minor contributions. Only the flight back to Germany was sponsored by Himmler's circle of friends. The begain from Germany in the spring of 1938. It reached Calcutta six weeks later. Then he started having difficulties. When Schaefer arrived there he must have noticed an article about himself in the "Voelkischer Beobachter" (the Nazi propaganda newspaper) which stated that he was undertaking a further expedition on behalf of the SS. An article in the international press was even headlined "A Gestapo agent in India." These articles caused him considerable troubles in negotiating with the British authorities. Later he received a telegram from the Consul General in Calcutta informing him that the government of Tibet refused to permit the entry of the expedition.

**Permission to Travel**

However, some months later, Schaefer and his crew were admitted to Lhasa, which was considered a great achievement in Germany. How then Schaefer did manage to get the permission to travel to Lhasa? Schaefer spent several months in Sikkim. But he did not get permission to go to

Tibet official channels were not helping because he was a German. He somehow tricked the British, following the personal advice of Francis Younghusband, "to sneak over the border". He successfully crossed into Tibetan territory for a short time and established friendly contact with local Tibetan officials, who forwarded an application directly to the Tibetan government. In this he referred to his personal acquaintance with the former Panchen Lama, and asked for permission to be the first Germans to enter Lhasa.

Some weeks later they received an official letter of invitation with five seals from the Kashag, which stated:

> "To the German Doctor Saheb Sha-phar:
>
> Thank for your letter of the 17th day of the 9th of the English month together with two boxes containing a gramophone, records and two pair of binoculars. Concerning you and the other Germans, Doctor Wienert, Mr. Krause, Mr. Beger, and Mr. Geer (altogether no more than five persons) who want to visit Lhasa and the holy Tibetan monasteries, please understand that no foreigners whatsoever are allowed to enter Tibet.
>
> Although we know if we allow you to enter, others might come the next time, it nevertheless appears from your letter that you intend only friendship and to see the holy land and its religious institutions..
>
> Acknowledging this, we deign to give you permission to go to Lhasa and to stay there for two weeks, on condition that you oblige yourself not to harm the Tibetan people and consent to not hunt any birds or game, which would deeply hurt the feelings of the Tibetan people, both clergy and lay. Please kindly keep this in mind.
>
> Sent from the Tibetan Kaṣhag on the auspicious 3rd day of the 10th month of the earth-tiger year."

**Sensational Letter**

For Schaefer and the authorities both, this latter was sensational. It was the first official invitation for a German mission to Tibet. It also certainly demonstrated some Tibetan independence from the British. We therefore have to see the German-Tibetan relations of the 1930s in the broader geopolitical context of the rather complicated and ambiguous relations between Britain and Tibet. The expedition included five members altogether: Schaefer as mammologist and ornithologist, Ernst Krause, entomologist and photographer and movie-operator, and ethnologist, Karl Wienert, geophysicist, and Edmund Geer, technical caravan leader. Some words about Bruno Beger, the anthropologist: he was one of the two true Nazis on the expedition and was strongly influenced by the then leading racist anthropology of Nazi ideology.

**Measuring Skills**

His actions in Tibet in regard to measuring people's skulls and taking masks of their faces was actually within the bounds of international scientific practice at that time. But his later actions in Auschwitz, where he carried out experiments on prisoners, discredited the expedition and contributed to its controversial image today. The actual purpose of the expedition can actually be characterised, in Schaefer's own words: "The expedition might be called a complete natural history expedition, comprising studies of terrestial magnetism, ethnology, anthropology, ornithology, mammology and partly botanies and of course geography. While in Lhasa, Schaefer successfully extended the mission's stay several times. Schaefer witnessed the Monlam festival and gave a most vivid and extensive description of it. The members of the expedition established official contact with the Kashag ministers and the Reting Regent. They also made contact with many aristocratic families. The person who fascinated them most was Dzasa Tsarong, whom they thought to be the only true politician. They valued him as highly as the British representative Hugh Richardson did.

And their Tibetan interpreters even had a short biography of him composed, having interviewed him for that purpose. But their most valuable informant, with whom they met almost every day, was Mondro, a high monk official, who had been one of the four boys who had been sent to Rugby school in England in 1913. Mondro was responsible for the police force, but he had been degraded from the 4th to the 7th rank after his motorbike caused a Kashag minister's horse to shy and throw him off.

**Completion of Expedition**

Schaefer completed his expedition in July 1939 and returned to India. When he expressed a desire to see the Viceroy, the permission was franted Linlithgow, the Viceroy of India, received Schaefer in a private audience in Simla during the first days of August 1939, just before Schaefer's return to Germany. Lord Linlithgow congratulated Schaefer on his great success. Moreover, referring to Schaefer's political skills, he told Schaefer that he himself at the same age would have acted just as Schaefer had done. He then revealed to him what Schaefer had suspected for a long time: Hugh Richardson had been sent to Lhasa in order to prevent the expedition's advance there. This act by the British needs to be understood in light of the ever increasing tensions between Nazi Germany and Britain. The Viceroy explained the British view to Schaefer in a very frank manner and asked him to transmit a personal message to Hitler.

**Seeing Hitler**

Shortly after his return Schaefer tried to see Hitler, but Himmler prevented him from doing so. When Schaefer turned to Canaris (chief of German intelligence) in order to deliver his message, Himmler soon learned of it and was upset. Schaefer was given a severe two-month education in the "SS-Leibstandarte" to break his "behaviour like a general" and to make him obedient. The German expedition to Tibet turned out to be highly successful in terms of the scientific material collected as well as in terms of the improvement of the political relations between Germany and Tibet. What were then the reasons for this success? Firstly, all the members of the expedition tried to learn Tibetan etiquette before they entered Tibet; they took with them to Tibet for this purpose a Sikkimese aristocrat, who also served as one of their interpreters.

Schaefer was also clever enough to create the idea of a shared collective identity of Germans and Tibetans by the use of the Swastika, with his motto of a meeting of the Eastern and Western Swastika. Thus a link between the two nations was drawn even on the symbolic level. Schaefer must have been an excellent negotiator. As is clear from his diaries he proved to be successful even when he complained about ill-treatment by the Tibetans. He also seemed to have been very much concerned about his honour, which he often connected with that of Germany.

Secondly, Bruno Beger, the anthropologist of the expedition, had undergone brief medical training that enabled him to treat members of the Tibetan aristocracy successfully.

**Lhasa Kanjur**

Every morning people queued in front of the government guesthouse where Schaefer and the other men were staying. For medical treatment of the famous Pha-lha family, they were even given a complete copy of the Lhasa Kanjur (Tibetan Buddhist scriptures). Finally, the Tibetans simply seemed to have liked and enjoyed the Germans' cheerfulness. According to Schaefer's diaries they were fond of the expedition members singing German songs. It is quite amusing to read about parties in the house of Tsarong. One can imagine the Germans linking arms with the Tibetans and swinging from side to side, singing the most popular songs from the Munich "Octoberfest".

Though the expedition was very successful Schaefer was a sad man. Soon after the return of its members to Germany World War II, broke out and Schaefer was prohibited from publishing his results and giving lectures because of political considerations. On the one hand, he was lionized, his expedition having been the first German mission to reach the "forbidden City" of Lhasa. On the other hand, Schaefer was considered politically suspect and thought to be some kind of a rebel. In 1941 he was sent to join the "Waffen SS" in Finland, with the order "to be forgotten" there. Because the "political myths" surrounding the alleged aims of the expedition have contributed greatly to the current notion of Tibet's "pro-Nazi attitude", some aspects of the expedition need to be studied in detail.

**German-Tibetan Relations**

German-Tibetan relations can best be analysed when we look at the picture Schaefer draws of the Tibetan Regent. Reting Rinpoche, and of Reting's attitude towards the members of the expedition, especially towards Schaefer. In his diaries Schaefer gives a lively and detailed account of his meetings with the Regent. He tells us that, although it was the rule that one had to request an audience at least three days in advance, and that even the prime minister had to wait a long time, Schaefer himself was soon able to have an audience whenever he liked. Though Richardson and various Tibetans told Schaefer that Reting Rinpoche would only grant "ten minutes audiences", Schaefer succeeded in staying with the Regent for more than three hours. During the German's visits the Regent would be sitting on his throne bed together with his favourite dog. There was always a Young boy present, the son of the new Kashag minister, whom he called his favourite. Reting was dressed in a yellow suede coat, with many German pistols and two golden Belgian pistols hanging above him.

According to Schaefer, he knew little about the outside world, and also little about Buddhism. Schaefer was very keen to learn more about Buddhism and was rather disappointed that Reting could not, or did not like to, respond to his curiosity. In the beginning Schaefer seemed to be impressed by the personality of the Regent. Schaefer invited him to Germany and they seriously discussed plans for the journey, while several other aristocratic young men also wanted to travel there. Reting wanted to be picked up by a German plane in Calcutta and flown to Germany, but apprently the Kashag would not give consent to the trip. Gradually, however, Schaefer's initial impression changed and his judgement of the Regent became increasingly negative, as the Reting Rinpoche was apparently always seeking some benefit from their contact.

Reting must also have been very fond of Bruno Beger, whom he wanted to engage as a bodyguard and it was rather difficult for Beger to get out of this situation without offending the Regent. Rating suggested that Beger stay in Tibet and that a Geshe ("Doctor of Divinity") go to Germany in exchange, in order to introduce Buddhism there. This might have been the first official attempt by the Tibetans to spread Buddhism in Europe. Perhaps the most famous outcome of the expedition is the letter the Regent wrote to Hitler. It has played a key role in the legacy of the expedition and the resulting judgement of German-Tibetan relations. Schaefer convinced the Reting Regent to write a letter to Hitler. Since the

Regent did not know much about the outside world, he did not anything Hiller either. The letter was addressed thus :

"To his Majesty Herr Hitler, Berlin, Germany

*'Jar man rgyal po har hi ti lar nonhog la 'bul rgyu bod kyi rgyal tshab srid skyong rwa greng ho thog thus sa yos bod zla dug I tshes 18 bzang bor phul"*

The letter in the original translation, (which omits something at the beginning) reads:

"To his Majesty Fuhrer Adolph, Hitler, Berlin, Germany.

From.

The Regent of Tibet.

On the 18th day of the first month of Sand-Hare Year.

Your Majesty,

I trust your Highness is in best of health and in every progress with your goodly affairs.

Here I am well and doing my best in our religious and Government affairs. I have the pleasure to let Your Majesty know that Dr. Schaefer and his party, who are the first Germans to visit Tibet have been permitted without any objection, and every necessary assistance is rendered on their arrival. Further, I am in desirous to do anything that will help to improve the friendly tie of relationship between the two Nations, and I trust your Majesty will also consider it essential as before:

Please take care of Your good self, and let me know if Your Majesty desire anything.

I am sending under separate parcel a Tibetan silver lid and saucer with a red designed tea cup, and a native dog as a small remembrance.

Sincerely Yours,

Reding Ho-Thok-Thu."

**Polite Correspondence**

The later is nothing but a polite correspondence. Tibetan diplomatic correspondence follows strict rules and upon visual inspection, this letter seems to have been written rather hastily. The lines run too close to the margin. There are no adorning attributes for Hitler and no seal on the letter itself, only on the envelope. There is no space of respect between inscription and introduction formula. The space between the lines is too big. According to Loden Sherab Dagyab Rinpoche it is not a letter to an equal but from someone slightly superior to an inferior. And *phul* is missing at the end in this letter.

**Published Translation**

Reinhard Greve in 1995 published a translation by Johannes Schubert, instead of the much more accurate one made by Helmut Hoffmann. Schubert was a Tibetologist from Leipzig who had sought in vain to enter the Sven-Hedin-Institute in the early forties and he might have thought it advantageous to try to translate this letter in Nazi terms. Thus he may have falsified the translation deliberately as a mean of propaganda for Nazi Germany. But his translation is simply wrong. He also added remarks that are not found in the original document. The most egregious interpolation is: "At present you [Hitler] are making all efforts in creating a lasting empire in peaceful prosperity based on a racial foundation," instead of translating correctly the usual Tibetan phrase: "Here I [Reting] am well and doing my best in our religious and Government affairs." Schubert's translation is relied upon by Neo-Nazis as propaganda for their cause, as they seek to demonstrate Tibetan sympathy for racist ideas. The left-wing parties of Germany tend to ascribe to the Tibetans an uncritical friendship toward the Nazis.

**Conclusion**

For years, professional and amateur scholars have imagined that the Schaefer expedition was steeped in occult Nazi ideology, and this fantasy has been deployed from both ends of the political spectrum. Some recent German publications on Tibet refer explicitly to the expedition, drawing a direct line from Blavatsky's Theosophy to Nazi occultism, citing the Schaefer expedition as evidence. They argue that since the late 1930s there have been occult and esoteric connections between Tibet and Nazi groups, leading to a direct influence on the Dalai Lama of Nazi ideology.

However, is clear that in the preparations and undertaking of the expedition, he approached this expedition as a scientist, seeking to collect scientific materials on Tibet. He did not approach this expedition nor he conducted it from Nazi point of view. The goals of the expedition were not political, esoteric or occult. Unfortunately, due to constant misinformation the fantasy of a "Nazi-Tibet-connection" among certain authors only adds to the already existing "myth" of Tibet, only this time stressing its dark sides. We encounter here what Donald Lopez called the "logic of opposites", in which a highly idealised image of Tibet transforms itself into its darker and equally distorted opposite.

**Discussion**

**A Nazi Mission?**

In discussion the question was raised as to the extent to which the popular understanding of the Schaeffer mission as a 'Nazi mission' was accurate. One factor that needed to be taken into account was the implacable hostility displayed towards the mission by Hugh Richardson, the then British representative in Lhasa, who clearly saw it in those terms. His judgement had been largely accepted, but the author's research suggested the need for a more nuanced analysis of the motivations of those involved.

In regard to the scientific results of the Schaeffer mission it was noted that they brought back to Germany about 2,500 ethnological objects, mainly those concerned with daily material culture. While some items had been destroyed in the war, the remainder was captured by the Americans in 1945 but eventually returned to Ethnological Museum of Munich, where they re still on display.

## A Brief Survey of Tibetan Relations with the United States

While unofficial contacts between Americans and Tibetans can be traced back to the early years of the 20th Century, it was not until the Second World War that there was to be any official contact.

In search of a reliable land route for war supplies from India to western China, the U.S. government authorized a mission to cross Tibet in 1942-43, ostensibly to ascertain the viability of such a route. The expedition produced nothing of substance and its true intent remains in dispute. Wartime exigencies aside, Tibet played no role in U.S. foreign interests and the first official U.S. statement on the status of Tibet, in 1943, declared:

> For its part, the Government of the United States has borne in mind the fact that the Chinese Government has long claimed suzerainty over Tibet and the Chinese Constitution lists Tibet among areas constituting the territory of the Republic of China. This Government has at no time raised a question regarding either of these claims.

The next official contact came three years later when Tibet, neutral in World War II but determined to end its centuries old policy of isolation, dispatched a "goodwill" mission to congratulate the allies on their victory. However, because the Nationalist (Guomindang, GMD) government of China considered Tibet a part of the Chinese state, the Tibetan delegates were denied visas and remained in India where they presented their congratulations to the foreign embassies.

The Lhasa government's next gesture was to send a "Tibetan Trade Mission" to several nations, including the United States, in 1947. Trade was vital to Tibet's economy and there were difficulties. Delegation leader, W.D. Shakabpa, claimed the expedition was designed to ease Indian restrictions on Tibetan trade, expand trade, purchase gold bullion to support the Tibetan currency, and "to demonstrate Tibet's independence and sovereign status."

Anglo-Indian officials believed the group's purposes was the enrichment of the participants. The Tibetans travelled on the first official passports issued by the government in Lhasa. Visas, however, were issued under circumstances which allowed each nation to permit travel but not to accord recognition to the passports, ultimately the mission failed to enhance Tibet's trade, end Tibet's isolation, or bring international recognition. Lhasa also tried inviting American journalists to visit the once forbidden land in an attempt to garner some favourable publicity. In that regard the visits were momentarily successful but they changed nothing of significance. On 1 October 1949 Mao Zedong proclaimed the establishment of the People's Republic of China (PRC) and promised the "liberation" of Tibet from western "imperialism" was imminent. There was every change Tibet isolation would be over.

**US Priority**

The communist China eventually took control of Tibet. Tibet became a greater priority for the United States. U.S. diplomats in the region urged relations with Lhasa to counter communism. But there were two problems; the U.S. alliance with the GMD who insisted that all relations with Tibetans be conducted only through the government on Taiwan and the reluctance of India to act against the PRC. Indian concurrence was considered essential, since India, in the words of the U.S. Ambassador in New Delhi, had a "practical monopoly on Tibet's foreign relations."

In 1949, American diplomats and Tibetan officials met in India. Tibetans were advised the United States was sympathetic to their predicament although it could not publicly demonstrate concern or involvement. Secret talks continued throughout 1952 but available documentation gives no hint of any aid being provided. Just about this time an unusual pamphlet surfaced in India. Entitled "Armed Forces Talk No. 348: Tibet—Roof of the World", it was published by the United States Department of Defense and "intended as a lesson plan for military unit commanders or their representatives to use in conducting troop education and information programmes," and, was a "part of a continuing programme on international awareness." The US government could not any background on this pamphlet from its records.

In the summer of 1950, after the outbreak of the Korean War, Washington began "to initiate psychological warfare and paramilitary operations against the Chinese Communist regime," to, in the words of a government memo, "foster and support anticommunist elements both outside and within

China with a view to developing and expanding resistance in China to the Peiping [Beijing] regime's control..."

> Consequently, the U.S. "...[was] now in [a] position [to] give assurances [to the] Tibetans re U.S. aid to Tibet," and that it was "reach to assist procurement and financing;" but only with Indian concurrence.

**Turning to United Nations**

At Washington's urging, and with its financial support, the Tibetans turned to the United Nations using a public relations firm and an international lawyer. But this also failed as the UN voted to indefinitely postpone the vote. The main concern of U.S. policy-makers was never Tibetan independence. "Historically, the United State Government has recognized a continuing claim by the Government of China to suzerainty over Tibet...," according to a government report. Yet at the same time, "the United States Government believes that "Tibet should not be compelled by duress to accept violation of its autonomy and that the Tibetan people should enjoy the rights of self-determination..." The obvious contradiction in this policy was never clarified because Tibetan independence was always secondary to other goals. the US government never had any interest in the middle hydom. It was a question of time. The PLA marched on Tibet. When the communist People's Liberation Army (PLA) reached the Tibetan border at Qamdo a battle of several days duration ensued in which the Chinese overcame Tibetan resistence. Several weeks later the Dalai Lama fled Lhasa for the town of Yadong, there the U.S. diplomats implored him to cross-over into India, where they thought he would be safe.

Ultimately the Dalai Lama returned to Lhasa which prompted negotiations with Beijing resulting in the "Agreement of the Central People's Government and the Local Government of Tibet" (Seventeen-Point Agreement). Ironically, Chinese insistence on such a pact demonstrated that Beijing understood that Tibet was not a Chinese province but an entity outside of China's boundaries that required official incorporation. Washington continued to pursue the Dalai Lama laying out terms in a secret 1951 letter. In return for a "disavowal" of the Seventeen Point Agreement and a public appeal for United Nations and U.S. aid, Washington would totally fund: his exile to another country; the organization and supply of a resistence movement (sending, "...light arms through India"); his brother, Thubten Norbu's travel to the U.S. under the auspices of the American Committee for Free Asia, a Central Intelligence Agency (CIA)—funded anti-communist organization; a propaganda campaign and a personal yearly allowance. The Pontiff rejected all U.S. offers. While these negotiations were in progress, another of the Dalai Lama's brothers, Gyalo Thondup, began conferring with GMD officials in Taiwan. Secret U.S. Tibet talks lasted until 1952 when the U.S. Department of State gave up its efforts to enlist the Dalai Lama into Washington's anti-communist crusade. While State may have given up on Tibet, the CIA was just getting interested.

**The Central Intelligence Agency**

The Central Intelligence Agency played a very controversial role in Tibet. For years the Dalai Lama and his followers denied the relationship existed. Chinese accusations of outside aid were met by the Dalai Lama with retorts that the reports were "completely baseless." In 1961 he was quoted as saying, "the only weapons that the rebels possess are those they've managed to capture from the Chinese. They have guns but they've even been using slingshots, spears, knives, and swords." In 1974 he was unequivocal: "The accusation of CIA aid has no truth behind it. My flight [in 1959] was conditioned by circumstances developing in Lhasa because of Chinese atrocities...." When Thubten Norbu, was asked by U.S. News and World Report, "Are you getting any weapons to resist the Chinese?" he replied, "There is nothing at all coming in from the outside." In fact, Gyalo Thondup had been receiving arms from the GMD since 1952 and from the CIA in 1956.

In keeping with long-held U.S. policy. the impetus for CIA involvement was not an independent Tibet but rather "...to keep the Communists off balance in Asia." By 1956 Chinese policies in the Tibetan areas of western Sichuan (Kham) had led to severe alienation of the local population that a major revolt broke out against Chinese rule. The CIA saw the revolt as an opportunity by which it could escalate its covert harassment of the PRC. There was not much the CIA could do. They just want Chinese to keep off-balance so that they ease the pressure on Taiwan in the far East.

**Gyalo Thondup**

Gyalo Thondup became the Tibetan liaison to the CIA arranging the first training missions. The first group was dropped back into Tibet in the autumn of 1957, from a plane flown by an American pilot. Their mission was to contact rebel forces and to urge the Dalai Lama to publicly appeal for U.S. assistance; only then could Washington publicly support him. The Dalai Lama's government was split; some supported the rebels while others elected to work with the Chinese. How much the Dalai Lama knew about the rebels' activities remains a mystery. Within Tibet proper the Chinese had promised that traditional Tibetan society would remain intact and it was, to a large degree, until March 1959. Consequently many of the Lhasan aristocracy was more intent on preserving their privileged lifestyles through compromise with the Chinese.

Dalai Lama never sided with CIA in their efforts. Despite their inability to get the Dalai Lama to join their cause, the CIA went ahead with training and equipping Tibetans rebels. The CIA's proprietary airline, Civil Air Transport, began flying from Thailand using Polish and Czech mercenaries as pilots. Some 25-30 missions dropped some 250-400 tons of equipment into Tibet from 1957 to 1961: arms, ammunition, radios, medical supplies, hand-operated printing presses and more. By 1958 the U.S. had established a training base at Camp Hale, Colorado and over the next 6 years some 170 guerrillas were trained there. In March 1959 the Dalai Lama fled Lhasa in a revolt whose origins remain unknown. By 1961 the last of the guerrillas were dropped into Tibet; a total of 49 men since 1957 of whom only 10 made it back out of Tibet; 1 surrendered, 1 had been captured and the remaining 37 killed.

In 1960 CIA a established a guerrilla base in Mustang, a small semi-autonomous feudal principality in Nepal. By early 1964 the Indian and American governments initiated a Combined Operations Center, funded by Washington, to oversee the Mustang operation. The U.S. supplied material and aid the Tibetans manpower, while India "controlled the territory and therefore the operations." From 1964-67, 25 teams were sent into Tibet with little success. Their activities were confined to ambushes of Chinese military convoys, sabotage of communication lines and the mining of roads and bridges. One foray did bring out some valuable Chinese government documents.

**US Propaganda**

For propaganda purposes the U.S. created supposedly popular organizations such as the American Emergency Committee for Tibetan Refugees, prodded its clandestinely funded "human rights" organizations (e.g., International Commission of Jurists) to prepare "official" report attacking China (some of the Tibetan aid groups were CIA-created fronts, others legitimate organizations penetrated by CIA agents Norbu paid for Tibetan delegations to travel to Geneva to press their case before international organizations and subsidized the establishment of offices in Geneva and New York to allegedly promote Tibetan handicrafts and to publicize the Tibetan cause but really to establish quasi-diplomatic offices for the Dalai Lama.

Tibet House in New Delhi was CIA funded. Money also went to Cornell University ($45,000 a year) to educate several Tibetans to prepare them for bureaucratic careers in Dharamsala, the seat of the Dalai Lama's administration in India. There were also direct subsides to the Dalai Lama himself; from 1959-74, US 180,000 a year for his personal use. At this point the Indian government established, with U.S. support, a Tibetan military unit called the Special Frontier Force. Eventually 12,000 Tibetans were trained by U.S. Special Forces (Green Berets) to operate from bases along the Kashmir frontier where they crossed into Tibet planting electronic listening devices.

For ten years CIA tried. It could not penetrate Tibet. By 1969 with very little to show, the CIA decided to end the Mustang operation. It lingered until Henry Kissinger's secret visit to Beijing in 1971 when all covert operations in that theater ended. After almost 15 years the guerrillas had been unable to create a sustainable, independent military force, nor a beachhead inside Tibet. When the U.S. prop was pulled out, the whole operation collapsed; the base at Mustang was abandoned.

The first phase of the U.S. Tibetan relationship ended in a betrayal of the dissident Tibetans. For all the money expended, there was never any intention of supporting a military force sufficient to achieve Tibetan independence; the military efforts, the propaganda, the phoney organizations were only intended to harass the government in Beijing.

## Recent Times

Suddenly in 1971 China underwent changes. In 1971, Lin Biao, Mao Zedong's designated heir, died mysteriously followed in 1976 by Mao himself, leading to a purge of a leadership group dubbed "the gang of four." Chinese policies changed dramatically; admitting past practices in Tibet were harmful, allowing tourists to visit, appointing Tibetans to positions with a modicum of power and permitting refugees to visit families. In February 1978, the Panchen Lama, second only in stature to the Dalai Lama in Tibetan Buddhism, was released from 14 years of house arrest and prison. The Dalai Lama responded to these changes by calling for the authorities to open Tibet to visitors which Beijing immediately did. The Dalai Lama then tempered his speeches by speaking less of Tibetan independence and more about the economic well-being of Tibetans; "if the six million Tibetans in Tibet are really happy and prosperous as never before,'' he declared in 1978, "there is no reason for us to argue otherwise."

For the first time Chinese took head of the world criticism. In December 1978, Beijing contacted Gyalo Thondup and talks resulted in an agreement to send an investigative delegation to Tibet. The Dalai Lama also began to travel around the world more to gain visibility for his cause visiting the Soviet Union, Mongolia and the United States, all for the first time.

In May 1980, the Dalai Lama sent his second and third delegations to Tibet.

## CCP Leader Travels to Tibet

Chinese Communist Party (CCP) leader Hu Yaobang travelled to Tibet. He found conditions so appalling he immediately ordered dramatic changes. These changes (only partially implemented), and the acknowledgment that there were serious problems in Tibet, continued to set a climate for compromise. In April 1982 the Dalai Lama sent another delegation to Beijing. Sadly, no accommodation was at hand as talks broke down. As long as the Dalai Lama was talking to Beijing, third party support was unnecessary. When talks stalled in the latter half of the 1980s the Dalai Lama had to rethink his options. The result was a plan calling for heightening awareness of Tibet by building popular support on moral grounds (independence, religions freedom, environment, etc.) and using the resultant popular protest to compel governments to line up behind the Dalai Lama by pressuring Beijing to be more flexible at the bargaining table. This strategy called for more openly political travel; establishment of support groups to lobby their governments; recruitment of parliamentary members from the major nations; peaceful civil disobedience inside Tibet and, continued appeals for dialogue with Beijing.

The International Campaign for Tibet was founded in Washington D.C. It was in March 1988. It sponsored visits by Congressional aides to Tibetan settlements in India and Nepal and published Tibet Press Watch, a compilation of news stories on Tibet as well as Tibet Forum, a Chinese language publication written by Chinese' educated expatriate Tibetans and aimed at the exile. Chinese dissident community

All of these efforts began to bear fruit, especially in the U.S. Congress where some members were already angry at China over trade imbalance, human rights issues in general, military sales, the export of prison labour, etc. In 1987 the Dalai Lama addressed the U.S. Congressional Human Rights Caucus and called for: (1) Tibet to be a zone of peace, (2) abandonment of ethnic Chinese migration to Tibet, (3) respect for human rights and democratic freedoms, (4) respect for the environment, and (5) negotiations on the future status of Tibet.

**Execution in Lhasa**

While the Dalai Lama was in the United States the authorities in Lhasa held a public trial, executing two Tibetans accused of being common criminals. That was perhaps to shows to the world that the Chinese did not care. Three days later Lhasa saw its first public demonstrations in 28 years. More disturbances followed on 1 October China's National Day which led to bloodshed. Five days after, in response to the turmoil in Lhasa, the U.S. Senate unanimously passed a resolution similar to the earlier bill in the House of Representatives which tied future military sales to China to the resolution of human rights abuses. In December, President Ronald Reagan signed the bill. But Congressional resolutions do not represent the official view of the United States. Deputy Assistant Secretary of State for East Asian and Pacific Affairs J. Stapleton Roy, testified to Congress that "...the United States Government considers Tibet to be a part of China and does not in any way recognize the Tibetan government in exile that the Dalai Lama claims to head." Moreover the Dalai Lama, "...is the head of a government in exile" No government had recognised the Dalai Lama as the head of any government.

On March 5, 1988 Lhasa saw its biggest demonstration ever. Several thousand Tibetans were met with tear gas and electric cattle prods. The Dalai Lama had hoped that a little civil disobedience in Lhasa and the internationalization of the Tibet question would help prod Beijing towards compromise. The plan backfired; unrest in a sensitive border area with a history of rebellion coupled with Western interference in what Beijing believes is an internal matter only served to buttress the arguments of those opposing compromise. Nonetheless, the Dalai Lama took a bold initiative. Speaking to the European Parliament (to highlight his international support) on 15 June he reiterated much of his earlier Five Point Plan and went one step further saying, for the first time publicly, that he would be willing to return to a Tibet that was less than independent. He proposed a Tibetan political entity "in association" with China. The speech called the Chinese bluff for he had agreed to the one condition China had always placed on the talks. Beijing saw through what the Dalai Lama was trying to achieve. The rejected the offer out right. The unrest. continued in Tibet.

Meanwhile unrest continued m Tibet and Chinese officials who supported less freedoms, more repression and no compromise with the Dalai Lama were becoming more vocal. "We must deal resolute, accurate and rapid blows against the serious crimes of a small number of separatists," read an editorial in Xizang Ribao (Tibet Daily), on 13 March 1988, "... [they] are the cause of this earthquake and a cancer cell in society." But not everyone agreed. "There are people who think it necessary to strike down the lamas and destroy the monasteries," the Panchen Lama said on 29 March. "We must not fall back to the errors of the past...I must seriously warn against people who have the idea of dealing merciless blows at the Lamas and closing all the temples."

As always happens, becuse of the liberalized policies, demonstrations continued and in March 1988 a political rally which culminated months of marches and protests led to a declaration of martial law in Lhasa and its environs which was to last until May 1990. Hu Yaobang had initiated a decade long liberalization of policies which resulted in increased use of the Tibetan language, the rebuilding of religious structures and a strengthening of Tibetan culture. The goals were to bring stability to Tibet and accommodation with the Dalai Lama.

**Thinking on Visiting Lhasa**

In January 1989 the Panchen Lama suddenly died and moderate officials invited the Dalai Lama to attend funerary rites in Beijing while letting him know that there would also be political discussions. He would not be allowed to visit Lhasa, what would he do if he was treated badly. The international Tibet campaign was also flourishing so; going later would give him more international support. The Dalai Lama gave a serious thought to it. At one point, it looked he was willing to accept the exortation.

But later it was turned down. Turning down the invitation was a grave error. In China the moderates were discredited, their policies had resulted in riots in Lhasa and the Dalai Lama refusing to visit Beijing. Hardliners who favoured more repressive policies now came to power over Tibet. For most of the next decade the CCP Party Secretary in Tibet, Chen Kuiyuan, opposed negotiating with the Dalai Lama believing that when the Pontiff died the international campaign would dissolve.

Economic development, Chen believed, would make Tibetans forget about the Dalai Lama so to that end he encouraged Chinese (Han) migration and substantial investment in the region coupled with a strict ban on displaying the photographs of the Dalai Lama, restrictions on religious institutions, cultural activities and political activities no matter how benign. While economic investment and tourism have brought material benefit to some Tibetans, the migration of perhaps hundreds of thousands of Han into Tibetan urban areas threatens the continued practice of Tibetan culture.

By the time Chen was reassigned, however, his policies had done more to increase ethnic tensions than to ameliorate them. In Washington the efforts of the Tibet Lobby continued to succeed with Congress passing legislation allowing for cash grants to Tibetan refugees and scholarships to students as well the establishment of a Cold War throwback called Radio Free Asia to beam U.S. propaganda to Tibet and countries of East Asia where government were seen as hostile to U.S. interests. But sensitivity to Tibet's status continued so even though the Dalai Lama has met the last three U.S. Presidents in the White House, the visits were "private" and he has never been formally invited to, nor allowed to sit in, rooms where state visitors are received.

**Non-acceptance of Chinese Proposal**

Dalai Lama had not accepted any Chinese proposal. The talks with China broke down completely with China blaming the Dalai Lama's intransigence on the independence issue and arguing that "...we have never changed our eagerness to hold negotiations" and the Dalai Lama insisting that he was searching for a middle way; "I am not demanding complete independence from China," he declared at a press conference on 1 August 1990, for that demand would be "a little unrealistic." Whatever the Dalai Lama did on the world form, or the Tibetans did in their homeland, it did not affect the Chinese much. In the beginning, the Chinese leaders' worst nightmare is that the Dalai Lama's efforts will contribute to the breakup of China or damage the Chinese economy through the elimination of trade concessions or boycotts. But for all the clamor on human rights foreign investment in China and the economy continue to grow at a healthy pace. In November 2001 China was admitted into the World Trade Organization. What China wants most in Tibet is stability and economic development. The Dalai Lama has the same objectives along with a reasonable measure of local autonomy so he can work to preserve and advance Tibetan culture. These are not conflicting intentions and the two sides are closer together than it may seem. But more than 20 years of failed talks has engendered considerable distrust on both sides. The internationalization of the issue has made Beijing defensive and weakened the influence of officials most willing to negotiate with the Dalai Lama.

A settlement would greatly benefit both sides; the Dalai Lama would return home, end anti-Chinese activities and preserve his culture and the Chinese government's international image would be considerably enhanced. Moreover, the Dalai Lama would attract considerable foreign investment, easing Beijing's current huge subsides to the region.

For the United States Tibet has no political, economic or strategic importance. Washington pays lip service to moral values but rarely acts on them. Up until 11 September 2001, there was a debate raging within foreign policy circles over U.S. policy towards China. No more. Now China is needed in the battle against terrorism, China's veto in the U.N. is essential to further U.S. foreign policy interests and there is always the issue of trade and that huge potential market. As Washington and Beijing find that their interests begin to converge, the Tibet issue will subside further and further into obscurity. United States has done more to betray the exile Tibetans community than to help them. It has become apparent that the United Indisputably the Dalai Lama's major success has been his ability to generate worldwide interest and enchantment with himself, his cause and religion.

**Unimagined Heights**

This allure has led to an infatuation with a romanticized and idealized Tibet as well as propelling it to heights unimagined by the originators of the international campaign; Hollywood movies, rock concerts, celebrities practicing Buddhism, have all combined to make the Dalai Lama and Tibet household words. There is a similar phenomena going on in China where the government's attention to Tibet has resulted in a different sort of a fad; an infatuation with Tibetans as 'noble savages' with their curious ways. Things Tibetan, such as traditional medicine, are becoming very popular. At first glance all the attention in the I United States and the West appears to be good for the anti-Chinese cause. But in reality it may be a Pyrrhic victory for American groupies feel far more about Tibet than they know. They would be deeply disillusioned by the real Tibet having created a "virtual" (in Orville Schell's word) Tibet as an icon, like so much else in American popular culture, a temporary fashion whose time will run out when something else becomes stylish. Tibetans—real people, with a real history, with a real struggle, will have been cartoonized by American (and Chinese) popular culture. It will be another popular misfortune for the Tibetans.

## Bibliography

Sh. Bira, "Khutagtai Setsen khun taijiin zokhioson negen huuliin tukhai" *(One law by Khutagtai Setsen khun taij)*. Ulanbaatar, 1970, No. 3.

BNMAU- iin tuukh *(History of MPR.)* Ulanbaatar, 1966, Vol. I.

D. Dashbadrah, "Altan Khan Tubdtei haritsaj baisan ni" *(Altan Khan had relationship with Tibet)*. Historical study, Vol. 22, Ulaan- baatar.

D. Dashbadrakh "Mangol Tubdiin uls tor, shashnuii khariltasaanii tuukh" *(History of Political and Cultural Relationships between Mangolia and Tibet)*, Ulaanbaatar, 1998.

Zaba Damdin "Umar zugiin Mongol orond deedsiin nom erdene garsan altan devter hemeegdekh oroshivo" *(Golden book which showed how to develop Buddhist teaching in North Mongolia)* Library of Historical Branch of Mongolian Sciences. Translated from Tibetan by Prof. D. Dorj.

Jamba, "Ligden khutagt khaanii tuukhen bair suuri" *(Historical view of Ligden Hutagi Khan)*, Social Science of Inner Mongolia, 1991, No. 6.

Rinchen Lhamo, "We Tibetans", New York city, 1985.

Yu. N. Rerih, "Mongoloy Tibetskii otnoshenity v XVI i nachale XVII v", Mongoliskii sbornik (economy, history, archaeology) (Relationship Mongolia and Tibet in XVI and in the beginning of XVII centuries), Moscow, 1959.

S. Purevjab, "Mongol dakhi shariin shashnii khuraangui tuukh" *(Brief history of Yellow Sect of Buddhism in Mongolia)*, Ulaanbatar, 1978.

S. Purejab, "Khubisgaliin omnokh Ikh Khuree" *(Ikh Khuree before the revolution)*, Ulaanbaatar. 1960.

Sagan Setsen, "Erdeniin tovch" *(Erdeniin Touch)*, Edited by Ts. Nasanbaljir, Ulaanbaatar, 1960.

L. Chuluunbaatar. "Mongoliin ard tumnii useg bichig, Tuunii tuukh soyoliin ach Kholbogdol" *(Mongolian Script, its historical-cultural importance)*, Dissertation, 2000.

"Erdeni tunamal herr sudar orshivoi" *(Sutra Clear Treasure)*, Edited by Zurenga, National Publishing House, Beijing, 1984.

Ya Khani Chjan, "Dalai lamiin namtar" *(Biography of Dalai Lama)*, National Publishing House, Beijing, 1992.

Ya Khani Chjan. "Banchin Erdeniin namtar" *(Biography of Banchin Erdene)*, People's Publishing House of Inner Mongolia, Hob Hot, 1990.

## References

1. BNMAU—iin tuukh. Ulaanbaatar, 1966, Vol. I, p. 229.
2. *Ibid.*
3. Rinchen Lhamo, *We Tibetans*, New York city, 1985, p. 21.
4. L. Chuluunbazatar, "Mongoliin ard tumnii useg bichig, tuunii tuukh soyoliin ach kholhogdol", 2000, p. 53.
5. Rinchen Lhamo, *We Tibetans*, New York city, 1985, p. 20.

6. Ya Khani Chjan, "Dalai Lamiin namtar". National Publishing House, Beijing, 1992, p. 24.
7. S. Purevjab, "Khubisgaliin umnokh Jkh Khuree". Ulaanbaatar, 1961. p. 15.
8. Sagan Setsen, "Erdeniin toch", Edited by Ts. Nasangaljir. Ullanbaatar, 1960, p. 222.
9. *Ibid.*
10. Zaba Damdin "Umar Zugiin Mongol orond deedsiin nom erdene garsan altan devter hemeegdekh oroshivo". Library of Historical branch of Mongolian Sciences. Translated from Tibetan by Prof. D. Dorj. p. 32.
11. Pauwels, Louis—Berber, Juques, *The Mòrning of the Magicians,* New York, Stein and Day, 1964, p. 198.
12. Angebert, Jean-Michel, *The Occult and the Third Reich,* New York, MacMillan, 1974, p.71.
13. "Der Spiegel", No.16 (1998), p. 111.
14. Suster, Gerald, *Hitler, the occult Messiah,* New York, St. Martin's 1981, pp. 191-192.
15. Feigon, Lee, *Demystifying Tibet,* Chicago, Elephant Paperbacks, 1996, p. 15.
16. Recently Martin Brauen did this in a somewhat different way in his excellent "Traumwelt Tibet", Berne (Switz.) 2000, pp. 53-81.

**Unpublished Sources:**

Ernst Schaefer: Tagebuccher (diaries), Berlin Bundesarc, Rì35/38-40.

SS-Ahnenerbe. Berlin Bundesarchiv, NS 21/682.

German Captured Records. Washington National Archives. RG 238, M-1270/R27; M-1019/R62.

**Published Sources:**

Bruno Beger: *Mil der deutchen Tibetexpedition Ernst Schaefer 1938/39 nach Lhasa,* Wiesbaden: Schwarz 1998.

Ernst Schaefer: *Fest der weissen Schleier,* Braunschweig: Vieweg 1949.

Ernst Schaefer: *Geheimnis Tibet.* Munich: Bruckmann 1943.

**Suggested Readings:**

Martin Brauen: *Traumwelt Tibet,* Bern: Haupt 2000: [English translation forthcoming, 2003. Weatherhill, U.K.].

Reinhard Greve: *Tibetforschung in SS-Ahnenerbe,* in: Thomas Hauschild (Ed.): Lebenslust und Fremdenfurcht, Frankfurt: Suhrkamp 1995, pp. 168-199.

Mark J. Rogers: *The SS-Ahnenerbe and the 1938/39 German-Tibet Expedition,*

Atlanta: Georgia State University, M.A. Thesis 2000. (This mainly contains a retelling of the above-mentioned "Geheimnis Tibet").

# 15

# Bhutan: Political Culture and National Dilemma

Political culture, as an inseparable aspect of larger values and beliefs, provides a package of theoretical and empirical orientations to understand national politics at one level and local politics at another. The recurrent themes in studies of political culture emphasise normative patterns such as roles, institutions, 'community', 'realm', participation, power and authority, rules of the game, symbols, scope of government, issue agenda, etc. The concept, though based on the *Anglo-Saxon* experience of a pluralistic tradition of communication and persuasion, consensus and diversity, change and continuity, is flexible enough to encompass the nuances of non-Western political systems. The present chapter first tries to identify some salient features of Bhutanese political culture.

On the basis of its history and traditions we shall endeavour briefly to track down the travail of the Bhutanese theocratic system to a near British colony. And finally, we shall comment on the present predicament, in which Bhutan must achieve a balance between its traditional political culture and the incomplete, process of an emergent Bhutanese nation state.

## Drukpa Political Culture

Bhutan is a frontier society away from the riverine centres of civilisation. Though pre-*lamaist* ethnic groups existed in the *Lh'o-Mon* (the classical name for Bhutan in Tibetan: Aris, 1980) it was the *Drukpa* (or *Druk)* theocracy that provided the social base of the contemporary Bhutanese social structure. On an apparent animistic and *Bonpo* social base, the Tibetan *Lamaist* missionaries— invariably house holding monks— were either engaged in magical/divine warfare, discovering lost holy texts, or fighting sectarian battles (Aris, 1980). The mainstay of the economy was pastoralism and barter trade, which was adjusted as per the demands of transhumance. *Dzongs*—initially significant structures for strategic purposes in Tibet—were adopted in Bhutan first for defence-cum-ritual purposes and then as administrative centres.

Shabdrung Ngawang Namgyal's charismatic leadership (1594-1651) laid the foundations of the Bhutanese system by providing a sound theocratic legitimacy and evolving a flexible status in the regional power structure and functioning of the Bhutanese system during the medieval period.

Some of the significant aspects of Drukpa polity were: ubiquitous oligarchic conflict, a shifting capital and seat of authority, duality of authority, and an extremely fragile and limited economic base (Sinha, A.C., 1991).

With a view to understanding this political culture, it is imperative to examine the traditional Tibetan pattern of government among the Shakya orthodoxy, which is closest to the *Drukpa* sect of Buddhist. The system of government was possessed of both *dharma (chhos*—religion) and *samsara (srid*—the world). While in an organisational sense *chhos-srid* meant a *dyarchy* of clerical and lay elements, in an ideological sense it meant a synthesis. In this view the norms *of dharma* and *samsara* were two sets of laws, one for the domain of the church and the other for the state. There were two sets of officials, monk and lay, not necessarily working to the exclusion of each other. One also finds monks and nobles closely connected and thus overruling the possibility of absolute separation between the spiritual and temporal estates (Sinha, N.C., 1967).

**Institution of Incarnations**

Furthermore, because of the institution of the incarnations and prince-abbotship, the sacred and secular roles were invariably mixed up. There was a provision that when a secular chief was elected to an office of the state, he was expected to take lower religious vows. The first Shabdrung *(Dharamraja)* himself began as a prince-abbot under the patronage of his grandfather and became a house-holding monk ruler over the estates of the Drukpa sect. Once his domain had been extended and established on a sound footing after various skirmishes with the Tibetan Gelugpa rulers, he appointed a *Je-Khan-po* (the ritual head), a *Deb Raja* (the secular head) and the *penlops* (regional governors). Since the Shabdrung's time there have been between five and eight Shabdrungs, 66 *Je-Khan-pos* and 55 *Deb Rajas* (Department of Education, 1974).

The system was simple enough, as there was no hereditary distinction of landed aristocracy in the rugged topography and harsh climatic conditions. Taxes were paid to the *penlops* and *dzongdas* (district heads) in kind for the consumption of the monk body at Punakha, Thimphu and other monastic establishments. Technologically, it was a simple system. Apart from climatic and geographical hardships, the small *Drukpa* society was also exposed to a number of diseases. In such a situation, gainfully employed persons were small in number, generating little economic surplus.

Apart from the maintenance of the monk bodies at the cost of the state exchequer, ubiquitous wars and feuds demanded the involvement of productive forces. A relatively isolated and near nomadic community such as the *Drukpa* had a limited appreciation of the settled plains people. This explains the continuous excursions of the *Drukpas* to the southern *Duars* (gateways to the southern foothills) to catch slaves and livestock and to collect economic surpluses and other consumer goods. The various sets of functionaries, with their limited exposure to the affairs of the state administration, remained on the periphery of the universal state and tribal polities. Needless to say, the *Drukpa* polity itself acknowledged nobody except its most immediate neighbours. Inaccesibilty to the East and deep in The South was another reason for isolation.

**Bhutan Under the British Colonial Fold**

In 1705, the first *Shabdrung's* death was made public. In 1903 the last official sovereign *Shabdrung* died. In these two centuries the *Drukpa* theocracy exhausted all its internal and external relevance. Internal requirements and geopolitical compulsions conspired to the emergence of this Wangchuks' dynastic rule in 1907, almost as a creation of British Indian frontier policy. The monarchy was created as a matter of expediency, without appropriate legitimacy and institutional props. This becomes obvious from the confusion that surrounded the institutions of the *Shabdrung* and *Deb Raja* after the establishment of the Wangchuk dynastic rule.

For example, though the office of the *Shabdrung* was reported to have been abolished after 1907, we are informed that Jigme Dorji (1905-31) was the *Dharamraja* born in Tawang region, who crowned the second Wangchuk Maharaja and died in mysterious circumstances in May 1931 (Sinha, A.C., 1991).

It is said that his reincarnation was discovered in the 1950s and is located at Rewalsar in the Manali district of Himachal Pradesh in India. Similarly, the institution of the *Deb Raja,* which was reported to have come to an end in 1905, finds its continuation in the form of the Wangchuk rulers as an afterthought in the 1970s. In this way, "the Wangchuk dynasty lacked the traditional ideological legitimation that has been so crucial to the survival of monarchies" (Rose, 1977).

It appears of late that there is an effort to discover theocratic legitimacy for the Wangchuk rule as the Druk Gyalpo. Uptil 1931, the British Political Officers in Sikkim and the Wangchuk *Maharajas* were unanimous in their view that Bhutan was an Indian principality within the British Empire. The *Maharaja* visited Calcutta to pay homage to the Prince and Princess of Wales, and attended the *Delhi Durbar* to pay homage to the King Emperor along with other rulers of Indian princely states. Similarly, the resident Political Officers took the second Maharaja to Guwahati, Calcutta and Sarnath (Banares) on conducted tours. The *Maharajas* and their second men in command—father and son Dorjis-Ugyen and Sonam Tobgyel—were decorated with British imperial titles like other princely dignitaries. In fact, on at least two occasions, Ugyen Wangchuk is reported to have said that Bhutan had become a part of the British Empire. Once when the treaty of Punakha was signed in January 1910[1] and again in 1923, when the Maharaja's request to increase his annual subsidy from 100,000 rupees to 300,000 rupees was turned down. On the latter occasion, he is reported to have remarked: "If they are unable to accede my request, I do not mind it, as it is by the kindness of the British Government that I have become what I am now."[2]

**Learning English and Hindi**

The British encouraged the Crown Prince to learn English and Hindi like other Indian princes. In fact, a number of Political Officers made it a point to report that the prince spoke good English and Hindi. Charles A. Bell, the Tibetologist and successor to John Claude White as Political Officer at Gangtok, was considered to be one of the architects of British policy in the Eastern Himalayan region in the first two decades of the 20th century. He was so close to the *Maharaja* of Bhutan that after learning that the former had filed papers for his retirement, the latter wrote, on March 2, 1919, that it was as if his own father had died. Bell had submitted a proposal, to the Foreign and Political Department on January 23, 1914 for the creation of a North Eastern Frontier Agency (NEFA) with its headquarters at Tawang, modelled on the North Western Frontier Agency (NWFA) at Peshawar. The Agency was to deal with political works connected with Sikkim, Bhutan, Tibet and the Assam hills (Arunachal Pradesh). Luckily for Bhutan, the British did not implement the proposal.[3]

Bhutan contributed to the War Fund during the two World Wars like other princely states in spite of its meagre financial resources. In fact, except for bureaucratic fussiness, the status of Bhutan as defined in 1911 remained unchanged: 'there is no doubt that Bhutan is a native state of India under the suzerainty of His Majesty's Government.' There appears to be a distinct change in the overall orientation of British policy towards Bhutan after the 1931 conflict between the second *Maharaja* and the last officially reported Shabdrung, Jigme Dorji. The Shabdrung considered the *Maharaja* to be a usurper of his authority, backed up by British support. He was not only in touch with the Indian National Congress leader, M.K. Gandhi, but was also in contact with the Dalai Lama in Lhasa.

**British Support**

The British used all their armery to support the Maharaja against the Shabdrung, so much so that the Shabdrung was quietly poisoned at the instance of the *Maharaja* with almost open British approval. Col. J.L.R. Weir, the then Political Officer at Gangtok, who guided the Bhutan *Durbar* on the Shabdrung crisis, did not crown himself with diplomatic glory. He lied to the Dalai Lama that the late Shabdrung was a born Bhutanese and he was convinced that he had died a natural death. No doubt a grateful Bhutan *Maharaja* confided to the Political Officer: "If an Indian were ever to be made Political Officer in Sikkim, he would never be invited to set foot in Bhutan". The report by Col. Weir was greeted with relief.[4]

British had ruled that part of India, i.e., Northeast for almost two centuries and ersualised what could happen. They British left a warning to the successor Indian Union in the form of a *Note*[5] prepared on August 10, 1946: "In practice it may well prove difficult to secure a tidy solution of the future of Nepal, Sikkim and Bhutan and even of the eastern marches of Kashmir. This will largely depend on the future policy and fate of China and hence of Tibet. The Government of the (Indian) Union must be prepared for complications on the North-East Frontier and evolve a policy to meet them. This may well have to be that of maintaining all the principalities in virtual independence of India but as buffer and, as far as possible, client states.

There may be greater advantages in according Sikkim a more independent status than in seeking to absorb Bhutan as well as Sikkim in the Indian Union, adding the communal problem of Buddhism to those of Islam and Hinduism ... the Government (of the Indian Union) would be well advised to avoid entering into fresh commitments with any one of those frontier states or seeking to redefine their status. Their importance is strategic in direct relation to Tibet and China and indirectly to Russia. Such adjustment of their relations with the (Indian) Union as can usefully be affected ... by those political strategic considerations ... account which it is hoped that the treaty will take rather than by constitutional niceties which do not help defence policy."

## Predicament of the Bhutanese Nation State

The reising tide of nationalism in India worried the British bureaucracy, especially the old Tibet experts such as F.M. Bailey, Basil Gould, and A.J. Hopkinson, appear to have had little faith in the *Maharaja* and the Indian democrats in the aftermath of the British withdrawal from India. They were apprehensive that the emergent democratic India might try to absorb Bhutan. They vainly pleaded that this imaginary issue should be taken to the United Nations Organisation and that Bhutan should be turned into a crown colony, or at least have some sort of British patronage. It is a tribute to the Bhutanese and Indian policy-makers that the transition from British overlordship to Indian assistance for a meaningful coexistence was a smooth and almost effortless enterprise.

For the first fifteen years after the British departure, Bhutan appeared prominently in the newspapers only twice: first when its second ruler expired in 1952 and again in 1958, when the Indian Prime Minister paid a visit to it. In between, the *Bhutan State Congress* raised a little storm in the placid Bhutanese tea-cup (Sinha, A.C., 1991) which was almost totally ignored by the newspapers. Meanwhile, the administration was run on an autocratic feudal pattern. The landlords controlled the bulk of the state's income and sent the residue to the Government treasury. The Government was in fact a body of about 130 semi-elected members, drawn even from the village headmen as official representatives of their districts. The Council "met once a year, if an emergency arose, or if the *Maharaja* had an announcement to make... the Government merely rubber-stamped the *Maharaja's* wishes.

There were no trained people and illiteracy was one hundred per cent... the Government was so scattered and isolated, (that) administration was limited to a few officials ... the 'capital' moved with the *Maharaja* and nobody bothered a great deal about anything. The hospitals and dispensaries were more often than not without medicine, which expired beyond their effective dates in storage through lack of interest or authority to issue. Schools were unattended because teachers were not paid and had to find other means to supplement their income. Even the 'Army' was subject to their feudal indifference, for while 'on paper' it was supposed to number two thousand five hundred with a ceiling of twenty thousand, it was really only a militia who were occasionally issued guns for firing practice for a few days, after which guns were returned to the headmen and the 'army' returned to the villages and field" (Patterson, G.A., 1963: 216-17). The nearly a hundred year-old Bhutanese dynastic rule of four successive kings may be divided into two broad periods. The first four decades and the regime of the first two *Maharajas* provided a typical picture of a distant, exotic, archaic family enterprise under the benign gaze of the British bureaucracy.

**Inputs from an Imminent Transition**

The regime of the third and fourth rulers over four decades from 1952 exhibits an effort to refurbish the old structure to receive inputs from an imminent transition. A period of transition is always painful and strenuous, demanding urgent decisions. All significant decisions affecting the course of the emergent Bhutanese nationhood were initiated during the reign of the third Wangchuk ruler (1952-72). He tackled the political challenge posed by the *Bhutan State Congress* in 1950s, invited the Indian Prime Minister (the first international leader to visit Bhutan) and took a far-reaching decision for the planned economic development of his country through Indian financial aid. Besides the introduction of transport, education, health care and other welfare and infrastructural schemes, he created various administrative bodies. It is said that he was engaged in a type of hurdle race in terms of human resource development. He sent selected trainees abroad for education and decided to go slow on having his own centres of higher learning.

Almost the entire development assistance for the first four Five Year Plans came from India, and since then India has remained the single largest donor of aid to Bhutan. Apart from India, Bhutan is very choosy about aid-givers and external relations. Apparently the Bhutanese do not want to flood their country with tourists and advisers from abroad who would adversely affect the small and ill-educated population. Thus, Bhutan chose either distant countries such as Australia, New Zealand, Canada and Japan, or small and mountainous countries such as Switzerland, Denmark, Netherlands, Sweden, Kuwait, etc. as potential foreign collaborators. Besides these countries, Bhutan joined various international fora for economic and social development. This all resulted in almost hundred per cent employment of its youth, a higher standard of living and a better quality of life for the average Bhutanese. However, in spite of all the precautions, geopolitics has conspired against the kingdom in its natural resource location. Because of the obvious southward orientation of the infrastructural network, most of the labour-intensive urban industrial enterprises were located in the southern 'negative land' of the past.

**Trading and Industrial Centres**

Thus, Samchi, Phuntsholing, Chukha, Geylegphug, Chirang, Lamidara, Sarbhang, Samdrup Jongkhar, and many more small settlements located on and near the Indian borders turned into limited trading and industrial centres, producing consumer goods and contributing to the exchequer in a considerable way. Most of the labour-intensive development projects were to be located in the south. A regional imbalance in the course of economic development is not unique to Bhutan. However, the ethnic policy of the country is that the Nepalese *(Lhotshampa)* immigrants are not permitted to settle north of an imaginary line drawn from east to west just behind the southern *Duar* foothills.

There has been another problem related to the ethnic policy and that is a 'politics of statistics,' if one puts it mildly, or rather 'a war of statistical figures' if one so desires. In a thinly populated, infras tructurally poor country such as Bhutan, which lacks transport facilities, it is no wonder that there has never been a formal census or enumeration of the population. The official statistics collected by village headmen are merely imaginary figures, as they are always reported to be the latest census estimates, with the last three digits invariably consisting of zeros (Sinha, A.C., 1988).

In the absence of a universally reliable and acceptable population figure, the claims and counter-claims of the size of the *Lhotshampa* population vary from sixteen per cent (Rose, 1977) to sixty-four per cent (Gurung, 1960) of the national population, depending upon the ethnic affiliation of the claimant. The thickly populated and intensively cultivated southern region of Bhutan presents a contrast to the thinly populated northern Drukpa pasturelands. In such a situation, a potential ethnic power-keg developed in the southern Nepalese ghetto in Bhutan, which ignited in 1988.

Kazi Ugyen Dorji, the chief of the King's household *(Deb Zimpom)*, the Royal Chamberlain *(Gongzim)*, and the Governor *(Dzongpen)* of Ha in western Bhutan, had encouraged large-scale Nepalese settlement in the south-western part of the country in the last decades of the nineteenth century. Charles A. Bell found 14,000 Nepalese on the Torsa river bordering India in 1903 (Bell, 1903). In no time, the land hungry Nepalese cleared the thick vegetation and organised themselves as cultivators in the southern *Duars.* Some twenty-five years later, Captain C.J. Morris of the *Gurkha Regiment* was commissioned to investigate the possibility of recruiting Bhutanese Nepalese in the *Assam Rifles Regiment* of the British Indian armed force.

**Captain Morsis Tour**

Captain Morsis made an extensive tour of the two Nepalese-inhabited districts of the south and made a crude estimate. 1,500 households of the eastern district and 4,000 households of the western districts contained a population of 60,000 out of a total population of 300,000, making the immigrants twenty percent in 1932. He remarked upon the largeness of Nepalese families within polygamous marital alliances.[5] Morris stated that the actual number of Nepalese settlers in Bhutan was much higher than his estimate, because he had not included Sipchu area to the extreme south-west. Nepalese immigration to Bhutan continued well into the present century even though there was a shortage of arable land. The government eventually banned further Nepalese immigration in 1958.

It is apparent that the bamboo and thatch houses of the Nepalese are less substantial than the multi-storeyed stone houses of the highlanders. The Nepalese areas are predominantly agricultural, producing rice, maize, wheat, pulses, oranges, pineapples, ginger, cardomom and so on.

Over the last 125 years or so or may be earlier the Nepalese migrated to Bhutan, Sikkim and Darjeeling in India. The Nepalese turned this 'negative land' into a productive bread-basket. They lead a frugal life. They are available for any type of work, and well suited to the extreme climate of the Bhutanese hills. In addition to agriculture, they have provided the workforce for recent development programmes. With the emergence of Samchi, Phuntsholing, Daga, Sarbhang, Geylegphug, Chirang and Samdrup

Jongkhar as the new commercial and (albeit modest) Bhutanese industrial towns of southern Bhutan, the role of the Nepalese in the national economy became more pronounced. Their food, dress, perseverance, industriousness and 'mercenary' character make the Nepali speakers one on an alien soil.

**India and Nepal**

They look to Nepal and India as the founts of their civilisation and historical achievements, and where their places of pilgrimage are located he they Hindu or Tibetan turned Nepalese Buddhists. Higher Nepalese Hindu castes practice ritual purity and shun beef, polyandry and widow remarriage. The Nepalese are new entrants in Bhutan and also occupy a lower economic and political status in national life. As residents of Bhutan, however, Nepalese do expect a share in the destiny of their new homeland and they have some genuine expectations from the Bhutanese nation state.

**Drukpa-Lhotshampa Ethnic Conflict**

The Bhutanese national dilemma can be identified at four different levels: national versus ethnic, the king versus the parliament, elitism versus populism, and frontier particularism versus universal modernisation (Sinha, A.C., 1991). Events beginning with the 1988 census enumeration have telescoped the entire dilemma into a conflict between Drukpa-ethnic-elitist-particularism versus Nepalese-ethnic-immigrant-populism. Never before has the Bhutanese polity put so much of its survival at stake. The total assimilation or outright rejection of the *Lhotshampas* appears to be the slogan of the day. In the absence of a creditable mass media, the publicity material produced by the Bhutanese establishment gives two aspects of the Bhutanese thinking. One aspect is a sad, forgiving, repentant and rather remorseful Druk Gyalpo (Hutt, 1992) and another is an aggressive, determined and vindictive Bhutanese bureaucracy (Ghosh, 1992). Are these postures two sides of the same coin?

Before we answer this question, it will he instructive to view the Bhutanese ethnic orientation towards the *Lhotshampas.* In the Bhutanese hierarchy, faith and loyalty to one's superiors goes unquestioned. A society of pastoralists and subsistence farmers was happy to leave trade, commerce and industry in the hands of the royal family. Bhutan's dynastic rule did not permit an aristocracy to emerge. Thus, today's *Drukpa* society consists of an all-powerful ruling family at the top, commoners at the bottom, and a monk body in between. The geographical compulsions of a mountainous country further isolated the *Drukpa* commoners from the shared experiences of a modern technological society. Under such circumstances, the urge for democratic participation practically does not exist.

**Semblance of Representation**

Any semblance of representation has to be sponsored from the top. The regime in Bhutan is notoriously intolerant of dissent. The stage was, thus, set for a conflict. While the *Drukpas* tried to impose an assimilationist policy, demanding oneness in language *(Dzongkha)*, dress *(Gho* and *Kira)* and cultural systems, Nepalese regarded themselves as culturally superior. The Bhutanese administration had always kept a careful watch on anti-feudal movements in Sikkim and Nepal, because the *Lhotshampas* have natural allies among them. It, therefore, came as a shock to the Bhutanese ruler when the 334-year-old Namgyal rule over Sikkim came to an end in 1975, succumbing to a movement organised almost entirely by Nepali-speakers. Even closer to home, the Bhutanese found an armed struggle in Darjeeling ending with the district also being governed by Nepali-speakers. The realisation dawned that, in the long run, New Delhi's commitment to prohibit anti-Bhutanese movements on Indian soil as per the provisions of the Punakha Treaty had no meaning. In a changed political scenario, the Nepali-speaking rulers of Nepal, Sikkim and Darjeeling could nullify New Delhi's assurances. This they could do by instigating, supporting or even financing agitation. Acting on these fears, the Bhutanese implemented an aggressive policy of cultural assimilation, starting with the implementation in 1988 of the *Driglam Namzha,* the *Drukpa* code of conduct.

**Refuges in Camps**

The rest is the story of the *Lhotshampas'* flight from their Bhutanese paradise. Bhutanese officials maintain that the refugees in various camps belong to three categories: (1) Indian refugees from Assam, Meghalaya and other eastern states; (2) illegal immigrants to Bhutan, who had no business to be in Bhutan (and were, thus, expelled after the 1988 census operation), and (3) *Lhotshampas,* who willingly surrendered their Bhutanese subjecthood and since then are busy in anti-Bhutanese terrorist activities. They say that none of the above has any claim on Bhutan and, thus, the Bhutanese have nothing to do with the *Lhotshampa* refugees residing in various camps: they are necessarily Nepalese and Nepal should take its responsibility seriously. They also view the Nepalese presence east of the river Teesta as a part of a Nepalese scheme to carve out a *Greater Nepal (Maha Nepal)* at the cost of Bhutan and India. And, thus, the Bhutanese and the Indians should ideally make common cause against such a nefarious design. India may decide to ignore the 'menace' of the Nepalese immigrants because of a Nepalese presence in India, treaty obligations, cultural and religious ties and its own huge plural ethnic base. With all this going on its territory and in the neighbouring countries Bhutan cannot afford to accept them as equal, as such an acceptance may threaten the very core of its ethnic and national identity.

**Nepalese Migrants**

The Bhutanese have adopted a number of strategies to deal with the crisis. They consider Nepalese identity to be a myth and portray the Nepalese as divided into small groups such as Tamang, Rai, Gurung, Kami, Magar, Damai, Bahun, Chhetri, Newar, Madesi, Sherpa, etc. They straightaway deny their presence in Bhutan prior to 1900. They paint the Nepalese as an anti-national mercenary menace to the legal regime. They have of late started to cultivate scholars and journalists, who could be more sympathetic to the cause of the last surviving *lamaist* monarchy in the world, and to invite such persons on conducted tours of Bhutan. In this context, they are concentrating of late more on Indian academics and journalists. They themselves have done their homework thoroughly and prepared illustrated documents to support their stand (anonymous, 1992). Lastly, they see to it that the representatives of the *Lhotshampa* refugees are not invited, wherever they make their presentations.

A classical theocracy turned into an exotic Wangchuk-ruled Bhutan had little experience of ethnic coexistence on its own soil. It has not been able to weigh the implications of its aggressive ethnic policy to assimilate an ancient, martial and substantive Nepalese commonwealth into its then relatively simple and recent *Drukpa* fold. Policy-makers such as the Foreign Minister appear to have an exaggerated image of their powers. They tend to forget that their aggressive ethnic policy and false sense of absorptive capacity is bound to affect the pace of economic transformation. The Bhutanese aberrations might slow but cannot stop the Nepalese expansion in the Eastern Himalayan foothills; rather, such antics as the Drukpa regime is currently engaged in may provide an impetus for a Nepalese resurgence in the region. The Bhutanese consider this to be a danger to their racial hegemony.

**Resurgent Ethnicity**

If nation-states turned out to the reality of the 20th century world political scene. By the same token resurgent ethnicity is going to be the concern of the first decade of the 21st century. There is hardly a nation-state in the world today that has no ethnic minority within its fold. Added to this is another aspect of the Himalayan states in the Asian heartland: the existence of numerous divided frontier communities across legal national boundaries. To date, no state has been able to completely resolve the vexed and overarching ethnic claims from across or within its frontiers. Bhutan, one of the world's smallest and least developed nations, is trying to achieve the impossible, i.e. the absorption or expulsion of *Lhotshampas.*

It should be in the interest of the Bhutanese to realise the limits of their aggressive ethnic policy. Once they do it, they may take the initiative in helping the SAARC countries to evolve a policy of ethnic coexistence without affecting national priorities. Once a regional consensus on ethnic policy has been hammered out, it may decrease the heat on Bhutan and morally bind Nepal and India to extend their support to it in its hour of crisis. In this way, the apparent conflict between Bhutan's national identity and the *Lhotshampas'* ethnic aspirations within the *Drukpa* polity may be resolved.

## References

1. India Office Library, London (I.O.L.) MSS: EUR: P: 1024, External/Secret 1, F80/SC: 22 Folios: 'Diary of My Mission to Bhutan', Charles A. Bell's personal papers, dated January 21, 1910.
2. I.O.L.: MSS: EUR: 4 P&S 5112/2225 No 814, Bhutan Affairs: Subsidies, etc., April 7, 1924.
3. *Ibid.:* F 80/5 d. 8 IH: 36 folios.
4. *Ibid.*, P 2: 32W1933 Confidential No. 6(10)-P/32, from Political Officer in Sikkim to the Foreign Secretary, November 11, 1932.
5. *Ibid.*, P.2 1854: 1934 Confidential. A Report on the Immigration of Gurkhas into Bhutan.

# 16
# Ethnic Stalemate and Crisis of Confidence

Among many proverbs prevalent among the culturally rich Nepalese is the following: "a son is born to go out in the world to earn wealth; and once he has earned it, he is to come back home (to Nepal) with it." "If you cannot defeat an enemy entrap him in a marital albance, goes a popular Dzongkha saying. These two words of old-world wisdom and experience may be taken symbolically representing two ethnic perceptions, relevant to the current ethnic strife in Bhutan. While the former may be taken as decisive and assimilative, the latter one projects to a limitless expansion from its base. These two statements may be ignored as gems of folk wisdom in normal circumstances, but when these two communities are engaged in a bitter conflict between themselves, these popular perceptions may be taken as functioning of the folk mind. Bhutan of 1990s appears to be no more an exotic, isolated and politically placid country.

A decade-old ethnic conflict continues to be in the news, to the extent that a series of academic international seminars were held on Bhutan; a number of concerned delegations visited the country; the *Tshongdu* besides deliberating on other issues spends most of its sessions in discussing the ongoing ethnic conflict and about a hundred thousand refugees kept on languishing in the various camps. A three-member delegation of the Amnesty International (AI) visited Bhutan in 1991 to learn about half a dozen *'prisoners of conscience'* and the International Committee for the Red Cross (ICRC) met the King on January 19, 1993 to understand the reasons of the ethnic strife.

### Population of Drukpa

The Royal Government of Bhutan always know the population Drukhpas in Bhutan. It is entirely another matter that they kept it to themselves. However, a small and distinctly *lamaist Drukpa* Bhutan could not afford the unlimited migration, because it was afraid that the immigrants would swamp it. The way the 'magic number' of 6,00,000, climbed down from 1,400,000 previous population figure of the country, came to be accepted is unknown. Nobody knows how it was arrived, who was its author and what are its various demographic features. However, the responsible functionaries of the state agree that the Nepalese ethnic elements constitute anything between 25 to 35 per cent of its total population. Bhutan is determined to correct the past 'statistical error' for all the time to come, as all its citizens are being given computerised identity cards.

Assertion to supremacy it is universally believed that the pace of economic development has been adversely affected because of the recent ethnic conflict, but it is considered to be an unavoidable passing phase. In the new dispensation everybody has to be a *Drukpa* in Bhutan and, thus, the *Lhotshampas* have to be assimilated in the dominant national fold. They had no reasons to complain against the assimilative policy of the state upto 1970s. It all started in a limited way, when Jit Bahadur Chhetri, a member of the Royal Advisory Council, began to issue certificates to the *Lhotshampas* seeking for jobs, licenses, contracts, admissions to academic institutions, etc. from the government as their sole representative in the *Council.* The *Lhotshampas* as well as the government functionaries accepted it as a convenient practice.

**Special Status**

But this practice initiated to emphasise on the special status of the *Lhotshampas,* an issue that contributed to ethnic clash. In mid- 1980s it was found that" a number of *Lhotshampas* were married across the borders in India or Nepal. Since wages were higher in Bhutan, a number of their kinsmen came with the newly acquired wives to work in the fields or help the households in various other ways. Besides that, some of the *Lhotshampa* heads of the households in their traditional ways had adopted some of their non-Bhutanese kinsmen as their sons/daughters for working as farm hands. In one extreme case a *Lhotshampa* head of the family had adopted as many as 14 young men as his sons, who were found working for him. The Bhutanese did not have workforce for rapid economic development, but within no time, the Government realised that the *Lhotshampas* were increasing abnormally.

With a view to be distinguishing the genuine Bhutanese from the aliens the king introduced the concepts of one man, one country' and 'code of conduct' *(Driglam Namza)* in public places. For that he did consult the *Lhotshampas.* As per the Bhutanese tradition, the public meetings were held at various places and the government position was explained to *Lhotshampas* and their consent was sought. As there was no open opposition and, in fact, some of the loyal *Lhotshampas* accused the government for its failure to bring them at par with the *Drukpas* in terms of the national dress, etc. The king asked the heads of the families (as per the Bhutanese practice, the state counts the views of the family heads in place of adult franchise) to give their consent on the code of conduct in writing, which was done in most of the cases.

**Silent Campaign**

These two steps led to a silent campaign among the *Lhotshampas* that they were being discriminated against. Then came the census operation 1988, in which efforts were made to establish the actual size of the Nepalese in the 'south'.

Since almost all the families had some 'illegal guests' from across the border, the state functionaries did adopt some highhandedness in identifying the recent migrants. The police was assigned extra duty to identify the illegal Nepalese residents and collect Rs. 100 as fine for every violation of code of conduct, which was to be shared on fifty per cent basis between the state and individual policemen. Moreover, there were some well-placed Nepalese bureaucrats, who were educated abroad and did not know *Dzongkha,* the official languages of the state. They made some feeble efforts to learn the language, but failed in their efforts.

**'The Green Belt Policy'**

That was when trouble started. Some of such articulate and educated Nepalese are reported to have stealthily organised themselves; moved from school to school preaching to the students and pupils alike opposition to the code of conduct and instigating the *Lhotshampas* to oppose the state ethnic policy. With a view to sanitise Bhutan from the alien intrusion in the form of Nepalese to the southern foothills, Bhutan began to consider an extremely innovative step since 1980s. It is said that even India's tacit support was secured. So much so that India had reportedly agreed to fund the endeavour in favour of environmental protection.

With sufficient preparation, the *Tshongdu* passed a resolution in its 69th session on March 19-20, 1990 to introduce "the Greenline Belt Policy" on its southern frontier adjoining India. It was intended to create a forest belt in all areas falling within one kilometre from the southern borders. Originally proposed in 1984, it was to be a two kilometre swath that would run along the Indo-Bhutan boundary.

It this green belt was intended to check erosion and flood and provide a distinct border between the two countries. The significant existing townships were not to be included, but the cultivators were to be displaced either by compensating them for their land or settling them elsewhere. The proposed rates for the land compensation were between Nu 15,000 and Nu 30,000 per acre for paddy fields and between Nu 8,000 and Nu 15,000 to the dryland. Alternately, one could opt for replacement of land for resettlement at sites in the interior areas of Samchi, Zhemgang, Dagana and Wangdiphodrang districts.

**Ban on Constructing Houses**

Much earlier construction of residential houses on paddy fields had been banned in the interior areas. Furthermore, a *Lhotshampa* fanner owned eight acres of land for paddy and maize cultivation besides his homestead and orchards. Were they to be provided that much of land among the Drukpa villages in the interior villages? It was certainly known to the Bhutan Government that the area was a most densely populated region of the country. These are the only plain areas available in the country, which were developed by clearing dense and wild forests during the last hundred years by the Nepalese settlers. Generations of the Nepalese had to toil hard against the difficult circumstances in these 'hot, humid and malarial black waters' *(Kalopani)* to reclaim the land for cultivation, orchard and the homestead.

This was the only land known to them, where many of their myths were created; children were born and married and ancestors were cremated. The *Lhotshampas* were stunned by this move and did not know-how to react to it. And it was not a question of rehabilitating some displaced families. The scheme affected as much as above one-third of the total *Lhotshampa* population, which could be anything between two to six lakhs souls. The Minister of Home Affairs, Royal Government of Bhutan was resolute to implement the scheme and it issued a memorandum to the Ministry of Finance on May 28, 1990 stating: "I shall, therefore, be happy if you will kindly purchase the lands from those falling within Green Belt (you will do so) entirely on their expressed desire and voluntary basis. The present acquisition should exclude those people, who wish to have land replacement or desire to be rehabilitated in the resettlement areas."

**Final Implications**

We have no idea whether the financial implication of the memorandum was examined; such lands and their willing owners were identified; budgetary provisions were made and sources of finance were identified before hand. It appears to be obvious from the memorandum that the Ministry of Home was implementing only a part of the proposed Green Belt Policy by buying land from persons willing to leave the country, and not from those who would stay in Bhutan. It was a perfect encapsulation plea for the *Lhotshampas.* Either they were to integrate themselves among the *Dukpas* by moving in the interior areas of Bhutan or leave the country at large, or in case they persist in staying back in their southern villages, the Government apparatus would do nothing for them.

There was no appreciable number of takers of the first policy. Volatile, emotive and exposed *Lhotshampas* took the second option and moved away from Bhutan with compensation amount for their properties or without. However, those of them who stay put on their homestead, they did at their own risk. Their children do not get admission in the schools; the health clinics remain closed; they have been removed from the government jobs and rest of the welfare provisions remain unavailable to them. This claimed innovative environmental plan was alleged to have been formulated with India's help and backing. However, once the ethnic agitation took the anti-government move and the *Lhotshampas* began to move out of the Dragon country after armed repression, there were no viable international sources to support it.

**Issues Involving the Lhotshampa Refugees**

Ultimately, at least at the overt policy level, the Royal Government of Bhutan was constrained to abandon the Green Belt Policy, as donors including India backed out of financing it. So the environment-friendly Drukpa regime was denied of this innovative environmental protection policy.

On the issue of the *Lhotshampas* flight to the refugee camps certain very contradictory developments are taking place. Firstly, the dissidents claim to be fighting for the cause of the Bhutanese Nepalese, but there are evidences, which suggest that some unruly and *Robinhood* type character among them are burning houses, terrorising and physically and sexually assaulting the loyal Nepalese left behind in Bhutan.

Many times the refugee leaders have charged that the police and army perpetrated the violence against the *Lhotshampas.* But those, who have been caught while indulging in violent activities, are invariably the persons of the Nepalese ethnic background. It is a fact that there have been some cases of individual violence such as beating, pushing around and rape, etc. but as a whole, state as such does not appear to be responsible for such an extensive violence and destruction of private and state properties in the 'south'. Another intriguing problem is against the *Druk-rgyalpo's* appeal to the *Lhotshampa* to stay back in their adopted land. And the dissidents encouraged the simple *Lhotshampas* to leave Bhutan for the refugee camps in Nepal. But now they maintain that they have full faith in the king, but it is the *Drukpa* bureaucracy, which is made responsible for the sad plight of the *Lhotshampas.* It is a double edge stretegy to foment unrest.

**Armed Dissidents?**

Who are the armed dissidents who are creating disturband which ultimately beas to violence. It is possible that the armed dissidents responsible for violence in Bhutan may not be directly linked with the BPP/BNDP/BCP or other organised political parties. It could be small time organised or other types of criminal gangs or extremists among the refugees. Who are doing all this for their own reasons. Similarly, the wild charges of financial irregularities, forgery, and criminal misappropriation against many of the deserting former bureaucrats and now political leaders in the refugee camps appear to be an after-thought of the Bhutanese establishment to defame and discredit them.

If such higher bureaucrats in the government were so much involved in the financial irregularities, the system should have evolved a built-in corrective measure and initiated steps much earlier than when they left Bhutan as political dissenters. It appears that the Bhutanese bureaucracy in its enthusiasm of 'Gorkha Phobia' forgot that education and awareness for democratic rights invariably go together. The King does not hide his dejection on the ethnic issue, as *Lhotshampas* walked on his pleas and assurances. It is commonly believed among the influential circle in Thimphu that the *Lhotshampas* had designed to change the Bhutanese political and ethnic scenario within next 25 years. They were determined to alter the citizenship laws and open up Bhutan for uninterrupted flow of the alien Nepalese. Then it would have been easier for them to extend their ethnic hegemony from Nepal to Sikkim, Darjeeling, *Duars* and, ultimately, to Bhutan. Even if the current ethnic conflict is resolved, the ethnic scenario is going to be difficult for Bhutan in the near future.

**The Divide**

The divide between the *Drukpas* and the *Lhotshampas* on the one hand and between the *Lhotshampas,* who continued to be in Bhutan and were deprived and subjected to all sorts of violence and the refugees, and those who will be supposedly coming back from the camps, is very much pronounced. Even if the king offers amnesty to the refugees after their return, so much animosity may been created by then that the *Lhotshampas* themselves may settle their scores for all the scorns heaped on them. Unrest and violence seems inevitable.

**The Drukpa Perception of the Nepalese Leadership**

Drukpas are unanimous in their thought that the Lhotshampas must assimilate with the Drukpas mainstream. There is no question of any compromise on this point. The Bhutanese consider the ethnic issue as their internal matter and do not desire any third party interference in it. Since the *Lhotshampas* have gone to refugee camps in Nepal, they are willing to talk to the Nepalese authorities to stop the ethnic strife. And here comes a serious difficulty. The Bhutanese find three shades of politics among the Nepalese at large with a bearing on the current ethnic strife. Firstly, the *'Greater Nepal' (Maha Nepal)* protogonists, a loose but unreasonable, expansionist cultural aspiration, which looks to the Nepalese past in grandiose manner and sees the occasional past armed sorties as unforgettable historical achievements.

While its historical aspect is as good as mythological, its cultural part is inspiring for the new generations. At the most it is at the level of a wishfulness and at the worst it is a foolhardly strategic design. It is the Nepali Congress and the various shades of the Marxist opposition parties in Nepal, which are at present of political significance in Nepal, who are relevant in terms of the *Lhotshampas.* The Bhutanese consider the then ruling party of Nepal (UML) consisting of administratively and even politically inexperienced and confused lot, who are tired old men burdened between old idealism and demands of real politics. On the other hand, the opposition political parties in Nepal are seen as an aggressively ambitious and impatient crowd of trouble suitors, which are more interested in settling their accounts with their arc rivals—the Nepali Congress.

**Potential Threats**

The immediate neighbours of the Bhutanese in the west, the Sikkim Sangram Parishad (SSP) of Nar Bahadur Bhandari and the Gurkha National Liberation Front (GNLF) of Subhash Ghising and their variants, are viewed as serious and potential threats to the Bhutanese state ethnic policy. It is felt that the SSP and the GNLF leadership in spite of their own squiblings are watching New Delhi and Calcutta leaders to take public postures on the refugee issue and then they may take an aggressive ethnic posture. To the utter surprise of the Bhutanese functionaries, the assurances given by New Delhi to discourage anti-Bhutanese activities from the Indian soil have no meaning in the changed political scenario. These Nepalese leaders in Sikkim and West Bengal are now in a position to instigate, support and even finance such agitations. With a view to counteract trans-border violence, the Bhutanese are coordinating their steps with the state governments of Assam and West Bengal at the highest levels.

The Lhotshampa leadership stands confused and in disarray. The Nepalese in their unreasonable bravado did not calculate for the Bhutanese aggressive and defensive stand to pursue their objectives The Bhutanese establishment maintains that they have a complete understanding with the Government of India on the ethnic issue and the latter had advised both the competing parties to solve the issue among them. The then Indian Prime Minister, P.V. Narasimha Rao, on a visit to Bhutan on August 21, 1993 expressed his confidence in the wisdom and ability of the leaders of Bhutan and Nepal to tackle and solve the difficult ethnic question. While he felt that the large-scale population movements over extended period of time were the most difficult and complicated problems to solve, he also found that "the quiet diplomacy between the two (countries) offered the best chances of resolving the refugee issue."

**Joint Agreement**

In this context, the Bhutanese are satisfied to sign a joint agreement with the Nepalese delegation led by the then Home Minister of Nepal to Thimphu on July 15,1993 to identify the Bhutanese nationals among the refugees. For that matter, both the countries identified and nominated three members each with a view to implementing the agreements. The Bhutanese felt that the refugees problem would be solved sooner provided the leaders of the Royal Government of Nepal were effective enough to contain the Marxists seating on the opposition benches in the Parliament. For the claimed terrorist attacks on the Bhutanese territory, the Bhutan Government tried coordinating its steps in consultation with the provincial Governments in Assam and West Bengal in India, which have long experience of anti-state violence unleashed by the AASU, ULFA, GNLF, BSF, etc.

**Categories of the Refugees**

The policy makers in India knew of this problem. It was there in Darjeeling where there was a sizeable Nepalese immigrant population. In the light of the above advice of the Indian Prime Minister, the outlook on the ethnic conflict appeared to be taking an affirmative turn. According to a press release issued on October 7, 1993 in Kathmandu, the Joint Committee set up by the Governments of Bhutan and Nepal agreed to identify the estimated 85,000 refugees into four categories: (i) bonafide Bhutanese, who were forced to emigrate, (ii) Bhutanese who emigrated at their own after disposing their properties, (iii) non-Bhutanese illegal migrant, and (iv) the Bhutanese subjects, who had committed criminal acts in Bhutan. The Committee proposed to meet in Thimphu in February 1994 to decide the mechanism for individual verification. And only then the two government proposed to specify their positions on each of the above categories of the refugees and evolve a mutually acceptable agreement, which might provide basis for a resolution of the ethnic problem.

The two Home Ministers, who were the elders of their respective delegations, expressed their determination to move forward with a sense of urgency to bring about a quick resolution to the present ethnic problem (*Kuensel,* Vol. VIII, No. 40). Since then half a dozen times, both the delegations have met in each other's land to sort out the ethnic conflict. One of the problems the Bhutanese faced was the changing policy-makers in Nepal, as a number of governments were formed in Kathmandu in mid-1990s. The Nepalese charge the Bhutanese of insincerity in their resolution and the Bhutanese feel that the Nepalese keep on changing their stand on the issue. The stalemate continues and the *Lhotshampas* suffer in the camps. The human misery and uncertain future of about a thousand-hundred human beings are left hanging between the distrustful delegations of the two countries.

## Declining of International Support

Meanwhile the international support to the cause of the refugees is declining in its vigour and volume. The immediate population in the neighbourhood of the refugee camps in the host country is turning hostile to the nuisance and intrusion of a huge idle population on their land. And the refugee leadership and the welfare administrators are suffering from fatigue of inaction. The recent ethnic conflicts have necessarily exposed the hollowness and limitation of the politics of consensus as a state policy in Bhutan. The *Drukpa* assessment that the King and the *Tshongdu* are good enough for their purpose and the voices, which do not fall in line with these two sacred institutions, are necessarily foreign-inspired, carry limited conviction in the comity of nations.

The argument that the 'southern Nepalese problem' is out and out an external conspiracy against the *Drukpa* state does not carry a universal conviction as well. It is a fact that the emergence of conventional democratic fora such as pressure groups, various sets of interest groups, political parties and institutions will have to wait for many years in the existing set-up in Bhutan. Till then the guided bureaucracy will continue to function as the conscious-keeper and trend-setter as well as the most orthodox forum of the legitimacy in Bhutanese public life. However, neither the *Tshongdu* nor the bureaucracy seems to provide the non-traditional alternatives. The primordial ethnic perceptions do not accept insubordination for all the time to come, and if the current ethnic stalemate is to be removed, Bhutan should evolve a policy of accommodating dissent. In this, *Drukpa* state will serve its own interests well, if it keeps its options open besides its policy of assimilation.

## Unsettling of the Ethnic Applecart

There was never any internal strife in Bhutan. They might fought battles with Tibetans or Sikkim, internagh Bhutan has always been peaceful. The last *Lamaist Buddhist* monarchy in the Himalayas, Bhutan was considered, less than a decade and half ago, as the ideal locale in which the Sri Lankan government and the country's rebel Tamils (LTTE) might negotiate a solution to their violent ethnic conflict. Within a couple of years, however, Bhutan itself had turned into another theatre of ethnic strife, this one pitting the dominant Buddhist communities in northern Bhutan against an immigrant Nepali Hindu community *(Lhotshampa)* in the southern third of the kingdom. The situation quickly became a stalemate: It continued to be the most significant political issue for the country in 1990s, although it was treated as a problem of law and order. If one reads the proceedings of Bhutan's *Tshongdu* (National Assembly) and speeches by its members, one really does not find a forward looking statement that rises above populism and xenophobia, nor has there been an honest effort to identify issues affecting the body politic.

## Democratic Aspirations

Democratic aspirations of the *Lhotshampas* have forced the *Drukpa* establishment to further withdraw to their ethnic particularism. However, it is handicapped in not providing a forum for dissenting voices. It goes without saying that structural reforms in the style of representation are badly needed. Visitors to Bhutan are told that political reforms are on the king's agenda but that he is unsure about the timing of their introduction and his subjects' response. Apart from the *Tshongdu,* most of the national fora are located in Thimphu, the capital. District Development Councils (DYT) continue to operate out of district headquarters, but under the benign gaze of the bureaucracy, and the village groups appear to suffer from development fatigue. But in what seems to be a step in the right direction, villages have been grouped into blocks *(geog)* for developmental purposes, and it is said that the most important development during 1990s was 'democratisation' at the block and village levels.

## Fiscal Health of Bhutan

It has reached the point, according to reports, that bureaucrats are now resigning their posts and contesting elections to the *Tshongdu.* Southern Bhutan, however, is totally paralyzed structurally, and development priorities have been adversely affected, if not shelved altogether. The government declared the 1993-94 financial year a success in terms of its statistical achievements. The total outlay for the year was Nu 4.2 billion (32 Nu = US $1), a 13 per cent increase over the projected figure. The government claimed it had collected internal revenue of Nu 1.59 billion against the current expenditure of Nu 1.606 billion, a deficit of just Nu 17 million. This means that the Royal Government had achieved its goal of self-reliance by meeting most of its current expenditures from internal revenue. Bhutan spends 30 per cent of its annual budget on social welfare programmes, mainly in rural areas.

## Education and Health Services

In Bhutan education and health services are free, while most other services are heavily subsidized by the state. Rural taxes amounted to just 0.3 per cent and income taxes on business only 3 per cent of total revenues. Bhutan had a hard currency reserve of more than US $100 million in 1993-94. Similarly, the annual report for the fiscal year, 1994-95 indicated that the total revenue of Nu 1,686 million was just short of 1.7 per cent for the hundred per cent expenditure for the year. Electricity (Nu 511 million), trade (Nu 346 million) and tourism (Nu 284 million) contributing two-third of the total revenue of the state were the most revenue-paying sectors in descending order. The top six *dzongkhangs* (districts) in order of revenue were Chukha, Thimphu, Samtase (Samchi), Samdruk Jongkhar, Paro and Sarpang (Sarbhang), which contributed 96 per cent of the revenue.

It is instructive to note that four of these districts were from the southern Bhutan besides Thimphu, the national capital, a predominantly Nepalese territory. Rest of the 14 districts in the northern and interior areas provided a mere 3 per cent to the exchequer, but they required a higher rate of investment and expenditure.

The Finance Minister announced in his 1998-99 budget report to the *Tshongdu* that Bhutan's foreign reserve had reached a record US $280 million, GDP had grown by six per cent and recurrent expenditure had been met from the domestic revenue for the sixth consecutive year. However, Bhutan's biggest revenue earner continues to be the Chukha Hydro Power Corporation (CHPC) followed by tourism and Bhutan telecom. So much so that in the light of above income, especially from the increased Chukha tariff that the King announced that the proposal of the personal income tax (PIT) was unnecessary. Tashi Commercial Corporation opened Thimphu's first supermarket in September 1999.

The Bhutanese are optimists to the bone have another way to look at the process of development: "For us in Bhutan, *Gross National Happiness* (GNH) is as important as the Gross National Product (GNP)" said Lyonpo Thinley Gyamtsho, the chairman of the Special Commission for Cultural Affairs and the Home Minister (and Chairman Council of Ministers—equivalent to the post of Finance Minister in 2000 A.D.), in Paris on 30th General Conference of the UNESCO. Drawing upon His Majesty, the King's brainchild, by the *GNH* he meant: "Development in Bhutan is characterised by a process that seeks to maintain a healthy balance between socio-economic progress, environmental sustainability and preservation of traditional, cultural and spiritual values".

**Riots and Acts of Terrorism**

However, the Finance Minister was candid in acknowledging that there were dark clouds hovering over the national economy. While project and programme implementation had been satisfactory, development activity—particularly in southern districts—had been hampered by frequent riots and acts of terrorism by *Lhotshampa* dissidents. Similarly, progress in trade and industry continued to be disrupted, as all major commercial and industrial centres are located in southern Bhutan. The government, thus, has had to engage a large number of security personnel to protect industries, service facilities, and forests, as well as people's lives. Till now no one knows for sure the exact population of Bhutan.

The controversial claim that Bhutan has about 600,000 bona fide subjects has helped the country achieve another miracle. The Human Development Reports issued by the United Nations Development Programme (UNDP) had listed Bhutan among the least developed of its 186 member countries. But by adjusting the claimed population figure, per capita income, literacy, and life expectancy, Bhutan's ranking went up from 162 to somewhere around 130. Bhutan, however, is one of the few countries in which statistics do tell lies. In reality, the social development undertaken is far more significant than the achievement rates indicate.

## Drukpa Reaction to the Lhotshampa's Flight to the Refugee Camps

By tradition, Bhutan is a Buddhist *Drukpa* monarchy; it is also a country in which predominantly Hindu Nepalese immigrants *(Lhotshampas)* have been living for nearly a century and half as subsistence farmers in the southern foothills. In other words, this *Lamaist* kingdom has a sizable immigrant population strategically located in a frontier zone over which the capital may not have complete control. The land-hungry Nepalese farmers have actively contributed to the economic development of Bhutan, turning the 'negative' southern area into a vibrant zone of prosperity. Many of them were educated and sent abroad on scholarships, and then returned to fill responsible government posts. They took advantage of the state policy of ethnic assimilation in which cash grants of Nu 5,000, further increased to Nu 10,000, were given by the government to encourage inter-ethnic marriages. This provision stands withdrawn now, which is a setback to the national policy of ethnic integration.

When Lhotshampas started goining ascendancy and slowly and steadily started occupying position of responsible, the Drukpa establishment saw a threat to the monarchy, the religion, and the laws of Bhutan *Driglam Namza*. It required the immigrants to accept the national traditions and be incorporated into the system. This resulted in an ethnic flare-up leading to the flight of thousands of *Lhotshampas* to refugee camps across the border of India, including many who left government positions. The argument goes on about their future return: What face will returnees show to those left behind in the camps and to those who did not leave Bhutan in the first place? Will the government rely on them again to fill responsible posts? Will the *Lhotshampas* in Bhutan, who have been subjected to *Ngolops*—anti-national—terrorist violence, accept them again?

How can those left the country willingly—even against the pleas of state functionaries and ever His Majesty, the King himself—even be termed as the refugees? In the face of worldwide uproar in favour of the refugees, the Bhutanese establishment, from the king to the last significant functionary, closed their ranks and made a concerted effort to counteract what they claimed was the Nepalese disinformation. Cabinet Ministers, High Court Judges, articulate members of the *Tshongdu,* senior bureaucrats, and above all, the king himself, worked aggressively to explain their point of view. They prepared reports and statistics and sent delegations to various fora, where the refugee issues were being debated. They invited scholars, journalists, jurists and concerned opinion leaders to Bhutan and welcomed representatives of the United Nations High Commissioner for Refugees (UNHCR) as well as dignitaries from the United States, India and other countries.

They engaged in various rounds of talks with the Nepalese government to try to resolve the deadlock. These efforts had paid off. The Bhutanese have successfully portrayed themselves as victims of a Nepalese *(Lhotshampa)* conspiracy, who has nothing to hide and whose only objective was self-preservation. The diplomatic offensive mounted by this small Bhutanese establishment has been so effective that the refugees have been left with no significant support voice in world fora. The Bhutanese policy-makers do not hide their rejection of some Western ideological and cultural concepts. At Bhutan's stage of national development, they feel that the Western concepts of representative democracy, competitive party system, consumer culture, and standards of human rights, as well as activities of Christian church-sponsored non-government organisations (NGOs) could pose serious threat to their traditions. They say that the economic growth required for the welfare of the population needs political stability and they fear religious plurality as going against the grain of age-old Bhutanese traditions in which life revolved around the institution of religion. Such ideological underpinnings have resulted in a kind of withdrawal syndrome.

During 1994 both the delegation held the third and fourth round of talks Bhutan had asserted it had almost been settled when the Nepali Congress Government in Nepal lost its parliamentary majority. The Bhutanese, who had developed a sense of confidence in their ability to handle the ethnic conflict in their own way, believe that the regular talks between the two countries had deflated the issue. Once the talks were underway, it became a game of numbers. The Bhutanese accept that some of the refugees will return to Bhutan, but many of them will remain in Nepal; some may opt for India, although India is not officially involved in the negotiation. The Bhutanese officials hasten to add, however, that those of them, who do return, are certain to face social, economic, cultural and even administrative problems. The Bhutanese worried about the role of the international NGOs especially associated with the Christian Church activities that have been active in the refugee camps, allegedly converting some of the refugees.

**Deserters**

The eighth round of talk between Foreign Ministers of Nepal and Bhutan were held on September 13-16 and November 1999 in Kathmandu in a satisfactory manner. From the Bhutanese point of view, the refugees in the Jhapa camps are deserters, who had not been subjected to any state-organised eviction. In support of this view, officials cite an account of the departure of *Lhotshampas* from Dorokha Block in Samchi (Samtse) District in April 1994 on the eve of the third round of Bhutan-Nepal negotiations. After 44 families (269 members) had filled their papers to leave Bhutan, officials advised them not to leave their country and reminded them they would lose their citizenship, if they emigrated. The king issued an edict *(kasho)* to the *dzongda,* his staff, instructing them to "meet with all the families, who have(d) applied to emigrate, and do your utmost to persuade them not to leave the country." Those, who withdraw their applications and returned to their villages, would be exempt from all rural taxes for three years. The king was every to keep them back. But they were adamant.

Just five families and two individuals listened to the above plea and decided to stay back in Bhutan and the rest left for the Jhapa camps in Nepal, and unlike in the past, most of them were Brahmins by caste. It is embarrassing for an observer to watch the 180 minutes long video cassettes on the unpleasant dialogue between a persuasive state establishment represented by the *dzongda* and the superintendent of police of Samtse and an impassive but determined heads of the households from Dorokha Block in April 1994. This raises the issue of the UNHCR's frequent letters about human rights violations to the Bhutanese representatives based in Geneva. It is noted here that Bhutan was elected to the High Commission in 1994 for the current term. What amazes the Bhutanese is the UNHCR's insistence on introducing international standards in prison facilities. For a country that is not in a position to provide basic necessities such as safe drinking water, health care and education to many of its rural subjects, and whose prison guards guarding the convicts and undertrials live in huts without plumbing.

It was hard to understand why it should spend more than four million rupees to provide amenities to deserters of the country, who were engaged in violence. The facilities included barracks with hot running water, medical care, waiting and sleeping rooms for visitors, newspapers and entertainment, what would be considered luxurious conditions by most of the Bhutanese. It is entirely another matter that Bhutan did not have jails in the past; a few serious criminals were simply put into a dungeon, and were left in an open village square shackled to a heavy log. Visitors are frequently reminded that the UNHCR provides what is regarded as lavish treatment in the refugee camps compared to the harsh realities of a mountain farmer's life.

**Plight of the Loyal Lhotshampas**

Sectarian and dissident violence has become the order of the day. It has continued against the loyal *Lhotshampas,* especially those with official status. In some of their villages, the loyal *Lhotshampas* cannot spend nights in their own homes. Up to mid-August, 1994, Sarpang District alone reported as many as 440 terrorist crimes—murder, kidnapping, rape, assault and damage to property—against *Lhotshampas.* One could see barren paddy fields, deserted villages and crumbling houses all over southern Bhutan, and the loyal *Lhotshampas* not only fear violence alleged to come from their former kinsmen and neighbours in the refugee camps, but they are also losing faith in the Bhutanese system as a whole. Although the king, the royal family, and a number of higher officials have been sympathetic to the *Lhotshampas* who stayed back in Bhutan, many *Drukpas* do not hide their pleasure at the plight of the Nepalese. From among the two southern districts of Samtse (Sanchi) and Sarpang (Sarbhang) with 45,000 and 50,000 estimated population respectively (and less than ten per cent Drukpas inhabitants), as much as 40,000 *Lhotshampas* emigrated to the refugee camps.

These *Lhotshampas* refugees were more from the newer villages than that of the larger and older settlements. However, there are villages such as Taklai in Sarpang district, which were totally deserted. All the villagers from this exclusively Nepalese village left for the camps or took shelter elsewhere, because the living conditions became difficult. It so happened that once they left their village in favour of a secured shelter even for a few days, their household properties (iron-sheets, tiles, doors, windows, wooden beams, shingles and frame and other building materials etc.) were removed by the various sets of people (thieves, bullies, businessmen and even more unscrupulous officials).

**Waiting for better days**

Many of them found the overall atmosphere so intimidating that they left their land unattended and ran to the camps with a cherished hope that they would come back to Bhutan on better days and on their terms and with self respect. Incidentally, this village was covered under one of the most developed small irrigation projects in the southern *Duars,* besides other infrastructure. One could see long stretch of arable fallow land—of late unattended for some cropping seasons—along the lush green well-cultivated paddy field and orchards in these southern districts. One of the issues in mid-1990s was in Bhutan, what to do with these deserted but developed agricultural fields. Naturally, the king was under a heavy pressure to allot them to his loyal *Lhotshampas* or to more than loyal *Drukpas.*

Another powerful lobby, encashing on the current international emphasis on environment canvassed that these agricultural fields, developed after generations of toil and sweat, should be permitted to turn into vibrant forests, which they were once upon a time. It is salutary to the King, who had seen to it that deserted agricultural lands were not unsurped by the more aggressive Bhutanese. However, this also led to speculation that even the *Drukpa* establishment at the highest level expected some of the *Ngolop* to come back to Bhutan. Moreover, these districts are located on such tropical sub-Himalayan topography where vegetation grows in abundance within no time, turning the agricultural fields into evergreen forests.

The resistance to settle the unattended dissidents' land could not continue for long. Of late, the *Tshongdu* has decided to settle them with shifting cultivators and landless marginal farmers from the interior of Bhutan. It is alleged that influential *Drukpas* have already taken over certain preferred land in a dubious way. Those of the *Lhotshampas,* who are left behind in the villages, are invariably from broken families living under a sense of panic, fear, uncertainty and continuous harassment. The officials are invariably cold to them; the fugitive relatives are hostile; and they cannot venture to their fields because of the lurking fear that they could be attacked by somebody from the nearby bush or forest. Rape, assault, arson, theft and all forms of violence are perpetrated on those, who have decided to stay behind in Bhutan.

**Spies**

Worst of all, many of them are considered spies by both the parties—the *Drukpa* establishment as well as the Nepalese in the camps. They rarely get the required support from any corner they desperately deserve. Their desperation may be assessed by the situation that they are not even hired by anybody as labourers. To the extent that the cheap and pliant Indian (alleged illegal Bangladeshi?) labour is being supplied on the construction sites by the contractor on fixed terms at the cost of the local Nepalese. On top of it all, the loyal relatives of the dissenters serving in the Bhutan Government have been removed from the jobs as a security risk. People are being attacked by terrorists from across the India-Bhutan border to create a situation in the south in which the loyal *Lhotshampas* flee away, leaving the economy totally paralyzed. For the Bhutanese, the ethnic conflict represents a problem of law and order, and left to themselves they would handle it in their own way. In the deserters' viewpoint, the real issue facing the kingdom are not illegal immigration, anti-national activity, or terrorism as claimed by the government, but rather the establishment of constitutional monarchy, political pluralism, democracy, and protection for human rights. And on these, the two sides do not see eye to eye.

A section of the Bhutanese feel that *Lhotshampas* had abused the royal trust reposed on them by going to the refugee camps. The Nepalese knew that it was a *Drukpa* country, with its own king, court, language, religion and laws. The immigrants must accept the national tradition and be a part of Bhutan, which they did to begin with. Once they do not accept the system and withdraw from it, they cease to have any claim for the Bhutanese indulgence. Unfortunately, for the Nepalese, there are a considerable number of the articulate senior bureaucrats, not necessarily from the *Drukpa* extraction, who hold such views. The *Drukpa* cultural door, which was kept ajar, is being closed for the Nepalese and an aggressive policy of Bhutanisation is being pursued. This may be seen in discontinuation of Nepali and Sanskrit teaching in the schools, stoppage of cash incentive to the inter-ethnic marriages and a move to change the Nepalese place names into Dzongkha: Samchi—Samtse, Sarbhang—Sarpang, Tashigong—Tashiyangtse, etc.

**Dissident's Plan of Action**

The refugees in the Camps strewn all over are trappeal The leaders of the refugees in camps show are slowing the signs of desperation and nothing is going well in their favour. International support base for their cause is shrinking. They appear to be far from happy with the patronage they received from their ethnic brethren, i.e., the Nepalese public and the Royal Government of Nepal. They are terribly upset with the continued cold public opinion in the world fora in their favour. They are equally puzzled and rather angry with the Indian media and democratic system for its total non-response of what the refugee leaders feel to be human rights violation in Bhutan. In such a situation, in spite of their proverbial factionalism and non-consensus among themselves, they have tried to do what is possible and logical to educate the world and the Indian public on their plight.

Thus, apart from participating in the various human rights and refugee related fora at the international levels, they held a series of public meetings in a number of important Indian cities such as Delhi, Calcutta, Patna, Siliguri, etc. During the negotiations with Nepal, the Bhutanese elite had a chance to appraise their counterparts and develop a working relationship; the fall of the G.P. Koirala Government and its defeat in the November 1994 elections confused the picture.

The Communist Party Government, as faction-ridden as the Nepali Congress, was equally inexperienced in inter-ethnic and international relations, and untested in dealing with inter-state affairs. The emergence of a new Nepalese administration meant difficult and protracted negotiations for the Bhutanese and new hope for the dissenting *Lhotshampas.* This point emerged after unstated failure of the round of talks between the representatives of two Royal Governments held in summer, 1995. It appears that the year 1995 saw a total stalemate on the issue of the Bhutanese refugees in the Nepalese camps. The Deuba Government in Kathmandu, a coalition of the desperate political parties, was perennially engaged in struggle for its survival and it hardly had time to spare to the cause of the refugees.

On the other hand, the refugees were divided into about a dozen of advocacy groups and political parties. And the Bhutanese continued to mount their known aggressive posture of defending their tradition of 'code of conduct' from the onslaught of the alien expansion. The Indian establishment remained apparently non-concerned on the assumed 'bilateral issue of the refugees' and, thus, dismissive of their role in the resolution of the ongoing conflict. This scenario gave birth to two complimentary moves. Firstly, the refugees in the camps started becoming restive and impatient with failure of the Nepalese establishment.

**Overtures to Indians**

They began cultivating a section of Indian Human Rights and Democratic Movement protagonists. They specifically turned their attention to their ethnic cousins in Sikkim, Darjeeling and *Duar* area of Jalpaiguri districts of West Bengal for a collaborative patronage. This is the strategic area through which they travelled from Bhutan to the camps and once more they presumed that the Indian Nepalese of the above districts would facilitate their reverse journey to the *Dragon Kingdom.* Secondly, both the Himalayan kingdoms, first the Nepalese in February, and then closely on the heels on March 4-7, 1996 the Bhutanese establishment, decided to court the Indian policy-makers in the first quarter of 1996. Both the visits were reported to be great success and the visitors expressed their satisfaction on the bonhomie between themselves. On their part, the observers could not miss the point that the visitors tried to court and solicit maximum support and commitment for their respective stands from an Indian regime, which was itself begging approval for its continuity from the Indian electorate.

However, one must add that so far the refugee tangle was concerned, nothing positive emerged publicly from the two state visits to New Delhi. In between, the political churning among the refugees led to the formation of the Bhutanese Coalition for Democratic Movement (BCDM)—a political forum—and the Appeal Movement Co-ordination Council (AMCC)—a human right action group—for the espousal of their cause. After holding rallies and press conferences in Kathmandu, Delhi, Calcutta, Siliguri and elsewhere, they decided to march from their camps in Nepal to Bhutan across Indian territory to petition to *Druk gyalpo* (the King) in their favour. The BCDM is an umbrella organisation demanding drastic democratic changes in the body politic of Bhutan. The AMCC appeals to the King for introduction of democratic rights and an early repatriation of the refugees, failing which they propose to file cases against the Royal Bhutan Government in the Bhutanese courts.

Apparently, while the former views the problems of the Bhutanese refugees originating from political crisis leading to arbitrary deprivation of subjecthood, the later regards the issue as basically that of violation of human rights. From January to March 1996 the refugees staged demonstration on borders of Nepal and India at Kakarvitta across river Mechi with their ethnic supporters from India and Nepal. The district administrations of Darjeeling and Jalpaiguri had declared their assembly and march to Bhutan across the Indian territory as illegal and imposed prohibitory orders on their movements. These steps forced the refugees to squat on the borders and court arrest.

By the end of the first quarter of 1996, as many as 537 persons inclusive of 62 women were arrested and sent to temporary jails. Cutting across the political affiliations, the Indian National Congress, CPM, and other political parties from the two districts expressed their solidarity with these stateless persons. The state Government of West Bengal was in trouble. It which bears the brunt of the refugees' march to Bhutan, approached New Delhi for more forces immediately and to find a way out to this political problem, as it is not an internal problem of the state. It is claimed that the *Druk gyalpos* Delhi visit underscored the current stalemate on the plight of the refugees in the camps and underlined the mutual interests of the two countries.

### Visit to New Delhi

For example, the Indian Home Minister's calling on the visiting Bhutanese sovereign to initiate an extradition treaty between the two countries assumed significance in the light of the Boro insurgents' sanctuary in eastern Bhutan and *Ngolops* continued attacks on the Bhutanese from the *Duars.* Signing of the agreement on Tawa hydro-electric project and Dungsum cement plant added to the strength of economic collaboration between the two countries. Oft-repeated plea of the Indian establishment that the refugee problem is a bilateral issue between the two kingdoms may be seen in the light of *Druk-gyalpo's* enthusiastic espousal of Indian candidature to the UNO's Security Council. It is difficult to miss the point that while the refugees had stepped up their agitation for repatriation to Bhutan, the Bhutanese decided to ignore it and concentrate on more pressing and lasting economic priorities. These in the international forum did not slow any interest in this new development.

### ULFA and BLTF: The Unwelcome Guests in Bhutan

An ominous development has taken place on eastern Bhutan which is a challenge to its stability as a state and its relations with the Indian Union. It so happened that flushed out of Bangladesh in 1996, the cadres of the United Liberation Front of Asom (ULFA), National Democratic Front of Boroland (NDFB) and Boroland Liberation Tiger Force (BLTF) have built their field headquarters in Bhutan at Gubanagand Sarsawen near the Assam border. They have established as many as 33 camps with 15 to 500 militants in each within a 600 km long arc from near Phuntsholing in the west to the Arunachal border beyond Samdruk Jongkhar in the east.

They move freely in Bhutan and buy provisions from the villagers on exorbitant rates. Apparently, thirty thousand strong Bhutan army is not in a position to evict them forcefully. It is rumoured that the Indian authorities do not like this new development. India would like Bhutan to allow the Indian army to flush the rebels out. But Bhutan is reluctant on the plea that they had a long-standing neighbourly relation with the Bodos and Assamese people, which might possibly be soured. The Indian armed forces are put on alert on the adjoining borders. Bhutan apprehends that their unwelcome guests on her land may even join hands with *Ngolops* (anti-nationals) in the refugee camps.

Thus, she opened a regional army training unit at Deothang in the eastern Bhutan; stepped up recruitment to the army and requested the Indian army to train the Royal Bhutan Army in appropriate skills of combat to engage these unwelcome guests. Both the governments have continuously been in touch with each other to coordinate their efforts in tackling the rebel menace.

**Council of Ministers**

The *Druk-gyalpo* issued an edict on June 30, 1998 on the eve of opening of 76th session of the *Tshongdu,* which stated: "To further enhance and strengthen our system of government, it is my wish and request to the members of the National Assembly to adopt a practice to register a vote of confidence in the Druk-gyalpo. A two-thirds vote of no-confidence by the Druk-gyalpo to abdicate in favour of the Crown Prince or the next in the line of succession to the Golden Throne." Further, the king commanded: "... The time has now come to further promote the people's participation in the decision-making process. Our country must always have a system of government which enjoys the mandate of the people, provides clean and efficient governance and has an in-built mechanism of checks and balances to safeguard our national interest and security. As an important step towards achieving this goal, the *Lhengyel Shungtshong* (the Cabinet) should now be restructured into an elected Council of Ministers that is rested with full executive powers to provide efficient and effective governance of our country." This was a very bold step the king had taken.

Under this system the Cabinet of Ministers would be elected through secret ballot by the National Assembly from amongst those who hold government posts of the rank of Secretary to the Government or above. A candidate must secure a majority of the vote cast to be considered elected. The King decides portfolios of the Ministers and the Cabinet Ministers would serve for a period of five years. All the decisions adopted by the Cabinet would be based on consensus. Though the Cabinet would have full executive powers for governance, it is also required to keep the King fully informed of all the matters concerning the security and sovereignty of the country. There is no post of the Prime Minister and the Chairman of the Council of Minister is the first among the equals.

**Joint Responsibility**

The edict is silent on the joint responsibility of the Council of Ministers. Many aspects of this far-reaching edict are yet to be worked out. A Council of Ministers was elected for five years by the 76th session of the *Tshongdu* in July 1998 and the King allotted them with the portfolios. The elected Ministers were: M/s Jigme Yozer Thinley (Foreign Minister and the Chairman of the Council of Ministers), Yeshe Zimba (Finance Minister), Khandu Wangchuk (Trade and Industry Minister), Thinley Gyamtsho (Home Minister), Sangay Ngedup (Education and Health Minister) and Kynzang Dorji (Agriculture Minister). Lyonpo Jigmey Thinley secured the highest vote cast, 136, and he was elected Chairman of the Cabinet for a year, and handed over the Chairmanship to Lyonpo Sangay Ngedup on August 16, 1999. All the Ministers are between 45 and 50 years of age and are educated in India. They have been known to be efficient and active in public affairs in the past.

This new structure (or the institution) will be carefully watched by all concerned for its initiative to solve the festering ethnic conflict and remove the Indian rebels from Bhutan. It appears that the King has carefully extricated himself from the state administration at this juncture. His moderating role as a sovereign appellate authority should provide him with much needed relief from the mundane involvement in the administrative chores to a bold initiative for a healing touch to the body politic of Bhutan. A report on 'Enhancing Good Governance' drawn up by a 25 member task force listed more than 90 specific recommendations for providing efficiency, transparency and accountability.

The report recommended creation of 10 Ministries by bifurcating Health and Education Ministry, splitting Communication Ministry into a Ministry of Communication and Information and Ministry of Construction, and Ministry of Trade and Industry into the Ministry of Trade and Industry and the Ministry of Energy and Water Resources. Based on recommendations of the Report, the Government undertook a number of administrative and institutional decisions. On later scruting, it was found they were in the right direction.

**Positive Changes**

The king was trying to bring in some positive changes. The 30th June 1998 edict of the King indicates an extremely significant development in the power structure of Bhutan. The *Druk-gyalpo* and the *Tshongdu* were known to be the joint sovereigns of Bhutan. With this new edict, the King has surrendered his sovereignty in favour of the *Tshongdu,* which is supposed to pass a vote on the continuity of the former's reign. It appears that the real power shifted from the King to the *Tshongdu* and the King has played a costly gamble. In reality, it is not so because of the two reasons. Firstly, the *Tshongdu* represents the most conservative elements of the country and the most articulate speakers among them are nominated to the Assembly by the King. There is no move to restructure its membership with a more open system of electoral process.

Secondly, there does not appear to be a move to permit political education of the masses by removing the disability to organise political associations. In the absence of an effective mass media and insufficient transportation to the various districts of the country, it is difficult to visualise an effective public opinion to influence the *Tshongdu* proceedings in a significant way. However, the King's edict is certainly a significant development impregnate with future possibilities. King's move to be the head of the State and Chairman of the Council of Ministers to be elected by the *Tshongdu* to head the administration may as well be seen conceding halfway the demands of constitutional monarchy and democratically elected government on the part of the dissidents.

In Shawian* tradition of conflict between the monarch and popularly elected ministers, the monarch wins handsomely every time, when personal ability and good sense are all equally divided, thus, upsetting the populist applecart. The wise king defeats the pompous, vain and arrogant populists. In case of the Bhutanese continuing ethnic conflict, who will upset whose applecart, i.e. the Bhutanese royalists or the populist *Lhotshampas?* Or in H.H. Risley's figurative clash between the *Drukpa's* prayer wheel and the *Lhotshampas' Khukheri,* the edge of whose weapon is sharper, will be tested only by the time. The answer to the above is anybody's guess. Moreover, in this process of one-upmanship, the ethnic stalemate is bound to continue for some more time.

# 17

# Gender Disparity in Level of Literacy: A Case of Uttaranchal

**Abstract**

Human resource development through education and skill upgradation is an important component of development strategy for any region in today's liberalized and competitive environment. Though education by itself does not generate socio-economic progress, a lack of it can certainly be an impediment in the development process. In the process of human resource development, literacy helps by better absorption of new information, by adopting improved production process and through all this promoting overall growth. In fact the role of education in human resource development makes it a crucial instrument of economic uplift and social welfare. Increased health care, hygiene and reduced fertility and birth rates add another dimension to human resource development through literacy. In this regard, the female literacy is even more important.

The problem of male out-migration, particularly from hilly parts is responsible for enormous social and economic responsibilities of women. As the women form the backbone of the economy and society of the region, the female literacy is an essential prerequisite for the over all development of the new state of Uttaranchal. Therefore literacy must occupy top priority as harsh geographical conditions limited employment opportunities and lack of infrastructure facilities have resulted in slow economic growth.

Uttaranchal is one of the better literate States of India and has shown continuous rise in literacy since 1951. In 2001, total population literacy rate has been recorded as 72.28 per cent which is more than 7 per cent than all India average. The female literacy rate is also high at 60 per cent. But the state still has a wide range of sex disparity in the level of literacy as is evident from the male and female literacy rate recorded as 84.01 and 60.26 per cent respectively. This disparity becomes more pronounced when we look at the district level data. While the gender-gap in literacy is 1.4 per cent in case of Dehradun it is 37.5 per cent in case of Uttarkashi. Six out of ten completely hill districts have recorded 30 per cent less female literacy rate as compared to male literacy. Apart from physical constrains of terrain, social and economic responsibilities of females from an early age, access to education institutions, economic condition of the family, work pattern of women in the society have been largely responsible for low female literacy.

The present paper is an attempt to analyse the status and spatial pattern of female literacy in Uttaranchal.

**Introduction**

According to National Literacy Mission (India), literacy is acquiring the skill of Reading, Writing, and aRithmetic (three R's) and ability to apply them to one's day to day life. UNESCO has defined literacy as essential knowledge and skills which enable a person to effectively function in a group and community and whose attainment in reading, writing and arithmetic make it possible for him or her to use these skills towards his or her own and community's development (www.youhelpindia.org).

Literacy is defined differently in different countries. In India some times a person is considered literate if he/she can put his/her signature on paper. In Finland a man can be called literate even if he has not studied in a school but can pass a test of literacy. Some countries exclude population below ten years of age from their literacy enumeration (Tikkha, 1993). According to Census of India (1981) "a literate person is defined as the one who can both read and write with understanding in any language". This understanding is not ordinarily achieved until one had some schooling or at least some time to develop these skills. It was, therefore, decided at 1991 census that all children in the age group 0-6 will be treated as illiterate by definition and population aged seven years and above only is to be classified as literate or illiterate. The same criterion has been retained at Census of India, 2001, (Census of India, 2001).

**What is Literacy**

Literacy is not simply the art of reading and writing. It is one of the important bases of every society. Literacy has helped the society world over to develop their productive forces and technological skills. Spread and diffusion of literacy is generally associated with essential traits of today's civilization such as modernization, urbanization, industrialization, communication and commerce. Higher level of education and literacy lead to a greater awareness and also contributes in improvement in economic conditions (Census of India, 2001). In fact, the role of education in human resource development makes it a crucial instrument of economic upliftment and social welfare. It is so because at given technological level, literacy helps in increasing productivity through better and intelligent organization and management of inputs, finance and marketing. No wonder, the trends in literacy are considered as an index of the pace at which socio-economic transformation of a society is taking place (Chandna, 2002). The stage of economic development and literacy pattern of a region are closely linked

(Kharkwal, 1993). A crucial dimension of literacy is the importance given to female literacy. It is common saying that if a male becomes literate, a single person becomes literate but if a female becomes literate the whole family becomes literate. Female literacy is considered to be a more sensitive index of social development compared to overall literacy rates. Female fertility is negatively related with fertility rates, population growth rates, infant and child mortality rates, and shows a positive association with female age at marriage, life expectancy, participation in modern sectors of economy and above all female enrolment (Nayar, 2002).

**Literacy in Uttaranchal**

In case of Uttaranchal literacy has a significant role to play because adverse physical conditions of the region. The region has limited scope for agricultural development because of rugged steep-slope topography, limited use of Green Revolution technology and traditional agronomic practices. Horticulture, a much-talked about sector for economic development needs large investment in infrastructure development, transport, processing and marketing. The region is also not suitable for setting up big industrial plants due to limitations of rugged topography, raw material, transport and lack of infrastructure facilities. Thus. literacy is the need of present economy of Uttaranchal for its overall development and better future of its population.

The lack of traditional avenues of employment and increased aspirations of people of this newly formed state can provide hope for new generation of Uttaranchal through education. The talks of skill-based employment and use of new technologies in different sectors make literacy the most essential requirement of Uttaranchal society. Joshi (1999) is of the opinion that Uttarakhand could perhaps do better by looking at education as the spearhead of development.

**Limitations of Agricultural Development**

Given the limitations of agricultural and industrial development, education, especially at tertiary level, could perhaps prove to be a major growth engine in Uttaranchal in future. Here again female literacy has its own importance because of high sex ratio and high female participation rate in local economy. Normally high out-migration of males from the region leaves female to manage not only their home and hearth but they have to interact with local officials for different administrative purposes. Plethora of development programmes in the region has to be carried through with women involvement. It is therefore imperative that female literacy is given utmost importance.

Uttaranchal is one of the better literate States of India and has shown continuous rise in literacy rate since 1951 (Table 17.1). In 2001, literacy rate increased three times (72.28 per cent) than that of 1951 (18.93 per cent). This overall literacy rate of the state is higher as compared to 65.38 per cent for the country. It is note7worthy that while male literacy rate has increased by a little over two and half times, the increase in female literacy is almost fifteen times since independence.

**Table 17.1**

**Sex Disparity in Literacy Rate of Uttaranchal since 1951 (in percentages)**

| *Year* | *Total literacy rate* | *Male literacy rate* | *Female literacy rate* | *Gender gap in literacy* |
|---|---|---|---|---|
| 1951 | 18.93 | 32.15 | 4.78 | 27.37 |
| 1961 | 18.05 | 28.17 | 7.33 | 20.84 |
| 1971 | 33.26 | 46.95 | 18.61 | 28.34 |
| 1981 | 46.06 | 62.35 | 25.00 | 37.35 |
| 1991 | 57.75 | 72.79 | 41.63 | 31.16 |
| 2001 | 72.28 | 84.01 | 60.26 | 23.75 |

*Source:* Census of India 2001, U.P. and Uttaranchal, Sahitya Bhawan Publications, Agra.

While the state has out performed the national average in overall literacy rates, a large variation exists within state. It can be observed that out of the total 13 districts, five districts namely Nainital, Dehradun, Pauri Garhwal, Pithoragarh and Chamoli have recorded more than 75 per cent of population as literate (Table 17.2). On the other hand Haridwar and Udhamsingh Nagar have only 65 per cent of their population in this category.

**Table 17.2**

**Spatial Pattern of Literacy in Uttaranchal 2001 (in percentages)**

| *State/District* | *Total literacy rate* | *Male literacy rate* | *Female literacy rate* | *Gender gap* |
|---|---|---|---|---|
| Uttarkashi | 66.58 | 84.52 | 47.48 | 37.04 |
| Chamoli | 76.23 | 89.89 | 63.00 | 26.89 |
| Rudraprayag | 74.23 | 90.73 | 59.98 | 31.15 |
| Tehri Garhwal | 67.04 | 85.62 | 49.76 | 35.86 |
| Dehradun | 78.96 | 85.87 | 71.22 | 14.65 |
| Pauri Garhwal | 77.99 | 91.47 | 68.14 | 25.33 |
| Pithoragarh | 76.48 | 90.57 | 63.14 | 27.43 |
| Champawat | 71.11 | 88.13 | 54.75 | 33.38 |
| Almora | 74.53 | 90.15 | 61.43 | 28.72 |
| Bageshwar | 71.94 | 88.56 | 57.45 | 31.11 |
| Nainital | 79.60 | 87.39 | 70.98 | 16.41 |
| Udhamsingh Nagar | 65.76 | 76.20 | 54.16 | 22.04 |
| Haridwar | 64.60 | 75.08 | 52.60 | 22.45 |
| Uttaranchal | 72.28 | 84.01 | 60.26 | 23.75 |
| India | 65.38 | 75.85 | 54.16 | 21.69 |

*Source:* Census of India (2001).

**Spatial Pattern of Female Literacy**

The overall female literacy rate in Uttaranchal is high at 60.26 per cent but this high share of female literate is not evenly distributed. Dehradun district has recorded highest female literacy (71.22) as against lowest female literacy in Uttarkashi district (47.48 per cent). Thus while in case of total literacy, the inter-district gap is 15 percentage point, it is nearly 24 per cent in case of female literacy. This shows great disparity in spatial pattern of female literacy.

On the basis of female literacy rate, Uttaranchal can be classified into following categories: -

(i) ***High female literacy districts (above 65 per cent)***
Three districts of the state including the two most developed districts have recorded more than 65 per cent of females as literate. These districts are Dehradun (71.22 per cent), Nainital (70.98 per cent) and Pauri Garhwal (68.14 per cent).

(ii) ***Medium female literacy districts (55-65 per cent)***
Completely mountainous districts of Chamoli and Rudraprayag from Garhwal region and Almora, Pithoragarh and Bageshwar from Kumaon region come under the category of medium level of female literacy.

(iii) ***Low female literacy districts (below 55 per cent)***
This category has the mixed of hilly and plain area of the state. Champawat, Uttarkashi, Tehri, Udhamsingh Nagar and Haridwar districts have recorded close to half of their female population as illiterate.

**Gender Disparity in Level of Literacy**

The above scenario obviously brings forth the worrisome feature of literacy in Uttaranchal – the large gender gap of 23.75 percentage point. No doubt the female literacy has taken a large leap since 1951 when it was only 4.78 per cent but still a wide gulf can be noted in male-female literacy rates. This becomes more acute when we look at the district level data. While the gender-gap in literacy is 37.5 per cent in case of Uttarkashi, it is 14 per cent in Dehradun.

On the basis of intra-state gender-gap data, the districts can be classified in three categories. These are:

(i) ***Large Gender Gap districts (more than 30 per cent)***
The districts of Uttarkashi, Tehri Garhwal, Rudraprayag, Champawat and Bageshwar are included in this category. Incidentally the last three are newly formed districts and all the districts have very small urban population.

(ii) ***Medium Gender Gap districts (20-30 per cent)***
In this category are included the districts of Chamoli, Pauri, Pithoragarh, Almora, Udhamsingh Nagar and Haridwar. While the last two are

heavily populated districts in the plain area of the state, in the former four except Pauri all are border districts spread over high mountainous tract.

(iii) ***Low Gender Gap districts (less than 20 per cent)***

The two districts of the state, namely Dehradun and Nainital have the lowest sex-disparity in literacy. These are economically developed and have well-developed infrastructure.

**Rural-Urban Disparity in Literacy**

Another important feature brought out by 2001 Census is the Rural-Urban disparity in case of literacy. While on the whole urban population has 12.56 per cent higher literacy rate as compared to rural population but in case of females this difference is more pronounced. The data shows that gender gap in literacy of urban population is 12.43 per cent where as it is more than 27 per cent in case of rural population.

**Table 17.3**

**Spatial Pattern of Gender Gap in Literacy in Uttaranchal 2001 (in per cent)**

| *District* | *Gender Gap (M-F) in overall literacy* | *Gender Gap in Rural areas* | *Gender Gap in Urban areas* | *Gap with in Female Literacy Rate by residence (Urban-Rural)* |
|---|---|---|---|---|
| Uttarkashi | 37.04 | 38.45 | 15.45 | 33.38 |
| Chamoli | 26.89 | 28.55 | 11.99 | 21.45 |
| Rudraprayag | 31.15 | 31.05 | 1.63 | 20.67 |
| Tehri Garhwal | 35.86 | 37.50 | 10.86 | 32.58 |
| Dehradun | 14.65 | 18.85 | 10.77 | 18.03 |
| Pauri Garhwal | 25.33 | 27.24 | 9.72 | 18.93 |
| Pithoragarh | 27.43 | 29.42 | 11.00 | 23.94 |
| Champawat | 33.38 | 36.38 | 14.52 | 20.75 |
| Almora | 28.72 | 30.16 | 6.79 | 29.37 |
| Bageshwar | 31.11 | 31.7 | 8.81 | 25.20 |
| Nainital | 16.41 | 20.03 | 9.84 | 9.55 |
| Udhamsingh Nagar | 22.04 | 24.42 | 16.97 | 12.38 |
| Haridwar | 22.45 | 26.41 | 13.63 | 26.36 |
| **Uttaranchal** | **23.75** | **27.22** | **12.43** | **19.25** |

*Source:* Census of India (2001).

**Spatial Pattern of Gender Gap: Some Tentative Conclusions**

- The gender gap tends to reduce in urban areas where this is 12.43 per cent, against more than 27 per cent in case of rural areas. Districts with low urban population such as Uttarkashi, Tehri,

Rudraprayag and Bageshwar with less than 10 per cent urbanized population have high gender gap.

- High gender-gap has been noted in the districts with high sex ratio as the districts of Rudraprayag, Tehri-Garhwal, Champawat and Bageshwar have sex ratio of above 1000 and gender gap of more than 30 per cent.
- The plain districts of Haridwar and Udhamsingh Nagar have performed poorly in case of overall literacy as well as female literacy but have lower gender-gap as compared to many hill districts.
- Districts with high literacy rates also have high female literacy and low gender gap (e.g., Dehradun, Nainital).

## Conclusions

The main reasons of gender disparity in literacy in Uttaranchal have been found to be the—lack of proper schooling facilities for girls, lack of female teachers, lack of urbanization, domestic workload and lack of importance to female literacy. The continuing gap between male-female literacy though represents an all India scenario but given the overall high rate of literacy it should be easier to fill this gap. Suggestions have been made to reduce gender-gap in literacy by focusing attention on female retention and achievement, by increasing the number of female teachers, by creating a more creative and gender-positive curricula and by dedicating specific attention to girls in the class-room (McDougall, 2000).

Education must be meaningful and relevant. It must reflect the overall needs of the society and fulfill the diverse needs of the local communities. Thus, education can become potent instrument for bringing in positive social, economic and political changes in Uttarakhand region. Therefore, multi-dimensional and dynamic educational programme is the need of the time to ensure quicker growth rates in all directions for better livelihood opportunities and allowing people to participate effectively in the process of development of the region (Mishra, 2001).

In order to reduce this disparity, priority in educational planning must be given to all girls having access to primary school with in habitation, separate girls high schools with residential facilities for students and teachers for a cluster of villages, only female teachers in girls' school, awareness programmes about positive impacts of female literacy, reservation of adequate seats for females in services such as teaching, medicine, local administration and developmental schemes etc.

## Strategy to Generate Employment in Uttaranchal Himalaya

Economic development and transformation of economy is not possible in isolation. It requires integrated efforts which brings break-throughs in the continuous process of development. It is not one day job but requires proper inputs and efficient functioning in every aspect of life building and income generation. Functioning in right direction depends on the active and creative governance of the strategies laid down for perspective and sustained growth in all directions, vertical and horizontal to take off.

Problem in the hill district are enormous. The government has not able to generate enough resouces. "Capital is necessary but not sufficient condition" (R. Nurkse). In the present state of polity and governance, one cannot expect the desired results with the limited resources when there is large scale of mismanagement in all stages of development/ administration. Performance and benefits having strong linkages with morally degraded ranks and files in the society which is responsible due to ignorant attitude, selfishness and longing for personal benefits and prosperity at the cost of others. Looking at the scenario of natural, financial and human resources, it is evident from the past that the strategies have been to create backwash effects rather than going for positive and creative spread effects. Economic transformation need proper strategy to utilise local natural, financial and human resources and to build up economy with the help of efficient managers having proficiency of constructive attitudes.

## Methodology

Secondary data/published/unpublished and relative literature have been taken into consideration and analysed on the basis of theoretical practices generally adopted in quantitative and qualitative terms. Personal field experience have been applied in formating the suitable strategy for manpower planning to eradicate the unemployment and poverty. Numerous ugly marks grimed the employment generation in the Uttaranchal. Those were political ill-will, topographical situation and environmental conditions. As a result, a large army of unemployed young workforce grew up. In this study, problem of unemployment is taken up to analyse its various types, basic nature, magnitude, causes and government policy and lastly, remedial measures have been stressed by suitable strategy keeping in view the local resources and environment.

## Types of Unemployment

Unemployment is taking serious turn in polluting the socio-cultural and economic structure. Therefore, the type of unemployment which is belenguring the State must be identified before finding out the ways and means for its eradication from the soil of Uttaranchal. Identified unemployment types have been discussed herein after: Kedarnath-Chandrabadni water divide is the primary development divide of Uttaranchal which divides the state into eastern and western blocks representing the moderately developing and retarded development areas. Contrast in the level of literacy is wide enough. Shadows of monarchic regimes are so deep that the area demand special development strategy for the erstwhile Tehri State. In the foot-hill zone 300 m contour is the secondary development divide of Uttaranchal. Plain and Terai belt, although economically self relient, progressing well in the area of industrialization and diversification yet poor in HRD. Agricultural economy of these areas appear to be a negative factor in social development as evidenced by general lower level of literacy.

The distribution of the literacy of rural population is strongly influenced by urbanization. In Nainital tahsil rural and urban literacy are 74.7 and 78.2 per cent respectively. Similarly rural literacy in Dehradun is 73.2. In Srinagar it is 71.0 and 86.7 per cent respectively. Only Almora is exception to this trend as it carries 55.8 and 90.1 per cent literacy in rural and urban areas respectively. In Pithoragarh, literacy is 68.4 and 86.4 per cent in respective areas. Areas infected by heavy out-migration also show moderately high literacy levels. Out-migration has been helpful in improving standard of living in such harsh terrain conditions. Joshimath (60.5), Munsiary (60.4), Pokhri (65.4), Tharali (60.5), Ukhimath (61.7), Dhoomakot (60.1), Gangolihat (64.1), Didihat (64.1) tahsils maintain higher literacy levels to this effect.

**Conclusion**

The present trend of population is suggestive of ongoing process of population redistribution. Population share of upper Uttaranchal is likely to fall in the each coming census, both the result of intra and inter-regional mobility of population. This pattern demand that state government should undertake serious steps to transform cereal dominant subsistence agriculture into viable market economy of the economically dormant hill villages. Migration is the most discussed theme of Uttaranchal and it is reflected in demographic and social fabric of the region. There is need to undertake long range strategy of employment generation in the hill village to retain 50 per cent of work force in 25-49 age groups. Western Uttaranchal requires formulation of special area programme to bridge the gap in literacy levels from eastern Uttaranchal.

**Conceptual Framework for the Holistic Development of Rural Womenfolks of Pravat Area of Upper Tons Basin, Uttaranchal**

The year 1997 marked the twenty-fifth anniversary of the UN Conference on the Human Environment held at Stockholm in 1972, as well as the fifth anniversary of UN conference on Environment and Development held at Rio de Janerio in 1992. A report prepared by the United Nations for consideration at the special session of the UN General Assembly convened in New York in 1997 to review the progress made since 1992 in giving operational contents to the concept of sustainable development warns that "the state of global environment has continued to deteriorate. Reversing the trend is more urgent than over". Also according to UNDP's 1997 Human Development Report the Human Development Index declined during 1996 in thirty countries more than any year since the First Report was issued in 1990. The world is, thus, still in search of methods giving practical shape to the concept of sustainable and equitable development. To achieve this, several forms of tensions, such as the following, need to be resolved:

- Between short-term opportunity and long-term stability.
- Between jobless economic growth and the livelihood security of the poor.
- Between resource extraction and ecological sustainability.

Only such kind of development, which can help to resolve the abovesaid tensions, will be sustainable in long run. Several Non-governmental Organisations around the world are successfully opposing unsustainable development. What, however, is equally important is proposing sustainable development options. This is particularly true of population rich but land-hungry countries like India, where millions suffer from extreme poverty and deprivation. For such a country, land degradation is a priority area for people-oriented sustainable development efforts, since rural societies by and large are dependent upon land-based economic activities. This applies to Uttaranchal as well.

**Peculiar Environment**

Focusing our attention on Uttaranchal Himalaya, one finds easily that hill development can no longer be regarded as a mere extension of the development methods employed in the plains. Since this region has its own peculiar environment, social and economic problems, it calls for environment oriented planning as a basic concept. Apart from the acute problem of deforestation, soil erosion, opportunities for limited agriculture and a money-order economy, the landman relationship in the hills is significantly different from that of the plains. The density of population is higher than that of the plains with poorer soil. However, the hills and the plains are not separate physical compartments of nature. There exist two ways flows of resources and people, which need to be balanced.

At present, apart from the inadequate resources of ill-considered governmental development plans, the only upward flow to the Hills is that of cash remittances sent by hill men employed in the plains. Far outweighing these two, is the catastrophic downward flow of soil nutrients, most of the water and hydrological resources, timber, minerals and, most of all, 'brain-drain'. To rectify this disastrous imbalance, environment oriented planning needs to generate a large flow of resources upwards into hill regions. Both nature and social justice demand this reorientation of the planning policy.

The Human factors of development in the hill call for special attention in the light of three important considerations at least:

(a) The youth of the hills have traditionally seen their future in the plains, and the hill, men who have sought employment in the plains are virtually ecological refugees.

(b) The health of the people in the hills has received meagre attention and has worsened with ecological degradation.

(c) Extension work in the hills has ignored the basic fact that women in the hills are responsible for 85 per cent of the farm operations.

**Study Area**

The study area is located in the upper catchments of Tons River within the *Govind Pashu Vihar Sanctuary,* and the National Park that was established on March 1, 1995 and its name coined after Pandit Govind Ballabh Pant, the first Chief Minister of Uttar Pradesh. It is situated between 31°18' - 33°51' North latitude and 77°49' - 78°55' East longitude, having an area of 957.97 sq kms which starts from the confluence of the Rupin and Supin Rivers at Naitwar and includes the entire drainage basin of these said rivers. Rupin and Supin rivers meet to form the Tons River, which is the most important tributary of river Yamuna in its upper reaches.

Thus, the area has a significant value as a major watershed for river Yamuna, which is a very important river of the Indo-Gangetic Plains. Administratively, this area comes under Mori Block of Purola Tehsil in District Uttarkashi. Within the Sanctuary area there are situated 48 villages ranging from an altitude of 1450 m (Naitwar) to 2600 m (Osla). Like other parts of the mountain region in the Indian Himalayan Zone as well as outside the country, the life of the local populace within the study area is hard, and every moment of life there is a constant struggle with their surroundings, yet the tremendous difficulties of the locality have not been able to suppress the initiative and adventurous spirits of the inhabitants. They have evoked a degree of adaptive skill and uncommon vigor, which is responsible for their economic condition.

**Parvatis**

In general, the people living in the Sanctuary area are known as 'Parvati', who follow their own culture and community life, and till recently were almost untouched by their so-called neighbours. These people have a short stature, fair complexion, and are strong as well as hard working. In this area the joint family system is in practice, probably, largely due to the age old practice of polygamy and polyandry prevalent in this area. The language spoken by the Parvati people is of an Aryan Group called Western Pahari. The dress of the people in the area is *Suttan* (Trouser), *Kurta* (Choli), *Farji* (Shirt and Blouse), *Pagar* (Pagri or turban), *Gatra*

(Kamarbandh), *Thapka* (Kardhani), *Khilka* (Longot), *Sitdak* (Waist-coat), *Paanchedi* (cloth which is worn outside the choli), *Ghagra* and *Dhoti*. These dresses bear more similarity with those of Himanchal rather than those whith of the Garhwal region. The popular system of marriage in the area is Rakshash and Paichash (known as *takka* marriage locally), which indicate a marriage on payment of bride price. In this system a bridegroom is expected to pay some amount of money to the brides family. Polyandry, polygamy and widow re-marriage systems are also practiced there.

Regarding the condition of women in the area, they are treated as man's property (socially in favour of her father). She is permitted to marry more than one person and also gets a higher status and value (price in cash) in the society with each re-marriage. Polyandry-Polygamy in the study area produces a picture in which the practice of re-marriage and divorce is common. Divorce is known as "chhoot", and one who is divorced would be called "Pundi" in local terminology. On remarriage, a wife's new husband shall have to pay the former husbands the demanded money in the form of compensation for "this act", which ranges from Rs. 20,000-80,000. However, the amount for the purpose varies in accordance with the nature of divorce, remarriage and other governing condition. There are various factors responsible for divorce. No final prescribed rules or regulations have been specified for this issue. Divorce takes place in the case an infertile woman automatically. She is in greater demand and, hence, the new husband has to pay high-bride price to the former one.

Besides this, a woman on her own initiative can abstain living with her husband if he is not providing her the expected facilities, the ornaments or other desired articles. Divorce is not necessarily required to be sought through the panchayats etc. Divorce has a procedure. During the period when the girt is at her *Malta,* the husband sends a message that she is no more needed back now. Otherwise, to make it effective or to get it implemented by her, she is subjected to harsh, ill treatment, and since then she is compelled to have a determination of remaining at her parent's village until she is further settled to another husband. For this, her father or nearest relatives reach her husband's house and settle the amount to be paid as compensation to them.

It is also seen that if a third party agrees to marry her, he has to pay all that her father demands. However, this practice of payment may result in some clever husbands possession of many young wives who may then divorce them (one by one) for the sake of monetary gains. But this is not the common practice. Many a time, he divorces them as he faces an artificial as well as biological disparity and enjoys the cause of remarriage. Women residing with her parents after having been divorced later on find the way to remarriage. Men, not women, enjoy most of the rights, hereditary or non-hereditary. The village Khumri deals with the division of family property in which father, eldest brother or both the youngest and eldest brothers choose their share. Leave the case of *Dhyantis* (married girl at Maita) use the enjoyment otherwise a woman is not entitled to any such share. A mother may simply choose to stay and thus live with any of her own son. Though the wife is the first to get up early in the morning, and the last to go to bed, yet she is denied all the rights of owing property.

Not only this, she has to leave all her ornaments with her ex-husband(s) in the case of divorce. This shows the low status of women in society. However, women are more active than men folk, and do most of the household drudgery, besides working hard in the fields and collect fodder and fuel.

**Made of Agriculture**

During the study, it has been observed that the terraced agricultural fields are situated adjoining the villages, however, some distant landholding is also located either in the Reserve Forest or may be bounded on three sides with forest. Such terraces are made across steep mountain slopes, generally have an outward slope (8-20°) and are poorly managed. Another type of land holding is usually subjected to rotational *jhum* cycles, locally known as the *Kuriala* system. Except the valley around the Naitwar and Sankri, the entire remaining land is cropped only once during a year, since such areas remain under snow cover for about four winter months. In such areas only Rabi crop is grown, whereas below 1700 m the climate supports, both, Rabi and Kharif crops. Amaranthus, Potato, Dolichos, Eleusine, Fagopyrum, Wheat and Paddy constitute the principal diet of the inhabitants.

As stated earlier, that agricultural produce hardly suffices for about three or four months. People procure wheat and paddy by selling their goats, sheep and woollen garments. Some of the non-conventional food items like flour made of *Aesculus indica* seeds (horse chestnut) and preparation of *Typhonium diversifolium* are also used in dire circumstances. The higher caste people own 0.48-3.61 hectare agricultural land on an average, whereas the lower caste families occupy less than 0.76 hect of landholdings within this region, the per hectare crop production is quite low, as depicted the Table 17.4. In spite of sufficient bio-fertilizers and more than adequate Human Muscle Power (HMP), the crop production is very low in the study area, which could be attributed to the vagaries of climatic condition, use of less decomposed bio-fertilizers and slopy agriculture land in which the top fertile layer is eroded easily. Therefore, the prevalent occupation of several families amongst the socially middle and higher caste is livestock rearing.

**The Professions of Hill People**

The existing forest areas and alpine *bugyals* (meadows) are tended to by the aboriginals of this area who have large livestock holdings, especially of sheep and goats, because cattle rearing is the means of economic subsistances. The domesticated animals of the area are cows, oxen, goats, sheep, buffaloes, horses, etc. Goats and Sheep are the commercial domestic animals of the area, as is the case with the Bhotiya tribes. With a sizeable number of goats and sheep one can measure the prosperity of a family in the area. It is primarily because the people get wool from the animals, and after spinning and knitting it they prepare fine woollen clothes. In addition to these means, illegal herbal collection, daily wages labour in P.W.D. and Forest Department, schemes as well as work as porters with trekkers are also other source of the economy of the area.

**Table 17.4**

**Crop Production (Q/ha)**

| *Crop* | *Naitwar (1450 m)* | *Osla (2550 m)* |
|---|---|---|
| *Amaranthus viridis*; ver. Jangli-Chaulai | - | 12.28 |
| *Brassica compestris*; ver. Sarson | 0.98 | - |
| *Dolichos uniflorus*; ver. Gaheth, Kulath | 1.11 | - |
| *Echinochloa colona*; ver. Jangli Jhangora | 2.01 | - |
| *Eleusine coracana*; ver Koda | - | - |
| *Fagopyrum tataricum*, ver. Phaphar | - | 21.65 |
| *Glycine max*; ver. Bhatt | 0.94 | - |
| *Lablab purpureus*, ver. Sem | - | - |
| *Oryza sativa*; ver. Dhan, Saatti | 6.0 | - |
| *Panicum miliaceum*; ver. China | 3.94 | - |
| *Sesamum indicum*; ver. Til | 0.97 | - |
| *Solanum tuberosum*; ver. Aalu | - | 20.25 |
| *Tritucum vulgare*; ver. Gehun, Gieun | 7.21 | 15.02 |
| *Vigna aconitifolia*; ver. Matki, Moth | 1.82 | |
| *V. mungo*; ver. Urd. | 2.03 | |

In totality, the 'Poorest of the Poor' are the women folk of the society of the study area, due to various social evils prevalent there like polyandry, polygamy, *takka* system of marriage, workload beyond their carrying capacity, and poor health facilities. Their domain is confined to the domestic affairs and they are denied any say in communal and social affairs. Unfortunately her condition is pitiable, both, at her parents and husband's home. At her parents home she suffers from illiteracy, because they think that if they send their girls to the school, they will lose the fetcher of water, wood and the caretaker of small children, particularly when the mother is working in the field or forests or does some odd jobs.

In her husbands house she is treated like man's property, as he has paid bride price for the marriage. Every dawn brings with it a long march in search of fodder, fuel and water. It does not matter whether women are old or young or pregnant, crucial needs have to be met. As the ecological condition worsens, the long march becomes longer and tiresome. Consequently, the women work for longer hours than men folk, not only in agriculture but also in household and other domestic chores. A woman's life is stretched between tbe scrutinies of men, because husbands of sound economic condition can marry as many times as he wants to. On the other hand, in a joint family with a poor economic condition, 3-4 brothers have a common wife.

**Effects of Migration**

However, due to the impact of visitors from the plains, as well as the immigration and out-migration process, such practices are losing their roots slowly. But the condition of women demands that we must be fast and steadfast in action with winning strategies to take care of the attitudes of the people and towards women in the community fabric. Another weighty point responsible for the backwardness of the inhabitants of study area is that there is only 13.29 per cent literacy. The worst hit of illiteracy are the women folk, since their literacy percentage is much more lower (1.49 per cent) in comparison to that of men folk (11.80 per cent). The poorer literacy rate among the women folk is only due to socio-cultural factors prevailing in the society.

As far as literacy amongst the menfolk is concerned, it has been noticed that there is an apathy is the minds of the local people towards the government policies of declaring their neighbour Jaunsaris as Scheduled Tribes. Being more backward, than the Jaunsari community, these people think that they have least chances of getting opportunities of a Government job. Therefore, to increase the literacy rate and generate strong will amongst the local people towards gaining education is needed, since in the struggle of existence, education is essential. In most part of the study area, agriculture is sub-marginal and inspite of more than adequate Human Muscle Power (HMP) the crop production is very low. The return from agriculture is on the decline and it is progressively and miserably failing to generate full time employment and adequate income to the people.

**Herbal Planks**

It is evident from the fact that the agriculture produce hardly feed the inhabitants for about three or four months. It is estimated that the earning per hectare through agriculture practices is less than Rs. 7,000 per annum. It is strongly emphasized that the cultivation of potential herbal plants can raise the economy of the people to at least five times the present level. The villages of the study area have been collecting medicinal plants from the forests and pastures from time immemorial for their traditional medicinal practices, as well as for economic gain by selling them. The medicinal herbs, which were being exploited commercially till 1991 have been totally banned since 1992, with the coming of the Wild-life (Protection) Amendment Act 1991. However, cases of illegal collection of medicinal plants do take place frequently. Such malpractices of smuggling of medicinal plants are not playing any vital role in their economic upliftment, because in most cases the personnel of either the Forest Department or the Police Department catch the local agents. The extracted medicinal herbs are seized at Check Posts, and these departments charge a heavy amount of penalty.

It is a common knowledge that the local agents ply this illegal trade with the connivance of the personnel of the Forest Department. The large part of the profit goes to the unscrupulous staff. Therefore, the inhabitants of the region are losing their wealth of phytodiversity without gaining any profitable return from it. The solution to the above said problem lies in cultivation of potential herbal taxa as an agriculture practice, which can become a leading cash crop.

The present approach, which refers to producers as beneficiaries has inbuilt seeds of patronage. The women folk are very poor because they do not have adequate assets and it is a matter of fact that the only assets they posses are time and labour. If the women are to be helped in improving their livelihood security, there is need for adding economic value and returns to their time and labour. This will be possible only if they acquire new skills. The skill, in turn, should be market driven.

In case of women who are often under paid and overworked, the strategy has to be based on reducing the number of hours of work and adding economic value to each hour of their work. Thus, the knowledge and technological empowerment pertaining to herb cultivation will be an asset for eradication of poverty and empowering the women within the study area. The species of medicinal plants for cultivation in the village situated at different elevation should be chosen in a manner that the environmental conditions are naturally favourable. It would be unfortunate if at every start a cultivation programme site is picked only on the basis of consideration of land.

Inhospitable or difficult sites will impose stress on the initial success of programme, which is likely to lead to delays or underachievement, opening the programme to sceptical critique. Hence, the cultivation sites should be promoted in a compact area by preferring cultivable fields over community land. Marketing operations occupy a central position in the rural economy and, therefore, must be provided highest priority in any scheme intended for their upliftment. A Women Growers Association or co-operative must be formed at the village level, because of its focus group promotion activities on self-reliance basis. Any attempts made towards the eradication of social evils and the suggested holistic development in terms of economic, social and political empowerment would greatly influence the life of women in the area.

## References


1. Bourai, Himanshu, 2001. Hill Women strength opportunities and problems, in *Garhwal Himalaya: Nature, Culture and Society*, Kandari, O.P. and Gusain, O.P. (eds.), Transmedia, Srinagar, Garhwal, pp. 293-306.
2. Census of India, 2001. State of Literacy, Provisional Population Totals, Chapter 7, Census of India, 2001, Series I, India, Paper 1 of 2001, p. 2.
3. Chandna, R.C. 2002. *Geography of Population: Concepts, Determinants and Patterns*, Kalyani Publishers, New Delhi, p. 331.
4. Dougall, Lori Mc 2000. Gender Gap in Literacy in Uttar Pradesh, *Economic and Political Weekly*, Vol. XXXV, No. 19, pp. 1650.
5. Garola, Ramanand 1997. Buniyadi Shiksha: Uttarakhand Ki Mahilaon Ke Sandarbh Mein Ek Vishleshan, in *Shikhraj*, Dhasmana, R. (ed.), pp. 108-110.
6. Golden, H.H. 1968. Literacy, in *International Encyclopedia of Social Sciences*, David L. Sills (ed.), Vol. 9, Macmillan Company and Free Press, London pp. 412-417.
7. Gosal, G.S. 1985. Spatial Perspective on Literacy in India, in *Contributions to Indian Geography: Population Geography*, Mishra, R.P. et al. (eds.), Vol. 6, Heritage Publishers, New Delhi, pp. 261-287.
8. Joshi, B.K. 1999. Education as a Thrust Area for Development of Uttarakhand, Centre for Himalaya Development Policy and Studies, Dehradun, pp. 12-13.
9. Kharkwal, S.C. 1993. *Physio-Cultural Environment and Development in U.P. Himalaya*, Nutan Publications, Kotdwar, p. 77.
10. Misra, A. 2001. Education, in *Garhwal Himalaya: Nature, Culture and Society*, Kandari, O.P. and Gusain, O.P. (eds.), Transmedia, Srinagar (Garhwal), pp. 329-342.
11. Nair, PR Gopinathan and Vaidyanathan, A. (eds.), 2001. *Elementary Education in RuralIndia—A Grass Roots View: Strategies in Human Development*, Sage Publications, New Delhi.
12. Nayar, Usha, 2002. Education of Girls in India: An Assessment, in *India Education Report: A Profile of Basic Education*, Govinda, R. (ed.), National Institute of Educational Planning and Administration, New Delhi, p. 36.
13. NLM, National Literacy Mission: Literacy and Women, NLM data on Literacy files\women.nun.
14. Ramchandran, Vimla and Saihjee, Aarti 2002. The New Segregation: Reflections on Gender and Equity in Primary Education, *Economic and Political Weekly*, Vol. XXXVII, No. 17, p. 1611.
15. Raza, Moonis and Aggarwal, Y.P. 1986. Inequities in the Level of Literacy in India, in *Spectrum of Modern Geography*, Shafi, M. and Raza, M. (eds.), Concept Publishing Company, New Delhi, p. 223.
16. Tikkha, R.N. 1993. *Economic and Commercial Geography, Resource Utilization*, New Publishing Co., Jalandhar.

017. K. Kumar et al, 1994. Rural Population Growth in the Western Himalaya A case study of Pauri Garhwal District (Uttar Pradesh), *Geog. Rev. of India,* Vol. 56, No. 1.

18. Kharkwal, S.C., 1993. *Physico-cultural Environment and Development in U.P Himalaya,* Nutan Publication, Kotdwar.

19. Nityanand et al. 1989. *The Holy Himalaya,* Daya Publishing House, New Delhi.

20. Kanka, S.S., 1984. *The Galloping Population and its components (1951-81): An inter-district analysis*

# 18

# The Role of Women in the Uttaranchal Regional Movement

## Introduction

In 1993 the Himalayan region of Uttar Pradesh witnessed an explosion of social protest centring on the demand for a separate State of Uttaranchal.[1] A turbulent period followed, and in 1998 the recently elected Bharatiya Janata Party (BJP) Central Government announced that a separate hill State would be created. These events raise many fascinating issues and questions, but in this paper I shall focus on just one dimension of the struggle, namely the role(s) of women within it. After a brief outline of the regional movement I shall explore the part that women played in the protests and demonstrations, the ideological positioning of and by women within the movement, and areas of difference and dissent amongst women in relation to the movement.

## The Separate State Movement

The aspiration for separate hill administration can be traced back to the late colonial period in the Princely State of Tehri Garhwal and the British Province of Kumaun. Elite groups in both areas opposed the joining of this hill region with the rest of the plains State of Uttar Pradesh at Independence, arguing (without effect) that it should form a separate State within the new Union (Bhatkoti, 1987; Rawat, 1989).[2] The issue remained a largely elite concern until about the late 1970s/early 1980s, at which point there is evidence of growing, if patchy, popular support, in 1979 a political party, the Uttarakhand Kranti Dal (UKD), was formed with the single point agenda of the creation of a separate hill held in various hill towns and in Delhi.

Significantly, a number of mainstream State and national parties also began to take an interest in the demand, suggesting that they viewed it as a popular and potentially vote-yielding issue. However, it was not until 1993 that the demand for a separate hill State attracted truly mass support. The trigger for this was the passing of a piece of State legislation on reservation (positive discrimination) for the Other Backward Classes

(OBCs) in Uttar Pradesh. This provided for 27 per cent reservation in Government posts and in educational institutes for the enormous number of artisanal and agricultural castes that make up an estimated 52 per cent of the population in Uttar Pradesh. Together with the 15 per cent for former Untouchables, the Scheduled Castes, and 7.5 per cent for the Scheduled Tribes, this brought the total reservation figure to just under 50 per cent.[3]

The problem was that the Uttaranchal region has an extremely unusual caste structure, in that over 70 per cent of the population are high caste Brahmins and Rajputs. According to the 1991 Census of India, Scheduled Castes make up 18 per cent of the rest of the population, and Scheduled Tribes 5 per cent. There are perhaps only 3-4 per cent OBCs in the hills (although it should be noted that these categories are far more fluid than is generally recognised). This legislation would result in half of the Government jobs and educational places available in the region being denied to most of its population—a crippling blow in an already poor economy, in which, in the absence of any significant private industry, Government jobs provide a major source of employment.

**Mandalisation**

The spectre of Mandal was looming large on Uttar Pradesh. The group that felt the immediate impact of the legislation were the students and prospective students in the region, who now had difficulties registering for the next academic year. Students have a long history of activism in India (Rudolph and Rudolph, 1987), and they were quick to move into confrontation with the State Government over the legislation. They were soon joined by many other groups and people in the region protesting over the impact of the OBC reservation on Government jobs, including Government employees, ex-Servicemen and vast numbers of ordinary men and women in villages and towns. But within the space of two or three weeks the agitation had shifted its focus from a mobilisation against the discriminating and insensitive OBC reservation legislation to contemporary political configuration in the State at the time, and the history of perceived maldevelopment and neglect of the region by the State.

First, the State Government of Uttar Pradesh at the time was headed by the relatively newly-elected lower and middle-caste Samajwadi Party-Bahujan Samaj Party (SP-BSP). The SP-BSP was widely believed to be antagonistic to this high caste region, and many argued that this was the worst in a long line of State Governments who had ignored or abused this politically insignificant part of the State. The second, and highly related, reason concerned development, with many claiming that the region has long been subjected to internal colonialism by the rest of the State. As well as this 'intentiona l exploitation' it was also widely felt that distant plains-based bureaucrats had been consistently unable to formulate suitable development plans for the hill region, resulting in inappropriate and often environmentally-destructive schemes.

## Separation from the Plains

In both cases, the 'answer' was separation from the plains while reaffirming ties with the Centre and the rest of India through the demand for a separate State. From July 1993 the movement developed with extraordinary vigour, rapidity and breadth. Protest included the familiar pantheon of Gandhian strategies, including readings of the *Ramayana*, relay hunger strikes, processions, *dharnas* (sit-ins), *rasta* and *rail rokos* (road and rail blocks), *bandhs* (strikes), *jail bharo andolans* (mass courting of arrest), effigy burning, and so on. *Nukkad nataks* (street plays) and *jan jagarans* (awareness raising programmes) help promote the movement and certain themes within it. Despite claims to the contrary, and the best efforts of many people, the agitation was pervaded by low level violence. Within a couple of months of the agitation starting literally hundreds of action groups were established all over the region and at no point could any one person or group be said to be leading it. This did lend the movement a great deal of robustness and flexibility, and it points to the genuinely spontaneous and locally-driven nature of the agitation. Many people were proud of the fact that it was a *'jan andolan'* (people's movement), and that it hadn't been co-opted by any political party or organisation. But as the months went by many Uttaranchalis became increasingly concerned by the loss of cohesion and direction in the groups, factions and parties were usually put down to ideological differences, they often owed more to a shameful jockeying of position in anticipation of the future rewards that Statehood was expected to bring.

## Women in the Uttaranchal Movement

Women played a key part at every level of the Uttaranchal movement: formulating, leading and participating in the protests and demonstrations; contributing to its ideological strength and direction(s); and acting as a point of *resistance* within the movement over certain issues. Gendered language was symbolically deployed within the movement by both men and women, and various idealised images of 'the hill woman' were foregrounded at different times within the agitation in pursuit of the moral high ground.

### *Getting Involved*

*Now listen to the voice of the women — give us our State.*
*The women of Uttarakhand are alight today — the hill woman*
*is revolutionary torch today!*

Slogans heard during demonstrations (1993/1994)

As many commentators have pointed out, the hardships associated with migration, environmental degradation, and economic deprivation are deeply gendered, with women often suffering particularly badly and particular ways (Agarwal, 1985; Kabeer, 1994). This is certainly the case for women in the hills, and helps explain why many of the general complaints of the regional movement, such as poor development and the inequity of the reservation order, attracted particular support from women. In December 1994, for example, a group of women sent an appeal to the MPs of Uttar Pradesh which outlined the specific difficulties women face in the 'mal-developed' hills, as well as the more general complaints of the agitation. The extra burden thrown onto them by the migration of so many of the region's men was especially noted, as were the rapes and molestation that had accompanied the State Government's repression of the movement.[4]

**Impact of Reservation**

As with most men in the movement, the key event that drew women into the struggle was the reservation order, given the impact that it would have on the education. We are involved because of reservation and the effects this will have on our children. They will be denied entrance to educational institutes, and this has made the women very worried. Without education there will be a lot of trouble. When they implemented this 50 per cent reservation in schools the women became furious. Our children are well-educated— BA and MA passed —but they are unemployed. The posts are being filled by plains people who are coming here for jobs. So this is the main reason behind women's participation—that it is their children who are unemployed. Also their husbands are away, and Lucknow is far from here—in this situation it is not possible to develop.

A village woman told me:

> Well, the mothers are fighting for the future of their children. They have educated them, but if the children remain unemployed, what can she do for their welfare? It is the same with the fathers — what is the use of giving education to the children if they can't get jobs.

**Women March Ahead**

Women often marched at the head of mixed rallies and occupied prominent positions on platforms and at *dharna* (sit-in) sites. There were special women's marches in most towns, and a large number of women's organisations were set up. Some of these were 'women's branches' of existing organisations and parties, such as the UKD, the Uttarakhand Sanyukt Sangarsh Samiti (set up to act as an umbrella organisation for the different groups involved in the agitation), and the BJP, while others were set up by and for women specifically in response to the agitation, such as the Uttarakhand Mahila Manch. On one occasion, recognising their distinct identity, and centrality in the agitation, the Chief Minister of the State, Mulayam Singh Yadav, appealed to "the women, students and political parties" to stop agitating.[5] Women were not just present as followers and supporters, but also emerged as leaders and directors at various levels.

However, like their male counterparts, some of high profile women in the agitation seemed more interested in internal politicking, rubbishing their opponents at every opportunity, changing parties depending on the chances offered them and iostling for future political gains in a separate state. Hills are comparatively independent and more free to travel than many women in the northern plains, and despite the fact that there were many specially organised women's rallies, protests and demonstrations, women were more restricted than men in when, how far and to where they could travel. This was exacerbated after a number of Uttaranchali women were molested and raped at Muzaffarnagar, resulting in many women being increasingly afraid to engage in direct protest or being prevented from doing so by their families.

Time was also a serious constraint for village women in particular, many of whom work (or are worked) incredibly hard, and who carry out the vast majority of agricultural, forest, and domestic tasks. A number of women told me that they simply didn't have the time to leave their fields and go and protest. Finally, there was no unitary position on the regional movement amongst the women of Uttaranchal. Women differed in their opinions with age, caste, region and community, as well as simply for contingent and personal reasons. Despite the popular claims that the movement was in no way exclusionary or parochial, the Uttarakhand movement *was* influenced by caste, communal and regional tensions, and women too shaped and were shaped by these differences and divisions.

**Gender, Identity and the Regional Movement**

During the regional agitation a number of semi-idealised constructions of the hills landscape and environment, and of hill people and society, were widely articulated. These strategies were intended to bolster the arguments that (a) the hills were very different from the plains, and thus legitimately required a separate State, and (b) that the hill people were peaceful and loyal citizens of India and thus represented no threat to the unity of the nation-state. One such 'theme' centred on women, and the celebration of their elevated position in a 'virtuous' hill society, particularly when compared with the situation in the plains.

The following comments were typical of those heard:

> Women are safe in the hills — our mothers, daughters and wives can go safely to the market and the jungle.
>
> We are safe here. Our women wear lots of gold, but in the plains it would be snatched away by *dacoits* (robbers).

Interestingly, these sorts of comments were almost always made by men, and while the images are based in the fact that hill women are generally freer to roam the forests and fields around their villages than their plains counterparts, it dues little justice to the harsh reality of life in the hills for many women, or the continuing inequalities of gender relations in hill society.

**Uttranchal or Uttrakhand**

A second way in which a gendered imagery was deployed in the regional movement was in the larger sense of the Uttaranchal's place in 'Mother India'. During 1994-95, the local and State apparatchiks of the BJP argued that the new State should be called Uttaranchal rather than the more popular (at the time) Uttarakhand. The semantic difference is interesting: *khand* means a discrete segment or piece of land, whilst *anchal* has more connotations of area or region. BJP politicians argue that 'Uttaranchal' is therefore more inclusionary and does not have the more separatist undertones of 'Uttarakhand', which should only refer to the three nothernmost border districts of the eight that are generally taken to make up the region. 'Anchal' can also mean the part of a woman's *sari* that falls over the shoulder — roughly where you would find Uttaranchal if an imaginary woman was transposed onto the map of India — again promoting the discourse and image of the (gendered) body politic.

Representations of the gendered body in Hindu nationalist politics has attracted great interest (Alter, 1994; Van der Veer, 1994) and the deployment of a bodily metaphor here is significant. But although 'Uttaranchal' fits the movement's non-separatist image and intent, many people do not use it. 'Uttaranchal' is a term with clear political affiliations while 'Uttarakhand' is more secular, and many hill people are adamant that the movement is not party political or driven by a (high) caste identity.[6] Most people I spoke to felt that these arguments only obscured the main issues.

**Dissent and Difference**

Many women were strongly motivated to join and take part in the regional movement because of the main issues at stake—concerns about reservation, and the longer-standing discontents over inappropriate and low levels of development in the hill region. There were also issues which, although by no means exclusively women's concerns, were particularly important in mobilising some women's support for the movement and activism in it, such as liquor. The region has a long history of protest against liquor, principally organised by women activists and *Sarvodaya* workers (Pathak, 1985). Women suffer from the alcoholism of their menfolk in a variety of ways. The household budget may be savagely cut into, the men might be unable to get work (resulting in a greater burden falling on the women to make ends meet from agricultural activities), and drinking is more likely to lead to domestic violence and abuse.

Some women made an anti-liquor commitment the key reason for their involvement in the regional movement. I none rally in Dunia (Pithoragarh), Radha Behn, a prominent and highly respected *Sarvodaya* worker, drew on an explicity Gandhian vision of a liquor-less Uttarakhand. 'Otherwise', she asked, 'what is the point of the separate State for women?' In December 1994, the Uttarakhand Mahila Manch (Uttarakhand Women's Platform) was formed, and at its inauguration Kamla Pant, the Convenor, stated that, on top of other issues, they would continue to fight the twin evils of drinking and gambling.

In January 1995, another organisation, the Uttarakhand Mahila Sangarsh Samiti (Uttarakhand Women's Protest Committee), delivered an ultimatum to dealers in liquor and lottery tickets in the region to adopt other trades by 15 January. If they did not do so voluntarily, the spokesperson said, women would launch a direct fight against them. The Uttaranchal region is perhaps best known for being the home of the Chipko protests in the 1970s and early 1980s. Women played a prominent part in these struggles, and some commentators, such as Vandana Shiva and Sunderlal Bahuguna, have suggested that Chipko represented a conflict of interests and ideologies between men and women in the region over the way in which the forests should be exploited (Shiva, 1988). I have argue against this and the differences and similarities expressed by men and women in relation to them.

Most people involved in the regional movement professed to be confident that the hill people could administer the hills better within a separate State, including in terms of natural resource management. Indeed, this argument formed part of the attempt mentioned above to convince the Central Government that a separate State for the region would strengthen, rather than weaken, the Indian polity. The environmental justification of the movement was sometimes related not only to improving development in the region, but to the Uttaranchalis' commitment to national unity and well-being.

In an interview with the *Amar Ujala,* UKD leader Kashi Singh Airi stated that :

> It is our duty to safeguard the environment of the Himalaya for the rest of India. If the forest and the environment of the Himalaya are damaged, it will result in disaster for the whole of India.[7]

**Environmental Tensions**

On deeper study it was found that environmental tensions certainly formed part of the larger protests. Two of the demands frequently listed in the agitation were that the 3-4 thousand cases registered under the Forest Conservation Act should be dropped, and that the Act should itself be changed. As we have already seen, complaints about the pace and type of development in the hills formed an integral part of the regional struggle, an issue which cannot be divorced from environmental concerns.

Not everyone is confident that a separate State will have a beneficial effect on environmental management in the region. One village man in Tehri Garhwal who had been very involved in the Chipko movement(s), told me that:

> I am completely against a separate State. If it was created I think the state of the forests would worsen—our so-called leaders would simply use the forests as a source of quick revenue. The separate State movement is completely politically motivated. It is a movement of politicians and leaders.

Sunderlal Bahuguna, the famous environmentalist, also felt that separate state would not provide a solution for the ecological problems economic growth, and nature viewed as a commodity to be 'cashed in' to fund that development:

> So they [a separate State's leaders] would need something, either taxes or production, but the people are poor. They cannot get anything out of property tax, or income tax, or other such taxes. So, the only means of income for the Government will be selling trees, extracting minerals, luxury tourism, and now that damming of the rivers in order to sell the water and the electricity, and unfortunately liquor. I think that the new State would exploit these things more.

For some, the future of a separate State rests on the hope that women will have greater decision-making and control within it, at the household, village, town and State levels. Chandi Prasad Bhatt, for example, the well-known social and environmental activist, situates his confidence for appropriate development (particularly in relation to the environment) in the growing political experience and assertion of women :

> I think forests will be good under a separate State. Women are now aware of their rights—they know in which way they have to develop the area... The Uttarakhand movement itself is deeply influenced by women. I have noticed that in the demonstrations and processions in Gopeshwar, 80 per cent are women. As their participation is so pronounced now, I think their participation in the Government [of a separate State] will be strong too, and their interests will be tied to the villages.

Environmental issues were not always the most prominent concern. Intensive research suggests that amongst both men and women there was a range of opinions on the subject, partly related to factors such as occupation, age, and economic status, but also in terms of individual experiences, viewpoints and concerns. Many women also wanted jobs and industrial development in the region, which is not to deny that many were deeply concerned about agro-environmental issues in the hills, but to recognise that this was allied with concerns about other forms of winning a livelihood in the hill region.

### Conclusions

Women have played an extremely important part in the struggle for a separate hill state, helping shape the nature, form and goals of the regional movement. With the prospect of a new State now almost certain, the hill region is set to embark on a potentially exciting period of change. If the optimistic claims are to be believed, this will include the establishment of a more sensitive and committed set of development planners and administrators, and a more democratically accountable set of politicians. These changes, it is argued, will facilitate *faster* development, and *better* development, which will be less environmentally destructive and of far greater benefit to local people in the region.

This is of particular importance to the women of the Uttaranchal region, given that the burden of under development and environmental degradation falls disproportionately on their shoulders. Unfortunately, there are many reasons to be sceptical, or at least very wary, of these glowing forecasts, but I would suggest that some hope may reside in the fact of the politicisation and experience of activism of tens of thousand of women in Uttaranchal over the last five years.

## References

1. The region is also known as the Uttarakhand. The differences between these names are discussed above.
2. Prior to 1947 Tehri Garhwal was an independent Princely State, while Kumaun and 'British Garhwal' had been part of the United Provinces ever since 1891, when it lost its Non-Regulation Province status. For more details, see Tolia 1994.
3. Reservation is an extremely complex issue, and this outline is highly simplified. For more details, see Galanter 1978 and 1984; Beteille 1992.
4. *Times of India,* 30.10.94; *Indian Express,* 6.10.94.
5. *Himachal Times,* 30.8.94.
6. I have always preferred Uttarakhand for this reason, but as the Central Government have said they will create Uttaranchal, it seems sensible to accept the change.
7. *Amar Ujala,* 10.10.94.

# 19

# Women's Empowerment: Types of Marital Relationship—Polygyny, Polyandry and Divorce in Himachal Himalayas

Marriage is preceded by betrothal in every Indian society though the customs and practices with regard to it differ. The parents regard it their duty to see their sons and daughters married and even if they are poor they would rather incur debts to do their duty than bear the opprobrium of society for shirking what as parents they are required to perform. The notion has a greater hold where the mass of population is uneducated and conservative. Whether a man can afford the expenses or not he must get his sons and daughters married so that he may not be looked down upon by society and fail in his duty to his own self. Thus many families incur debt and court poverty because of the marriage expenses but they cannot tolerate the idea of having an unmarried boy or girl in the family.

They would prefer death to this humiliation. The same idea has penetrated into the trans-Giri society where people are found to carry it to excess. While in the plains the age for betrothals and marriages is going up everywhere these people stick to their old practices and ideas. Betrothals take place very early. In some parts of the trans-Giri territory a betrothal is arranged before the child attains the age of one year. As soon as a child is born it is sometimes betrothed. Not only that, betrothals are known to take place even when the children are in their mothers' wombs. The understanding in such cases is that if the babies belong to opposite sexes they are to be wedded to each other. The actual ceremony is, however, performed after the birth of the babies. (The table overleaf elucidates the point.)

### Child Marriage

Even when the children were only one-year-old, 44 of them had been married. Their betrothal must have taken place sometime before

**Table 19.1**

| | *Population* | | | *Unmarried* | | | *Married* | | | *Widowed* | | |
|---|---|---|---|---|---|---|---|---|---|---|---|---|
| *Age* | *Persons* | *Males* | *Females* | *Persons* | *Males* | *Females* | *Persons* | *Males* | *Females* | *Persons* | *Males* | *Females* |
| Total | 139,031 | 76,922 | 62,109 | 42,766 | 26,239 | 16,527 | 83,471 | 45,650 | 37,821 | 12,794 | 5,033 | 7,761 |
| 0-1 | 3,230 | 1,658 | 1,572 | 3,186 | 1,617 | 1,569 | 44 | 41 | 3 | | | |
| 1-2 | 3,179 | 1,631 | 1,548 | 3,073 | 1,542 | 1,531 | 106 | 89 | 17 | | | |
| 2-3 | 3,541 | 1,761 | 1,780 | 3,353 | 1,625 | 1,728 | 186 | 136 | 52 | | | |
| 3-4 | 3,611 | 1,771 | 1,840 | 3,267 | 1,562 | 1,705 | 342 | 208 | 134 | 2 | 1 | 1 |
| 4-5 | 3,566 | 1,804 | 1,762 | 3,102 | 1,540 | 1,562 | 457 | 261 | 196 | 7 | 3 | 4 |
| 0-5 Total | 17,127 | 8,625 | 8,502 | 15,981 | 7,886 | 8,095 | 1,137 | 735 | 402 | 9 | 4 | 5 |
| 5-10 | 15,394 | 8,246 | 7,148 | 11,257 | 6,224 | 5,033 | 4,097 | 2,001 | 2,096 | 40 | 21 | 19 |

Source: *Sirmur State Gazetteer*, Part B, 1931.

they were born. There were 106 married persons of the age of 1-2 and 188 of 2-3. The figure goes up in the case of persons of 3-4 years: they number 342 while persons of 4-5 years number 457. Thus between 0-5 years of age we find 1,137 married persons and most of these belong to the trans-Giri territory. Between the ages of 5-10 we find the figure rising to 4,097 out of which 2,001 were males and 2,096 females. It is thus clear how very early betrothals and marriages take place in this country.

Children are married when they are yet in their cradles and it is interesting to find persons who are widowed before they leave their cradles. There were two widowed persons (one male and one female) between 3-4 years and seven (three males and four females) between 4-5 years. It would be sheer cruelty if in these circumstances no widow marriage were sanctioned by society and girls were forced to live as widows all their life. Naturally widow marriage in such society is a common and daily occurrence. The betrothal ceremony is a simple affair. The bridegroom's people send their *Purohit* (family Brahmin) and barber with some ghee and a lump of sugar to the bride's place. If the bride's people after consultation accept these articles the proposal is complete.

**Dowry**

Some people send clothes, myrtle, *mauli* or *paranda* (red, yellow, and white threads stitched together) and even cash. The bridegroom's parents must present clothes to the bride at every Diwali after the betrothal ceremony till the actual marriage otherwise the betrothal will not stand. The boy is at times made to work with the parents of the girl when he is too poor to make any presents. Betrothals are of two kinds: (i) *kachhi*, i.e. preliminary and (ii) *pakki*, i.e. final. All that is necessary for a preliminary betrothal is that a man is sent by the parents of the boy (if he has none living, he goes himself) to the girl's parents with some *kachha* ghee, a few rupees, and a *bheli* (a lump of coarse sugar). No particular relation or person need carry these things for the boy. If these are accepted, the matter ends there.

At the time of final betrothal some money in cash, a *bheli*, a pair of silver bangles, a *hansli* (tight necklace), and three garments—*kurta* (loose shirt), pyjama, and *chaddar* (sheet) to cover the head—are sent through a pandit and two men to the house of the betrothed girl. Paranda and *mehndi* (henna powder) are also taken. The girl's side is represented by a pandit and two of her relations. The pandit from the girl's side puts on her arms the pair of silver bangles *(kangan)* sent by the boy. A pujan is held. Swasti-bachan, Ganesha Puja, Khotshe Matrika, Kalash Nwagrah, etc., are also performed. After the betrothal till the marriage is celebrated the boy or his parents send one complete suit consisting of *kurta*, *pyjama*, and *chhadar* to the girl thrice a year at Diwali, Bishoo (1st of *Baisakh)*, and Rihali [from *hariyali* (greenery), held on the 1st of Sawan every year]. If no separate pakki betrothal is held, the ceremony of giving the bangles, etc. is performed at the time of marriage. In cis-Giri the age at betrothal varies from five to 15, but Rajputs, Bhats, and Kanets celebrate betrothal and marriage between 15 and 20, both ceremonies being performed simultaneously.

**Bride-price**

It is customary in trans-Giri to take bride-price, only Rajputs avoid the practice. Brahmans and Banias as well as Kolis and other artisans and trading castes practise it. This money is paid to the bride's father or the nearest male relative by the bridegroom. Pun marriage, in which the parents of the bride receive nothing in cash or kind from the bridegroom, is confined to the upper classes, but the rest consider themselves entitled to receive some compensation for the upbringing of their daughters. Even when anything is received as compensation, the amount is not very high and only marriage expenses are charged. The Bhats and Kanets usually avoid it but their indigence forces some of them to have recourse to this help. Insanity, leprosy, or any other incurable physical defect in the boy or the girl entitles either party to cancel betrothal. Otherwise it is regarded as an offence to cancel a betrothal without sufficient and cogent grounds. Great offence is done in wantonly cancelling a betrothal but the discovery of physical defect in the boy or the girl is held to justify it.

Betrothal followed by marriage at an age of one to ten years may seem to be a horrible practice and grave consequences may naturally be apprehended. But the custom does not materially affect the social life of the people for the girl is not allowed to cohabit with her husband before she attains puberty. Though women here are at the mercy of their husbands and can be deprived of the marital protection at any moment, they enjoy great personal liberty. Their status here is in certain respects superior to that of the women in the plains. The natural result of early betrothal and marriage would have been the permanent slavery of the girl-wife under her husband and members of his family and she would have found it impossible to extricate herself out of this intolerable life. But what actually happens is that when she attains majority or understands her own interests she can dissolve the marriage contract by paying compensation to the husband and go over to the man after her heart.

**Remarriage**

She thus gets back to her home, arranges marriage with someone else, pays compensation to the husband in the form of Reet, and goes to live with the new husband. No marriage is legally valid without the payment of compensation or Reet to the first husband. The origin of early betrothal and marriage is very difficult to trace but certain advantages are claimed for them. It has to be remembered that these people are practically agriculturists and the utility of a wife depends upon her interest and training in household and field work. It is claimed that one advantage of this custom is that the mother-in-law finds it very easy to train her daughter-in-law when she gets her under her disposal at so young an age. She is impressionable then and the training imparted to her is sure to last her for her life. Her services in agriculture can thus be utilized from her childhood. At times in the plains, where the custom of child marriage was once prevalent but has now been superseded by adult marriage, the mothers-in-law complain against their daughters-in-law.

They say that they find it difficult to train the grown-up daughters-in-law who have developed different habits and would not pay heed to their advice while in the days of early marriage they could mould them as they pleased. The girl-wife was given instructions in every household and outdoor work and she took part in everything which concerned the family. She could help her mother-in-law from the early years of her life and thus got a proper understanding of every household duty while a wife who came late had most probably been spoilt by too much caressing from her mother. Further, through early marriage the couple live together from childhood and great intimacy naturally develops between them and they are able to understand each other very well which would not be possible for grown-up people. The girl-wife would after some time learn to regard the relations of her husband as her own and a very wholesome and healthy atmosphere would be created. Such, in brief, are the advantages claimed for early betrothal and marriage. There is some truth and force in the assertions, but the drawbacks of early marriage are numerous and outweigh the advantages.

**Child-wife**

The child-wife finds life very hard for her. The mother-in-law is not usually, and cannot naturally, be so kind to her as her own mother. It is sheer cruelty to deprive a girl of tender age of the love and affection of her own mother in the interest of a practical training for the benefit of her mother-in-law. It is the mother's care which a child holds dearest in her life and which cannot be replaced by anything. Rudimentary education is also denied to her for her mother-in-law would never care for her education as her parents could. But the worst of it is that the couple are not really so happy as they are claimed or expected to be. Serious differences develop between the husband and wife as time passes and the numerous cases of dissolution of marriage give a conclusive proof that early marriage does not strengthen the marital tie. The custom of Reet could not have existed and prospered if such marriages were happy.

As soon as the girl grows up and finds things intolerable for her, her spirits rebel against her marriage. She goes home, arranges an alliance with someone else more to her liking, pays compensation to her husband, and lives with that man. This custom seems to be a very old one and people stick to it because of their conservatism as also because there is no other way out of the difficulty. We may thus surmise that the need of women as partners in agriculture, their services at home, and the necessity of training them in discipline and loyalty to their mother-in-law might have led to early betrothals and marriages. The evils associated with infant marriage are probably responsible for the introduction of the custom of Reet by which a woman may escape the hard lot to which otherwise she would have been permanently bound.

**Betrothal Customs**

In Simla, Chamba, Suket and Mandi, Chakrata, betrothal customs are similar to those of Sirmur. In Chakrata, however, a few customs similar to those of trans-Giri are found, while in other places cis-Giri customs preponderate. Early betrothal and marriage are, however, a common feature in all these hill areas and there is practically no difference in the ceremonies performed. Early betrothals are common in Kullu too but often the marriages do not take place till the parties are of an age fit to cohabit. Early marriages are, however, not forbidden and do take place in the interior. The betrothal ceremony is quite simple here too. The father of the boy goes to the girl's father with presents. Promises are exchanged. The girl's father agrees to give her in marriage if the boy's father is prepared to give him a certain sum. If the boy's father agrees the betrothal is complete.

It is noteworthy that while in Kullu the boy's father has to give money to the girl's father it is not necessary to do so in Sirmur. It is not in every case that a girl's father realizes money from the other side but only those who cannot afford marriage expenses do it. In Lahul, however, a slight difference is noticeable in the betrothal ceremony. There the negotiations for a betrothal are carried out by the father and the maternal uncle of the boy. The girl is first selected by the parents or by the boy if he is in a position to do it. The father and maternal uncle then take a pot of *chang* (a local drink, made out of barley) to the parents of the girl selected. There they disclose the purpose of their visit to the father of the girl. The mother is then deputed to obtain the consent of the daughter. If she agrees to the proposal her parents also accept it and partake of the *chang* brought by the visitors.

If she does not agree to the preferred hand the parents refuse to drink the *chang* which means a final rejection of the offer of marriage. If, however, they accept the proposal and drink the *chang* it is sent to them on two further occasions and at the third time the payment and acceptance of a rupee settles the matter.

**Lahaul Custom**

The Lahaul custom, though differing in the matter of drinking *chang* which is not done in Sirmur, resembles the *kachhi* and *pakki* betrothal ceremony of trans-Giri. As in Lahul, betrothal proceedings are conducted in Sirmur too generally by the father or the maternal uncle of the boy though friends or other relations too may do it at times. Throughout the Simla hills, Kangra, and Sirmur polygyny is widely practised. It is prevalent in all the Himalayan tracts as well as in the plains. But the spread of education and a consequent change in outlook has placed this custom at a discount in Hindu society. Such, however, is not exactly the position in the hills for no stigma attaches to a man who has more than one wife. It is not everyone who can afford a wife in the hills where the mere possession of more than one wife signifies distinction and prosperity. The possession of many wives in a tract where the number of males is considerably higher than that of females would seem improbable.

**Polygyny**

Polygyny is usually practised where there are more females than males. But in a place where there are fewer females, this custom cannot be widespread for the majority of the male populace would have to remain unmarried. Thus it is that polyandry is prevalent in Kullu and Saraj, Bashahr, Simla hills, and Sirmur and so even those who cannot afford to have a wife separately manage to do so jointly. It is only the rich or well-to-do who have more than one wife. The rich sometimes keep as many as four wives and moneyed men with two wives are quite common. The *Sirmur Settlement Report* (1881) mentions that the majority of Rajputs, Kanets, Bhats, and Kolis were accustomed to keep more than one wife.

The most important reason behind the adoption and continuance of polygyny in the hills was the importance of women as partners in agriculture. In the past it was not possible in the hills to carry out the household and field work without the assistance of someone else. For that purpose Dhialtas or tenants had to be engaged and they had to be paid quite decent sums of money to settle on the lands. Instead of getting a Dhialta or tenant it was cheaper and more useful to get a wife who could in addition satisfy a man's sexual appetite.

If the first wife is childless or has only female issues she insists on her husband's marrying another woman, preferably her own sister, or he may do it on his own initiative without giving offence. When the wife is living a comfortable life, according to the local standard, and is happy with her husband, she might ask him to marry her sister so that the latter too might be as happy as herself. Or again where she finds that she cannot carry on the household and field work singly she might ask her husband to marry someone else too.

All this goes to show that polygyny is not by any means a sign of feminine inferiority or felt as a degradation by the women concerned. Nor is the husband in most cases prompted to take a second wife by an excessive libido but by his first wife's eagerness to shift part of her household duties ôn other shoulders. The opportunities of satisfying one's sexual desires are so ample that in legal marriage with a second wife the sexual motive plays an insignificant role.

Such marriage also becomes a badge of distinction and a sure sign of prosperity in the family, for a man having more than one wife is not only in a better position to manage his household and field work but has very little work to do himself and can entertain his guests much better. A land holder or a householder benefit socially and economically by having more than are wife. It may seem inevitable that two or more wives which one may have would be always quarrelling and fighting and making one's life miserable. But an examination reveals that this apprehension is not justified by the actual state of affairs. Since it is only the rich who can afford the luxury of many wives the husband has generally at least two rooms in his house. Only the wife whom he would like to have with him for the night would sleep in his room though in cases where the wives have no feelings of jealousy they may sleep with him in the same room.

**Home for Second Wife**

Quite often the husband has a dochhi where he keeps his cattle and he keeps one wife at his house and the other at the dochhi. He lives in the house and at the dochhi and performs his duties towards them. Since the women married him not under any coercion or pressure they generally have good relations with each other and in case differences grow the injured wife may leave her husband and marry someone after her heart. Sporadic instances of jealousy must of course be expected everywhere but where the second wife is brought at the suggestion of the first wife the risk is minimized though, at times, it makes its appearance later. Sisters are likely to quarrel less as co-wives than unrelated women but even the latter pull on wonderfully well. We came across cases in the hills where children treated their mother and their step-mother, who was not their mother's sister, on the same terms and had no reason to dislike her but were rather more attached to her than to their mother. This is of course by no means common but it has to be admitted that on the whole the relations of the co-wives are not so bad as they are generally painted.

The ceremony by which a second wife is taken is quite simple in Sirmur. At the wedding the second wife is made to sitin one corner of a room, the first wife sits in the opposite corner, while a woman with a lighted lamp in her hand stands by each of them. Then the family Brahman or an elderly woman stands in the middle of the room, and he or she joins their hands and they give each other a rupee. The lamps are lighted to prevent the shadow of the one falling on the other. This custom is common in the hills on both sides of the Giri. A similar ceremony is practised in the other hills too.

**Polyandry**

Polyandry of the fraternal type is extensively practised in Bashahr, Kullu, Jubbal, Keonthal, and the trans-Giri tract of Sirmur. It is not peculiar to any particular caste or tribe. Since it is a phenomenon of vital importance it will form the subject-matter. Various forms of marriage are practised in the trans-Giri tract. The economic, social, and regional factors all combine to determine the form of marriage and we shall discuss below the nature and origin of the forms of marital relationship in these parts. The ancient Hindu law recognized eight forms of marriage of which four were approved and four unapproved. The four approved forms were: (*i*) Brahma, (*ii*) Daiva, (*iii*) Arsha, and (*iv*) Prajapatya. The four unapproved forms were: (*i*) Asura, (*ii*) Gandharva, (*iii*) Rakshasa, and (*iv*) Paisacha.

Where the father or other guardian of the bride gives the bride in marriage without receiving any consideration from the bridegroom, the marriage is called Brahma. It is commonly called Pun marriage now. When the girl is given in marriage to the officiating priest it is called Daiva and where the father of the girl receives from the bridegroom a pair of cows it is called Arsh a and where the father gives his daughter to the bridegroom saying: "You two be partners for performing secular and religious duties," it is called Prajapatya. For many centuries these were intended for Brahmans who are high caste in Hindu hierarchy. With the passage of time and more so in the later half of twentieth, the century, they ceremonies have became liberal. Now Hindus belonging to any caste may marry either in the Brahma form or the Asura form.

Where the father receives any consideration which is technically called *sulka* (bride's price) for giving his daughter in marriage, the marriage is called Ausra even though it may have been performed according to the rites prescribed for the Brahma form. What distinguishes the one from the other is that in the Brahma form it is a gift of the girl pure and simple while in the Asura it it a sale of the girl for pecuniary consideration. The test in each case is whether any consideration was received by the father or the other guardian for giving the girl in marriage. The mere giving of presents to the bride or to her mother as a token of compliment does not mean that the marriage is Asura.

**Gandharva Marraige**

The Gandharva is a marriage by mutual consent, the Rakshasa is a marriage by forcible capture, and the Paisacha is the marriage of a girl to a man who had ravished her when asleep or when flushed with strong liquor. In fact, the Asura form was permissible for Vaisayas and Sudras but not for Brahmans and Kshatriyas. The Gandharva and Rakshasa forms were peculiar to Kshatriyas. The Paisach form was regarded as the most debased and was strongly condemned. All these forms except the Brahma and the Asura have, however, gone out of use.

A passing reference to them was necessary because some traces of the defunct forms may still be found to exist. Any class may now marry only according to the Brahma or the Asura form. Thus a Brahman may contract an Asura marriage and a Sudra may contract a Brahma marriage. The most common form of marriage in the polyandrous trans-Giri tract of Sirmur is Asura. Whether this form of marriage by purchase was of Aryan origin or was handed down by indigenous earlier generations is not clear but it marks a stage in advance of the system of marriage by capture, though a few relics still seem to connect it with the latter.

In trans-Giri as also in cis-Giri the act of taking away another person's wife whether by force or by mutual consent is called *har lana,* which suggest that marriage by capture must have been practised by these people. Since the dominance of Rajput influence in these tracts, the Kunnindas and then other orthodox Rajputs having held them in their sway, marriage by capture or Rakshasa marriage which was permissible only to Kshatriyas might have been in vogue. The *Simla District Gazetteer* (1904) also notes that "among the higher castes if a man forcibly makes a woman his wife the marriage is called *Har* and considered illegal, but among Kanets and lower castes it would hold good." One fact seems, however, to have been overlooked by the *Gazetteer,* namely, that the event is followed by a settlement with the husband or his people and unless they agree to free her from her marital obligations, whether after receiving any consideration for it or not, the marriage would, irrespective of any caste high or low, be illegal in case the woman was married.

**Illegal Connection**

If no settlement is made with her former husband, her connection with her seducer would be illegal. She cannot be the wife of two persons at the same time unless they are living jointly. She must therefore have the matter settled with her husband or her new choice would be liable to conviction under Secs. 497 or 498, I.P.C. for adultery and enticing her away. If the woman was unmarried no such difficulty would arise but even then the parents of the girl would strike a bargain as far as possible. *Har* could originally have been possible because of the aggressor. But now, except in rare cases, *Har* is possible because of the mutual consent of the man and the woman and because it resembles the Gandharva form which was permissible for the Kshatriyas only. We noticed a case of Har when Bhalku and others of Poka village, Paonta tehsil in the trans-Giri tract of Sirmur, took away Noopi, wife of Harnam of Sara, Paonta tehsil.

The accused Bhalku and his brothers had struck a bargain for the hand of Noopi with Harnam brother but neither Harnatn nor his wife were agreeable to it. While Noopi was going to her parents Bhalku and others waylaid her by the banks of the Giri and carried her by force to their village. There they made her put on their clothes and ornaments and, since the family was polyandrous, kept her as a common wife. The aggrieved husband had to move the authorities for redress. We thus find that the working of their social customs and practices suggests that marriage by capture as also by mutual consent may have been common there.

## Marriage Precedence

The carrying of guns, the beating of drums, and the firing of shots in a marriage, which give it a warlike picture, suggest that marriage by capture preceded the present form of marriage by purchase. The essential and binding part of the marriage ceremony among the Hindus consists of the *phera* (circumambulation of the sacred fire) which is held to imply the consummation of the vows in the presence of *agani* (fire) and the other sacrificial gods. This ceremony had been held important according to the Hindu law. The Brahma or Pun marriage has come to be associated with it and it is considered odd to accept any consideration while giving away a girl in marriage according to the phera. Formerly marriage was not at all performed according to the orthodox Hindu custom. The phera marriage was all but unknown in the trans-Giri tract of Sirmur.

Things have now changed. It is found that the well-to-do and respectable Kanet and Bhat families perform the phera ceremony. This has been due to their contact with the cis-Giri people and those of Nahan and other areas. In order to raise themselves from their inferior position and to prove that they are of the same status as the Rajputs and Brahmans of the plains they are now everywhere gradually adopting this custom. The Kanets and Bhats living just on the other side of the Giri river have customs more of the cis-Giri than the trans-Giri type. In the cis-Giri, however, phera is a necessary custom and even Kolis observe it. Some of the Koli families of the cis-Giri would not marry except according to the orthodox phera ceremony.

## Types of Marriage in trans-Giri

In the trans-Giri tract of Sirmur we find three types of marriage: (i) phera, (ii) Jhajrah, and (iii) Reet. These types, with slight changes, are prevalent throughout the Himalayan tract under consideration. In Bashahr they are called: (i) Biah or regular marriage, (ii) Jhajrah, and (iii) Gadar or Paraina; in Kullu (i) Brahma, (ii) Arsh or Asura and (iii) Gandharb; in Chamba (i) Biah, (ii) Jind-Phuka or Gandharb, and (iii) Jhanjarira or widow marriage. Though some differences are found in the ceremonies the main types resemble one another. We shall see how these resemble or differ from the forms of marriage in other polyandrous tracts like Chakrata, Kulu, and Lahul. Phera marriage is a recent innovation in this territory but the most common form of marriage is the Jhajrah.

The term *Jhajrah* is used for the marriage of a widow in Kangra and Kulu as well as in Chamba. Apparently the term means "putting the *nath* (nose-rising) in the bride's nose" but in Kulu and Kangra it stands for widow marriage. But in the trans-Giri territory of Sirmur regular marriage is termed Jhajrah, in contradistinction to Reet. After the betrothal the bridgegroom's father (or in his absence some near relative) goes to the bride's house with a *pundit* and a barber and two or three other persons, the number of persons being three or five or at the most seven taking with him a nath and as many ornaments as he can afford. Among the Kanets and Bhats gold ornaments like nath and murki and silver ornaments like dandiyan, jhummack, sis-phul, janjir, har, mala, tandtu, paploche, dulri, and bulyan are presented. The nath is an indispensable ornament, while it rests with the bridegroom's father to offer in addition any of the above-mentioned ornaments. The Kolis and other low castes were not allowed by society to use any gold ornaments, especially the nath. The bridegroom's father and his party are very cordially treated by the bride's people.

An auspicious moment is selected by the *pundit* when he recites the *mantras* and in certain places near the Giri, women sing the wedding songs. The Shant ceremony takes place a day before the bridegroom's relatives reach the bride's place. A *pujan* is held at this time and whoever wants to present anything to the bride at that time can do so. Her maternal uncle presents her with a complete suit of clothes, a *thali,* and a *lota.* Failing her maternal uncle, her father gives these articles to her. The bride is asked to sit before the *thapa* (quaint lines drawn with cowdung on a wall) and five seers of grain placed in a vessel. *Pujan* takes place and the *pundit* recites some mantras or incantations. This ceremony is called *sohag lagana.* After the *sohag* ceremony or putting on the nose-ring they sing songs and perform their native dance or gee. The pandit reciting the mantras puts the *nath* in the bride's nose, a *paranda* or *mauli* is tied round her wrist, and *gur* or *shakkar* (raw sugar) is distributed among those present on the occasion.

**Marriage Arrangements**

It is then decided as to how many men should accompany the *jhajri* (bride) so that arrangements could accordingly be made for them by the bridegroom's people. The bride clad in a red garment follows the visitors to her husband's place accompanied by the *pundit*, barber, and the *jhajroos* or *baratees* (wedding guests). Ordinarily the *jhajri* goes with the jhajroos or her relatives and friends. When she reaches her husband's place she stays in her husband's village with her own people and dines with them till the Ghrastni ceremony which is performed only at an auspicious moment. Generally the jhajri and the *jhajroos* reach the bridegroom's place in the evening when a *dham* (feast) awaits them.

At times the bride reaches in the morning and the jhajroos follow in the evening. If, however, a death occurs in the village or some other accident takes place the *jhajri* is sent to her husband's place and the *jhajroos* go there after about 10 or 15 days and then the ceremony takes place. In the cis-Giri and in Nahan the bridegroom and the bride are commonly carried in *palki* or *doli*. But it is to be noted that in the trans-Giri the bridegroom's father or some other relative goes to fetch the bride and not the bridegroom himself. The bride, when she comes to her husband's house, comes on foot and not in a doli or palki as is the custom elsewhere. If she is of very tender age she is carried on a man's back and in case she is a child her mother goes with her to suckle her. The *Sirmur Gazetteer* states that it is counted as an ill omen to go in a *palki* or *doli* in this tract because it is only the dead that are so carried although this could not be corroborated by investigation.

The bride enters her husband's house at 'an auspicious moment fixed by the pundit when a pitcher of water is placed and Swastikas are painted on the walls and a *diwa* (earthen lamp) is put near a place called *thapa*. A raised square platform is made of each about two inches high on which turmeric and small images are placed in the centre. The bride and the bridegroom sit in front of the platform and incense is burnt. The whole affair is managed by the pundit (*Bhat*) who gets one rupee and four annas as his fee besides four or five seers of grain. The bride takes her seat to the left of the bridegroom. The nuptial knot is symbolized by tying some part of the dress of the bride with the shirt or turban of the bridegroom. Both are made to stand up and *gath-jora* (union of knots) is tied to unite them for ever. They now change sides and the husband comes to the left.

**Phere Ceremony**

This is the only *phera* that was known to these people before the regular *phera* ceremony was introduced. *Gur* or *shakkar* is then given to the bridegroom by the *pundit*. The bridegroom puts it in the bride's hand and she eats it. Next gur is given to the bride who gives it to the bridegroom who also takes it. This completes the marriage ceremony and the custom is called *Ghrastni*. *Gur* or *shakkar* is also distributed among those present. We may note in passing how the *gath-jora* ceremony of the trans-Giri tract resembles the Lai Lui ceremony of Kulu. In Kulu, as in trans-Giri, the bridegrooms plaid is fixed in a knot with the bride's *dopatta (chaddar,* i.e. head cover). The bride and the bridegroom are then carried round the altar on which the worship of Ganesh has been celebrated. This is performed at both houses and this tying of knots is called *Lai*

*Lui*. A vessel of water is consecrated and the *balli* (nose-ring which corresponds to the wedding ring of Christians) is solemnly purified. The young couple and the guests, or at any rate the members of the bride's escort, receive a *tikka* mark on their foreheads, generally from the hands of the bride.

Then follows the marriage feast which often includes a goat which is killed for the occasion. A very close resemblance is thus found between the marriage ceremony, especially the Lai Lui of Kullu and gath-jora and jhajra of trans-Giri. Reverting to the trans-Giri Jhajra celebrations, it is found that the Bajgi is sent by the bride's people to all those whom they want to invite at the wedding. He goes to them and informs them of the marriage and invites them to join the function. This is considered a formal invitation. The Bajgi is given some grains by those who are invited and a person who lets him go without giving him anything on such an occasion is considered ill-bred. The relatives of the bride who accompany her to her husband's house fire guns. Such sport is called *mohalla*. The custom of carrying guns and fire-arms seems to be a survival of a time when marriage by capture was the rule. But it is noteworthy that in this tract it is not the bridegroom's people that take these guns but the bride's. In other parts of the state in the cis-Giri territory, in Sain and other places, the bridegroom's party carry guns with them and before reaching the bride's place fire them in sport.

**Celebrations**

They beat drums and blow clarions. Naquaras are played and the particular tune of the music on this occasion is called *Jang* and *Pholanian*. This custom of firing guns and all those celebrations on the wife's side suggest that the custom may be a legacy of a time when society was matriarchal. The procession reaches the bridegroom's house in the evening and the *jhajroos* on reaching there take their dinner. In earlier days, at the dinner shakkar and ghee were distributed extravagantly, about 40 or 50 maunds of shakkar, 20 to 30 tins of ghee, and 60 to 70 maunds of wheat flour being consumed on the occasion. This is thus a purely vegetarian dinner. In the morning the *jhajroos* are served with non-vegetarian diet and huge quantity of rice and eight to ten goats are consumed at this feast. These are no doubt the maximum figures. The non-vegetarian dinner is called *gulti* (meat) and *bhat* (rice).

**Neota**

The above figures indicate the expenditure on marriage and how hard it is for the poor to meet the expenses. The *jhajroos* do not sleep but in honour of the wedding they dance throughout the night. This dance is called *Gee*. Men dance singly or in twos. The *Dholki* and the *Naquara* or *ghara* (earthen pitcher) are played in accompaniment with the dance and the songs. Women too dance and keep very good rhythm with the music. The whole night they dance and smoke hookah. The *neodharis* or *nadharis* (guests of the bridegroom) offer presents to the bridegroom's parents in the morning before the second dham is given to the *jhajroos*. This custom, called *Neota,* is of great importance because of its economic significance. Every neodhari gives either two rupees or one rupee to the bridegroom's parents and a *lotku* (small earthen pot) full of ghee.

In certain parts it is the custom to give one rupee in return for that which the Neodhari had received from the bridegroom's parents at his own marriage or any marriage in his family which is called *aton* and another rupee which is called *gahon* or *agehun* (advance). In certain parts only one rupee is presented to the bridegroom's parents. No written account is preserved of these presents but the bridegroom's parents keep them in mind for they will have to pay to others in their marriage ceremonies. This custom of Neota is important in as much as it shows the solidarity of these people. The *Neota* is given so that the money thus received might financially help the bridegroom's people in conducting the marriage. It considerably helps the poor people.

**Neota Dalna**

Thus it is of economic benefit to the family which has to meet the heavy expenditure incurred in this behalf. The custom of paying money to the bridegroom's parents is called *Neota Dalna.* It is not necessary that the present must be in cash. It can take the form of grain or ghee. If one feels that he may need ghee, rice or wheat at the time when he will have to perform a marriage ceremony he may present ghee, rice or wheat and not cash. This is even more in harmony with the needs of the people and it is a direct help to them. The maternal uncle is expected to bear the expenses of the morning meal. If he is rich enough he may bear all the expenses of these meals but ordinarily he brings a certain quantity of rice and some goats. The other expenses are borne by the bridegroom's parents. As opposed to *Jhajra* or the regular form of marriage there is also *Reet* or the irregular form of marriage. Reet literally means custom. It is not a recognized form of marriage and is outside Shastric prescriptions. It is never the first marriage in Sirmur in the case of a woman though it can be so in the case of a man.

**Rites of Jhajra**

The first marriage of a woman in this tract is always performed according to *Jhajra.* It is only after the first regular form of marriage that *Reet* may take place. Elsewhere the people who observe *Reet* consider it a form of marriage which can be contracted by payment of a lump sum of money. No ceremonies of a Hindu marriage are observed. The payment of a certain sum of money to the father or the guardian of the girl if she is a *virgin,* or to her husband if she is married, is all that is required. This done, the purchased girl becomes the legal wife of the buyer. The price of a woman acquired by this means varies according to her natural dower of beauty from Rs. 100 to Rs. 500. Sometimes the price in the case of an especially prized woman is as high as Rs. 2000.

This custom has robbed marriage of its character of sanctity and inviolability and a system of divorce has in this peculiar form come to be widespread. Under its influence all domestic ties have been weakened and either the husband or the wife has got a free hand in dissolving the union. More often than not they are seen to separate on trifling pretexts. It will be found from the above that Reet is more of a form of divorce than of marriage. Its importance has increased because of its effects on the life of the people of this tract in particular and of the other tracts in general.

During the existence of the feudal states in the region one other marriage tie was also noticed, namely, that between a ruling chief or a high class Rajput and his khawas wives. A khawas was generally more than a concubine and she was always treated with respect in the palaces, especially if she be the mother of a son. There were three classes of khawas. The highest was a Kanet maid-servant or attendant of a rani who in the phera ceremony had accompanied her mistress in her seventh round of the fire. The second was a Kanet woman brought into the palace in order to be a khawas. In her case a ceremony similar to the *Jhajra* is performed when she enters the palace.

**Reet and Polyandry**

The third was a concubine introduced without any particular ceremony. It was not necessary that only a Kanet woman could be kept as a khawas. Bhat women were also kept as khawas. We find polygamy and polyandry both existing in the tract. Since the matter of widow marriage is so intimately connected with the working of *Reet* and *polandry* it will be appropriate to deal with it while discussing them. No account of marriagein these parts of the Himalaya would be complete without a reference to Lahul which lies on the borders of Tibet and where naturally Tibetan civilization and culture have a great influence. The bridegroom does not send any of his representatives to fetch a bride in Lahul but he has to go himself to bring her and perform the ceremonies.

On the day fixed the bridegroom's family and relations go in a body to fetch the girl. The fetching ceremony takes place at night. On arrival at the bride's house the bridegroom accompanied by his companions has a little encounter with the servants of the house who will not let him in unless he has paid them a fee. Once inside, the bridegroom exhibits his gifts. The *chang* is passed round and all the bride's relatives receive a part of the cake he has brought. This consists of roasted barley flour kneaded into a stiff dough with butter and also bits of the dried ribs of a sheep. Then the bride's dowry is presented which is called *zori* or *istridhan.* It may consist of sets of clothings up to eight or ten, a sum of money, utensils required for her new home, a cow, a hybrid yak, and a pony or two.

The husband also gives her a dower called *gotam* which is recoverable by him in case she leaves him. Thakurs and even Kanets at times give land to he held by her for life. By such means her position is made stable in her husband's house and the husband does not have any inducement to neglect her or divorce her though divorces seem frequent. The bridegroom then takes the wife home but cannot enter the house unless he performs ceremonies by which all the evil influences the pair may have brought with them are supposed to be destroyed. The Thapa, or spiritual medium, is engaged to counteract the evil influence of the demons.

**Customs**

After invoking the benevolence of the Lama this man throws from top of the house a live sheep in front of the wedding party, and its heart and liver are quickly torn out, cut up and eaten raw, the pieces being scrambled for by all the friends present. The Lama meanwhile proceeds with the reading of the Chos which are calculated to scare away the evil spirits. He brings with him a small pot with dough effigy of the demon inside it. He eventually breaks it and kills the demon in the effigy. Then the party enters the house and partakes of the marriage feast.

Closely allied to Lahul is the Kanaur valley where Buddhism is the dominant faith but where the social customs of the people generally resemble those of the Hindus although the observances bear Tibetan names and the rituals are conducted in that language. Here the marriage customs resemble those of the Tibetans. Brothers marry a joint wife, the Lamas solemnizing the wedding by chanting certain hymns, worshipping the gods or goddesses and sacrificing goats. It is here that we find a group of brothers marrying one woman only. The wedding is quite a simple affair. One of the brothers, usually the one who is the bride's equal in age, goes with some of his relatives to the bride's house on the day fixed by the Lama. There they are well entertained and the Lama solemnizes the wedding by reciting some *mantras* in Tibetan after the Tibetan manner. Next day they return to their own house with the bride richly dressed and adorned. On reaching home the bride is cordially received by the mother-in-law.

After a religious ceremony the bride's right hand is held by all the brothers who are deemed to have married her. A feast is then given to all who are present and the Lamas and musicians are paid their fees. This marriage is a valid one. The bridegroom's father or the guardian gives a dheri to the bride's guardian. The amount of the dheri is usually high, varying from Rs. 100 to Rs. 1000. The *dheri* prevents a woman from going over to another man. It is a sum paid to the bridegroom and must be refunded to him if at any time the marriage ties are dissolved. If the wife leaves her husband and goes off with another man the latter has to refund the amount to the husband.

The Lahulis of Chamba-Lahul have a system of joint marriage resembling to some extent that of the Kanauris. While the bridegroom brings the bride home, his younger brother accompanies the bride on her ceremonial return home which is called Phirauni in Chamba-Lahul, Garnoon-Phernoon in Sirmur and *Gauna* or *maklawa* in the plains. The younger brother presents a rupee to the girl's mother and this establishes his rights as a second husband. More than two brothers are not allowed. While considering marriage one has to remember that the various kinds of marriage from the Brahma to the Gandharva can take place only between those castes who are permitted to intermarry.

Thus no Bhat or Kanet, male or .female, can marry a Koli or Chanal, male or female. The barriers of caste are held intact and any deviation from them results in ex-communication or some other form of chastisement. While marriages between Bhats and Kanets are not uncommon the twice-born Brahmans, Bhats, Rajputs, and Kanets cannot marry persons of any low caste. If, however, anyone does marry, he or she at once sinks to the caste of the lower one. The sale therefore takes place between persons of the same caste and not between a person of a higher caste and another of a lower one. In the same caste, however, one may give his daughter to one who is superior to him in status. One generally wants to marry in a family which is superior to one's own but one cannot get out of one's caste except in the case of Bhats and Kanets who at times intermarry on equal terms.

**Forms of Marriage**

A study of the different forms of marriage leads to the conclusion that three main forms of it are practised in the Himalayan region. The Brahma form is always held in great esteem and people want to come as near to it as possible. The first marriage in the case of a virgin, in a vast majority of cases, irrespective of caste or creed, is of the regular kind though it may have different names. It may be performed according to Jhajra as in Sirmur, Jubbal, and Bashahr, according to Arsh, Asura or Gharbiah in Kulu; or according to *Biah* or *Bedi biah* as in Chamba and Simla district. But some religious ceremony is always necessary of which Ganesh Puja forms an essential part. From Chakrata and Sirmur to Jubbal, Keonthal, Kulu, Saraj, and Bashahr with its Buddhist population of Kanaur and Lahul, we find the worship of Ganesh to be an integral part of the marriage ceremony. It will also be noticed that the marriage tie is very loose and is rarely considered to be of a permanently binding nature. That is why divorce is easy and no particular restrictions are attached to it. How the system of divorce under the name of *Reet* works and affects these people will be seen to hereafter. The facility of divorce on flimsy pretexts and subsequent remarriage which is not at all considered disreputable, together with other regional factors, have affected the morals of the people. Reet is an institution which serves as marriage to some and divorce to others or again simply as marriage to some or remarriage or widow remarriage to others. It is a very complex custom and needs consideration from various angles. Divorce is not known to the traditional Hindu law for the reason that a marriage, from the Hindu point of view, creates an indissoluble tie between the husband and the wife. Neither party, therefore, can divorce the other unless divorce is allowed by custom in a particular community or tract.

Exactly the same state of affairs is found in other parts of the Himalayas as also in the trans-Giri tract of Sirmur where the difference in the number of widows and widowers is thus easily explained. Reet has been traced by some people to the custom of forcible capture or marriage of a woman by a Rajput, called *Har* in the hills and Rakshasa according to the Hindu law. But mutual love resulting in elopement of the woman, backed by her economic importance, may have prevailed upon society in giving her a release from her previous husband if she recompensed him for his loss and in this manner divorce may have been introduced to facilitate the working of society.

**The Custom of Karewa**

Some people, however, trace it to *karewa,* a form of widow remarriage. Karewa appears to be an off-shoot of levirate. According to levirate, it is only the deceased husband's brother who marries his brother's widow and looks after her. But when the husband dies without leaving a brother his nearest cousin may condescend to look after her and marry her. Even greater laxity is allowed to her and failing a cousin of her husband she may marry any man from the same village or community. It is a custom which is prevalent practically throughout Punjab and even in other parts of India.

In castes which practise karewa, a widow, after her remarriage, would almost invariably live for the rest of her life with her second husband. If he also dies she would rarely remarry and would remain a widow. But the women of the hills very often could not pull on with their husbands. The independence which they had gained in return for their services gave them the inducement and opportunity to look for a change. They would always find someone who would be prepared to marry them and compensate the husband. This fact and their importance in the house and on the field kept them always in demand. In the cis-Giri and other parts the common blessing which a married woman receives at the hands of elders is *budh sohagin,* i.e., get old as a married woman.

A Hindu woman cares for nothing more than the life of her husband. He is her protector, lover, and all that is dear to her. Her status and prestige in the house are derived from him and with his death she loses practically everything. Strictly speaking, she has to give up all her interest in the material world and shun all worldly enjoyments. A widow is considered to be a most unfortunate woman. She is even considered inauspicious and cannot, for example, perform many of the ceremonies at the time of the marriage of her sons simply because she is a widow. The greatest blessing, therefore, which can be given to a Hindu woman is *budh sohagin*. The women of the hills are, however, not content with merely getting old in their capacity as married women. Their ideas of married life are different. The blessings which they expect from one is not *budh sohagin* but *sada sohagin* (remain a married woman for ever). In other words, they want always to enjoy the status of a married woman right up to their death and, if widowed, would regain their status at their will.

**A Relic of Times**

This may as well be a relic of the times when polyandry was in vogue in practically the whole of the Himalayas and, since several brothers had a joint wife who could not be a widow so long as even one of the whole lot remained alive, this blesssng may have been literally true in a majority of cases. The prevalence of child marriage is also said to be at the root of this custom. As we noted before, the result of child marriages in many cases is that the husband and wife cannot get on with each other and daily quarrels and troubles make family life impossible. As the girl-wife comes of age and finds things intolerable she 'goes to her parents' home and refuses to return to her husband. The parents too need someone to help them in the management of their affairs and so they do not resent a helping hand. She remains there for some time and enjoys herself. The poor husband, deprived of the services of his wife, not only finds life miserable but cannot manage his agricultural operations. He married her in expectation of her services on the field and in the house and with her departure the need for a" helping hand is renewed.

He has two courses open to him. He may either induce her to come back or marry someone else. He cannot recover her because she is not prepared to live with him and he cannot marry again because he has no money. The only course left for him therefore is to come to an agreement with her and renounce his claim over her in return for some compensation. Thus a means is devised whereby divorce comes to be sanctioned by society. The wife goes to her parents, arranges marriage with another, pays the compensation to the first husband, and starts living with the second. This payment of compensation determines the dissolution. It thus serves as a divorce for the first husband and a marriage for the second. There is no other form of divorce except this. It is performed according to Reet which, as noted before, acts as marriage, divorce or widow remarriage as the case may be.

**Sexual Morality**

If any of the parties finds his or her partner unbearable because of some other reason he or she asks her or him to dissolve the marriage. Sexual morality is commonly lax in the hills and if one comes to detect it in the other divorce according to Reet is the only way out. If the husband finds that his wife does not act according to his wishes or if the wife in turn finds that her husband has no respect for her wishes they decide to part and the wife goes home and arranges another marriage after paying *Reet*. There is also a rupture when a wife does not get sufficient clothes and ornaments. A hill woman is very fond of them. She asserts that if, in spite of her hard work in the house and on the field, her husband cannot supply her with plenty of clothes and ornaments she is not prepared to live with him.

Quarrels between the relatives of the husband and wife also result in the dissolution of the marriage of the couple. In such circumstances the woman is asked by her parents to stay with them and marry someone else. The wife's relations scarcely persuade her to return to her husband. They arrange for *Reet* with her husband and let her marry again. Physical unfitness is also the cause of dissolution. Where the husband suffers from leprosy, insanity, or some other incurable disease the wife has the option of marrying another man though *Reet* has to be paid. She has however every facility extended to her in case the husband suffers from physical unfltness. We came across a case in Pachhad where a young Koli boy about 25 years old was in the grip of Bright's disease. In spite of all the medical aid which the poor boy could get he could not regain his health and was unfit to discharge his duties as husband towards his young wife. His parents did all they could for the unhappy wife and gave her all the clothes and ornaments which a woman of that class values.

**Agony**

For a time she tolerated every thing but then, having despaired of his health, she went to her parents and told them she wanted to be relieved of her husband so that she could find another who could properly keep her as a wife. I happened to be present when the final bargain was struck between the parties. The husband, the wife, their parents, and other close relations and a Panch were all there and the matter was put before the gathering. The girl's father narrated the awkward situation in which he had been placed. He did not relish severing his connections with the family but could not help it in face of the troubles of his daughter. She narrated her story and then her husband was asked if he had to say anything. The poor boy loved her and did not want to part with her and said he wanted to have her as his wife till he lived. He was well aware of the misery that his illness had caused her but, in order not to lose her, he went to the extent of suggesting that he would not mind any laxity on her part if she continued to live with him. The girl and her parents did not agree to this and finally the boy accepted Rs. 240 as *Reet*.

One fact which has to be noted in the working of *Reet* in Sirmur is that it is always the privilege of the husband to accept *Reet* or not. No *Reet* can take place without the husband being a consenting party to it. The consenr of the woman, however, is not essential and she can be given away in marriage according to *Reet* even if she does not want it or agree to it. I saw a Dumra woman in Pachhad entreating her husband not to give her in *Reet* to another. She implored him not to part with her but to let her serve him and his family all her life. But the fellow was adamant and since the law was in his favour he gave her away in marriage and accepted the *Reet*.

After the death of her husband a woman can contract another marriage according to *Reet*. If the husband has any brother she is passed on to him as wife. If his brother does not want to keep her as his wife, which is unusual, she can marry any other man and pay him the *Reet*. When her husband has no brother and she has small children she might choose to stay where she is to bring them up. But if she cannot get on with her sons when they come of age she may leave the house and remarry. When the child is very small she may take it with her to the second husband, rear it, and send it back when he has grown up.

Whether a child is to return to her former husband or not is decided at the time of settling *Reet* and if it is not to be returned its price is taken into consideration at the time of fixing the *Reet*.

It is interesting to come across this particular form of marriage called *Reet* in this Himalayan region. Many authorities have treated it as a form of marriage but one finds no essential feature of marriage in it. When we take the whole region of the Himalaya into consideration where this custom prevails it may appear to be a form of marriage. But when we consider only the trans-Giri tract or even the whole of Sirmur we cannot take it as a form of marriage. In Kangra district, Bashahr, Kulu and Saraj, Lahul, Jubbal, and Koomharsain it might be treated as a form of marriage. But in Sirmur, especially in the trans-Giri tract, though the custom is in all other respects the same as in other parts of the region, it differs on a vital matter which points to its being a form of dissolution rather than marriage.

While Reet marriage in other parts of the region can be contracted by paying from Rs 100 to Rs. 500 or even Rs. 2000 to the guardian of the girl if she is unmarried or to her husband if she is 'married, in Sirmur an unmarried girl cannot be married according to *Reet*. We have stated that Pun marriage is not very common and the parents of a girl receive some compensation for bringing the girl up in the case of Kolis and Dumras and other low castes while the Kanets and Bhats receive it only as marriage expenses. But the first marriage of a girl is always performed according to the Jhajra even in trans-Giri. There can be no Reet marriage in the case of a virgin in Sirmur. That is where *Reet* in Sirmur differs from the custom in other parts. Though the bridegroom or his guardian may pay some money to the bride's father at the time of her first marriage, it is never done according to the *Reet* but it is called Patta. It is not everybody who receives the sum, which is given to defray the marriage expenses, but even those who do cannot receive any sum more than Rs. 24 for this'purpose. This sum can be anywhere between Rs. 4 and Rs. 24. No father or guardian of a virgin could thus receive more than Rs. 24 at her first marriage and this payment is called *Patta*.

One may secretly receive a higher sum but it is considered highly undesirable and if one does so he may incur the displeasure of his caste and may have to pay for it. But even when *Patta* has been received the marriage is to be performed according to Jhajra. After a Jhajra marriage a woman may contract as many marriages according to *Reet* as she pleases. A man can have a wife by Reet at his first marriage but a woman cannot marry for the first time according to *Reet*. A man too does not like to marry for the first time according to *Reet* and would prefer a Jhajra marriage but if no virgin girl is to be had he has to content himself with one by *Reet*. When for any of the reasons indicated above the couple cannot pull on they decide to break off and the wife goes back to her parents.

If a rapproachment is possible the latter may try it; otherwise it is announced by them that their daughter has given up her husband and is prepared to marry again. The parents in a majority of cases do not offer the girl any sane advice in the matter. On the contrary, very often they help her in this dissolution and remarriage. If no one comes for her hand her father or brother, some maternal relation and a responsible man of the village go to her husband and ask him to fix the sum of money he is prepared to accept as *Reet* for his wife. They would then come and announce the sum agreed upon. In case no one is willing to pay that sum her parents ask her husband either to keep her or give her a maintenance or reduce the *Reet* money. When it is announced that she is prepared to remarry and a suitor makes his appearance he has to offer Rs. 2 to the woman in her parents' or brother's presence. If she consents to become his wife, after consulting her parents or brother, she accepts this sum which is called *Sotha* or *Dwas*.

If the husband has not already fixed the Reet for her the suitor would name the amount of Reet money he is prepared to pay and if the amount demanded exceeded that sum he would withdraw his suit. After receiving the *Sotha* or *Dwas* her father or brother, some relation from her mother's side, and a respectable man go to her husband. If the husband wanted to get rid of the woman he would fix a reasonable figure and if it tallied with the amount undertaken to be paid by the suitor the matter would be settled. A day would be fixed when he would be paid the *Reet* money. Word would be sent to the suitor that his suit had been accepted and that he was to send money by a specified date. When the money arrives the ornaments that were given to her by her first husband are taken off from her person and given back to him. But the ornaments and other articles given to her by her father, brother or any other relative ori her father's or mother's side are kept by her as they form her *stridhan* and are not returned to him. Her father or brother and one or two respectable men take the money and ornaments to her husband. They return his ornaments to him.

The price of vessels that were given to her in dowry is deducted from the *Reet* money at the rate of Rs. 1 per vessel. If any money was given to her in cash at the time of marriage that too is deducted. After deducting all such sums the balance is paid to the husband. He now gives a receipt for the total sum, inclusive of the money deducted, and this receipt is commonly called *Bhar Pai,* i.e. full payment of consideration. They now return home and ask the suitor to come to take the woman. He comes with a *pundit* and brings ornaments like nath and some clothes. On an auspicious day she puts on the nath and a *paranda* is tied round her wrist. She is then taken to her second husband's house either on foot or on a man's back but in cis-Giri in a doli. On reaching there gur or *shakkar* is distributed but no *phera* ceremony takes place.

Sometimes, though rarely, Ghrasni is also performed. Sometimes a feast is also given, as in Jhajra, but on a much smaller scale. She now becomes a legal wife and lives as such so long as she wants to live with her new husband, the slightest provocation giving her cause to leave him for another.

But in this connection it may as well be noted that it is not always that the woman has to do the job of finding a suitor and then accept the *Dwas*. What really happens in most cases is that the woman had already formed an intimacy with some neighbour to her liking and had obtained his promise to marry her if she left her husband. Even the parents are all the time aware of it and do not often discourage her. On the strength of his promise she goes to her parents and after announcing her intention to remarry accepts *Dwas* from her suitor and thus tries to dissolve her marriage. The husband too is aware of the situation. He knows very well that she is not going to live with him as his wife but also knows that someone is pulling the strings from behind and so demands a pretty high price. Many a visit is exchanged to settle the matter and he may still be adamant.

A good deal of haggling takes place and in the end he is able to strike a good bargain. If, however, he is not much interested in her he may accept a reasonable price. There are cases when no suitor is to be had or the woman does not want to remarry but does not want to remain the wife of her husband. Such cases arise where the father of the woman wants his daughter to live with him and serve him for which he gives her his property. I have come across cases of this kind which have given rise to law suits filed by the father's reversioners. In such circumstances there can be no question of any *Sotha* or *Dwas* but the father of the girl goes and settles the *Reet* money with his daughter's husband. If he agrees to the same, which he has to in order to run his house successfully, he pays the husband the *Reet* money he has demanded and his daughter lives with him.

Now that woman would be free to marry anyone she pleased because her husband gives her a receipt of dissolution of their marriage and permission to her to remarry. She, however, scarcely marries during her father's lifetime though she may be in liaison with one or more persons at his place but may marry with his permission during his lifetime or at her free will after his death. The deserted husband, however, has to perform certain duties. After receiving the *Reet* money, called *Zara-Reet*, he goes to the *Patwari* (village accountant) and informs him of the dissolution of his marriage and the amount of money received in compensation.

It is evident from the above that *Reet* is a contract and is based on custom.

In the Simla hills, Kulu, Kangra, Chamba, Kanaur and Lahul even unmarried girls are given in marriage according to *Reet*. In Bashahr the *Reet* system of marriage is applicable to Jhajra and Gadar marriages. If a wife wishes to leave her husband the marriage can be annulled by the latter's acceptance of the amount of *Reet* and a rupee which is called *Ched Karai*. An additional ceremony is also at times performed. The husband gives the wife a small stick, called *dingi*, to break it. If she breaks it the divorce is complete. The ceremony is practised in the upper hills by all castes except the highest Rajputs and Brahmans.

A similar ceremony is found among the Lahulis of Chamba. Usually two or three persons are present at the time of a dissolution of marriage. The husband and the wife hold a piece of thread between them and break it by pulling it in opposite directions. It both are consenting parties no money payment is made; otherwise payment is made by the party wishing the divorce and is called *man*. It is an improvement on the custom of *Reet* in as much as a woman has been given the same rights as a man. While in other hills a widow has to marry her husband's brother, in Chamba-Lahul she cannot be forced to do it and can appeal to the court for protection.

The Kanauris have tried to check this evil in their own way. Among them the bridegroom's father at the time of marriage pays a sum varying from Rs. 100 to Rs. 1000 to the bride's father which is called *dheri.* This *Dheri* later works as Reet money for he alone can take the woman who has paid this sum to her husband. Otherwise she has to stay with him. In Sirmur, if someone runs away with the wife of another, the husband, if he does not want to retain the woman as his wife, receives Reet money for her. Otherwise he may proceed under Section 497 oi 498 I.P.C. against him. He cannot claim any special damage because of this Har. In Bashahr, however, he is entitled to an additional penalty for it called *harkaran.* The adulterer has to pay the husband a penalty varying from Rs 6 to Rs 12 in addition to the amount of *Reet.* He may get it through the law courts. In case of widows in Bashahr, the second husband is ordinarily a younger brother of the first. No special ceremony takes place. When the widow's second husband is a stranger, it is usual for him to pay one or two rupees as *Reet* to the first husband's family. This special *Reet* is called *Makhtal.* If a man died without direct heirs or near relatives and his widow wished to marry again, it was the custom formerly to pay the *Makhtal* to the state. By remarrying, a widow, as elsewhere, forfeits all rights to her first husband's property which belongs to his sons, whether by her or by another wife. Her children by her first husband are generally supported by the latter's brothers, if any, whether she remarries or not. *"The Himalayan Tragedy of Marriage,"* as the late Thakur Surat Singh calls this custom, is a most suitable epithet for *Reet.* The tragedy is Himalayan not only literally but also metaphorically. Fully conscious of her utility to her husband as a field worker and a domestic drudge, as well as a mother, the woman is the mistress of the situation, for if her husband proves distasteful there is nothing to prevent her from eloping with a neighbour of her choice. She may pass on to several husbands in her lifetime as there is no permanent bond of union between the husband and the wife. The result is loose morals. Women can be very easily tempted and thus promiscuous life originates.

Where domestic life is so disturbed, where the marriage tie is so loose, and where it can be dissolved at the mere whim of either of the parties there can be no peace in the household. When differences arise the wife does not take the full share of responsibilities in the house. She is then concerned with her own person and must get all that she requires while she does not properly attend to the household and field work. In case the husband wishes to keep her, he tries to meet her demands and thus incurs debt and consequent poverty.

We have discussed how this institution has resulted in the indebtedness of the masses and has put them in a position from which they do not see any means of extricating themselves. We may here note that the husband has to remarry if he wants to carry on at all. He has to spend money again and get another wife. But if he has any children by the first wife the second one would scarcely give them a mother's care and they may be deprived of all that a child needs most in this world. The evil results of this custom may be classified under three heads: *(i)* domestic, *(ii)* moral, and *(iii)* economic. We will discuss here briefly the domestic and moral effects while economic results have already been reviewed.

As a result of the pernicious working of the *Reet*, all domestic ties have become loose and marriage has come to have a very insignificant position in the stability and upkeep of society. While a woman is free to leave her husband at her sweet will she has much liberty in choosing her friends and companions and spends much of the time, which is badly needed for the management of her husband's household, in her idle pursuits. Thus, it is common for women to have a rather gay time when they go out to fetch fuel or grass from the jungle. They sing native songs, the Jhoori, Ghoogtu, Nati, etc., engage in singing competitions with their paramours and after having a good time come back home. The slightest pretext is enough for them to go to their parents and torment the husband by depriving him of her services.

Her indiscriminate relations may result in her catching syphilis or gonorrhoea from one of her friends which she in turn passes on to her mates. Even supposing that she has no lapses after a marriage we may see how, getting the disease once, she may affect a number of families. In a polyandrous family she may transmit the disease to all her husbands and on getting a divorce from them may do the same to the next family and so on. She would in that way be the cause of the ruin of many families. In the case of a non-polyandrous family too she would pass on the disease to one husband after another. When we remember that she may marry any number of times successively the consequences can be easily realized. Shini of Naini Dhar, Sirmur, Pachhad tehsil, married as many as 16 times. Had she contracted one of these diseases she would have been instrumental in transmitting the disease at least to 16 families. Another woman in Bhatgar, Renka tehsil, had eight husbands in her lifetime. It is not very easy in the trans-Giri tract of Sirmur to find women who have had only one husband in their lives. On the contrary it is common for women to have three or four husbands during their lifetime. When the facts of their laxity in sexual matters and extra-marital unions are taken into consideration one may be tempted to presume that every person suffers from one or the other of these sexual diseases.

It is one of the most common complaints that wives do not stay with their husbands but remain for months together with their parents. The husband has to pay a number of visits to her before he can induce her to come back. Her parents hardly have the decency to ask her to go and live with her husband. On the contrary they welcome her, because, while she helps them in their daily work, some young suitor or suitors may come and lend them their services in the hope of getting her in marriage or at least having a good time with her. Such lapses are scarcely discouraged and some families have earned a notoriety for thus using their daughters. Since the marriage tie is weak she knows she can always force her husband either to accept *Reet* or go without her services.

If she marries another man her first husband can have his revenge or at any rate his compensation for he can proceed against her new mate in the court of law under Section 498, I.P.C. But if she simply goes to her parents and lives there and develops intimacy with men who give her clothing and ornaments, the husband can hardly do anything. He can certainly proceed under Sectiom 497 and 498, I.P.C. against them but since there has been no formal marriage it is very difficult for him to establish his case. All the evidence has to come from the girl's village but none would be prepared to say anything against a co-villager. The poor fellow is thus left without any redress and has to accept her *Reet* and give her a free hand to remarry. It may take months or even years to come to a final settlement and by that time the husband's domestic affairs are thoroughly upset. It is needless to say that the children of such a union cannot in such circumstances receive any education or training. They are left to themselves and grow to manhood in an improper moral atmosphere.

The social effect of this institution has been no less marked than the domestic. It has affected not only the morals of girls or boys but also that of their parents and of the whole village community. The natural result of such easy divorce and remarriage as is provided by the institution of *Reet* is the laxity of sexual relations and the total disregard of the laws of chastity. While making that generalization one must bear in mind that even in the midst of such wide corruption one may find a number of women who have been true to their traditions of chastity and can compare with the best that any society can produce.

In brief, this custom is more responsible for the steadily increasing degeneration of the people than all other evils put together. Under its malicious influence domestic relations have been torn to shreds, marriage has lost its sanctity and society has been deprived of all that makes it a means of civic welfare. It allows too wide a latitude to the people in selecting or divorcing their mates and, unrestricted by any moral scruples, the sexual instinct in them finds free play. A destructive social outlook thus gets hold of the people who revel in it without incurring any moral or social stigma. What Lord Krishna about moral comes very true.

# Index

## D

## H

## Q & R

## Y



## Z